FUNCTIONS AND USES OF DISCIPLINARY HISTORIES

SOCIOLOGY OF THE SCIENCES

A YEARBOOK

Editorial Board:

VOLUME VII – 1983

FUNCTIONS
AND USES OF
DISCIPLINARY
HISTORIES

Edited by

LOREN GRAHAM

*Massachusetts Institute of Technology,
Program in Science, Technology and Society,
Cambridge, Mass. 02139, U.S.A.*

WOLF LEPENIES

Institut für Soziologie, Freie Universität Berlin

and

PETER WEINGART

*Fakultät für Soziologie und Forschungsschwerpunkt
Wissenschaftsforschung, Universität Bielefeld*

D. REIDEL PUBLISHING COMPANY

A MEMBER OF THE KLUWER ACADEMIC PUBLISHERS GROUP

DORDRECHT / BOSTON / LANCASTER

Library of Congress Cataloging in Publication Data
Main entry under title:
Functions and uses of disciplinary histories.

    (Sociology of the sciences ; v. 7)
    Includes index.
      1. Science—History. 2. Social sciences—History.
3. Classical philosophy—History. I. Graham, Loren R.
II. Lepenies, Wolf. III. Weingart, Peter. IV. Series.
Q125.F86   1983   907′.2   83–4588
ISBN 90–277–1520–3
ISBN 90–277–1521–1 (pbk.)

Published by D. Reidel Publishing Company,
P.O. Box 17, 3300 AA Dordrecht, Holland

Sold and distributed in the U.S.A. and Canada
by Kluwer Academic Publishers,
190 Old Derby Street, Hingham, MA 02043, U.S.A.

In all other countries, sold and distributed
by Kluwer Academic Publishers Group,
P.O. Box 322, 3300 AH Dordrecht, Holland

TABLE OF CONTENTS

Acknowledgement   vii

Introduction   ix

Biographical Statements of the Contributors   xxi

PART I

The Natural Sciences

M. NORTON WISE – On the Relation of Physical Science to History
in Late Nineteenth-Century Germany   3

PETER GALISON — Re-Reading the Past from the End of Physics:
Maxwell's Equations in Retrospect   35

BERNADETTE BENSAUDE-VINCENT — A Founder Myth in the
History of Sciences? – The Lavoisier Case   53

RACHEL LAUDAN — Redefinitions of a Discipline: Histories of
Geology and Geological History   79

ROLF WINAU — The Role of Medical History in the History of
Medicine in Germany   105

PART II

The Social Sciences

ROBERT ALUN JONES — On Merton's "History" and "Systematics" of Sociological Theory   121

MITCHELL G. ASH — The Self-Presentation of a Discipline: History of Psychology in the United States between Pedagogy and
Scholarship   143

ULFRIED GEUTER — The Uses of History for the Shaping of a
   Field: Observations on German Psychology   191
BOB SCHOLTE — Cultural Anthropology and the Paradigm-Con-
   cept: A Brief History of their Recent Convergence   229

PART III

The Humanities

REINHART HERZOG — On the Relation of Disciplinary Development and Historical Self-Presentation — the Case of Classical
   Philology since the End of the Eighteenth Century   281

Epilogue   291

Name Index   297

Subject Index   305

ACKNOWLEDGEMENT

The editors would like to thank the 'Stiftung Volkswagenwerk' for the generous support of the conference on "Die Selbstthematisierung von Disziplinen. Zur Historiographie von Disziplinen und ihrer Auswirkung auf die Disziplinenentwicklung", which was held September 18–20, 1981, in preparation of this volume.

We also want to thank the Center of Interdisciplinary Research (ZiF) of the University of Bielefeld for having been host to this conference, thus supporting once more endeavours in the interdisciplinary study of science.

INTRODUCTION

Edward Gibbon's allegation at the beginning of his *Essay on the Study of Literature* (1764) that the history of empires is that of the miseries of humankind whereas the history of the sciences is that of their splendour and happiness has for a long time been accepted by professional scientists and by historians of science alike. For its practitioner, the history of a discipline displayed above all the always difficult but finally rewarding approach to a truth which was incorporated in the discipline in its actual form. Looking back, it was only too easy to distinguish those who erred and heretics in the field from the few forerunners of true science. On the one hand, the traditional history of science was told as a story of hero and hero worship, on the other hand it was, paradoxically enough, the constant attempt to remind the scientist whom he should better forget.

It is not surprising at all therefore that the traditional history of science was a field of only minor interest for the practitioner of a distinct scientific discipline or specialty and at the same time a hardly challenging task for the professional historian. Nietzsche had already described the historian of science as someone who arrives late after harvest-time: it is somebody who is only a tolerated guest at the thanksgiving dinner of the scientific community.

The traditional history of science, when noticed at all by the practitioner of the discipline, was in most cases nothing but a "preface history" (Kuhn); whenever the present discipline changed its cognitive content, the disciplinary past took on another shape and was rewritten in an almost automatic way. Today this situation has changed considerably. A growing concern for the disciplinary past can be found in different fields, ranging from physics to the human and social sciences, including the humanities. In many cases, this new interest in the history of scientific disciplines is combined with a critical evaluation of the "traditional" history of science.

Historians of science have — as one can well understand — probably been the last to take note of the allegation from critics, notably sociologists, that they often reproduce an ideology of science which mainly reflects the interests

Loren Graham, Wolf Lepenies, and Peter Weingart (eds.), Functions and Uses of Disciplinary Histories, Volume VII, 1983, ix–xx.
Copyright © 1983 by D. Reidel Publishing Company.

in legitimation of the scientific profession. Thus, an 'Ideologiekritik' of the history of science could easily point out that the reconstruction of scientific development which focuses on the "great men" and on the linear and accumulative sequence of discoveries represents a distorted picture of which not only the epistemological implications and assumptions could be drawn into question but which also coincided all too neatly with an idealized picture of the scientific enterprise. To reveal the ideological function of the history of science can hardly come as a total surprise since the ideological functions of general history are widely recognized.

To assume however that all historians of science are deliberately serving to legitimate the cause of pure science and its elites would be far-fetched. How, then, can one account for that happy coincidence? Evidently one has to ask what the (possible) relations are between science, i.e. individual disciplines or groups of them, and the histories that are being written about them. The stories presented in this volume are varied, complex and sometimes, we think, even amusing. In order for the reader to appreciate some of the generalizations that we have drawn from their messages it is necessary to present these first.

The Natural Sciences

It is not by accident that we have begun with case studies from the natural, the "hard" sciences where, as the lore of science has it a connection between the development of the discipline and its historiography is only conceivable as a one-sided dependence of the latter on the former. To some extent that point is made in Peter Galison's article on the Re-Reading of the Past from the End of Physics. But Galison identifies all together three functions of the reinterpretation of past accomplishments in physics: pedagogic, heuristic and justificatory ones and the examples he gives lend support to the thesis that at least in the case of the latter the writing of history affects the advancement of the discipline itself.

Norton Wise looks at the history of physics from the perspective of the history of ideas and establishes the case that the physical scientists in Germany participated in the late nineteenth century reaction against materialism. This means in part an attempt to build new bridges between the historical disciplines and the natural sciences. In particular, Ernst Mach and his positivism and the energeticists around Wilhelm Ostwald adopted as an 'ideal of explanation' in the physical sciences several premises traditional in German historicism. The modes of connection between physics, its history and the general political context perhaps remain implicit in this analysis but should not be overlooked. Wise suggests the disciplinary debate between the 'Natur' — and 'Geisteswissenschaften' both on the level of the universities and in a national political context and the dominance of the historicist paradigm in conservative-liberal political philosophy as two such modes.

Bensaude's article on Lavoisier looks at the historiography of chemistry from a different perspective. How does one proceed from the notion of revolution to that of foundation, from historic talk to mythical narrative? she asks and goes on to show which factors, epistemological, historical, philosophical and socio-political, accounted for the erection of Lavoisier as an 'immortal monument', for the establishment of the founder myth. Lavoisier himself was a party in this process by taking the strategic move in the opening remarks of his *Traité élémentaire* of *not* mentioning his predecessors at all and instead presenting his work as an entirely new basis, a radical foundation of chemistry. A consequence of this was that "all those concerned described the chemistry of the nineteenth century as an extension of the Lavoisian enterprise". The founder myth had consequences not only for the history of chemistry but for chemistry itself, as Bensaude shows in the reluctance of the reception of atomism in France which she attributes to the system of authority in French chemistry based on the commitment to Lavoisier at the time.

Laudan's account of the relation between 'Histories of Geology and Geological History' focuses on the legitimizing role of history writing but she can identify at the same time how, depending on the particular state of the discipline, the specific form in which that takes place may vary. Thus Lyell's historical introduction to the *Principles of Geology* was intended to promote a revolution in geology by showing how the methodology adopted in the past had prevented geology from becoming a respected science. In the early histories of plate tectonics such as Wilson's and Cox's the goal was the reverse insofar as the revolution which by now was interpreted in Kuhnian terms had to be stabilized. This was attempted by showing that the revolution of plate tectonics was very much like other revolutions in science and merely proved that geology was a true member of the community of scientific disciplines.

In a very similar way Winau demonstrates the variety of functions which the history of medicine can fulfill. In a first phase, ranging from antiquity to the nineteenth century, the history of medicine served to secure the image of a true science by an appeal to the authorities of the past. In a second phase, that of scientific medicine from the middle of the nineteenth century on, the history of medicine was bestowed with a function from outside, namely to represent a counterweight against the prevailing materialism in medicine. A third phase is characterized by the antiquarian interest of doctors in their own past, beginning at the end of the last century and extending into the present. A fourth phase, which has its beginning in the 1920s and increasingly determines the profile of the history of medicine, is characterized by the attempt to locate it as an important factor in history at large and to reveal its connections with social and cultural history.

The Human and the Social Sciences

In the human and the social sciences the growing interest in the disciplinary past has many reasons: these are different from discipline to discipline and from one national scientific culture to the other. Some common causes however may be identified. Among these are a new idea of the process of scientific developments where a thinking in discontinuities has become prevalent; the re-structuring of sub-disciplines and specialties in various sciences which have to be justified not only by systematic reasons or external demands but also through historical reasoning; last but not least the changes in the self-image of several disciplines which are most obvious perhaps in the behavioral and social sciences and which are closely connected to the processes of social change which occurred in all industrialized countries since the 1960s.

The continuity of disciplinary development, especially in the natural sciences, which had been the basic assumption of the traditional history of science did not call for sociological explanations. History of Science and History proper shared the conviction that there was not much need for either a philosophy or a sociology of the sciences. The discussion which Thomas Kuhn's book *The Structure of Scientific Revolutions* (1962) provoked, however, made abundantly clear that a proper history of the sciences could not be conceived without theoretical reflections and that these, in turn, needed sociological explanations for the development of academic disciplines as their complement. That was exactly what the later so-called social studies of science intended to do: to bridge the gap between the hitherto separated fields of the *philosophy*, of the *history* and of the *sociology* of science.

Yet it is astonishing to see how long it took even the social sciences, above all sociology, to give up a pure Whig historiography which concentrated on a mere chronology of dogmas and theories and completely lacked all sociological elements of a disciplinary history: the analysis of the social, economic and cultural milieux in which these theories were produced and selected.

Since the 1960s most of the social and behavioral sciences have undergone a quite substantial change of their self-image. With the rapidly diminishing belief in the irresistible progress of Western civilization a growing skepticism and a loss of disciplinary self-confidence can be identified in many sciences. One form of reaction and, sometimes, consolation consists in the re-historicization of a field. In retrospect, hitherto neglected and hidden alternatives to the mainstream of scientific developments become visible and attempts are made to re-interpret the cognitive identity of a discipline or even to re-invent it as a whole as it has been the case with anthropology. The semantics used to describe the development of disciplines has changed: the narrative of quasi-natural growth has in most cases been replaced by the vocabulary of political conflict in which the decadent 'anciens régimes' of established theory traditions are overthrown by a coup d'état or a scientific revolution.

Attacking some of the traditional histories of sociology which normally are 'written by sociologists, about sociologists, and for sociologists', Robert Alun Jones identifies common disgraceful practices in the historiography of sociology by retracing the various ways in which Durkheim's *Elementary Forms* have been read and (mis-) interpreted by different schools of sociological thought. Jones argues that even Kuhn's lesson for the historian of the social sciences did not change these practices — at least not in sociology where the best histories are still written by historians not by sociologists. As early as 1957 Robert K. Merton had suggested distinguishing between the history and the systematics of social theory in order to pave the way for a better, i.e. a social history of sociology. Using examples from the history and the sociology of religion, Jones discusses Merton's proposal and tries to clarify it, mainly referring to the opposition between approaches of continuity vs. discontinuity in historiography and to the distinction between the natural and the social sciences and its consequences for history writing in these fields. Though he seems rather reluctant to hope that the practice of writing the history of sociology might be improved in the near future, Jones stresses one major and important role which the history of the discipline can play for sociology; namely to 'restore our concepts and ideas to the social, historical, and linguistic contexts within which they once made sense.'

The papers by Mitchell G. Ash and Ulfried Geuter focus on the history of psychology in the United States and in Germany. They both demonstrate how important it is to take into consideration specific socio-cultural contexts in analyzing the role which the history of a discipline has played and still can play for the discipline itself. Mitchell Ash distinguishes several forms of (internal and external) self-presentation of a discipline through its history, by giving special emphasis to the so-called pedagogical self-presentation, a legitimation strategy mainly aimed at beginning or more advanced students in a discipline. To pay attention to this form of self-presentation seems to be especially important in the United States, the only country "where the history of psychology is an institutionally organized subspecialty of the discipline". Ash discusses the functions which pedagogical self-presentation fulfilled in the history of American psychology. The establishment of the history of psychology as a subdiscipline was combined with the emergence of a hitherto unknown systematic scholarship in the field and finally led to important revisions in both the form and the content of traditional textbook history.

Geuter's analysis concentrates on another function of the history of psychology: its use to back up diverse standpoints "within controversies on theory and method in the discipline". Geuter distinguishes three phases in the history of German psychology in which attempts at reconstructing its disciplinary past have been equally important: the emergence of psychology as an independent field of teaching and research, the methodological debates of the 1950s which were closely connected to questions about the role of psychology during the Nazi regime and the so-called 'crisis of relevance' which psychology underwent in the 1960s. The distinction of these periods enables Geuter to show how the function of the historical recourse in psychology changed accordingly with the development of the discipline, its subject matter, its basic theoretical assumptions and its standard methods and procedures.

In the last decades, a considerable change of its cognitive and institutional identity has marked the development of cultural anthropology. More perhaps than in other fields a renewed interest in its disciplinary past has been an indicator of this change, as Bob Scholte shows in his essay. The intellectual-historical message of Thomas Kuhn has been extremely important in this respect and Scholte concentrates on the question why Kuhn's approach should have appealed to cultural anthropologists and why it still does. It becomes obvious that the notion of paradigm, in its existential, sociological, philosophical and historical aspects served 'to reorient the reflexive study of anthropological traditions along anthropological lines'.

The humanities could almost be defined as those disciplines in which the reconstruction of a disciplinary past inextricably belongs to the core of the discipline. In the case of classical philology, Reinhart Herzog identifies interdependencies between the history of classical philology and the development of the field on several levels of analysis. Almost all paradigmatic shifts in classical philology have been connected with a rewriting and with a re-assessment of its disciplinary history. Since the end of the eighteenth century, historiography of classical philology has not the least been used to plan future research whereby contexts of institutional history and rather complicated politics of research have played an important role. So far, the case of classical philology seems to illustrate the functions of disciplinary history which are known from the natural and the social sciences. However, classical philology seems to be unique insofar as it regards itself, at least in parts, as finished and past, thus demonstrating the 'phenomenon of a programmatic post-disciplinary history of science within the discipline itself'.

Functions of Disciplinary History

Histories of science make no exception to history writing in general in serving the function of legitimation. But that function is too general to add to the understanding and interpretation of the diverse cases we have at hand and it is necessary, therefore, to look for differentiations of that broad category.

One that comes immediately to mind is to look for the addressee of legitimations, or, in other words, the 'clienteles' of disciplinary histories. In the case of science, one distinction is obvious: legitimations are directed to those who support it, in a very general sense the lay public and more specifically governments, foundations and other sponsors engaged in science policy. The legitimation of science with arguments of utility or of its cultural value has as long a tradition as the development of modern science itself.

Legitimations of this sort typically assume the format of popularized accounts of heroic achievements and adventures at the frontiers of knowledge. In contrast to the 'socializing' function of disciplinary histories directed to the novices which appear in the first chapters of standard text books they have an 'educative' function directed to the lay public. They are powerful instruments because the lay public lacks the knowledge with which to evaluate disciplinary histories critically.

In some cases the general public becomes the target of a battle between disciplines for recognition, e.g. biology reaching out to acquire the place of physics or at least to step out of its shadow. But there is also the general concern on the part of science as a whole with a public that has to become educated enough in science in order to continue to grant privileges and resources, and not to become influenced by irrational forces which would eventually destroy sciences. This theme together with attempts at popularization has, of course, been a part of science's relation to the public since the Enlightenment, and even since Bacon. But it is rarely reflected to what extent it shapes the contemporary professional history of science, let alone at a time when fears and criticisms and a revulsion against scientism are gathering momentum.

In other cases, when the establishment of new research areas and pleas for institutional support are at stake, retroactively constructed histories of the continuous and cumulative development of such fields are a typical form. Lazarsfeld's construction of the history of empirical social research is here a case in point. One can formulate the hypothesis that nowadays disciplinary histories become increasingly "externalized", i.e. that the discipline is no longer the frame of reference for the writing of its history but that its development is interpreted and explained in terms of the social and political environment in which it takes place.

The essence of these 'external histories' does not seem to be legitimation with utility in competition with legitimations of the cultural value of knowledge for its own sake but rather a less obvious type of legitimation. While the "internal" histories serve to immunize science as an activity from outside interference, the "external" histories legtimate just that; by undermining the aura of heroic achievements and the sanctity of elitism they transmit an image of science as an everyday, social activity which is not aloof from challenges of democratic accountability. Thus, the "social studies of science" are not really "histories" of disciplines but systematic analyses which focus on the conditions of the historicity of scientific development.

The other side of the distinction is, of course, that legitimations are directed to the disciplinary community, i.e. inwardly and with respect to it our case studies reveal a number of different functions that disciplinary histories may serve.

One function of such histories is that of legitimating "political" interests often pursued by the authors of such histories themselves. Histories of disciplines are being written and rewritten, to extend the present (or what is to become the future) as far as possible into the past, thereby constructing an image of continuity, consistency and determinacy. In battles for supremacy in a field, in times of uncertainty of orientation, or in conflicts over the truth claims of contradicting schools of thought a history of the discipline serves to rearrange the relative impact of past achievements, the proper evaluation of founding fathers and disciplines, heroic discoveries and consequential mistakes. Histories thus serve to legitimate new paradigms and to delegitimate old ones. A different periodization, the mentioning of some, hitherto less known, and the ignoring of others, hitherto highly respected scholars will change the image of a discipline's history, it will restructure the memory of the past and, by way of socialization, structure the future.

Histories of disciplines can serve conservative or progressive functions. They may be written to justify revolutions in a field, as was the case in molecular biology, where accounts of the discovery of the double helix were written while the dramatic development of molecular biology was still going on. It was the history of a specialty which emerged on the margins of biology but revolutionized the discipline by becoming the center and is now considered the 'natural' direction that the development of biology had to take. The men who wrote these histories did so partly glorifying their own role but also to stabilize the revolutionary achievements and the new sense of identity.

Histories may also be written to counteract and, if possible, prevent change. Although, not surprisingly, examples for this conservative function are probably much less numerous, elements of this may be found in the history of medicine in Germany which once was supposed to provide a counterweight to the growing 'scientification' of medicine by retaining its humanist and historical orientations.

Another type of legitimating function may be set aside by pointing to examples where histories of disciplines were and still are intended to establish the image of a true science which seems to have been the case in geology and the integration of the 'plate-tectonics'-paradigm. Similarly, histories of classical philology convey the impression of a succession of attempts at re-establishing the field by demonstrating that the preceding tradition of the disciplines has been superceded, or even that the development of the discipline has come to an end.

It is obvious that all these functions which can be subsumed under the broader category of legitimation (or delegitimation) of cognitive strategies imply the rewriting of disciplinary histories. The extent to which they do this constitutes a continuum: from the re-writing of the entire history which is to re-arrange the entire field to the reformulation of specific parts. In all cases historiography is used strategically which suggests that it is as powerful and political a tool in science as it is in society at large.

To speak of the strategic use and thus functions of disciplinary historiography directs attention to those who produce histories of disciplines. Does the distinction between different types of producers of such histories give us more insight into the ways of history writing in science than we have gained from looking at their functions? At least one such distinction which must be considered is that between professional historians of science and amateur historians of disciplines. The writing and rewriting of disciplinary histories for strategic purposes is mostly done by practitioners from the field, namely those who have their own stake in engaging in writing history. They are not to be confused with professional historians of science with scientific training of some sort who still are considered the only truly qualified members of their guild but practitioners who turned amateur historians of their field without much concern for the profession and its standards. These have, as we shall see, other motives for writing histories of their disciplines than merely to reconstruct past developments and events. Unless they have only the amateur's antiquarian interests their work is always linked to their field in some "political" way. When, as some of the stories of this volume show nicely, a practitioner in a discipline decides to write a history of that discipline it is usually directed to his own colleagues with an imaginary supporting public back stage. His colleagues are to take over and accept a new image of the discipline's development, or perhaps to remain firm in the belief that had constituted their identity and which is threatened by new challenges. In these cases the clientele is, in the first instance, the discipline itself. Thus, for them the discipline is the frame of reference.

In contrast to this group there are the professional, academic historians of science. Although the history of science itself has a long and quite distinguished past, the establishemnt of a distinct field of research and its endowment with chairs, degree programs and a sizeable number of students is a post war phenomenon. This is important to remember because it means that most professional values and standards of the writing of history of science, and notions of objectivity and disinterestedness in particular, are equally as recent phenomena. While the practitioner-turned-amateur-historian of the discipline directs his accounts to the colleague-scientists, the professional historians will normally write for other members of their own profession. In this way the field develops, quality standards emerge and serve to judge new work to distribute the rewards available. However, one can surmise that professional historians of science more than the members of any other of the meta-scientific disciplines, are directing their own work to the scientific community as a whole and to the disciplinary communities under study in particular. They attempt above all, to give a correct picture, one that is acceptable to the practitioners, and sometimes perhaps even with an educative motive in mind. Why would one want to study the history of science if one cannot learn from it for contemporary practice? Orientation to the scientific community and dependence on its judgment, it is plausible to deduce, lead to an internalization of the community's values, to adaptation and idealization. A close and systematic look at the profile of research foci, at the aspects of science which are neglected, at the self-image of historians of science and their professional identity especially vis à vis the sciences would have to substantiate that thesis.

To distinguish, then, between different groups that produce histories of science, different "publics" to which these are directed, and different uses for which they are written, in looking upon the historiography of disciplines proves to provide a surprisingly fruitful, new perspective of the interrelations and interactions between the development of the sciences and their histories. On the one hand we learn why the history of science and the historiography of disciplines reflect ideologies of science, epistemological theories, and sociological belief systems. This is not so much to denounce the value and the standards of historical accounts of science, which certainly vary widely, but to lay open a fundamental condition of historiography of science as an intellectual activity. On the other hand we also learn about the uses and functions of the history of science for scientific development proper. That historiography is a medium through which the supposedly most rational of all intellectual activities seeks to establish its legitimation and identity by continuously reconstructing its past may not be a surprise. But the ways in which this medium is shaped by the theoretical, epistemological and "political" concerns of disciplines and in which it affects the disciplines by virtue of its power to structure perception are largely unknown. Finally, we learn about a particular mode in which science relates to different publics in order to establish legitimation. In this attempt at legitimating themselves by establishing accounts of their histories can be seen one of the most important mechanisms by which the sciences as intellectual enterprises are linked to the socio-cultural and political contexts to which they belong.

WOLF LEPENIES and
PETER WEINGART

BIOGRAPHICAL STATEMENTS OF THE CONTRIBUTORS

MITCHELL G. ASH, born 1948, Ph.D. Harvard University, History. Fulbright scholar in history at the Free University of Berlin 1978 – 80. At present Research Associate of the Psychology Institute of Mainz University, FRG, working on a project 'Psychology in Exile', supported by the German Research Council (DFG). Author of several articles on the history of psychology, co-author with William Woodward, *The Problematic Science – Psychology in 19th Century Thought*, Praeger, New York, 1982.

BERNADETTE BENSAUDE-VINCENT, born 1949 in the South of France, graduated in philosophy. Gave courses of lectures in history of science at the Sorbonne and at the École Polytechnique. State Doctorate in 1981 with a thesis on 19th century history of chemistry. Currently working on a project of the future Science and Industry Museum of La Villette.

PETER GALISON is a Junior Fellow at Harvard where he is completing Ph.D. requirements in the History of Science and Theoretical Physics. His historical research is on the changing role of experiment in modern physics. In physics his interests lie in high energy particle physics. Beginning in September 1983 he will be an Assistant Professor of Philosophy at Stanford University.

ULFRIED GEUTER, born 1950, studied German literature and psychology at the universities of Bonn and Berlin. He received his diploma in psychology from the university of Bonn in 1974. Since 1978, he is a "wissenschaftlicher Assistent" (assistant professor) at the "Psychologisches Institut", Free University of Berlin. Geuter has specialised on the history of psychology in Germany during the 20th century. His Ph.D. (1982) deals with the professionalization of German psychology during the Nazi-period.

LOREN GRAHAM is professor of the history of science in the Program in

Loren Graham, Wolf Lepenies, and Peter Weingart (eds.), Functions and Uses of Disciplinary Histories, Volume VII, 1983, xxi–xxiii.

Science, Technology and Society at the Massachusetts Institute of Technology. He is the author of *Science and Philosophy in the Soviet Union, The Soviet Academy of Sciences and the Communist Party*, and *Between Science and Values*, as well as numerous articles on the history of biology and physics. He is currently working on a book on the history of Russian science since 1860.

REINHART HERZOG, born 1941, was educated in Western Germany. He studied history, philosophy, law and classical philology at the universities of Berlin, Paris and Kiel from 1959 to 1966. Assistantship (science of literature/ classical philology) in Konstanz until 1971. Professor of the science of literature and classical philosophy at the university of Bielefeld since 1971. Research work and publications in late antiquity.

ROBERT ALUN JONES is associate professor of sociology and religious studies at the university of Illinois. His essays have appeared in the *American Journal of Sociology*, the *Journal of the History of the Behavioral Sciences*, the *Annual Review of Sociology*, and elsewhere. He is also a former coeditor of *Knowledge and Society: Studies in the Sociology of Culture, Past and Present*. He is presently writing a book on secularization and disenchantment in Victorian Scotland.

RACHEL LAUDAN is assistant professor of history at the Center for the Study of Science in Society at Virginia Tech. She has published a number of articles on the history of the earth sciences, and is completing a monograph on Charles Lyell's *Principles of Geology* with M. J. S. Hodge and L. Laudan. She is also concerned to develop a theory of technological change.

WOLF LEPENIES, born 1941, is professor at the Department of Sociology, Free University of Berlin; Directeur d'études associé at the Maison des Science de l'Homme, Paris; currently long term member at the Institute for Advanced Study, Princeton, N.J. Publications include *Melancholie und Gesellschaft* (1969); *Das Ende der Naturgeschichte* (1976).

BOB SCHOLTE is a cultural anthropologist with an interest in the history and theory of the discipline, especially from a critical and dialectical point of view. He has taught at the universities of California, Pennsylvania, and the Graduate Faculty of the New School for Social Research. He is currently associate professor at the University of Amsterdam.

PETER WEINGART, born 1941, is professor of sociology of science and science policy at the University of Bielefeld since 1973; author of *Die amerikanische Wissenschaftslobby* (1970); *Wissensproduktion und soziale Struktur* (1976); author, co-author and editor of numerous books and articles in the area of sociology of science, technology and science policy studies.

ROLF WINAU studied philosophy, history and German literature at Bonn and Freiburg, medicine at Mainz. 1963 Dr. phil., 1970 Dr. med., 1972 habilitation for history of medicine at Mainz, 1976 professor ordinarius for the history of medicine at the Free University of Berlin.

M. NORTON WISE has worked primarily on problems of concept formation in the physical sciences, e.g. "The Flow Analogy to Electricity and Magnetism, Part I: William Thomson's Reformulation of Action at a Distance," *in Archive for History of Exact Sciences,* **25**, 1, 1981, 19–70, and "German Concepts of Force, Energy, and the Electromagnetic Ether: 1845–1880," in *Conceptions of Ether: Studies in the History of Ether Theories, 1740–1900,* G. N. Cantor and M. J. S. Hodge (eds.), (Cambridge University Press, 1981) 269–307. He is currently studying interpretations of thermodynamics in Germany in relation to social-political change. He is associate professor of history at the University of California, Los Angeles.

PART I

THE NATURAL SCIENCES

ON THE RELATION OF PHYSICAL SCIENCE TO HISTORY
IN LATE NINETEENTH-CENTURY GERMANY

M. NORTON WISE

Department of History, University of California, Los Angeles, CA 90024, U.S.A.

> "The history of science is science itself."
> Goethe, *Farbenlehre* (1)

With these words Goethe asserted the priority of an historical mode of knowing over an abstract, analytical mode. That is, one could know nature only directly, by experiencing it as a participant. No radical disjunction between the knowing subject and the object of his knowledge would be fruitful, for one could only know the object through concepts, concepts which were themselves contingent and historical. To be true to nature, therefore, the concepts would have to stand in direct relation to it. Goethe's sweeping polemic in the *Farbenlehre* against Newton's mechanical reduction of whole white light to supposedly more fundamental discrete colors has stood as a reference mark for the two-cultures debate since the beginning of the nineteenth century. In Germany that debate was traditionally one between the *Geisteswissenschaften*, or historical and moral sciences, and the *Naturwissenschaften*, or natural sciences. Within the debate one can trace a long series of popular lectures that evaluate Goethe's status as a scientist, a genre that continues to the present (2).

In 1941, for example, Werner Heisenberg discussed "The Teachings of Goethe and Newton on Colour in the Light of Modern Physics", concluding that "in the field of exact science we shall, for the time being, have to forgo in many instances a more direct contact with nature such as appeared to Goethe the precondition for any deeper understanding of it" (3). But Heisenberg argued also that our attempts to objectify nature by analytic reduction suffer inherent limitations, on two fronts. With increasing abstraction the

3

Loren Graham, Wolf Lepenies, and Peter Weingart (eds.), Functions and Uses of Disciplinary Histories, Volume VII, 1983, 3–34.

'objects' of science become increasingly subjective constructions whose 'objectivity' rests only on their constant reappearance in sophisticated experiments set up to detect them. Goethe had already recognized that aspect of abstraction. But through his Uncertainty Principle, Heisenberg raised a wholly modern objection to the concept of a material world definable outside our thought and action. Our notion of particles possessing precisely determinate positions and velocities in space and time was now shown to violate any possible experiment made to realize that notion, for the knower necessarily interfered with his object in the course of knowing it. On both counts Heisenberg echoed Goethe, "our experiments are not nature itself, but a nature changed and transformed by our activity in the course of research" (4).

With this stress on the necessary interpenetration of subjective and objective, Heisenberg also recognized the historical nature of science: " . . . every scientific theory arises in a certain mental climate . . . . This background is often conditioned by the historical development of the science concerned and the author of the theory may be only vaguely conscious of it". Having entered on a course of development, furthermore, such as that of analytic science, there could be no radical turning away from it until its potential had been realized. "We have to reconcile ourselves to the fact that it is the destiny of our time to follow to the end of the road along which we have started" (5).

In all of these remarks Heisenberg makes evident his own continuity with the nineteenth century tradition of comparing historical knowledge and natural-scientific knowledge. The tradition seems to have depended for its long life on the historically and philologically oriented education of nearly all German academics at the classical Gymnasia. Heisenberg provides a stereotypical product of that training in another lecture "On the History of the Physical Interpretation of Nature". Adopting a simplified philological style, he analyzes the conflict between Goethe and modern science in terms of the Greek words used by Plato, in his analogy of the cave, for different stages of perception. Thus 'ἐπιστήμη is Goethe's preferred "immediate and direct understanding" while διάνοια is Newton's (and more recently Helmholtz's) 'analytical' comprehension by .reduction (6). These are the same categories employed in the nineteenth century disciplinary debates between historical and natural sciences. They are the historians' *verstehen*, to understand, versus the scientists' *erklären*, to explain.

It is not my purpose in this paper to recount the entire disciplinary debate from Goethe to Heisenberg. I shall restrict myself to the late nineteenth century, aiming only to present an example of how historiography has been important in physical science. I emphasize one hundred and fifty years of continual discussion to indicate, first, that my example barely scratches the surface of the problem, and second, that even in its limited form the example must be treated temporally. It must be treated too in both positive and negative dimensions, for the historical sciences provided both positive and negative models for physical science. Thus the example will be complex. For that reason I shall further restrict myself to one side of it, the side discussed by scientists, ignoring major developments in historiography itself. And only in conclusion shall I suggest overarching issues in the educational, social, and political context with which any larger treatment would have to deal.

Qualified in this way, the example will revolve around Helmholtz and Mach as leading figures, Helmholtz reacting negatively to traditional historiographical concerns and Mach reacting positively to the tradition but negatively to Helmholtz. I shall begin by schematizing a number of central features of the nineteenth century German tradition in philosophy of history, commonly labelled *Historismus*, or historicism. That will introduce also the debate between *Geisteswissenschaften* and *Naturwissenschaften*, which will carry through the paper, providing its continuity. The following section on Helmholtz will then suggest a reinterpretation of the historical periodization of the conflict. I believe that widespread concern over a fundamental incommensurability of the two cultures only appeared around mid-century, with the strident claims of Helmholtz and his party for atomistic-mechanical reduction of nature. I shall follow the fortunes of their program within electrodynamics and thermodynamics, arguing that the program had lost its momentum by the mid-seventies and pointing out internal issues that seemed ammenable to an historicist alternative. That will lead to discussion of the historicist aspects of Mach's positivism and the closely related ideas of the Energeticists, such as Ostwald and Helm. These aspects may be indicated by Mach's claim that, "The choice of fundamental facts [in natural science] is a matter of convenience, history and custom" (7).

1. Essentials of Historicism

Those aspects of *"Historismus"* which are relevant here might be developed

from a wide variety of sources (8). The basic categories and attendant ideas
were enunciated quite clearly by Kant and Hegel. They were further articulated by Droysen and Dilthey, among others and, in general, formed an
integral part of neo-Kantian philosophy. For the quite common features that
I shall list below, therefore, it matters little whether one looks to philosophers
like W. Windelband or to historians like Treitschke. All were concerned so to
establish the foundations of historical knowledge that history retained its
legitimacy as *Wissenschaft* and so that no unbridgeable rift appeared between
Geisteswissenschaft and *Naturwissenschaft*. For ease of reference and lucidity
of presentation I shall largely follow Droysen's *Grundriss der Historik* of
1868, and particularly his appended essay on 'Natur und Geschichte' which
was Droysen's most precisely formulated contribution to the debate between
the disciplines.

(1) Our minds are both spiritual and sensuous at the same time. Concomi-
tantly, we have two *a priori* intuitions, space directed externally and time
directed internally. All our perceptions are both in space and in time, but we
can nevertheless choose to isolate the one factor or the other and in so doing
we isolate Nature from History. This isolation produces two different senses
of time. The time that we associate with Nature is the time of mechanical
processes that continually repeat themselves in space, such as the revolutions
of the planets, the oscillations of a pendulum, or even the cycles of generation
in biology. These cycles divide the line of time into units to be counted,
thereby defining its quantity. The time of History, however, is its quality,
measured in terms of progress toward realization of the purpose of the
universe, its *Idea*, or its *Reason*. The highest form of this Idea is developed
in the progress of man's Spirit toward true morality, which is Freedom. Thus
the *Geisteswissenschaften* are at the same time historical sciences and moral
sciences.

To summarize this point, the two senses of time are *mechanical* and
teleological. They are associated in the following series of dichotomies.

circle   vs line
space   vs time
matter vs spirit
Nature vs History
Naturwissenschaft vs *Geisteswissenschaft*

(2) It must be emphasized that teleology and mechanism are not incompatible in this scheme. Following Kant they differ as regulative and constitutive principles (9). Teleology guides development without altering in any way the mechanisms through which development is realized.

(3) Since a course of development is the working out of an idea, each new form of the idea contains the previous form within it. That is perhaps the core of historicist epistemology. As Droysen put it, each new form "is conditioned by [its predecessor], grows out of it, ideally takes it up into itself, yet when grown out of it contains and maintains it ideally in itself" (10). This notion has several corollaries.

(4) An idea, abstract, universal, and empty in itself, attains content only through its realizations in particular instances. For Kant and for post-Hegelian historicists that meant that history must be an empirical science. The historian can only know the idea through his experience of it, not *a priori*. Preliminary knowledge of it, however, which means limited knowledge of the purpose within the idea, can help to discover the underlying mechanism for, and logic of, its realizations.

(5) Because each new form of the idea contains the previous forms within it, one can only understand later forms through the knowledge of earlier ones. This is, in the first instance, knowing by understanding a thing in all its facets, rather than knowing it by explaining it from first causes. A fact, then, is understood only in its relation to other facts, or simply put, we know only relations.

(6) The basic mode of understanding historically is analogy, analogy of forms. Externally, "things are numberless individuals in ceaseless change," as Droysen said. Internally, in the mind, they "stand forth fixed and classified according to their similarities, affinities, and relations" (11).

(7) Our analogies, however, are always limited, for our experience and our minds are finite. Thus our understanding is related to the totality of the things that we immediately perceive as "the polygon is to the circle". The polygon remains incommensurable with the circle, according to Droysen, no matter how many little straight lines compose the latter (12).

These several features constitute the 'form' of historicism, which I shall assimilate to analogous forms of argument in the natural sciences. The form, however, is ideal, and oversimplified. For a more elaborate argument than the one I shall present both variation and development of the form would have to be included. In particular, historicism in the late nineteenth century became increasingly positivistic, and with that, relativistic. With adoption of Ranke's creed, to describe history *"wie es eigentlich gewesen"*, the Idea of universal history and of progress toward universal morality sought by Kant and Hegel gave way to description of the "ideas" of various cultures (13). As has often been noted, to pluralize the Idea meant to bring relativism to the moral sciences. The sociologies of Max Weber and Karl Mannheim, with their 'ideal types' and 'entelechies', exemplify both the positivist and relativist features of late historicism. These features parallel quite closely developments in the natural sciences, where we shall see a similar form of positivist idealism. It would be valuable to follow the parallel developments more closely, but that would greatly expand and complicate my case, without, I think, adding anything essentially new to the description of historicism in physical science. This is not to say, of course, that the parallels would not enrich our understanding of the relation between the disciplines and thereby increase substantially our belief that such relations existed in a form that was of immediate significance for natural science. To this last question I shall return in concluding remarks.

2. Helmholtz's Reductionist Program, the Alternative of Weber and Fechner, and the Decline of Atomism

2.1. *The Relevance of Helmholtz's Program for History*

The issue of an inevitable conflict between the *Naturwissenschaften* and *Geisteswissenschaften* became significant for most German natural scientists only when the program of atomistic-mechanical reduction of nature had gained some momentum. That occurred in the late eighteen forties and early fifties under the leadership of Hermann von Helmholtz and Emil du Bois-Reymond. Earlier there had been conflict, but largely over issues of method, with the scientists arguing in perceived self-defense that nature could only be investigated empirically, rather than *a priori*, as in Schelling and Hegel's speculative philosophy. Practicing historians and philologists, however, employed the same self-defense, so that the conflict was not so much between the disciplines as within them. Helmholtz and du Bois-Reymond raised the issue to an altogether new level, I believe, by hardening into an impermeable wall Hegel's distinction between the disciplines based on ideal content, i.e. matter vs. spirit. And where those two realms had traditionally interpenetrated, in biology and psychology, they attempted to reduce the operations of *Geist* to material processes. That required as a concomitant a radical distinction between the *Natur-* and *Geisteswissenschaften*. To support these claims I shall cite several popular lectures by Helmholtz, taking his views as representative of the reductionist program.

In recounting the development of the disciplinary schism in a general lecture at Heidelberg University in 1862, "On the Relation of Natural Science to Science in General", Helmholtz blamed that schism on Hegel's attempt to subsume nature under pure thought. He praised what he saw as the return of the moral sciences to "experimental investigation of facts", which reduced the antagonism. Nevertheless, he asserted, the opposition "has its foundations in the nature of things, and must, sooner or later, make itself felt". For the two groups of sciences differ both in 'intellectual processes' and in 'subjects'. Concerning the former, Helmholtz provided an analysis of the methods the two branches employ to attain generalizations from their evidence. "The natural sciences are for the most part in a position to reduce their inductions to sharply defined general rules and principles; the moral sciences, on the other hand, have, in by far the most numerous cases, to do with conclusions arrived at by psychological instinct." Helmholtz suggested, therefore, characterizing the former process as *'logical induction'* and the latter as *"aesthetic induction*, because it is most conspicuous in the higher class of works of art" (14). Thus the historical sciences were strongest in the degree to which they were like art. What Helmholtz thought of art as a mode of *scientific* knowledge, he could not fully betray in this lecture, given his capacity as Rector of the University with the responsibility of encouraging all branches of it. But he had developed that theme in a much earlier lecture of 1853, "On Goethe's Scientific Researches". Comparing Goethe's insistence in the *Theory of Colors* that Newton's researches contained 'absurdities', with the incredulous insistence of Goethe's contemporaries in physical science that the supposed absurdities were fully accounted for by Newton's hypothesis, Helmholtz said: "So flat a contradiction leads us to suspect that there must be behind [it] some deeper antagonism of principle, some difference of organization between his mind and theirs, to prevent them from understanding each other." Indeed, Helmholtz found a thorough incommensurability of modes of investigation. The poet, instead of trying to subsume phenomena of nature "under definite conceptions, independent of intuition . . . sits down to contemplate them as he would a work of art, complete in itself, and certain to yield up its central idea sooner or later, to a sufficiently susceptible student". His error, which he shares with Hegel and Schelling, lies in supposing that there is "in the phenomenon the direct expression of the idea" and "that Nature shows us by direct intuition the several steps by which a conception is developed". Goethe proceeded by analogy, analogy of form, to show, for example, how through a series of transformations the leaf of a plant became a blossom, complete with stamen and pistil. In such transformations Goethe saw the realization of the potential of the leaf form; he saw its purpose unfolding itself. Such a teleological understanding, furthermore, could be gained only by tracing by analogy the succession of *complete* forms, for any analysis into parts would destroy the form wherein lay the teleological principle (15).

Claiming that by the method of analogy one could prove anything and therefore nothing, Helmholtz argued that the investigator of organic nature had so to define the physiology of the plant's separate organs that the transformations of form could be followed in a series of cause and effect relations. One thereby attained a 'scientific conception' with 'definiteness and meaning'. While Goethe required "that the observed facts shall be so arranged that one explains the other, and that thus we may attain an insight into their connection without ever having to trust to anything but our senses", the scientist had to employ 'abstract conceptions' (16).

To the degree then that practitioners of the *Geisteswissenschaften* relied on the skills of the artist — and to Helmholtz those were their most valuable skills — they were not scientific at all. The method of analogy could produce penetrating insights, but without further explanation of the analogies through rigorous causal connections, it was art, not science. That conclusion lies, too, only just beneath the surface of Helmholtz's 1862 address. While allowing all due credit to the factual material that philologists and historians had unearthed, to insights they had obtained, and to the lofty nature of their task, he nevertheless concluded that "not only have they something to learn from [the natural sciences] in point of method, byt they may also draw encouragement from the greatness of their results". Among the lessons to be learned were, "the effort to detect in all cases relations of cause and effect, and the tendency to assume their existence, which distinguish our century from preceding ones . . . " (17).

Now, to be told that his method was not that of science but of fine art would have been inflammatory enough to any representative of the *Geistes-wissenschaften*, but Helmholtz's program had an ultimately more polarizing effect in separating the disciplines radically by subject. "There is no denying", he said, "that, while the moral sciences deal directly with the nearest and dearest interests of the human mind, . . . the natural sciences are concerned with dead indifferent matter." What then of the intermediate cases, such as psychology of perception and physiology, Helmholtz's own realm? In a lecture of 1869, on "The Aim and Progress of Physical Science", Helmholtz made his case quite clear. All natural science was to be physics, and was to require reduction of every description of form to causal mechanics, in fact to laws of attractive and repulsive force between elementary particles or atoms acting "without arbitrariness, without choice, without our cooperation, and from the very necessity which regulates the things of the external world as well as our perception" (18). Helmholtz leveled his attack most directly against vitalists in biology but also against the closely related advocates of a psychophysical 'preordained harmony' in sensory psychology. Both groups mystified science, in Helmholtz's view, by linking physiology to mind through loose analogy rather than through causal analysis. Thus vital forces determined the purposive development of organisms 'like' our mental processes control our actions. Our perception of space, similarly, 'corresponded' innately to physical space, whereas Helmholtz would have that correspondence learned, i.e., caused.

In a forthcoming study of German physiology Timothy Lenoir has shown how Helmholtz and his party systematically distorted mainstream vitalism by linking it rhetorically to the notion of active powers that interfered with physico-chemical processes, suspending and reactivating them. Such effects could violate conservation of force. Leading physiologists, however, held a much more subtle view in which vital forces acted as forces of form or of constraint, deriving from distribution of matter. They guided mechanical

processes without in any way interfering with the causal chain. Labelling this
doctrine 'teleo-mechanism', Lenoir has shown how it refers back to Kant's
analysis of vital processes in his *Critique of Judgement*, where Kant distinguishes teleology and mechanism as regulative and constitutive principles,
respectively (19).

Even this form of vitalism, however, came under Helmholtz's attack,
for he sought "to eliminate the incidents of form and distribution in space
. . . by resolving the forces of composite masses into the forces of their
smallest elementary particles" (20). Such attractive and repulsive central
forces, acting only between pairs, Helmholtz regarded as the necessary
basis for universal conservation of force. He recognized no possibility of
essentially multiparticle forces depending on arrangement nor any other
possible realization of the teleomechanist's belief.

In this we can see why Helmholtz's stance in physiology required as
a concomitant his sharp separation of the *Naturwissenschaften* from the
Geisteswissenschaften, for the same 'teleomechanist' position adopted by
contemporary vitalists operated as well in history. I need only point out
here that Kant's description of the biological problem parallels closely his
analysis of progress in history, according to which political-social development fulfills the teleological idea of freedom but is worked out via the
mechanism of man's 'unsociable sociability', his simultaneous attraction
to and repulsion from society (21). In driving his reductionist wedge between
teleology and mechanism, therefore, and correspondingly between reasoning
by analogy and reasoning by causes, Helmholtz pried natural science apart
from historical science on the ground of both content and method. No
longer would purpose be seen in nature, but only 'dead indifferent matter'.
In natural science, "to understand phenomena" would be "to find the law
by which they are regulated", i.e., "to seek out the *forces* which are the
causes of the phenomena" (22). To understand, would not be, as in history,
to see a complex of events in their multiple relations to prior, contemporary,
and succeeding events and thereby to grasp as a whole their teleological
significance. For historical science to improve itself, furthermore, it should
do what Helmholtz decreed for natural science: give up purposes and analyze
causes.

Not many of Helmholtz's contemporaries, not even in physical science,
shared his radical distinction between purpose and cause, between *Geist*

and *Natur*. Indeed, his program did not remain long in the ascendency before new accommodations between the disciplines appeared, though deeply affected by that program. Before considering Helmholtz's decline it will be instructive to examine an alternative construal of mathematical physics contemporary with Helmholtz's and against which he campaigned.

2.2. *The Physics of Weber and Fechner*

Helmholtz's program was radically materialist in that it required the reduction both of vital function and of sensory perception to material processes. Other physicists, just like many physiologists, agreed with Helmholtz about the necessity of reducing nature to cause and effect, but they were not materialists. Prominent among them were Wilhelm Weber and Gustav Theodor Fechner. I shall here only briefly summarize their view, extracting those elements relevant to historiographical concerns.

Weber and Fechner preserved their non-materialist stance, even while reducing physical processes to atoms and forces, by emphasizing a positivist and relativist perspective. Atoms were to be conceived simply as points in space and time, without any properties in themselves except inertia. All properties of matter derived from forces between the atoms; but the forces did not derive from individual atoms, they represented relations between the atoms in space and time. These Weber called 'given relations', that is, given by experiment in the present state of science. At a later time different relations might be given that were more general (23).

The fundamental law of force (*Grundgesetz*) upon which Weber and Fechner built their natural philosophy, and which Weber is famous for having discovered in 1846, depends not only on relative spatial position but also, implicitly, on time, for it depends on relative velocity and relative acceleration. From it Weber was able to derive all known electromagnetic relations; and he set out to construct an electromagnetic model of nature. This *mechanical* law is peculiar, however, for it provides an *organic* picture of nature. Because it is acceleration dependent, the relation between two atoms depends on the effect of any third atom. Although Weber was able in 1848 to derive the force from a strictly two-body potential, neither he nor Fechner ever gave up the idea that higher-order, multibody forces might act in nature. Weber suggested that the effect of the third body in the law of force might

explain catalytic action. As Lenoir has shown, that was one of the key
models of the teleomechanists for a vital force, which would depend on the
organization of parts in a body, on its form (24). Thus the positivist emphais
on forces as "given relations in space and time" led quite naturally to teleo-
mechanism and to an organic conception of matter:

> If material essences that are spatially and temporally separated interact, then the basis
> of this interaction lies in the essence of both *as a whole*. The interdependent parts of
> this *whole* exist in different points of space and time. If there are *material* essences that
> as wholes cannot be localized to a point of space and time, then that is far more true of
> *spiritual* [geistige] essences (25).

Fechner put the point somewhat more poetically. "*Geist* steps up [to the
atoms] and asks, what have I to do with you? And the atoms say: we spread
our individualities under your unity; law is the commander of our band, but
you are the king in whose service he leads" (26). For Weber and Fechner
the laws were God's laws of relation and the unity his unity. As Weber said,
"the capacity for sensation, thought, and recollection is bestowed on us.
With it we acquire generally a world of ideas, in particular a world thought
of in causal connection, materially and spiritually. The causal connection
leads to a final cause — God" (27).

This perspective is teleomechanist in that it supposes a teleological goal
worked out mechanically. It is more specifically historicist in tone because
it supposes that later stages of development not only develop out of earlier
stages but also *contain* the earlier stages. That is a direct consequence of
Weber's law of force. Because it is implicitly time dependent, a given relation
between any two atoms depends on how that relation was established. For
example, velocity dependence implies that the relation between two atoms
at a given distance of separation depends on whether or not that distance is
changing, so that atoms arriving at the given separation along a line between
them will relate differently than atoms moving perpendicular to that line.
The present relation of the atoms depends, as Weber says, on the "continua-
tion of their motion in their preceding paths" (28). That is a statement that
would make an historicist proud, for it means that the past lives in the present; consequently, we can only understand the present in terms of the past.

Out of this view of nature Fechner and Wilhelm Weber's brother Ernst
Heinrich Weber developed during the sixties the subject known as psychophysics. They attempted to determine quantitative relations between physical

stimuli and perceived sensations, thereby putting teeth into the psycho-physical parallelism that Helmholtz found so egregious. I shall not discuss this subject further here except to note that it connects the positivism of Weber and Fechner directly to that of Ernst Mach, which I shall take up shortly.

2.3. *Heyday and Decline of Atomistic-mechanical Reduction*

During the fifties and sixties it looked to many, particularly from outside the physical sciences, as though the materialist program of atomistic mechanical reduction led by Helmholtz and his friends would sweep all challenges before it (29). That seems to have been as much because this group had a 'strong program' which they vociferously pushed on the scientific community as because of their success in carrying through the reduction in a wide variety of cases (30). Granted that Helmholtz had founded the law of conservation of energy on an analysis of central forces acting only between pairs of atoms, and granted that this provided a powerful conceptual basis for the mechanical theory of heat, still it was quickly shown by others that nothing in either area depended necessarily on atomism. Within the biological sciences Helmholtz thought he had finally found the ultimate weapon against teleology when Darwin's theory of evolution was published. But again, his argument was more nearly an internal political power play than it was a logical argument. In the course of his 1869 lecture, "On the Aim and Progress of Physical Science", Helmholtz strongly suggested — through his argument that law implies cause, that all natural causes are forces, and that "we must endeavour to eliminate the incidents of form and distribution in space ... by trying to find ... laws for the operation of infinitely small particles" — that evolution too was merely mechanical. He did insist that evolution resulted "from a blind rule of a law of nature without any intervention of intelligence" (31). But as has been pointed out before, there is difficulty in this, for in referring to a blind rule Helmholtz meant "the law of transmission of individual peculiarities from parent to offspring" (32). The 'law' of variation of those peculiarities he treated as in itself unproblematic. For neither effect did he or could he give any semblance of a reduction that would be independent of 'form and distribution' of matter. His arguments, therefore, had no logical force whatever against teleomechanism but expressed only his program. The unusual strength of this program has yet to be thoroughly investigated in its political dimensions, either internal to science or externally.

In the area of electrodynamics Helmholtz recognized Weber's time-dependent law of force as a threat to the elimination of teleology. But because the law could be derived from a potential, it satisfied conservation of energy, which left Helmholtz with no effective weapon against it. He mounted an outright attack only in 1871 in the course of showing that electromagnetic equations for the propagation of light could be derived from an action-at-a-distance law of force, as opposed to Maxwell's derivation from continuous fields of energy with action only between contiguous parts (33). A field view satisfies all the conditions for an organic whole, in which the parts can be defined only in terms of the whole. Thus it does not allow elimination of considerations of 'form and distribution'.

Since the same objection applied to Weber's law of force acting at a distance, Helmholtz developed an intermediate case, where instead of beginning with interacting atoms of electricity in motion, he began with the interaction of infinitesimal elements of electric current. The law of this interaction is not time dependent. Again, however, there is duplicity, because Helmholtz did not say what a current was. In his own conception of nature it had to be the motion of atoms, but in those terms time-dependence would enter again through the velocity of the particles. Without mentioning his dilemma Helmholtz went on to attack Weber's force law on the ground that two particles moving relative to each other at a speed greater than that of light would acquire an infinite velocity in a finite distance. Among a variety of replies Weber suggested that the velocity of light might be a limiting velocity in nature (34). This depended for him on the relativistic notion that space, time, and matter were not independent. The further debate produced little more than polemics.

Helmholtz's paper of 1871 marked the last gasp in electrodynamics of theories of action at a distance between atoms. Conceptual incongruities in the paper itself helped to stimulate field theories in Germany. Already by 1874 Stefan had suggested from a critique of Helmholtz's paper, that the supposed sources of electromagnetic force, the electric atoms, should be treated as singularities of variable strength determined by the state of the energy field in which they occurred (35). The energy of the field, then, would be the fundamental concept in its description rather than the atoms.

This paper was a forerunner of the electromagnetic view of nature that emerged in the last decade of the century (36).

A case more immediately tied to the issues of historicism is that of thermodynamics. The subject began as the mechanical theory of heat, and thereby seemed tied inextricably to the mechanical law of energy conservation. The Second Law of Thermodynamics, however, the law of entropy increase, soon proved itself resistant to atomistic-mechanical reduction. Clausius, Helmholtz, and others tried to apply the most powerful tools of mechanics, particularly the principle of least action, but still it proved intractable. We may note in passing, once more, Helmholtz's duplicity in the 'Aim and Progress' paper, for there as elsewhere he failed to mention that the 2nd Law was of a very strange kind and that it had already in 1852 been tied to teleology in a famous paper on the heat death of the universe by his friend William Thomson (37). Again, Helmholtz's argument against teleology was largely a statement of a program.

The fortunes of necessary mechanical causality seemed for a short time to be reviving when in 1872 Ludwig Boltzmann made the first of several powerful attempts at incorporating the 2nd Law within kinetic theory. Through his famous H-theorem, he attempted to reduce the approach of a gas toward its equilibrium state to the average behavior of an ensemble of atoms colliding mechanically. In 1876, however, Joseph Loschmidt argued that no such derivation could be valid, because all the laws of mechanics are reversible in time. For every state of a system moving toward equilibrium, therefore, there is another state in which it will move in the opposite direction. To this rather obvious but deep objection Boltzmann responded with his statistical interpretation of 1878. In it he proposed that a system moves in the direction of increasing probability, that is, in the direction in which there are the most states with identical energy distributions. This probabilistic interpretation is now regarded as the most fundamental basis of the 2nd Law, but Boltzmann thought it could be derived from the mechanics of atomic collisions (38).

At that point Max Planck entered the community of professional physicists with a series of quite original papers on the foundations of macroscopic thermodynamics, thermodynamics considered independently of the constitution of matter. He developed the idea that the 2nd Law should be regarded as in essence a statement about irreversible processes. Previously, it had been

developed in terms of reversible cycles, or ideal processes that never occurred
in nature. The natural irreversible processes had been seen as processes that
more or less approached the ideal ones. On the basis of his reinterpretation,
and perhaps with Loschmidt's reversibility paradox in mind, Planck concluded
a paper in 1882 with the following statement.

Consistently developed, the 2nd Law of the mechanical theory of heat is incompatible
with the assumption of finite atoms. It can therefore be forseen that the further development of the theory will lead to a battle between these two hypotheses in which one
of them will perish. An attempt to predict the conflict's outcome with precision at this
time would be premature. Nevertheless, a variety of present signs seem to me to indicate
that the atomic theory, despite its great success, will ultimately have to be abandoned
in favor of the assumption of continuous matter (39).

To Planck, a derivation of the 2nd Law meant a derivation of irreversibility.
He thought that in a mechanical continuum, such as in an electromagnetic
ether field, where every part is tied to every other part like an organic whole,
the derivation might be possible, though just why he thought this is problematic (40).

In any case, Boltzmann came to see Planck as one of his most biting critics,
as having accused him of wasting his energies in an area that could not hope
to yield results. That was in 1894. Shortly afterward when Planck had been
forced to adopt Boltzmann's methods in toto for his quantum calculations,
and when Boltzmann had committed suicide, Planck blamed the whole affair
on old Mach, to whose influence he had too long been subject (41).

In 1895 another major figure, Wilhelm Ostwald, moved the entire subject
of irreversibility out of the realm merely of the 2nd Law and attached it to
the real home of teleology, organic nature. In a paper on "The Victory over
Scientific Materialism", which crystallized many issues of the day and which
aroused a stormy conflict with Boltzmann, Ostwald pointed out that "In a
purely mechanical world there would be no earlier and no later in the sense
of our world; the tree could again become the shoot and the seed . . . the old
man could change into a child . . . . The actual irreversibility of real natural
phenomena proves therefore the presence of processes which are not repre-
sentable by mechanical equations, and thereby the judgement of scientific
materialism is spoken" (42).

Planck no doubt sympathized with some of Ostwald's conclusions, but in
the paper, as I shall discuss below, Ostwald attempted to reduce all of natural

philosophy to energy considerations. Planck could not accept that and wrote a paper saying so. His assistant Ernst Zermelo, however, sought to rid physics of mechanics entirely, whether it be atomistic mechanics or Planck's continuum mechanics. He published a paper in 1896 that brought the historicist tradition to the doorstep of physics. In it he proved the so-called 'recurrence paradox', that any mechanical system, given long enough, will return arbitrarily close to its initial state. "In such a system", Zermelo wrote, "irreversible processes are impossible" (43). Thus mechanics could never be the basis of physics for, indeed, it dealt only with cyclic processes. Such cycles, according to the 2nd Law, and especially to Planck's interpretation of it, were not *natural* at all. The physicist's time, just like the historian's, would have to be defined not by recurring cycles but by unique states of ever increasing entropy along an infinite line.

3. Rise of the Opposition: Positivism, Relativism and Historicism

I have summarized the decline of atomistic mechanics and have pointed out some of the ways in which ideas associated with that decline might be seen as having to do with historiography. The relations, however, have been nothing more than analogies of form, precisely the sort of analogy that Helmholtz claimed could prove anything and nothing. By surveying now the rise of a part of the opposition to Helmholtz's program, I shall show that this part of the opposition did, in fact, adopt methods and epistemological claims that were the stock in trade of the historicists. I shall survey, then, Ernst Mach's positivism and the position of the energeticists as represented by Wilhelm Ostwald and Georg Helm.

Mach's sphere of problems is closely associated with the psychophysics of Fechner and Ernst Weber. But rather than study the quantitative *parallel* between an objective physical world in which stimuli are produced, on one hand, and our subjective response to those stimuli, on the other, Mach sought to analyze our knowledge of both worlds through the middle term between them, our sensations. Naturally that eliminated any possibility of a radical distinction between the object of study in physics, nature, and the object of study in psychology, mind. They were merely two ways of organizing sensations.

Mach's early ideas on this subject, in its bearing on physics, are contained in a small book on *The History and Root of the Principle of Conservation of Work* [Energy] published in 1872. It was the first of several such analyses of physical concepts, *"historisch kritisch dargestellt"*. They are, in a sense, not histories at all, for they aim not at an understanding of the past, but at an understanding of the present through the past. It is precisely in that sense, however, that they are historicist. As Mach put it: "History has made all; history can alter all. Let us expect from history all . . . . " He meant that we can only understand our concepts historically. "There are only two ways of reconciling oneself with actuality: either one grows accustomed to the puzzles and they trouble one no more, or one learns to understand them by the help of history . . . . " (44). We should note carefully the sense here of 'understanding' for it is the historicist notion of *Verstehen* acquired by immersing oneself in history so as to see the development of an idea. It is the opposite extreme from 'explanation' by reduction to supposed fundamental physical entities like atoms and forces. Many physicists before Mach had expressed the positivist view that the task of physics was not to explain but to describe, e.g., Weber, C. Neumann, and Kirchhoff, to name some of the most prominent, but Mach emphasized the historicist dimension of positivism in ways that they had not. His attack on Helmholtz's claim of the priority of mechanical reduction was in essence the attack of a cultural relativist. "It is the result of a misconception", he said, "to believe . . . that mechanical facts are more intelligible than others, and that they can provide the foundation for other physical facts. This belief arises from the fact that the history of mechanics is older and richer than that of physics, so that we have been on terms of intimacy with mechanical facts for a longer time". In the future electrical and thermal phenomena might be more familiar. "The choice of fundamental facts is a matter of convenience, history and custom." Or again, "What we represent to ourselves behind the appearances exists *only* in our understanding, and . . . varies very easily with the standpoint of our culture" (45). Thus to understand was necessarily to understand historically.

That I have not exaggerated the historicist dimension of Mach's epistemology can be established from his central argument on the root of the conservation law. Helmholtz had tried to demonstrate that conservation was founded on the principle of excluded perpetual motion and that this principle in turn was founded on mechanics. But Mach argued, on purely historical grounds, "it is clear that the principle of excluded perpetual motion cannot be founded on mechanics, since its validity was felt long before the edifice of mechanics was raised" (46). I must reiterate the radical nature of this claim: because excluded perpetual motion preceded mechanics historically, mechanics cannot be its foundation. Though no positivist today would be able to see the force of this reasoning, Mach let his reader know, by repeating it several times, that it was the core of his claim.

On what then is the principle of excluded perpetual motion founded? On the *law of causality*, answers Mach, but this root he calls a logical root. He has no clearly historical evidence for it. He suggests that the law of causality in some form is as old as human culture itself. It is only that it has taken time for history to give it positive content. This he illustrates with an example of how every child at present learns what only the greatest minds had had access to earlier. That is one form, of course, of the notion that ontogeny recapitulates philogeny. It is specifically the historicist claim that logical concepts attain their reality by being worked out through history. "Without positive experiences", Mach tells us, "the law of causality is empty and barren". The same is true of any other formal law, such as that of perpetual motion, sufficient reason, or inertia. History teaches us their content (47).

There is another aspect of Mach's positivism that connects it with historicist claims: the essential wholeness of nature. Because to Mach all our knowledge of nature is knowledge of relations, or "knowledge of the connection of appearances with one another", time and space too are relative. They are "determinations of phenomena by means of other phenomena" (48). In particular they are determinations of relations of masses. This leads, through an analysis of the problem of inertia, to the view that space, time, and mass must be thought of as an interrelated whole. Each can be thought of as a function of the other. No notion of isolated atoms could properly exist in such a world. This wholeness extended for Mach not only throughout nature but also to the psychic life of man, for of course, our sensations extend in both directions. Thus he stated in another connection his opposition to the separation of the physical sciences from the historical sciences claiming that "both these sciences are simply parts of the same science, which have begun at different ends" (49). In this he could hardly have agreed more with Hegel and Droysen.

There is one very important aspect, however, in which Mach and other positivists among physical scientists disagreed with the older historical tradition; that is *teleology*. "To us investigators", said Mach, "the concept 'soul' is irrelevant and a matter for laughter" (50). Yet he rested his entire historicist argument on the progressive development of ideas through history. What controlled that development? Mach's substitute for soul was the *'principle of economy'*. Nature, including man's nature, operates always in the most efficient way, whether it be in producing the shape of a soap bubble or arranging our eyes for three-dimensional vision. In addition man progresses in the direction of greater economy of thought. To Mach as a physical scientist, that meant subsuming ever more various appearances under ever more general laws relating those appearances. Thus he replaced teleology by an equally elusive principle of change, but one more nearly suited to a late nineteenth century industrial state and to Mach's liberal political position. Throughout his writings on the principle of economy he illustrated it by examples of the operation of a capitalist political economy and the role of the businessman in it.

Turning now to the energeticists, we find a program that develops many of Mach's ideas but which aims directly at turning on its head Helmholtz's mechanical reductionist program. "We ask no longer", Ostwald concluded in his 1895 address on the victory over scientific materialism, "after the forces which we cannot demonstrate between the atoms which we cannot observe; but we ask, when we want to judge a process, after the kind and quantity of the outgoing and incoming energies". We can only know, in Ostwald's view, relations of appearances through sensations, and all sensations register "differences of energy states relative to our sense apparatus". This implies a totally relativistic view of the pictures of reality that men form, with the resulting moral, "Thou shalt make no image nor any likeness" (51).

The energeticist scheme denies not only Helmholtz's physical pictures but also his separation of *Naturwissenschaft* from *Geisteswissenschaft*, for supposing all knowledge to express relations of energy states implies that external and internal perceptions are the same in kind. Thus the methods of *Wissenschaft* must be universal. In a parody of Helmholtz's strictures against Goethe's arguments by analogy of forms, Ostwald began his paper: "In order to find our way about in the infinity of the world of appearances, we use always and everywhere the same scientific method. We juxtapose like to like and seek what is common in the multiplicity." Goethe, and Droysen too, understood this method of analogy as the prototypical method of history. To Ostwald it implied for science an idealism of mathematical forms discovered through history.

The most obvious clue, in fact, to the relation of energeticism to historicism lies in the historical style of its presentation. As the foundation for his public promotion of the energeticist program, Ostwald had completed in 1894 a book on *Electrochemistry, its History and Theory*. He announced that he intended to carry out an experiment, to test preliminarily by analyzing the history of development of a limited subject, whether it would be possible to set up general laws for historical development. He concluded that the historical record pointed toward an ever more significant role for analysis of electrochemical processes according to the energy transformations involved. Generalizing from there, energetics was the idea of the future. Where Helmholtz had rested his program on what seemed to him the logical force of his reduction, we now find Ostwald resting his antithetical program on history. In a truly Hegelian manner Ostwald contended that "the historical course of development of an area in general coincides continuously with the logical course" (52). Thus history could teach the logic of science.

That should serve to indicate how radically historicist Ostwald's epistemological position was. His teleology reinforces the impression. If intellectual history were controlled by logic, where did man's freedom of choice lie, and what about organic development? Ostwald's answer requires some elasticity of thought. Though all scientific laws are deterministic they nevertheless do not determine the course of nature. That is because the laws describe processes in the ideal world, rather than the real. They are ideal types, to use Max Weber's term. They describe what will always happen if a certain very limited set of circumstances repeat themselves. But in the actual world there are an infinity of variables and the same circumstances never recur. Thus science can determine a certain broad path that natural events will follow; but "which of the infinitely many possibilities within this path will afterwards become reality can never be uniquely determined by human powers". That is why we have the consciousness of acting freely. There is no objection, Ostwald argued, to a fundamental determinism which explains this feeling of freedom by saying, "that a part of the causal chain lies within our consciousness, and that we sense these processes (in themselves determined) as though we ourselves determined their course . . . " (53).

The teleology of organic development is similarly determined, but by the process of adaptation, which Ostwald ascribes even to inorganic contrivances like clocks and violins. They must be 'broken in' before their full qualities are realized. This is an extreme form of the theory of evolution, where adaptation determines survival. Even our concepts, according to Ostwald, derive from adaptation. Thus we are perfectly justified in regarding all mental activities as connected series of increasingly manifold and purposive actions proceeding from the same physico-chemical and physiological foundations (54). With this slippery set of notions, which seeks to integrate Hegel with Darwin, Ostwald replaced the idea of a soul and thereby rounded out his natural philosophy in a properly scientific spirit.

Ostwald received considerable support in his advocacy of the energeticist program from Georg Helm. Since Helm's arguments add little that is new, however, I shall use them here to summarize the historicist aspects of the program.

(1) *Historical presentation*. Helm entitled his major energeticist works: *Die Energetik nach ihrer geschichtlichen Entwicklung* (1898) and *Die Theorien der Elektrodynamik nach ihrer geschichtlichen Entwicklung* (1904).

(2) *Historical justification for the program*. "To whoever appreciates the perspective of historical development ... this book will decisively protest against the view that as *Energetics* one designates only a single branch, or even the refuse, of that unitary [historical] development − as its enemies have attempted to do. This creation of thought [energetics] must be understood as a whole, as a great turning point in the human conception of natural processes."

(3) *Knowledge derives in the first instance from analogies, which are then superceded at a higher level*. "Wherever our mind encounters relations, which show similarities with already known relations, it is the first step of comprehension to make the new understandable through the old, to portrary through them; the last step, however, is to sweep forth to what is common in the old and the new relations and to grasp them in a higher concept under which then all those relations are subsumed."

(4) *The new always contains the old, from which it grew*. As in (3), plus the idea that history allows one to recognize the 'inner connections' of "manifold modes of consideration and representations, ... which allows all these circles of thought to appear as terms in one and the same chain of development."

(5) *We learn fundamental principles of physics from history.* "If any development of physical ideas can teach an onlooker, the history of electrodynamics can teach him that all facts are relations and that anything absolute, insofar as it is thought of as absolute, corresponds to no fact."

(6) *Mathematical Idealism.* "The equation $\nabla^2 \phi = 0$, for example, appears in such various areas of physics, that it appears justifiable to treat it as a mathematical object cut loose as a 'pure form'" from every physical application and representation (55).

4. Conclusion

Throughout the preceding discussion of the relation between the natural sciences and historical sciences I have referred to certain forms of argument as historicist. I have shown how such historicist thinking among one important group of scientists, served as the basis for launching a reform program, providing even its rationale. Yet one may object that the connection thus suggested between historiography and physical science is gratuitous, that it follows merely from defining the term historicist and has little to do with real relations. More particularly, the suggested connection has little to do with real causes of change in science. I have given an analogy of form without supplying any mechanism of interaction. Helmholtz himself would surely have made this criticism, advocating that history, like physics, should make "the effort to detect in all cases relations of cause and effect" (56). Because nearly all reactions to this paper have involved objections of that sort, I shall take the opportunity in conclusion, of examining in what direction the present description could most fruitfully be expanded. I shall argue for extension of the analogies as the primary desideratum rather than the search for mechanisms of causation.

Let me first summarize what sorts of connnections to historiography have so far been drawn. We have seen that the claims of Mach and Ostwald were explicitly historical in presentation and epistemology, resting on arguments typically historicist in form. We have followed the debate between the disciplines as a continual theme, with the terms of the debate deriving from historicist categories. We have seen that Mach and Ostwald developed their ideas in opposition to the reductionist program, which Helmholtz enunciated as itself a reaction to an imperialistic historicism that threatened to annex

natural science. Discussion of these issues, finally, has indicated that developments in the physical sciences cannot be treated separately from those in
the biological and historical sciences. Each can be followed separately in
its own development and its own internal problems, but the separation is
artificial, as the examples especially of Helmholtz, the Weber brothers,
Fechner and Mach show. The areas they investigated, biophysics and psychophysics, continued to involve issues central to the relation of the disciplines,
a fact which they discussed.

These connections to historiography do not satisfy the critic who wants
rigorous causal analysis. At the level of individuals, he wants to know which
historians or philosophers of history influenced Mach and how. Perhaps
biographical evidence of that sort exists. If so it would certainly lend credibility to the discussion. The point I wish to make here, however, is that
even if no such evidence existed, even if Mach had had no direct contact
with historians whatsoever, his work would still be historicist and dependent
on the historicist tradition. It is precisely for this reason that I have developed
the case historically, as a tradition of debate in which Mach was a participant.
But also, I hope to have indicated that the issue of historicist argument was
much larger than the individuals here discussed. Piecemeal biographical
evidence, consequently, could only be anecdotal and exemplary, showing
how individuals related in detail to the general issue. It is doubtful, furthermore, that such evidence could be fruitfully collected in support of a causal
argument without having first surveyed, at the macroscopic level, the breadth
and depth of historicism.

Two factors, then − that the issue is essentially temporal and that it sweeps
across many disciplines − have led me to adopt a mode of presentation which
is itself essentially historicist and which points toward an extension of that
mode. Thus the connections I have drawn are not causal in the sense in which
external bodies or forces (historiography) act on other bodies (physicists)
which have been isolated from their surroundings for the sake of observing
their response to the forces. Rather, I have described temporal variations in
attitude among physical scientists both with respect to problems in their
own local context and simultaneously with respect to the much wider debate.
This should suggest not response to, but participation in, the surroundings.
On this view issues that transcend the local context are nevertheless worked
out within it, in its own language and with respect to its own problems. The

general ideas thereby attain their content, their meaning, through the process of becoming particular instances. To attain a full understanding of the particular case, therefore, one should compare it to other cases of similar kind worked out over a different ground and with respect to different problems. In this ideal of intellectual history, each facet of a political, social, cultural, and disciplinary context would illuminate the others without determining their content. Though that is an ideal particularly of nineteenth century German historicism it is one also with prominent adherents today (57).

Applied to the present case this perspective suggests how one might approach answering the question of why the German historiographical tradition was important to an influential group of late nineteenth century physical scientists. We should not be seeking reductive causal explanations – whether intellectual, social or otherwise – but contextual understanding that merges a variety of factors, none of which should be supposed definitive but each of which can be shown relevant to one or another of the actors involved. In what follows I shall suggest the range of factors that need consideration without attempting to elaborate their action. They provide a set of interrelated reasons why we might have expected to find historicist thinking in physical science. And they will suggest where further research might seek a deeper understanding.

The historical background I have sketched to Mach's and to Ostwald's positions has been intended to suggest the operation of a kind of historical logic. Helmholtz and his party promoted their program of materialist reduction in opposition to existing research schemes that were linked closely to historicist ideas, ideas that maintained an intellectual unity between the disciplines. Weber and Fechner in physics and the teleo-mechanists in physiology are examples. The reductionist scheme was short-lived, however, and never eliminated its competitors. They resurfaced with a new face. One could think of this as the pendulum of history, with older views reemerging on the promise of solving problems that have resisted the current mode of explanation. But a description more appropriate to the present narrative would emphasize a dialectic in which the poles of strict materialist-mechanist causality and of historical organicism merged with Mach and Ostwald into a new synthesis of causality and history. Gone was the previous connection of causality with mechanism, and gone too was the connection of organicism with *Geist*. In Mach's psycho-physics, sensations, as the elements of a scientific analysis, replaced both atoms and *Geist*. Causality became a recurring relation of phenomena and scientific laws became historical and conventional. Heat or electricity, Mach thought, might serve as well as mechanics as a reductive basis for physics.

This metamorphosis of world view depended, of course, on very real and pressing internal problems. I have summarized a number of these in physics. The internal problems alone, it could well be argued, suggested a new approach with strong affinities to traditional historicist concerns but which nevertheless did not depend on that tradition. In electrodynamics, both the time dependence of Weber's force law, with its attendant implication of interconnectedness, and the wholistic nature of field theories were amenable to such treatment. Thermodynamics provided a similar motivation because of the seeming impossibility of reducing the Second Law to atomistic mechanics. It demanded an interpretation that would allow unique progress of natural processes in time. Granting these immediate causes, however, they are still not sufficient to explain the new positivism. They provide only a problem situation in which Mach's and Ostwald's theory choices seem reasonable. Others chose differently.

The search for internal causes can easily be extended to natural science as a whole, to include, for example, Darwin's theory of evolution, which is known to have been important for Mach (58). But evolution was important too for Helmholtz and for Boltzmann, on very different grounds. Its effect on Mach's thinking can only be understood contextually in that realm where causes and effects coalesce into interactions.

An obvious point of entry for scientists into traditional historicist concerns was their education at the classical Gymnasia, where all of them imbibed a strong dose of history and philology. Those disciplines provided the central focus of the curriculum. Access to basic historicist ideas, then, is relatively unproblematic. More interesting is the fact that debate over school modernization raged throughout the second half of the nineteenth century. That debate pitted advocates of more mathematics, science, and modern languages against those wishing to maintain the traditional humanist emphasis on classical languages, literature, and history. That is, it pitted the natural sciences against the historical sciences and thereby kept very much alive the problem of their relation. Many prominent scientists entered the public debate, including Helmholtz, Mach, and Ostwald (59). The latter two, with

Helmboltz, supported modernization, but in a form that minimized the conflict between the disciplines by making them parts of the same science which began at different ends to arrive at the ultimate source of all our knowledge in sensations. Even before Mach, of course, Fechner and Ernst Weber had sought through psychophysics to make of subject and object two sides of one reality, to parallel *Geist* with *Natur* and thereby to maintain the unity of science.

In this context it is relevant to note that disciplines other than the physical sciences engaged in internal debate over the basis of their science. Historians like Droysen, Ranke, and Dilthey participated in an ongoing internal dialogue that questioned the methodological foundations of history at the same time as they responded vehemently to outside attacks on what Helmholtz labelled "aesthetic induction" in history. Droysen in 1862 levelled his counterattack at H. T. Buckle who had tried, in his famous *History of Civilization in England*, to model history on the laws of natural science and statistics. Historians pilloried Karl Lamprecht on the same grounds in the 1890's (60).

Economics offers another such example, with the so-called 'historical school' led by Schmoller, Brentano, and Wagner battling the analytic school in a well-known *Methodenstreit*. The historical school emerged in the 1870's, during the consolidation phase of Bismarck's government and particularly during the early phases of the great depression. They sought to combat the excesses of mechanistic, free-market economics, based on universal law, and to redress the social evils that attended it. Although operating from a wide variety of political perspectives, members of the historical school generally regarded economics as a culturally dependent study. From their midst arose the new discipline of sociology, represented most prominently by Max Weber, whose positivist, relativist, and idealist conception of sociological analysis could be compared at many points with positivism in physical science.

The more disciplines one examines, in fact, the more ubiquitous seems the debate between historical and analytical 'schools'. That does not necessarily suggest any direct influence between the disciplines, but it does at least suggest a context of academic politics within which each of the disciplines debated its own issues. Just how such an ambiance affects individual thinkers deserves much more research. We have one important example of how to proceed in Paul Forman's study of Weimar academic culture and quantum mechanics (61). I would find his discussion more satisfying, however, if the physicists appeared as active members of that culture rather than as a separate group who capitulated to its overwhelming force.

The issue of academic politics cannot be left at the academic level, for academic politics was at the same time national politics. I will note here only that historicists like Droysen provided an intellectual support base for Prussian dominance in the Second Reich as well as for the limited form of political liberalism that guided the National Liberal Party. Similarly, the historical school of economics saw itself as a social policy group as well as a research school. And again, the school debate itself became a major national issue in the 1890's, with Kaiser Wilhelm taking active part. In all of these ways, as in a multitude of others, questions of historical versus analytical understanding translated into political-social terms.

To conclude, the historicist mode of knowing enjoyed strong political, strong social, and strong academic sanction in late nineteenth century Germany. In such a situation it would seem highly anomalous if physical scientists did not respond within their own discipline. But that statement leads only to the first premise of the sociology of knowledge as applied to science: namely, we must learn to see scientists as participants in political and social movements at the same time as we see them as producers of rational scientific knowledge. I have provided only one more case study to motivate the premise, but with this addition: by presenting a basically historicist account of historicist thinking in German physical science, I hope to have argued for an approach to the sociology of science that will unite temporal (i.e., historical), internal, and social-political dimensions in a single structure of meaning. I would turn our attention away from discovering causes, whether internal or external, and toward enriching contexts. That is not because causes do not exist or are not discoverable but because they are too easy to discover. There are too many of them. More importantly, they do not act independently, but in an overdetermined network of mutually interacting and constantly shifting factors. Thus the notion of a single cause having an effect is meaningless outside of its context. In this situation, the context as a whole must be regarded as the cause. There can be no question, furthermore, of an exhaustive causal explanation, but only of a more or less rich understanding.

Another way to put this point would be to advocate discarding, as our model of a 'scientific' explanation, Helmholtz's ideal of mechanical causation.

If we should model social science at all on physical science it should be on field theories, for field theories are always interaction theories. That is, a body interacting with a field may be said to be acted on by its own effect on the field, or by its participation in the field. To change any one part of the field, similarly, is to change the whole field, for it is defined in terms of the temporal and spatial relations between its parts. That much is typical of the nineteenth century field theories that Helmholtz opposed. If we moved to more modern field theories of elementary particle interaction we would find it even more difficult to distinguish the objects and their fields. We would also find increased willingness to accept alternative representations of the interactions. But though the field metaphor offers useful insights it does not help with the problem that seems to me most fundamental to the sociology of knowledge: to describe the field in the first place. It is through the description that we can expect to answer such questions as that raised in this volume: under what conditions does historiography become significant for scientists.

Notes

1. J. W. Goethe, *Zur Farbenlehre* (1810), in *Goethe: Gesamtausgabe der Werke und Schriften*, Stuttgart: J. G. Cotta, 1956–60, XXI: 18.
2. E.g., Gernot Böhme, 'Ist Goethes Farbenlehre Wissenschaft?' *Studia Leibnitiana* **9** (1977), 27–54.
3. Werner Heisenberg, in *Philosophic Problems of Nuclear Science*, F. C. Hayes (tr.), London: Faber and Faber, 1952, p. 75.
4. *Ibid.*, p. 71.
5. *Ibid.*, pp. 65f, 71.
6. *Philosophic Problems* (Note 3), pp. 32, 29.
7. Ernst Mach, *History and Root of the Principle of the Conservation of Energy*, P. E. B. Jourdain (tr.), Chicago: Open Court, 1911, p. 57.
8. A convenient survey is Georg G. Iggers, *The German Conception of History: The National Tradition of Historical Thought from Herder to the Present*, Middletown, Conn.: Wesleyan U. Pr., 1968.
9. Discussed most generally in Kant's *Critique of Judgement*. Timothy Lenoir provides a lucid account of this issue for biology which I shall draw on below, 'Teleology without Regrets. The Transformation of Physiology in Germany: 1790–1847', *Stud. Hist. Phil. Sci.*, **12** (1981), 293–354. For its importance in history see Kant's essays, 'Perpetual Peace', esp. 1st Supplement, 'Of the Guarantee for Perpetual Peace', and 'Idea for a Universal History from a Cosmopolitan Point of View', in L. W. Beck (ed.), *On History*, Indianapolis: Bobbs-Merrill, 1963, pp. 106–114, 11–26.

10. J. G. Droysen, 'Natur und Geschichte', in R. Hübner (ed.), *Historik: Vorlesungen über Enzyklopädie und Methodologie der Geschichte*, 3rd. ed., Darmstadt: Wissenschaftlich Buchgesellschaft, 1958, p. 411; translation from *Outline of the Principles of History*, E. B. Andrews (tr.), Boston: Ginn, 1897, p. 98.
11. *Ibid.*, p. 408; Andrews, p. 94.
12. *Ibid.*, p. 415; Andrews, p. 104.
13. The mix of positivism and historicist idealism in Ranke's work is well described by Leonard Krieger, *Ranke: The Meaning of History*, Chicago: Univ. Chicago Pr., 1977, pp. 1–31.
14. H. von Helmholtz, Ueber das Verhältnis der Naturwissenschaften zur Gesamtheit der Wissenschaften', *Philosophische Vorträge und Aufsätze*, H. Hörz and Siegfried Wollgast (eds.), Berlin: Akademie Verlag, 1971, pp. 86, 93; translations from 'On the Relation of Natural Science to Science in General', *Popular Lectures on Scientific Subjects*, E. Atkinson, (tr.), new ed., 1st Series, London: Longmans, Green and Co., 1895, pp. 8, 14. Atkinson gives *Geisteswissenschaften* as 'moral sciences'.
15. H. von Helmholtz, 'Ueber Goethes Naturwissenschaftliche Arbeiten', *Vorträge* (Note 14), pp. 31, 32: 'On Goethe's Scientific Researches'; Atkinson, pp. 39, 40. Cf. Helmholtz's lecture of 1892, 'Goethes Vorahnungen kommender naturwissenschaftlicher Ideen', *Vorträge*, pp. 337–364. No longer feeling himself under the threat of imperialistic *Geisteswissenschaften*, Helmholtz here presents a much more respectful and sophisticated analysis of the disciplinary divisions. His basic ideas, however, remain unchanged.
16. *Ibid.*, p. 37; Atkinson, p. 45.
17. 'Ueber das Verhältnis' (Note 14), p. 101; Atkinson, p. 21.
18. *Ibid.*, p. 86; Atkinson, p. 8. 'Ueber das Ziel und die Fortschritte der Naturwissenschaften', *Vorträge* (Note 14), p. 160; Atkinson, p. 326.
19. Above, note 9. See also Lenoir *The Strategy of Life: Teleology, Mechanics and the Development of Nineteenth Century German Biology*, Dordrecht: D. Reidel, 1982.
20. 'Ueber das Ziel', (Note 18), p. 161; Atkinson, p. 326.
21. 'Idea for a Universal History', (Note 9), p. 15.
22. 'Ueber das Ziel', (Note 18), pp. 160, 161f; Atkinson, pp. 325, 326.
23. Wilhelm Weber, 'Elektrodynamische Maassbestimmungen: Ueber ein allgemeines Grundgesetz der elektrischen Wirkung', *Abhandlungen bei Begründung der kaiserlichen sächsischen Gesellschaft der Wissenschaften*, Leipzig, 1846, in *Wilhelm Webers Werke*, Berlin, 1892–94, III: 149f, 214. Gustav Theodor Fechner, *Ueber die physikalische und philosophische Atomenlehre*, Leipzig, 1855, pp. 106–118. For a summary of Weber's and Fechner's physics see my 'German Concepts of Force, Energy, and the Electromagnetic Ether: 1845–1880', in G. N. Cantor and M. J. S. Hodge (eds.), *Conceptions of ether: Studies in the history of ether theories, 1740–1900*, Cambridge U. Pr., 1981, pp. 269–307, esp. 276–287.
24. *Ibid.*, Weber, 'Grundgesetz', III: 212f. Lenoir, *The Strategy of Life* (Note 19), Chapter 4.
25. Weber, 'Aphorismen', *Werke* (Note 23), IV: 631f.
26. Fechner, *Atomenlehre* (Note 23), p. 65.
27. Weber, 'Aphorismen', *Werke* (Note 23), IV: 632.
28. Weber, 'Grundgesetz', (Note 23), III: 212.
29. E.g., Hermann Lotze, *Streitschriften von Hermann Lotze*, Leipzig: Hirzel, 1857.

30. Another such 'strong program' of causal analysis is advocated for the sociology of science by members of the Edinburgh Science Studies Unit, e.g., David Bloor, *Knowledge and Social Imagery*, London, 1976. I shall discuss an alternative, somewhat analogous to modern alternatives to Helmholtz, in the conclusion below.

31. 'Ueber das Ziel' (Note 18), p. 174; Atkinson, p. 338.

32. Lenoir, *The Strategy of Life* (Note 19), Chapter 5.

33. H. von Helmholtz, 'Ueber die Bewegungsgleichungen der Elektricität für ruhende leitende Körper', *Journal für die reine und angewandte Mathematik* **72** (1870), in Helmholtz, *Wissenschaftliche Abhandlungen*, I: 545–628. I have analyzed Helmholtz's arguments in 'German Concepts' (Note 23), pp. 295–301.

34. I have discussed this in 'Atomism and Wilhelm Weber's Concept of Force', in Charlotte Schönbeck (ed.), *Atomvorstellungen im 19. Jahrhundert*, Paderborn: Schöningh, 1982, pp. 57–66.

35. Joseph Stefan, 'Ueber die Gesetze der magnetischen und elektrischen Kräfte in magnetischen und dielektrischen Medien und ihre Beziehung zur Theorie des Lichtes', *Sitzungsberichte der kaiserlichen königlichen Akademie der Wissenschaften zu Wien* **70** (1874), 589–644.

36. Russell McCormmach, 'H. A. Lorentz and the Electromagnetic View of Nature', *Isis* **61** (1970), 459–479.

37. 'On a Universal Tendency in Nature to the Dissipation of Mechanical Energy', *Proc. Roy. Soc. of Edinburgh* (1852), in Thomson's *Mathematical and Physical Papers*, Cambridge Eng.: Cambridge U. Pr., 1882 I: 511–514.

38. For a lucid analysis of Boltzmann's concerns and those of Planck presented below see Thomas S. Kuhn, *Black-Body Theory and the Quantum Discontinuity*, 1894–1912, Oxford: Clarendon Pr.; New York: Oxford U. Pr., 1978, Chapter 2 and pp. 11–37, respectively.

39. Max Planck, 'Verdampfen, Schmelzen und Sublimieren,' *Ann. d. Phys.* **15** (1882), 474f; translation from Kuhn, *Ibid.*, p. 23. A footnote to Maxwell is omitted.

40. Kuhn, *Black-Body Theory* (Note 38), pp. 23–29.

41. See the interchanges between Planck and Mach in the *Physikalische Zeitschrift* **10, 11** (1909, 1910), reprinted in Stephen Toulmin (ed.), *Physical Reality: Philosophical Essays on Twentieth Century Physics*, New York: Harper & Row, 1970, pp. 1–52.

42. Wilhelm Ostwald, *Die Ueberwindung des wissenschaftlichen Materialismus*, Leipzig: Veit & Comp., 1895, p. 21.

43. Kuhn, *Black-Body Theory* (Note 38), pp. 26–28. E. F. F. Zermelo, 'Ueber einen Satz der Dynamik und die mechanische Wärmetheorie', *Ann. D. Phys.* **57** (1896), 485.

44. Mach, *History and Root* (Note 7), pp. 18, 16f. The translator gives *Arbeit* as 'Energy' to conform to modern usage.

45. *Ibid.*, pp. 56f, 57, 49.

46. *Ibid.*, pp. 41, 59.

47. *Ibid.*, pp. 65–71; quotation, p. 65.

48. *Ibid.*, pp. 49, 60; also pp. 78f on the wholeness of the universe.

49. Ernst Mach, 'Why has Man two Eyes?' (1867), in T. J. McCormack (trans.), *Popular Scientific Lectures*, 3rd ed., Chicago: Open Court, 1898, p. 87.

50. Mach, *History and Root* (Note 7), p. 48.

51. Ostwald, 'Die Ueberwindung' (Note 42), pp. 32, 29, 22.
52. Wilhelm Ostwald, *Elektrochemie, ihre Geschichte und Lehre*, Leipzig: Veit & Comp., 1896, p. vi. For date of completion (1894) see p. viii.
53. Wilhelm Ostwald, *Grundriss der Naturphilosophie*, Leipzig: P. Reclam jr., 1908, pp. 58, 60.
54. *Ibid.*
55. Georg Helm, *Die Energetik nach ihrer geschichtlichen Entwickelung*, Leipzig: Veit & Comp., 1898, pp. iiif; *Die Theorien der Elektrodynamik nach ihrer geschichtlichen Entwickelung*, Leipzig: Veit & Comp., 1904, pp. 154, iii, iv, 155.
56. 'Ueber das Verhältnis' (Note 14), p. 101.
57. E.g., Carl Schorske, *Fin de Siècle Vienna: Politics and Culture* New York: Knopf, 1980. Schorske would insist, however, on a concrete biographical grasp of the various facets.
58. I thank Michael Heidelberger for raising this issue.
59. Mach, Note 49 above and, in the same collection, 'On Instruction in the Classics and the Mathematico-Physical Sciences' (1886), pp. 338–374. Ostwald, *Wider das Schulelend: Ein Notruf*, Leipzig: Akademischer Verlagsgesellschaft, 1904.
60. J. G. D. Droysen, 'Erhebung der Geschichte zum Rang einer Wissenschaft', from von Sybels *Zeitschrift* 9 (1863), later appended to *Grundriss der Historik*, in *Historik* (Note 10), pp. 386–405. See also another appended essay, 'Kunst und Methode', in which Droysen defended historical method as Wissenschaft rather than art.
61. Paul Forman, 'Weimar Culture, Causality, and Quantum Theory, 1918–1927: Adaptation by German Physicists and Mathematicians to a Hostile Intellectual Environment', *Hist. Stud. Phys. Sci.* 1 (1970), 1–115.

RE-READING THE PAST FROM THE END OF PHYSICS: MAXWELL'S EQUATIONS IN RETROSPECT

PETER GALISON*

Department of Physics and Society of Fellows, Harvard University, Cambridge, Massachusetts 02138, U.S.A.

I. Introduction

For the working physicist, the past and future of physics are thoroughly intertwined. With each set of goals the discipline has posed for itself comes a new gloss on prior accomplishments. As a result there is no unique or simple fashion in which the history of physics (as viewed by physicists) is related to their research priorities. In this brief essay I would like to illustrate some examples of the many ways in which the past is re-read, and then to speculate on some of the functions this constant reinterpretation plays.

By the 'history of physics' I am not referring to the relatively recent professional history of physics of the sort that appears in journals like *Historical Studies in the Physical Sciences, Archive for History of Exact Sciences*, and so on. Physicists as a rule do not read this literature and in any case it has not yet existed for a long enough time for there to be any meaningful assessment of their effect. Rather, I have in mind history as it appears in textbooks, as it is repeated from generation to generation of physicists, and in general the version of the past physicists learn from those primary and secondary sources they actually read.

I take the self-thematization (*Selbstthematisierung* as it appears in the original title of the conference in preparation of this volume) to mean the establishment of programmatic ideals for physics: the articulation of what it would take to provide an adequate account of natural phenomena. This articulation has occurred not once but several times within modern physics. The argument to be presented here is that each of these reorderings of explanatory ideals has been accompanied by a new perception of past accomplishments, at least in the minds of working physicists.

Loren Graham, Wolf Lepenies, and Peter Weingart (eds.), Functions and Uses of Disciplinary Histories, Volume VII, 1983, 35–51.

Unfortunately in a mature science like physics, the participants in research are not given to explicit pronouncements on their over-arching explanatory goals. There is, however, a fascinating exception to this general tendency towards problem-solving rather than goal-defining. Several times in the history of modern physics there have been moments of an almost hubristic optimism about the future. Claims have been made that the fundamental laws of physics are all known and that the future will lie in applications of detail. In these moments we can glimpse the broad goals of physics: for to state that the end of physics is near is *a fortiori* to provide an idea of what would constitute such a triumph.

2. Histories and Futures: Maxwell's Equations through Continuum Physics

This discussion will be limited to examples of the reinterpretation of Maxwell's equations from the time of their invention by Maxwell to the present. Maxwell inherited two very different traditions which up until his time had coexisted in European thought without productively interacting. The first, Cartesian physics, supposed that all phenomena could be explained by the mechanical pushing and pulling that matter at one point exerts on matter at neighboring points. Within this scheme, Descartes contended, he "could set out here many rules to determine in particular, how and how much each object's motion is diverted, augmented or diminished by its collision with others. Taken together these would comprise all the effects of nature ..." (1).

The other mechanical legacy from the 17th century came of course from Newton. Unlike Descartes, in his theory of gravity Newton was unwilling to propose specific mechanisms by which gravity would operate, instead preferring to state simply the mathematical relations by which the motion of celestial objects could be calculated. So successful was his strategy that some Newtonians such as C. L. Berthollet were later moved to argue that even molecular attraction and gravitation were but "one and the same property" (2).

Newton's central force law formed the ideal for explanation in the 19th century as J.-B. Biot, F. Savart, and J.-M. Ampère turned to the newly discovered electrodynamic phenomena of the early nineteenth century. All of their discoveries were couched in the language of distant-action force laws. Biot and Savart sought laws for the action of magnetic poles on other magnetic poles; Ampère found the distant effects of current elements on other current elements. Maxwell, by contrast, formulated electrodynamics in such a way that he could maintain the precision of a Newtonian theory in a near-action form. Instead Maxwell proposed that charged objects act upon one another by first affecting states of an intervening substance which provided a continuum throughout space. For Maxwell his equations offered a comprehensive and quantitive measure of states of this continuum.

For example, in one formulation of his theory Maxwell represented the effects of magnetism as being analogous to an array of linked vortices through the ether. (See Figure 1.) Imagine a wire pq in which balls rotating clockwise

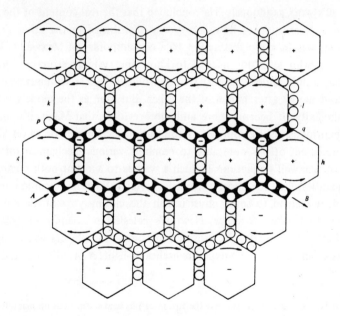

Fig. 1. Maxwell's Etherial Vortices (1861). Current in line pq causes vortices to form in the ether above and below the wire. Source: Maxwell, *Scientific Papers*, 489.

in place represent a current. The current causes motion of the vortices on either side of the wire. These motions can then have physical effects on other wires (such as AB) just as a magnetic field induces currents in moving wires (3). Quite generally Maxwell felt the mechanics of the ether "must be subject to the general laws of dynamics, and we ought to be able to work out all the consequences of its motion, provided we know the form of the relation between the motion of its parts" (4). In fact the dynamical analogies Maxwell established between the electromagnetic continuum and a mechanical continuum played a crucial role in his discovery of the electromagnetic nature of light (5). Maxwell's success in this regard led him and many of his followers to pursue the continuum mechanical analogies with great interest. In the course of his work Maxwell proposed many different models of the ether, leaving his followers to sort out what they took to be the essence of his theory. Here there was much disagreement.

J. H. Poynting, one of the first group of Cavendish students (6), studied Maxwell's work assiduously. He concluded that the real content of the theory was in a description of how energy was distributed in the ether (7). This approach was in sharp distinction to a contemporary of Maxwell's, William Thomson, who felt "one needed to know the system's structure" in detail in order to fully understand it (8). In the following years Thomson and others proposed model after model of the ether. But even as the models increased in complexity, it became more and more evident that Maxwell's equations were enormously successful. Hertz found the electromagnetic waves Maxwell had predicted, others were able to combine various mechanical interpretations of Maxwell's equations in such a way as to account both qualitatively and quantitatively for a host of electrical effects. What more could one want? Indeed, it seemed to some physicists in the closing year of the nineteenth century that taken together, Newton's celestial mechanics and Maxwell's equations indicated that the prospect of completing physics was in sight. As the pre-eminent American experimentalist on light, A. A. Michelson, declared in 1894:

While it is never safe to affirm that the future of physical science has no marvels in store even more astonishing than those of the past, it seems probable that most of the grand underlying principles have been firmly established and that further advances are to be sought chiefly in the rigorous application of these principles to all phenomena which come under our notice. It is here that the science of measurement shows its importance – where quantitative results are more to be desired than qualitative work. An eminent physicist has remarked that the future truths of physics are to be looked for in the sixth place of decimals (9).

Many late nineteenth century Maxwellians saw Maxwell's electromagnetic synthesis as a triumph of dynamics. Of course they recognized problems, but these were expected to be surmountable. Not everyone was of such a mind. In 1900 Wilhelm Wien became a spokesman for a new movement that hoped to reverse the effort to explain electromagnetic effects by the dynamics of the ether. Wien argued that,

It is doubtless one of the most important tasks of theoretical physics to unite the up until now isolated fields of mechanics and electromagnetism, and to derive their relevant differential equations from a common foundation.

However Wien insisted that his predecessors' dream of finding a mechanically based synthesis was misguided.

More promising as a foundation for further theoretical work is the opposite task: to derive the mechanical from the more general electromagnetic equations (10).

For those physicists after 1900 who sought a unified 'electromagnetic world picture', such as H. Minkowski, H. Poincaré, H. L. Lorentz, and M. Abraham, Maxwell's equations were a starting and not an ending point. No longer did they view the ether as a mechanical object (or as fundamentally analogous to a mechanical object) in which stresses and strains could be identified with electromagnetic fields. Instead, as reformulated by Lorentz, the ether was completely distinct from charge. Thus electrical current simply became the movement of charge instead of a complicated state of the ether. Furthermore, the mechanical models of the ether were entirely abandoned and electrical and magnetic fields simply became specifications of states of a purely electromagnetic continuum.

In the years following Wien's program of 1900, Lorentz and others hoped to eliminate the concept of mechanical mass as a fundamental concept. They sought to show that what we call mass is nothing more than the inertia associated with electric fields in the ether. The mass of an ordinary object was ascribed to the aggregate inertia of the object's constituent charged particles. This was what was meant by explaining mechanics in terms of electrodynamics (11).

The ambitious program of the electromagnetic world view found a fascinated observer in the person of the young Albert Einstein. Even in his days as a student at the Eidgenossische Technische Hochschule (and despite the lack of interest displayed by his teachers) Einstein felt that

The most fascinating subject at the time I was a student was Maxwell's theory. What made this theory appear revolutionary was the transition from forces at a distance to fields as fundamental variables . . . . It was like a revelation (12).

Even Planck's work of 1900 on energy quanta seemed of interest to Einstein principally insofar as it would clarify the problem of the electromagnetic foundation of physics (13).

But after considerable thought the young physicist concluded that "neither mechanics nor electrodynamics could ... claim exact validity", and thus neither should be derived from the other. "By and by", Einstein recalled, "I despaired of the possibility of discovering the true laws by means of constructive efforts based on known facts. The longer and the more despairingly I tried, the more I came to the conviction that only the discovery of a universal formal principle could lead us to assured results" (14).

Einstein's 'formal principle' became the foundation of the theory of special relativity. It can be stated briefly: Maxwell's equations and more generally all laws of physics should have the same form in all frames of reference. (This was already true for mechanics.) This meant that the Lorentz interpretation of Maxwell's electromagnetic theory of light would no longer do. For Maxwell's equations predicted the light wave to have a velocity of $c = 3 \times 10^{10}$ cm sec^{-1} in the rest frame of the ether. Therefore some other, different set of equations would have to replace Maxwell's equations in a frame of reference moving with respect to the ether. On philosophical-aesthetic grounds Einstein rejected this possibility. There should, he believed, only be one set of electromagnetic equations (15).

As can easily be understood, Einstein's epistemological criticisms of the usual interpretation of Maxwell's equations were not easily assimilated into physics. The person most responsible for the acceptance of Einstein's work was perhaps Hermann Minkowski, through his reformulation of Einstein's theory into a geometrical language. Minkowski's expectation was that one day physics could be expressed as a series of geometrical statements about lines and surfaces in four-dimensional space-time. As a start on this program, he re-expressed Einstein's formulation of electrodynamics in this goemetrical scheme (16).

At first Minkowski's highly mathematical (geometrical) point of view seemed alien and unnecessary to Einstein. Little by little though, Einstein came to Minkowski's point of view as he discovered that his own work on the general theory of relativity could not even get started without the idea of space-time. Eventually, the stunning success of general relativity made Einstein a thorough-going convert to the geometrical program.

From 1915 to the end of his life Einstein attempted to create an even more general geometrical theory that would incorporate both the general relativity theory of gravity and suitably generalized Maxwellian electrodynamics. Thus Einstein's vision of Maxwell's equations was of a component of a more general geometrical theory of space-time. Einstein even came to believe that such a generalized geometrical theory could be so formulated that quantum effects would be explained by a more fundamental physics of the continuum. As is well known, in this belief Einstein maintained a minority position against his contemporaries.

Some very interesting physics has been built upon the Einstein-Minkowski idea. One intriguing recent project has been the attempt by J. A. Wheeler *et al.* to pursue a 'geometrodynamics' in which all physics would be built upon the dynamics deduced from geometrical considerations. (They did not, however, expect to derive quantum effects as Einstein had hoped.) Part of their program included the writing of a now very popular text on gravitation which they began by summarizing their motives. First they wanted to display the results of much interesting astrophysics. They then added:

Of quite another motive for the study of the subject, to contemplate Einstein's inspiring vision of geometry as the machinery of physics, we shall say nothing here because it speaks out, we hope, in every chapter of the book (17).

One of these chapters, naturally, is on Maxwell's equations which are interpreted as simple geometrical objects in space-time (akin to elongated wine bottle boxes). (See Figure 2.) Of course no physical object exists which looks like Figure 2; Wheeler and his colleagues are simply saying that such hypothetical objects can be used to calculate electrodynamic effects such as the force on a moving charged particle.

3. Histories and Futures: Maxwell's Equations and Quantum Physics

As discussed earlier, Einstein set his geometrical program against the view that held quantum mechanics to be the basis of a complete physical theory.

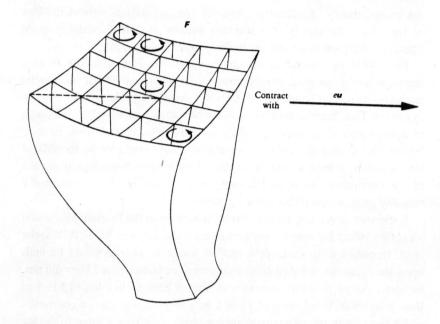

Fig. 2. Space-Time Geometrical Representation of Maxwell's Equations. Misner, Thorne and Wheeler show how a vector representing the velocity of a charged particle (the arrow) can be combined with a two-form (the wine-box object) to yield the force on on a moving particle. Source: Misner, Thorne and Wheeler, *Gravitation*, 104.

Since then the quantum mechanical approach has been accepted almost universally as the proper foundation of physics.

It was already clear in 1905 (when Einstein first hypothesized that light was made up of quanta) that discrete particles of light would wreak havoc on Maxwell's differential equations. How could these equations about continuous entities describe a granular reality? The answer at least for the then known massive particles — electrons and protons — came in the 1920's as quantum mechanics was developed. Since electrons and protons were thought to make up all matter, the future path of physics seemed well charted. Bertrand Russell was optimistic enough to claim in 1925 that:

Physical science is thus approaching the stage when it will be complete, and therefore uninteresting. Given the laws governing the motions of electrons and protons, the rest is merely geography — a collection of particular facts filling their distribution throughout the portion of the world's history. The total number of facts of geography required to determine the world's history is probably finite; theoretically they all could be written down in a log book to be kept at Somerset House with a calculating machine attached which, by turning a handle, could enable the inquirer to find out the facts at other times than those recorded. It is difficult to imagine anything less interesting or more different from the passionate delight of incomplete discovery. It is like climbing a high mountain and finding nothing at the top except a restaurant where they sell ginger beer, surrounded by fog but equipped with a wireless. Perhaps in the times of Ahmes the multiplication table was exciting (18).

For three years following Russell's prophecy there was extraordinary excitement in the physics community as it became clear that quantum mechanics was a very new kind of physical theory. Heisenberg, Schrödinger, and Max Born set out the elements of the new theory which was brought to what seemed a conclusion by Dirac in 1928. Dirac brought together relativity and quantum mechanics in the equation that bears his name. Max Born apparently was so exuberant over these heady developments that he announced to a group of visitors to Göttingen: "Physics, as we know it, will be over in six months" (19).

Part of Born's enthusiasm for the relativistic quantum mechanics was based on theoretical and experimental success that from the beginning promised to be spectacular. But another element of Dirac's theory that inspired statements such as Born's was grounded in a fundamental misunderstanding of what Dirac's equation meant. Dirac, it should be added, shared this misapprehension (20). The issue was this. Dirac's equation for the electron unambiguously also predicted the existence of a positively charged particle. This particle seemed to have the same mass as the electron (as well it should — we now call this particle the positron) but no such particle was known. It was thus widely assumed that someone would find a reason why this particle was the proton.

Naturally this would have been a success beyond anyone's expectation: a single equation would have accounted for both known particles and simultaneously reconciled quantum mechanics and relativity. It seemed obvious to many research physicists at the time that Maxwell's equations would easily be integrated into this system. Leon Rosenfeld later recalled that,

After Dirac's great paper on the theory of the electron one had the impression that all the fundamental features of atomic physics had been neatly incorporated into the new conceptual structure, and with characteristic eagerness the other pioneers of the atomic world Heisenberg and Pauli, leaving to lesser fry the polishing off of details, turned to the major remaining task of apply the new methods of quantization to the electromagnetic field. It is difficult to those who did not witness it to imagine the enthusiam, nay the presumptuousness, which filled our hearts in those days. I shall never forget the terse way in which a friend of mine (Now a very eminent figure in the world of physics) expressed his view of our future prospects: 'In a couple of years', he said, 'we shall have cleared up electrodynamics; another couple of years for the nuclei, and physics will be finished. We shall then turn to biology' (21).

Needless to say physics did not end — only a few years later the neutron, positron, and muon were discovered, none of which fit neatly into the naive interpretation of the Dirac equation. In addition Maxwell's equations were not quantized nearly so easily as Rosenfeld and his contemporaries expected. Both problems came to be seen as more, not less difficult during the late thirties — the number of particles continued to increase and the difficulties inherent in constructing a self-consistent and physically interpretable quantum electrodynamics became more evident.

After World War II, largely through the work of R. Feynman, J. Schwinger, S. Tomonaga, and F. Dyson, quantum electrodynamics was put in a form that was both predictively successful and (more or less) coherent. Together they presented an interpretation of quantum electrodynamics in part by jettisoning the 1930's hope that quantum equations could describe the motion of individual particles. In the new scheme any physical interaction could involve an arbitrary number of particles. Let me give an example. In electrodynamics before quantum mechanics one electron repels another by creating a field, the field causes the second electron to feel a force. In quantum electrodynamics one says the force between two electrons is due simultaneously to many processes, each of which occurs with a certain probability.

Most probable is that a photon (γ) travels from electron 1 (e_1) to electron 2 (e_2).

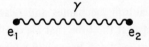

Fig. 3.

Less probable is that the photon, en route, creates an electron-positron pair

e^+e^- which then annihilates creating a second photon which is absorbed by electron 2.

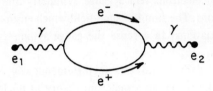

Fig. 4.

Indeed there is an infinite series of such possible processes which grow less probable as they grow more complicated. Adding together all possible diagrams gives us the total probability of electron 1 bouncing off electron 2. Maxwell's equations are thus given by infinite series, like the one just sketched of possible quantum exchanges between electrons.

Inspired by the success of quantum electrodynamics, physicists hoped that by analogy a quantum theory of the weak and the strong nuclear forces could be formulated. Some new particle or particles would take the place of the photon as carrier of the force. In 1967 S. Weinberg and A. Salam proposed a theory along these lines that explained both the weak and electro-dynamic forces. They did so by making use of a new kind of symmetry.

The coordinate system in which one studies a phenomenon seems extrinsic to the phenomenon itself. For this reason Einstein postulated that it should be a goal of physics to make physical laws independent of changes of coordinate systems, even as one passed from a still to a moving system. Because coordinates are external to the objects of study, equations that remain unchanged when one changes coordinates are said to have an *external* symmetry.

Other kinds of symmetries are possible. For instance in the 1930's it was discovered that for some nuclear physics experiments nuclear effects were the same if one switched every neutron with a proton. This is an operation affecting the objects under study themselves. There the equations that remain unchanged even when one switches neutrons for protons are said to have *internal* symmetry.

Internal symmetries had been explored ever since Weyl's work in the

1920's, but in the 1960's a particular kind of internal symmetry, gauge symmetry, became the focus of a good deal of attention. Several physicists including Weinberg were very struck by a remarkable fact. If one demanded that the quantum theory of electrons had a gauge symmetry one had to add a new field to the equations. The simplest such field which ensured gauge symmetry gave Maxwell's equations! In a sense the gauge symmetry yielded the laws of electrodynamics.

Weinberg and Salam found this fact tremendously encouraging. They guessed that in order to obtain a quantum theory of nuclear forces it might suffice to demand a new, more general kind of gauge symmetry. Theories with this more general symmetry were hard to find, but not impossible. As Weinberg later recalled,

Limitations of this sort are after what we most want; not mathematical methods which can make sense out of physically irrelevant theories, but methods which carry constraints, because these constraints may point of way toward the one true theory (22).

In 1967 Weinberg constructed a theory that satisfied these symmetric 'limitations', and properly yielded both Maxwell's equations and a weak interaction theory. Building on these ideas, H. Georgi, S. Glashow and others exploited an even larger gauge symmetry condition to build a theory that would encompass the Weinberg-Salam theory and the strong nuclear forces — in short all of fundamental physics except gravity. These theories have been dubbed GUTS for grand unified theories. Experimentalists are now working in many international groups to test these ideas. But already the theoretical virtues of these models have precipitated another period of great optimism among physicists. Glashow introduced the First Workshop on Grand Unification by arguing that

. . . . we have for the first time an apparently correct theory of elementary particle physics. It may be, in a sense, phenomenologically complete. It suggests the possibility that there are no more surprises at higher energies, at least at energies that are remotely accessible . . . . Theorists do expect novel high-energy phenomena, but only at absurdly inaccessible energies. Proton decay, if it is found, will reinforce belief in the great desert extending from 100 GeV to the unification mass of 10^{14} GeV. Perhaps the desert is a blessing in disguise. Ever larger and more costly machines conflict with dwindling finances and energy reserves. All frontiers come to an end.

You may like this scenario or not; it may be true or false. But it's neither impossible, implausible, nor unlikely (23).

But even before the grand unified field theories were developed it was clear that the basic machinery of quantum field theory, together with the new ideas about internal symmetries offered a profound new insight into the nature of matter. For the first time, in the early 1970's there was a real hope that a unification of all the fields could be accomplished without reducing physics to electrodynamics or geometry.

The pedagogical organization of physics has begun to reflect the new ideal of the gauge theorists. In his text on gravity and general relativity Weinberg, like Wheeler, began by acknowledging the intrinsic interest of astrophysical phenomena. He added that it was true that the geometrical approach,

.... *was* Einstein's point of view, and his preeminent genius necessarily shapes our understanding of the theory he created. However, I believe that the geometrical approach has driven a wedge between general relativity and the theory of elementary particles. As long as it could be hoped, as Einstein did hope, that matter would eventually be understood in geometrical terms, it made sense to give Riemannian geometry a primary role in describing the theory of gravitation. But now the passage of time has taught us not to expect that the strong, weak, and electromagnetic interactions can be understood in geometrical terms, and too great an emphasis on geometry can only obscure the deep connections between gravitation and the rest of physics (24).

Stephen Hawking, whose work lies on just this boundary between gravity and particle physics has helped advance physics towards the still distant goal of uniting gravity with 'the rest of physics'. In fact he (more than some particle physicists) is concerned that any 'final' theory of physics include gravity. Nonetheless Hawking expects that GUTS can be expanded to do the job. In his inaugural lecture as Lucasian Professor at Cambridge University Hawking began by discussing,

The possibility that the goal of theoretical physics might be achieved in the not too distant future, say, by the end of the century. By this I mean that we might have a complete, consistent and unified theory of the physical interactions which would describe all possible observations (25).

After cautioning that such hopes have been raised before he added:

"Nevertheless, we have made a lot of progress in recent years and, as I shall describe, there are some grounds for cautious optimism that we may see a complete theory within the lifetime of some of those present here (26).

Like many physicist-prophets before him Hawking finished by contending that a sufficiently large computing machine would be capable of all future calculations of applied problems.

So maybe the end is in sight for theoretical physicists if not for theoretical physics (27).

If so, in the future Maxwell's equations will be viewed as the consequence of some small corner of the vast internal symmetry that determined the final theory of physics.

4. Re-Ordering the Past

Clearly there are a great many reasons why physicists reinterpret past accomplishments in physics. For purposes of discussion I want to call three of these functions pedagogic, heuristic, and justificatory. A pedagogic function is served for example, when earlier well-known results can be explained to students in the vocabulary of a new theory. Thus now virtually all texts on gauge theories and unified field theories begin by deriving Maxwell's equations from symmetry principles as a simple example of a much more powerful technique. One of the most popular of these pedagogic presentations adds almost apologetically after such an observation,

It is supererogatory to observe that the photon was not discovered by gauge invariance. Rather, gauge transformations were discovered as a useful property of Maxwell's equations (28).

Or, to give another example: in the Misner, Thorne, Wheeler text, *Gravitation*, the authors carefully develop Maxwell's theory in terms of differential geometry in order to point out the differences and similarities between the (geometrized) Maxwell equations and Einstein's geometrical gravity equations. Furthermore both in the case of quantum gauge theories and geometrodynamics the authors want to instruct the student in methods that will later be applied to more general and difficult cases. It would be interesting to trace systematically the entire pedagogical history of Maxwell's equations. At least at the best level of instruction I suspect such a history would closely parallel (though lag behind) research concerns.

Reformulation of the past often plays a role not just in the education of students but in the advancement of the discipline itself. Now we see the goals of the mechanical and electromagnetic world pictures as misguided; nonetheless, we can recognize that these older interpretations of Maxwell's equations led to much productive physics. To give another example: in later life Einstein commented that Lorentz's reformulation of Maxwell's equations in terms of charges and fields in the ether "simply had to lead to the special theory of relativity" (29). Elsewhere Einstein asserted,

The special theory of relativity owes its origin to Maxwell's equations of the electromagnetic field. Conversely, the latter can be grasped formally in a satisfactory fashion only by way of the special theory of relativity (30).

Yet another example comes from the case of weak interactions. Weinberg recalls being very impressed by the possibility of deriving Maxwell's equations from a symmetry constraint. This contributed to his hope that some analogous constraint might prove productive in finding a theory of nuclear interactions.

Finally, there is a justificatory role played by re-reading the past. It always gives added weight to a current research program if older, established theories mesh with the new theories in a natural way. For the late nineteenth century ether-mechanicians Maxwell's equations fit into a larger mechanical world view. For the reductionist electromagnetic program of the early 1900's the history of physics was up until then a series of fortunate approximations, the true basis of which was only beginning to be understood. In their eyes there was an ever decreasing number of fundamental entities — they hoped to show ultimately that there would only be electricity in the world. When Einstein was developing the special theory of relativity, Maxwell's equations represented but one of several physical theories which, when properly reinterpreted, would co-exist with (not replace) relativistic mechanics.

In recent times we see the progress of physics very differently — as a long road marked by ever increasing symmetry. We have in mind an inexorable climb up a ladder of symmetries: Galilean, Lorentzian, global gauge, local Abelian gauge, local non-Abelian gauge. The study of the reinterpretation of the past in physics is therefore integrally linked to the ideal of progress in the physical sciences.

The example I have given here of Maxwell's equations is of course not typical of all older physical theories. But I do hope to have left the reader with some sense of how the past feels to working physicists. It is certainly not the past of the historian, but neither is it the stale textbook anecdote forcibly put in Baconian form. The past in physics is an ever-changing legacy, constantly reinterpreted at the forefront of physics.

Acknowledgements

I would like to thank R. Daston, G. Holton, E. Mendelsohn, A. I. Miller, S. Schweber, S. Weinberg, and participants in the conference for helpful suggestions.

Note

* Research supported in part by the Harvard University Society of Fellows, and the National Science Foundation under Grant No. PHY 77-22864.

References

1. Descartes, *Oeuvres de Descartes*, C. E. Adams and P. Tannery (eds.), Paris: L. Cerf, 1897–1910, Volume 11, p. 47.
2. Cited in R. Fox, 'The Rise and Fall of Laplacian Physics', *Historical Studies in the Physical Sciences* 4 (1974), 89–136, on 98.
3. J. C. Maxwell, *Scientific Papers*, New York: Dover, 1965, 485ff. Two excellent secondary sources are the book by C. W. F. Everitt, *James Clerk Maxwell, Physicist and Natural Philosopher*, New York: Charles Scribners, 1975, and the article by J. Z. Buchwald, 'The Hall Effect and Maxwellian Electrodynamics in the 1880's Part I: The Discovery of a New Electric Field', *Centaurus* 23 (1979), 51–99, esp. 54ff. See also note 7.
4. J. C. Maxwell, *Scientific Papers*, 533 (Note 3).
5. E. W. F. Everitt, Maxwell, 98–99 (Note 3).
6. J. Z. Buchwald, Hall Effect, 66 (Note 3).
7. J. Z. Buchwald, *Matter, the Medium and Electrical Current*, unpublished Ph.D. dissertation, Harvard University, 1974, 427.
8. *Ibid.* See also the excellent article by M. Norton Wise, 'William Thomson's Mathematical Route to Energy Conservation: A Case Study of the Role of Mathematics in Concept Formulae', *Historical Studies in the Physical Sciences* 10 (1979), 49–83. Wise shows how Thomson's mathematical work led him to give the 'physical analogies more weight'.
9. A. A. Michelson, from an address of 1894 excerpted in a publication of 1898–1899. Cited in L. Badash, 'The Completeness of Nineteenth Century Physics', *Isis* 63 (1972), 48–58, on 52.
10. W. Wien, 'Über die Möglichkeit einer Elektromagnetischen Begrundung der Mechanik', *Annalen der Physik* 5 (1901), 501–513, on 502.

11. For more on the electromagnetic world view, see items in Note 15 and 'R. Mc-Cormmach, Einstein, Lorentz and the Electron Theory', *Historical Studies in the Physical Sciences* 2 (1970), 69–81; Tetu Hirosige, 'Theory of Relativity and the Ether', *Japanese Studies in the History of Science* 7 (1968), 37–58; P. Galison, 'Minkowski's Spacetime: From Visual Thinking to the Absolute World', *Historical Studies in the Physical Sciences* 10 (1979), 85–121.
12. A. Einstein, 'Autobiographical Notes', in P. A. Schilpp (ed.), *Albert Einstein: Philosopher-Scientist* 1, La Salle: Open Court, 1969, 32.
13. *Ibid.*, 47.
14. *Ibid.*, 53.
15. There is a vast literature on the history of special relativity. The reader should refer to A. I. Miller, *Albert Einstein's Special Theory of Relativity: Emergence (1905) and Early Interpretation (1905–1911)*, Reading: Addison Wesley, 1981, and G. Holton, *Thematic Origins of Scientific Thought*, Cambridge: Harvard University Press, 1973 for further references.
16. See P. Galison, 'Minkowski', (Note 11).
17. C. W. Misner, K. S. Thorne, and J. A. Wheeler, *Gravitation*, San Francisco: W. H. Freeman, 1973).
18. B. Russell, 'What I Believe', reprinted in R. E. Egner and L. E. Denonn (eds.), *The Basic Writings of Bertrand Russell*, New York: Simon and Schuster, 1961, 367–370, on 367–8.
19. Stephen Hawking, *Is the End in Sight for Theoretical Physics?* Cambridge: Cambridge University Press, 1980, 1.
20. See for example, P. A. M. Dirac, *The Principles of Quantum Mechanics*, Oxford: Clarendon Press, 1930, 236.
21. L. Rosenfeld, 'Niels Bohr in the Thirties', S. Rozenthal (ed.), *Niels Bohr: His Life and Work as Seen by His Friends and Colleagues*, New York: Wiley, 1967, 118–119.
22. S. Weinberg, 'Conceptual Foundations of the Unified Theory of Weak and Electromagnetic Interactions', *Reviews of Modern Physics* 52 (1980), 515–523, on 517.
23. S. L. Glashow, 'The New Frontier', from *First Workshop on Grand Unification*, Brookline, Massachusetts: Math. Sci. Press, 1980, 3–8, on 3.
24. S. Weinberg, *Gravitation and Cosmology: Principles and Applications of the General Theory of Relativity*, New York: John Wiley, 1972, vii.
25. S. Hawking, 'End in Sight?' 1 (Note 19).
26. *Ibid.*, 2.
27. *Ibid.*, 26.
28. E. S. Abers and B. W. Lee, 'Gauge Theories', *Physics Reports C* 9 (1973), 1–141, on 10.
29. A. Einstein, 'H. A, Lorentz, His Creative Genius and His Personality', in H. A. Lorentz, *Impressions of His Life and Work*, Amsterdam: North Holland, 1957, 5–9, on 7.
30. A. Einstein, 'Autobiographical Notes', 62 (Note 12).

A FOUNDER MYTH IN THE HISTORY OF SCIENCES? THE LAVOISIER CASE

BERNADETTE BENSAUDE-VINCENT

Science and Industry Museum of La Villette

The history of French chemistry is dominated by the figure of Lavoisier. Even now, two centuries after the famous revolution in chemistry, he still reigns supreme as the uncontested father of modern chemistry. Indeed, in the mind of more than one student, his name has eclipsed that of all other chemists in history. Nonetheless, his privileged status has been questioned by several historians of the subject. Maurice Daumas, in particular, reexamined the importance of Lavoisier, by reinterpreting his system in the light of the knowledge of his time, and by calling attention to the cognitive tradition that Lavoisier preserved (1). More recently, H. Guerlac's work, widely renowned in France, has tempered the idea of radical innovation by presenting Lavoisier's revolution as the fruitful reunion of two separate trends in chemistry (2).

But even these scholarly analyses have not succeeded in diminishing the prestige of such an established figure, whose social image has been protected by a long-standing tradition. Indeed, this tradition was primarily developed by the French chemists of the nineteenth century, who in their treatises devoted as much space to the history of their discipline, as to the problems of chemistry proper (3). Their commitment to history, in fact, always focuses on Lavoisier. For in their eyes, he was not merely the hero of a scientific revolution, who set up a new 'paradigm' and 'normalized' science; he did not revolutionize chemistry, he founded it. This is manifest in their writings which lay greater emphasis on the theme of the advent of a new world than on the problem of discontinuity with the past. Architectual metaphors proliferated, religious connotations abounded, even at the expense of the historic subject matter; and the Lavoisian edifice thus took on an unexpected dimension, that of a truly founding myth. The revolution was all the more remarkable as it suddenly confined to distant prehistory the recent history

53

Loren Graham, Wolf Lepenies, and Peter Weingart (eds.), Functions and Uses of Disciplinary Histories, Volume VII, 1983, 53–78.

which in some instances had been experienced by some of the commentators. A New era had begun. But how does one progress from the notion of revolution to that of foundation, or from historic talk to mythical narrative? Such is the aim of this analysis. The intent then is not to take stock of Lavoisier's specific contribution, but rather to point out the various factors — historical, epistemological, philosophical and socio-political — which led to the production and functioning of such a myth.

1. The Genesis of the Myth

The precocious emergence of the myth, even as events occurred, constitutes the most salient feature of the case. The myth itself was conceived by Lavoisier's disciples and furthermore encouraged by the man himself.

Guyton de Morveau, for example, was one of its main exponents. Indeed, as early as 1786, at the time when he was writing the first volume of the *Dictionnaire de chimie* of the *Encyclopédie Méthodique*, Morveau penned a second Foreword, in which he presented Lavoisier as a true Saviour. Initially, this was probably the expression of inward relief, as Guyton de Morveau had been struggling for quite some time to produce the article entitled 'Air', when his task was suddenly facilitated by Lavoisier's startling remarks concerning phlogiston. But the rhetoric employed in the portrait of Lavoisier is even more revealing: here Lavoisier is already endowed with the traits of the hero of the popular legend. He is portrayed as the champion of truth, the staunch enemy of dogmatism and of error, who had succeeded, by his merit alone, to dethrone a powerful doctrine founded on the authority of a cult. The means used to achieve this hagiographic representation is in fact reminiscent of that employed by another prestigious hero, Descartes. Guyton posited that Lavoisier would have had as a principle:

cette maxime trop oubliée du grand Descartes, que celui qui aspire à connaître la vérité doit, une fois dans sa vie, s'appliquer à douter de tout ce qu'il a appris (4).

The cartesian reference favours the idea of a shift from the concept of revolution to that of foundation. Thus Lavoisier, sifting through the whole of chemistry in a spirit of total scepticism was able to rebuild knowledge on firm and secure foundations. By imposing on chemistry the demands of clarity and precision, Lavoisier thereby ushered in the age of reason, namely that of modern science.

The idea of foundation is subsequently reinforced by a theme borrowed from ancient cosmologies: viz., the demiurge which established order from chaos. Before Lavoisier, confusion, doubt and darkness reigned; after him there was light and a peaceful road leading straight to truth. Guided by this metaphor, Morveau could then affirm that the order established by Lavoisier was immutable and eternal, as it was none other than the very order imposed by nature:

Dès qu'on a abandonné l'hypothèse d'un combustible unique, on voit tout rentrer dans l'ordre conforme à la nature des choses (. . .). La postérité verra s'élever l'édifice dont ils [les premiers chimistes] n'auront pu poser que les premiers fondements; mais elle ne pensera à détruire ce qu'ils auront fait que quand, avec les mêmes matieres, dans les mêmes circonstances, la nature cessera d'opérer les mêmes phénomènes (5).

Hence, as soon as 1786, Morveau regarded Lavoisier's achievement sub *specie aeterni*, and commented on its peculiarity: the revolution had scarcely encroached on history only to vanish from it. It had erupted into it but escaped the wear and tear of time. The history of chemistry had hardly begun, but already its structure was outlined, inscribed from the outset in the plans of the Lavoisian edifice. The future held no surprises, consisting as it did of a continuity of accumulated progress:

Les points fondamentaux éclairés, il reste sans doute beaucoup à faire dans une science où chaque découverte semble n'être qu'une route tracée vers un but éloigné; mais notre marche sera plus sûre et nous n'aurons plus de sujets de craindre de revenir sur nos pas (6).

Even before the death of Lavoisier, his work had been described in terms of an everlasting foundation. However, it must be pointed out that this metamorphosis of history into myth was not a usual occurrence. For if all the disciples of Lavoisier concurred in emphasizing the importance of the event, some, such as Fourcroy, clearly opposed the propagation of the myth. In his article entitled 'Chymie', written in 1792, for the same *Encyclopédie méthodique*, Lavoisier was not accorded the customary place of honor. For, according to Fourcroy, the decisive factor in the chemistry revolution was not so much Lavoisier himself, but the advent of pneumatic chemistry (the study of gases). Lavoisier, it was alleged, was merely a good theoretician who was able to assemble and reorganize various facts already elaborated by his contemporaries (7). How is one to explain then such a divergence of interpretation? It does not seem to be a simple case of historical perspective, as this contradiction is already apparent in the actual body of Lavoisier's work. Indeed, he successively presents two contrasting points of view of his work, in which that associated with continuity was by no means relegated to a secondary position. Perhaps it was Lavoisier himself who was the main instigator of the myth? After all, he had always been acutely conscious of his role as a revolutionary, as his laboratory notes of 1777 indicate:

L'importance de l'objet m'a engagé à reprendre tout ce travail qui m'a paru fait pour occasionner une révolution en physique et en chimie. J'ai cru ne devoir regarder tout ce qui a été fait avant moi que comme des indications; je me suis proposé de tout répéter avec de nouvelles précautions, afin de lier ce que nous connaissions sur l'air qui se fixe et qui se dégage des corps avec les autres connaissances acquises et de former une théorie. Les travaux des différents auteurs que je viens de citer, considérés sous ce point de vue, m'ont présenté des portions séparées d'une grande chaîne; ils en ont joint quelques chaînons. Mais il reste une suite d'expériences immense pour en former une continuité (8).

For Lavoisier then, revolution was synonimous with continuity. He reckoned ideas had to be assembled, linked and coordinated. However, just as the system was beginning to take shape, the historical significance of the revolution changed. It was doubtless clear in the memoires of 1777 that progress was contingent upon adjustment and correction. Hence, the memoire *Sur la combustion des chandelles dans l'air atmospherique et dans l'air éminement respirable* proceeded from a critical survey of former work, at the end of which Lavoisier concluded:

Ces réflexions m'ont obligé à prendre une autre route (9).

Apparently then, the revolution was inspired by the mistakes and failures of contemporaries. It consisted of a reorganisation, a systematic rereading, a better approach, but its effect was not yet that of a devastating and final upheaval.

However in the Mémoires which followed, and especially in the notorious *Traité élémentaire de chimie*, Lavoisier abandoned all notion of continuity with regard to his predecessors and contemporaries. This sudden reversal was visible right from the start of *Réflexions sur le phlogistique pour servir*

de suite à la théorie de la combustion et de la calcination publiée en 1777,
a memoire in fact published in 1783. However, this title is misleading, for
with regard to its link with the past, far from adding to his ideas of 1777,
Lavoisier has completely revised them. There is no longer any question of
offering a better or more plausible approximation or more plausible hypothesis. Rather Lavoisier's theory took the shape of a radical innovation,
a sudden illumination which at once banished all shadows:

J'ai déduit toutes les explications d'un principe simple (...). Ce principe une fois
admis, les principales difficultés de la chimie ont paru s'évavouir et se dissiper, et tous les
phénomènes se sont expliqués avec une étonnante simplicité (10).

Strengthened by this new principle, Lavoisier then literally invited all chemists
to forget about the past, and return to a state of ignorance and innocence,
so as to better receive his message:

Je prie mes lecteurs, en commençant ce mémoire, de se dépouiller autant qu'il sera
possible, de tout préjugé; de ne voir dans les faits que ce qu'ils présentent, d'en bannir
tout ce que le raisonnement y a supposé, de se transporter aux temps antérieurs à Stahl,
et d'oublier pour un moment, s'il est possible que sa théorie a existé (11).

The *Discours Préliminaire* of the *Traité Élémentaire* emphasised this position.
In it, Lavoisier set out his method and aimed to justify the originality of
his work. Seemingly though, this originality lay more in what was omitted
than in which was actually said: no mention is made of affinity, for example;
nor of the elements of matter, since everything that has already been said
on the subject was but a hotbed of errors and prejudices, masking the truth.
This double silence, moreover, implied a third: nothing was said about the
history of chemistry. Lavoisier wanted to sever all links with the past, and
present his work as an entirely new basis, a radical foundation for chemistry.
It was to be the work of one man alone, and Lavoisier justified this by
saying:

Ce n'est ni l'histoire de la science, ni celle de l'esprit human qu'on doit faire dans un
Traité élémentaire: on ne doit y chercher que la facilité, la clarté; on en doit soigneuse-
ment écarter tout ce qui pourrait tendre à détourner l'attention (12).

The rejection of history was necessary for pedagogical reasons; namely to
avoid confusion and cluttering and so facilitate the teaching of beginners.
It is the same motive that in 1777 led Lavoisier, at the beginning of his

memoire *Sur la combustion en général* to criticise empiricism and warn of
its dangers; an analogy, which shed light on Lavoisier's concept of history.
He saw it as a sort of empiricism, a sterile and disordered accumulation of
quotations and events (13) Needless to say in any science, facts are always
necessary, even if they are not in themselves sufficient; they are retained
in order to be classified and sorted. This distinguishes it from history, which
is characterised by a parade of opinions which are quite simply discarded.
But at this point it is important to ask whether there are not other reasons
for the exemption of history, besides the alleged pedagogical ones?

Firstly, if Lavoisier was genuinely afraid of encumbering information,
why did he burden his paper with philosophical reflexions which were seemingly just as remote from the concerns of elementary chemistry? Evidently,
the insistance on clarity and simplicity was applied quite selectively! For
although Lavoisier wanted to disassociate himself with the past in chemistry,
he nonetheless enjoyed pointing out the philosophical affinities of his work
with the *Logique* of the Abbé de Condillac. Indeed, two long quotations at
the beginning and at the end of the *Discours Préliminaire* reveal his intent
to place the *Traité Elémentaire* under the esteemed patronage of the philosopher. Hence Lavoisier set out to confirm, on his own initiative, the validity
of Condillac's theses, as if he wanted to place the chemical revolution at the
service of this philosophy. But if he chose in this way a spiritual guardian
from outside the field of chemistry, was it not precisely in order to justify
his own ambitions as a founder of his discipline? Indeed, Lavoisier found
in the works of Condillac what he needed to legitimize his desire for discontinuity in chemistry, and his project of global reform. In a sense, this
constituted a purely negative conception of history, as was evident in the
long quotation that closed the passage:

Au lieu d'observer les choses que nous voulions connaître, nous avons voulu les imaginer.
De supposition fausse en supposition fausse, nous nous sommes donc égarés parmi
une multitude d'erreurs; et ces erreurs étant devenues des préjugés, nous les avons
prises pour cette raison pour des principes; nous nous sommes donc égarés de plus en
plus (. . .). Quand les choses sont parvenues à ce point, quand les erreurs se sont ainsi
accumulées, il n'y a qu'un moyen de remettre de l'ordre dans la faculté de penser; c'est
d'oublier tout ce que nous avons appris, de reprendre nos idées à leur origine, d'en suivre
la génération, et de refaire, comme dit Bacon, l'entendement humain (14).

By introducing Lavoisier to the therapeutic virtues of such oblivion, Condillac

enabled him to despise all previous literature on the subject and present
himself as the unique founder of chemistry. Yet, since it was vital to replace
literary knowledge by an immediate concern with facts, the new chemistry
would be the product of an intimate dialogue between Lavoisier and nature.
Hence the justification for ignorance and naiveness, which together supplied
the alibi for this so-called 'elementary' treatise, intended for 'beginners'.
In addition, Lavoisier also finds in his contemporary's philosophy a model
for his own project of global reform in chemistry. This simple method, which
consisted of acquiring knowledge by proceeding only from the 'known'
to the 'unknown' took on a new meaning with Condillac: that of proceeding
not from already acquired knowledge towards new cognition, but of starting
from actual sensation – the only recognised basis of understanding – to
construct ideas of growing complexities. Lavoisier transmitted this sensory
theory in his discussion of method: the chemist must follow the natural
course in the development of ideas in individuals:

Lorsque nous nous livrons pour la première fois à l'étude d'une science, nous sommes
par rapport à cette science, dans un état très analogue à celui dans lequel sont les enfants,
et la marche que nous avons à suivre est précisément celle que suit la nature dans la
formation des idées (15).

Hence the genealogy of ideas could replace the archeology of knowledge.
So it was essential to efface the past. An intellect that was receptive to
nature was independently capable of reconstituting knowledge: and, being
thus the unique founder of an entirely new science, it was therefore assured
of having produced a definitive work. Condillac's *Logique*, articulated as
'natural' logic, was consequently infallible. Lavoisier too was protected
from all error, in spite of some recognised lacuna. Admittedly, the proposed
system contained its flaws, but no severe defects could be found in it. This
conviction was clearly reflected in Lavoisier's discussion of nomenclature
which was strongly influenced by Condillac's ideas on the role of words:

Nous sommes bien éloignés sans doute de connaître tout l'ensemble, toutes les parties
de la science; on doit donc s' attendre qu'une nomenclature nouvelle, avec quelque
soin qu'elle soit faite, sera loin de son état de perfection; mais, pourvu que ce soit une
méthode de nommer, plutôt qu'une nomenclature, elle s'adaptera naturellement aux
travaux qui seront faits par la suite, elle marquera d'avance la place et le nom des
nouvelles substances qui pourront être découvertes et elle n'exigera que quelques ré-
formes locales et particulières (16).

It is clear from this, that Lavoisier's own texts were naturally inclined to favour the birth of a myth: the idea of an absolute beginning, an *ex nihilo* creation, which at the outset carved its mark in eternity, and made of Lavoisier a solitary founding hero, later to become a sacrificial victim through the various accidents of history.

2. Towards an Apotheosis

The myth is then enriched by a very old symbol, that of fire: Indeed, the theory of combustion has traditionally been regarded as the focal point of Lavoisier's revolution, as it was the issue over which the revolution's proponents and detractors were most divided. And yet, the revolutionary aspect of this theory is by no means obvious; for, even if it is with fire that Lavoisier began his destruction of the old chemistry, the theory he replaced it with was an inversion more than a revolution: for Stahl, burning an element meant breaking it down and releasing the phlogiston; whereas for Lavoisier, it entailed combining it with the oxygen in the air and releasing the caloric.

This did not escape the notice of several chemists of the day, such as Macquer, who minimized the revolutionary implications of this thesis (17). Later too, Macquer was regarded as a narrow-minded conservative, but one must admit that the fate of the chemical revolution did not hinge on this single experiment. If however, the controversy focused precisely on this point, was it not due to the symbolic significance of fire? Theories of combustion seem, in fact, to have always held a privileged position in the context of chemical doctrines, as indeed A. Comte affirmed:

On a souvent remarqué, et avec beaucoup de raison, que par sa nature, l'étude de la combustion constitue, pour ainsi dire, le point central du système des considérations chimiques (18).

The theme of fire seems then to have always been at the heart of chemistry. It so effectively characterized an age, that as Comte put it, it was possible to define the history of chemistry through a parallel study on fire: phlogiston typified the metaphysical age of chemistry, as Lavoisier's theory of combustion did its positive state. As for Berthelot, he further increased the standing of the concept of fire, by making it the very source of all scientific doctrines:

L'intervention de la chaleur, c'est à dire du principe du feu, dans les phénomènes de la nature, est trop frappante et trop considérable pour avoir été jamais méconnue, et la manière de la comprendre a été à l'origine de la plupart des théories physiques et physiologiques qui se sont succédé depuis l'antiquité jusqu' à nos jours (19).

It was thus that the experiment of 1772 on combustion became the symbol of the chemical revolution, just as the storming of the Bastille symbolized the French revolution. The event became replete with significance and the controversy between different schools of thought took on the dimension of a quasi-theological conflict, each faction denouncing the intolerance and sectarism of its opponent. Once converted to Lavoisier's views, Morveau, for one, was quick to attribute the triumph of the phlogiston doctrine to the dogmatism, enthusiasm and intransigent commitment of Stahl's disciples (20). In rebuttal, Priestley described the French school as a sect or "synod" in which the reign of terror had exorcized all freedom of thought (21).

Later, well after the final victory of the Lavoisians, J. B. Dumas arrived at a near deification of the 'founder of chemistry'. But it was in his *Leçons sur la philosophie chimique* that the myth was rendered its finest tribute. To begin with, the lesson devoted to Lavoisier was delivered on the "douloureux jour anniversaire de la mort de Lavoisier" (7 mai), in a solemn oratory style which was well-suited to the funeral occasion. In it, Dumas evoked the life and works of the great man, proceeding from a psychological portrait of the precocious genius to his transformation into a cult-like figure. Dumas started off with a chronological description of events: after Scheele and Priestley, then came Lavoisier. But from the moment he entered scientific circles, the young Lavoisier already stood out. Lavoisier was already Lavoisier. He already mastered the instrument which was to revolutionize the whole of chemistry: the balance. According to Dumas, the idea for its application originated from a native intuition destined for a great future:

(Ce n'est) "point à la légère qu'il a choisi cet instrument. S'il l'adopte c'est qu'il est guidé par une pensée nouvelle et profonde. Pour lui tous les phénomènes de la Chimie sont dus à des déplacements de matière, à l'union et à la séparation des corps. Rien ne se perd, rien ne se crée, voilà sa devise, voilà sa pensée; et dès les premières applications qu'il en fait, il efface une grande erreur" (22).

It is surprising that Dumas, who was usually so careful to trace the genealogy of chemical ideas, made no attempt to identify the origins of Lavoisier's "Rien ne se perd, rien ne se crée". Apparently, this idea suddenly loomed into his mind, as a sort of illumination, a "instinct merveilleux", the origin of which was to remain a mystery. This is, in fact, how Dumas resolves all questions of antecedence, for if Lavoisier responded only to personal inspiration, he was endebted to no one:

On lui a prêté des faits; mais son point de vue primitif, demeuré pur ne s'est altéré d'aucun emprunt (23).

Dumas thereby achieved the double exploit of intensifying the revolution and dramatising history: not only was it the work of a single man, but it was inspired by a creative intuition that was entirely elaborated in the initial stages of his research programme. From then on, logic demanded that Lavoisier's life may be summed up in religious terms: the initial inspiration imposed a mission and called for the sacrifice of the solitary founder hero; whereupon the lesson ended with the pitiful account of Lavoisier's death, and Dumas solemnly vowing to do his utmost to amend this crime:

— Permettez-moi d'ajouter, et ce n'est pas là une vaine promesse arrachée par l'émotion dont je suis accablé, permettez-moi d'ajouter que je publierai cette édition des oeuvres de Lavoisier; que je doterai les chimistes de leur *évangile* (24).

Dumas regarded himself then as an apostle who had to preach the gospel of the Saviour. For, according to him, Lavoisier was truly a God, and one with a gift for creation:

Un mot sur Lavoisier, que je vous présente au moment où prononçant son *fiat lux*, il écarte d'une main hardie les voiles que l'ancienne chimie s'est vainement efforcé de soulever, au moment où, docile à sa voix puissante, l'aurore commence à percer les ténèbres qui doivent s'évanouir aux feux de son génie (25).

Dumas' religious fervour, however, was not simply the product of the rather emphatic and elevated style of his lectures given at the Collège de France. Nor for that matter was it a publicity ploy used to boost the sales of the forthcoming publication. On the contrary, the entire message expressed Dumas' global vision of history. He traced the history of great men, and of chemists in particular, more than of chemistry itself; and this, despite having intimated in the first lecture his intent to deal with the philosophy of chemistry, and the evolution of methods in particular (26). The discrepancy between this initial project, designed to provide a certain "formation de l'esprit scientifique", and what turned out to be in fact a collection of por-traits, can nonetheless be explained: it was the inevitable outcome of the eternalist concept with regard to chemical methodology:

Il existe entre les chimistes actuels et les anciens chimistes quelque chose de commun: c'est la méthode. Et quelle est cette méthode, vieille comme notre science elle-même, et qui se caractérise dès son berceau? C'est la foi la plus complète dans le témoignage des sens (27).

That constitutes a nice paradox: Can one construct history from fixed and eternal elements? It compelled Dumas to designate the important figures who embodied the Spirit of chemistry across time. For history was just a long procession of the successive updatings of the one eternal essence. This did not imply, however, that it necessarily remained stationary, for according to Dumas, chemical methodology was critical and revolutionary by nature. Wherever it figured, it rose up against the established order (28). Chemistry, it seems, has always harboured a revolutionary irresistible force, and Lavoisier is depicted as the latest reincarnation of this revolutionary trend. Indeed, he conformed so well to the projected model, that alone he represented the condensed image, the scaled-down model of the entire history of chemistry. Due to this perfect compatibility then, Lavoisier may be regarded as the true founder in the discipline, whatever the merits were of past generations. And, whilst making history, Lavoisier also destroyed it: he erected an immortal monument, for eternity. Hence, continuity was assured after him. In chemistry, work must be conducted under the sur-veillance of the Father and if anyone dared tarnish his memory, Dumas was quick to retaliate:

On vous a dit souvent: la théorie de Lavoisier est modifiée; elle est renversée! Erreur, Messieurs, erreur! Lavoisier, est intact, impénétrable, son armure d'acier n'est pas entamée (29).

Here is a god cased in steel who watches over his kingdom. The Lavoisier of Dumas embodied so convincingly the irresistible force of chemical discord, that he seems to have definitively excluded the possibility of future con-troversy in the discipline; the revolution in chemistry is at an end!

3. Political Stakes

Did the chronological proximity of both the French and the chemical revolution have any effect on the development of the Lavoisian myth? It is certainly
tempting to combine the two. We know, for instance, that in Germany,
the fear of revolutionary contagion from abroad was one of the main reasons
why Lavoisier's chemistry was kept at bay (30). It is highly likely then,
that in this case, the coincidence of the two events intensified the quarrel
in the 1790's. But this theme extends beyond the eighteenth century, as
when, a hundred years later, Berthelot again refers back to it. In *La Révolution chimique, Lavoisier*, written in 1889, he commemorated the double
anniversary and underlined the interconnection. Why the reminder? At first
sight, it seemed innocent enough; it was just a pretext, a good opportunity
for publishing a work on the master. Moreover, after a brief attempt to
parallel both revolutions, Berthelot devoted himself exclusively to the study
of Lavoisier's work. The book was a sensitive, well documented analysis,
avoiding the effusions of a Dumas. In fact, rather than insisting on Lavoisier's
so-called intuition, he instead drew attention to the role played by his predecessors and contemporaries, and was bold enough to depict the revolution
as a skilful exploitation of other peoples' work, in effect a seizure even, of
the capital amassed over the years by past generations of chemists. Hence
the notion of a radical innovation or cult was dismissed. Instead, Berthelot
sought to destroy the religious aura surrounding scientists, and even condemned the belief purporting their infallibility:

La prétention à l'infaillibilité scientifique ne prouve guère autre chose que la vanité
de celui qui la met en avant (31).

But if Berthelot demystified Lavoisier in this way, why did he persist in
according him a central role in the development of the revolution? Why,
considering he professed a determinist philosophy of history, did he persistantly exalt the role of the genius?

Les idées qui ont triomphé ne sont pas une oeuvre collective, contrairement à une
opinion trop généralisée et qui tendrait à décourager l'effort personnel du génie. Si le
progrès insensible du temps finit par tout éclaircir, il n'en est past moins certain qu'un
homme tel que Newton ou Lavoisier peut le devancer et épargner à l'humanité le travail
indécis et sans guide de plusieurs générations: les conceptions qui ont fondé la chimie
moderne sont dues à un seul homme, Lavoisier (32).

The firmness of tone underlying this statement might indicate that it was made in response to some attack. Indeed, the glorification of the genius, took on, in 1889, a particular significance. The quarrel was rekindled, and became fiercer than ever before. On the one hand, the cult phenomenon was given a new lease of life. On the other, opponents criticized, blasphemed, and denigrated him, and provocations and denunciations grew in number.

What explanation can be given then for the resurgence of what had after all been a long-closed matter? Why, after almost a century of calm, were people again prepared to topple Lavoisier from his pedestal? The great man certainly bore the brunt of a long and turbulent history. Indeed, he seems to have become the emblem of French power, so that all the nationalist militancy stirred up between France and Prussia due to the politics of the day focused on his person. So it was that the legend of a chemist became one of the stakes in a complex game of political rivalry. To understand this phenomenon, it is fundamental to recall that the revolution provoked by Lavoisier shifted the geographic center of gravity in chemistry from Germany, Stahl's native land, to France. Thus France clinched the title of the cradle of chemistry from Germany; but this was only temporary, for after the 1850's, Germany reacquired its leading position, following its pioneering work in the domain of organic chemistry and its application. It was precisely then, therefore, that the rather humiliated French chemists brandished the memory of Lavoisier and claimed their right to the ownership of chemistry.

In 1869, on the eve of the Franco-Prussian war, a Alsatian chemist, A. Wurtz, advanced a provocative formula:

La chimie est une science française: elle fut constituée par Lavoisier, d'immortelle mémoire. Pendant des siècles elle n'avait été qu'un recueil de recettes obscures, souvent mensongères, à l'usage des alchimistes et plus tard des iatrochimistes. Vainement un grand esprit, G. E. Stahl, avait essayé, au commencement du 18ème siècle, de lui donner une base scientifique. Son système ne peut résister à l'épreuve des faits et à la puissance critique de Lavoisier (33).

A single master, a single nation; this was the creed of the French chemist. On the other side of the Rhine, however, Kolbe and Volhard protested so vigourously, that the Russian Chemical Society, and Mendeleev in particular, saw fit to intervene (34). In fact, Russian chemists sided so strongly with the French, that as a result, they completely forgot about their kinsman, Lomonosov (35). This incident so weakened the noble universalist conception

of science as the instrument of peace among men that the ideal did not resist
a second flair-up of the Lavoisier controversy, especially on the eve of the
1914 war. The collapse of this ideal is perhaps most manifest in the disputes
between French and German scientists; a dispute triggered off by the famous
Manifeste des 93, which in turn provoked a French counter-manifesto entitled
La Science Allemande. It was hardly surprising, therefore, that Lavoisier
became a prime target in the conflict, especially after the publication of
W. Ostwald's celebrated work, *L'évolution d'une science, la chimie*. Like
many German chemists, Ostwald aimed to minimize the historical significance
of Lavoisier. He devoted but a few lines to him, presenting his work as the
culmination of findings by Scheele and Priestley and reminding his readers
of previous forerunners, such as J. Mayow. Indeed, he only attributed to
Lavoisier the merit of correctly chosing between two rival theories, and even
this choice, he commented, had nothing definite about it:

So erheblieh dieser Fortschritt genannt werden muß, so hat man doch seine Bedeutung
meist übertrieben. Denn das eigentlich Wesentliche, die Systematik der Verbrennungsreak-
tionen war bereits durch die Phlogistontheorie geleistet worden und es war jetzt nur
nötig, Betrachtungen einfach symmetrisch umzukehren, soweit sie sich auf die Auffassung
von Zusammensetzung und Zerlegung bezogen. (36)

Hence, Ostwald set out to erase the image of the founding father: All that
Lavoisier had achieved was to resurrect the Stahlian doctrine. Not that he
entirely succeeded here either, since his system still retained many internal
contradictions. Nor did Ostwald hesitate to underline the inconsistency of the
introduction of caloric to a doctrine which condemned imponderable and
uncontrollable elements in experiments. Far from considering this a simple
accident, a harmless error, Ostwald derived from this analysis a sort of general
law, a theorem on the structure of scientific revolutions, which can be formulated thus: the greater the change, the greater the influence of the past.
Hence Ostwald demystified both the foundation and the Lavoisian revolution.
Needless to say, this attitude was enough to offend the national honour of
French scientists. P. Duhem, for one, interpreted Ostwald's remarks as being
an insult against France. So in 1916, he launched a counter-offensive in the
form of a short document, the revealing title of which was: *La chimie est-elle
une science française*? Of course, in it, Duhem reaffirmed the existence of a
'revolution', but went one step further when he showed by a brief genealogy

of Lavoisier's ideas, the essential contribution of French scientists even prior to Lavoisier. Duhem's strategy was subtle, for initially, he pointed out the limitations of Lavoisian novelty, even going as far as to denounce the excessive praise attributed to Lavoisier, which according to him, disguised historical realities. (37) Having criticized in this way the wholehearted followers of Lavoisier, Duhem then appeared as an impartial judge of history. He could now embark on a long analysis intended to neutralize all German claims to chemistry, and even denied it the distinction of having been the fatherland of phlogiston;

Une fois de plus, grâce à Rouelle et à Macquer, l'esprit de notre nation avait joué le rôle qui, si souvent au cours des siècles, lui avait été dévolu; l'étranger lui avait transmis une pensée; mais de celle-ci, la beauté et la fécondité se cachaient sous un monceau de considérations confuses, obscures, inutiles ou erronnées; cette pensée, il l'avait dégagée de ce fatras; il l'avait rendue simple et pure, puis il l'avait offerte à l'admiration du monde; à l'idée allemande, larve de théorie, il avait donné des ailes françaises (38).

In his conclusion, Dumas called forth an impartial arbitration of the question, but perhaps most astutely, he terminated with a citation from Priestley, Lavoisier's most fierce critic, the final words of which were 'système français'. What better way to demonstrate that chemistry was and always has been a French invention!

The figure of Lavoisier is consequently replete with a host of associations, both nationalistic as well as religious. All that remains now is to examine the influence of these imaginary dimensions on the history of chemistry, and on chemistry itself.

Faced with the magnitude of the Lavoisian cult, history somewhat loses its credibility, at least when it is related by French chemists. Indeed, how are such historians to be judged, who, contemptuous of the past, recognized in Lavoisier's work a radical foundation; and contemptuous of the future, saw in it a permanent foundation? Does this not entail the refusal of historical residues overly abundant in the Lavoisian system, as well as the rejection of more recent discoveries which actually disproved the master's theses?

4. The Historian Pitfall

And yet, even the most ardent defenders of Lavoisier give indications of the limitations of his system in their writings. This dimension is not presented overtly of course, but it is nonetheless conveyed. Literary style can indeed prove treacherous: In extolling the greatness of Lavoisier, it may be that some 'unavowable' aspects of his work are accidently revealed. The poetic glorification of the founder hero required traditional rhetoric, and more or less legendary images, which notably revealed the obsolescence of the system. For example, in order to highlight the simplicity and yet grandeur of the concept of oxygen, Dumas presented Lavoisier as an illusionist, performing conjuring tricks;

Présent dans tous les phénomènes naturels, sans cesse en mouvement, il revêt mille formes; mais je ne le perds jamais de vue et puis toujours le faire réapparaître à mon gré, quelque caché qu'il soit; dans cet être éternel, impérissable, qui peut changer de place, mais qui ne peut rien gagner ni perdre, que ma balance poursuit et retrouve toujours le même, il faut voir l'image de la matière en général (39).

By underlining the omnipresence of oxygen, Dumas suggested a parallel with the traditional elements and principles, which were once regarded as the universal intermediaries in chemical reactions. In attempting therefore, to stress the novelty of Lavoisier's theory, he evoked, quite unwittingly its similarity to the old system. Berthelot too provides a striking example of this when, in a bid to demonstrate the importance of oxygen, he advanced a hazardous comparaison:

L'air vital devenait ainsi le principe acide par excellence, cet acide universel tant cherché depuis un siècle. De là le nom d'oxygène que Lavoisier ne tardera pas à lui imposer (40).

It is impossible to demonstrate more effectively how originality, far from destroying past objectives, complements and concretizes them. Berthelot once again reproduced this ambiguity when he noticed an analogy in structure between the old theory of the four elements, and Lavoisier's system. Air, water, and earth, are contained in the three states of matter; and fire continues to exist under the name of caloric:

Le feu n'en resta pas moins sous cette nouvelle forme le premier principe du mouvement dans les êtres inanimés, aussi bien que dans les êtres vivants, et le lien des trois états généraux de la matière pondérale; de même qu'il était réputé autrefois l'élément actif de toutes choses et le lien des trois autres éléments (41).

In the process of commenting upon Lavoisier's doctrine with the intent of amplifying its strength and coherence, the French chemists occasionally got to the stage where they quite involuntarily reduced its revolutionary status.

5. Continuity at All Costs

If continuity with the past is scarcely evoked, continuity with the future is strongly underlined. This was an inevitable consequence of the founding myth: through a single sovereign act, Lavoisier endowed chemistry with solid and lasting foundations; hence his work was at the basis of all future endeavour. The result was that all those concerned described the chemistry of the nineteenth century as an extension of the Lavoisian enterprise. The project, however, encounters two difficulties: the first concerned certain of Lavoisier's essential theses, which were quick to be falsified; the concept of oxygen as a fundamental acidifier was contested less than twenty years later by Davy; similarly, the theory of caloric was to succumb within the following half century after its appearance. But how can such inaccuracies coexist with the assertion that Lavoisier's system is immutable? The second difficulty lies on the periphery of the Lavoisian system: in 1805, the English chemist Dalton adumbrated a hypothesis which was to have a great future, the atomic hypothesis. Yet this hypothesis, based on the two laws of definite and multiple proportions, was conceived outside the Lavoisian frame. These theories moreover, and the research on which they were based, were unknown in France, as they had been overshadowed by the glory of Lavoisier. Given this fact, is it still possible to argue that Lavoisier's system was at the heart of all modern chemistry?

With regard to its inaccuracies and inadequancies, the attitude of French chemists was quite plain: they played them down and considered them as mere readjustments of minor details. Thus the concept of oxygen as an acidifying agent, was, in Berthelot's eyes, just a slightly exaggerated thesis which Davy had then put right. Yet this was not a secondary thesis in the system. Indeed, it represented here a definite reversal of Lavoisier's ideas on muriatic acid (hydrochloric acid). Like all other acids, it was supposedly composed of oxygen and an acidifiable base, as yet unidentified, but which Lavoisier called radical muriatic. However, in 1785, Berthollet demonstrated that this radical was in fact oxygenised muriatic acid. Following this,

Gay-Lussac and Thénard strongly suspected that they were dealing with an element, but had not dared deal such a blow to the doctrine of the master. Finally, it was Davy himself who announced that muriatic acid did not in fact contain any oxygen and that radical muriatic acid was after all the simple agent: chlorine. This reversal of Lavoisier's ideas strangely resembled Lavoisier's own treatment of Stahl's notions, when he demonstrated that a metal before calcination was a simple body and not a radical combined with phlogiston. And yet one speaks of revolution in one case and of correction in the other. Concerning caloric, the interpretation is equally nuanced. Wurtz, in 1875, did not hesitate to speak about a deep conception that modern science adopted in a different form (42). The shift from a substantialist concept of heat to a mechanistic theory was not apparently recognized as being a basic change, but merely a variation in form! As for Berthelot, he persists in seeing only minor excesses in Lavoisier's work: he speaks of a "too great generalisation", and the only reproach that he permits himself to make dismisses all suggestion of error:

Le ferme esprit de Lavoisier lui-même n'est pas exempt d'un côté romanesque quand il cherche à trop approfondir ces questions (43).

It is thus by adventuring too far into the unknown that Lavoisier nearly reperpetrated past errors. A genius only sins through excess. Let posterity get the measure of things and preserve his monument. One thing seems clear though: there will be no future revolution of the magnitude of Lavoisier's.

6. History and the Present

The history of the atom emerges powerfully from this sermon of fidelity to Lavoisier. Without a doubt too, the celebrity of Dalton is diminished by that of Lavoisier: one scarcely acknowledges his merit as a founder; at best, he is praised for his ingenuity and skill, although it is true that even Dalton never regarded his work as revolutionary; he presented in all modesty his hypothesis, and this only after praising Lavoisier at great length (44). It is also true that his hypothesis did not immediately transform the existing ideas contained in chemistry and that the version of atomism finally adopted in the mid-nineteenth century was that of Avogadro and Ampère, backed by the works of Gerhardt, Cannizzaro and Wurtz, and not that of Dalton. The effects of the atomic theory were thus slow and gradual, forming a marked contrast with the abrupt and striking nature of the Lavoisian revolution. It is important to ask, however, to what extent the Lavoisian structure did not actually hinder the development of atomism. It is not a question of blaming Lavoisier for the tardy acceptance of atomism by French scientists. The century-long delay in the atom's institution in France was probably the consequence of other causes, which are too elaborate to analyse here. The phenomenon is complex, and cannot simply be explained in terms of a screen-effect, stemming from the Lavoisier cult. At the beginning, moreover, chemists did not intentionally snub atomism: Gay-Lussac even supported its wide-spread acceptance – though admittedly he was not in accordance with Dalton – and Dumas remained for some time an ardent advocate of it. Hence, the rejection of the atom was not immediate. Moreover, as was noticed later, the few rare supporters who remained faithful to it in France were also the most fanatical adepts of Lavoisier.

For the Lavoisian tradition sustained its influence in a more devious way: it did not openly attack atomism, but sought to minimize its impact by reducing it to an accessory component in the Lavoisian edifice. Once again, what mattered was to preserve the idea of continuity at all costs; and this the chemists achieved, with the aid of numerous expedients which they varied according to the age and circumstance. Three cases can be chosen to characterize the range of reactions: those of Dumas, Berthelot and of Wurtz; the first two were reputed for their anti-atomism, whereas the third was remembered for his staunch support of the atom. How then is atomism presented by each party, and how exactly does it figure in post-Lavoisian history?

Despite a cult-like devotion to Lavoisier, Dumas acknowledged that the atomic hypothesis was the product of research done outside the master's system. He even deplored that the fame of Wenzel had been slighted by the success of Lavoisier (45), and even went as far as to suggest that the figure of Lavoisier could have constituted an epistemological obstacle:

On peut même assurer aujourd'hui que, tant qu'on se serait occupé exclusivement de l'examen des corps que Lavoisier et ses contemporains étudiaient avec tant d'ardeur et de persévérance, la théorie des équivalents devait demeurer inaperçue (46).

Will Dumas end up by disparaging the glory of Lavoisier? On the contrary, he upheld it and what is more, safeguarded the theme of continuity. If the evolution of chemistry occurred on the periphery of the system, this was because Lavoisier had more pressing questions to deal with: first, he wanted to study categories of general phenomena, and one can only praise the wisdom of his choice. Indeed, from a study of air, water, and carbonic acid, Lavoisier dealt with the fundamental questions about nature, life and even feeling. And no one would contend that such complex problems required a life-time's work! Indeed, it is quite clear to Dumas, that, had Lavoisier had the time, he would have discovered the laws of Wenzel:

Il existe des lois que Lavoisier n'a point connues et qu'il aurait pu découvrir néanmoins si les grands phenomènes à l'étude desquels il avait consacré sa vie n'eussent absorbé toute son attention, ou peut-être si sa vie se fût assez prolongée pour lui laisser le loisir de les aborder (47).

It is thus purely accidental that the renown attached to the theory of equivalents was not attributed to Lavoisier, for there was no discontinuity or breach with his system:

Cette théorie des équivalents chimiques, (...) cette théorie des atomes (sont) nées, comme la doctrine de Lavoisier, d'un emploi soutenu de la balance et (...) tôt ou tard se fussent offertes à son esprit attentif ou seraient sorties de ses expériences si minutieusement exactes (48).

The theory of equivalents takes us back then to Lavoisier's great primitive intuition, which was the irreproachable source of his discoveries; although the former is actually a by-product of the Lavoisian system. Hence Dumas managed to preserve continuity. Furthermore, he associated this stance with his own work: notably his famous declarations condemning atomism testified the current validity of Lavoisier's principles. He proclaimed that one should not diverge from experience, or seek to compensate for the absence of facts. It was by having contravened the father-founder's commandments that the young chemists had lost their way: they had forgotten the warnings of the Discourse Préliminaire and succumbed to the temptation of hypotheses; whereas Dumas, the prodigal son, had returned to the house of his father and had sworn to him an undying fidelity. Berthelot, for his part, never suffered the temptations of atomism. Always obedient, and submissive to the precepts of Lavoisier, he does not even raise the problem of continuity: according to him, it had never been seriously threatened, and in any case, it was inevitable.

The chief idea of Berthelot is that the venture of Lavoisier remains incomplete. The necessity governing history leads the chemists' work.

So let them complete the edifice. Hence Berthelot is driven by the force of things, to pursue and elaborate Lavoisier's programme. Lavoisier had made of chemistry a science of analysis. Well! But that was only the start of things; it was the first stage, and only half the objective:

Lavoisier fut conduit, il y a près d'un siècle, à définir la chimie la science de l'analyse. Cette définition est incomplète, elle laisse de côté la moitié du problème. En effet, lorsque nous avons pénétré l'essence des corps pondérables par la voie de décompositions successives, nous sommes conduits à recomposer ce que nous avons séparé, à refaire les corps que nous venons de détruire: c'est cette puissance de la formation synthétique qui assigne à la chimie son caractère véritable (...) La chimie est aussi la science de la synthèse (49).

Lavoisier was then nothing more than the founder. But, also interesting to note, is that by drawing attention to the limitations of the Lavoisier system, Berthelot also ingratiates himself. Admittedly, he presents himself as a successor, but this does not prevent him from comparing himself favourably to the master. And, as promoter of synthetic chemistry, he can claim the accolades of a cofounder. Indeed, the whole of chemistry can eventually be summarized in terms of the twin-influences of Lavoisier and Berthelot.

This vision of things, however, hardly soothed the susceptibilities of the atomists. Berthelot even questioned the need to mention the notion of atom, so slight was its impact on history. In fact, from the atomic theory, Berthelot only accepted the retention of the concept of atomic weight. So, although he accepted the Daltonian atom, deemed useful by him, he nonetheless rejected all subsequent progress (50). Having been reduced and weakened, the atomic theory could now easily be treated as a mere refinement in Lavoisier's ideas. For Berthelot, then, it represented an effective but accessory progress, the atomic weight only serving as a criterion for the characterisation of simple substances. Happily, the importance of atomism then lay in its potential to complete the Lavoisian chemistry of the simple substance. But here again, the path of progress was dictated by Lavoisier himself. There is no question of an outside contribution, for, as Berthelot put it, without Lavoisier's simple substances, it would have been inconceivable to look for equivalents or atomic weights. Ergo, continuity is safe.

The rigidity of history and reluctance with regard to the hypotheses seem therefore, to have been the direct effect of the Lavoisian monopoly of French chemistry. But as in the case of Wurtz, the Lavoisian cult could also be mobilised in defence of atomism. Wurtz took up the militant cause not only at the Congress of Karlsruhe in 1860, but also in several of his works which were devoted to the developments of atomism. He accorded Lavoisier a central role, and refused to grant Dalton the status of a founder, even in the domain of the atomic theory, which-according to Wurtz he had only updated. Lavoisier is hailed the "maître éternel, fondateur d'une base immuable" and even appeared as the true author of the atomic hypothesis. Wurtz even managed to integrate the atom into the general plan of the Lavoisian edifice, thanks to two types of argument.

The first, formulated in 1864, in *La Théorie atomique*, was very direct: it was known that the atomic hypothesis rested on two pillars, the law of fixed proportions and that of multiple proportions. The discovery of the latter definitely belonged to Dalton, but Wurtz attributed the first to Lavoisier:

La loi de la fixité a donc été expressement admise et clairement énoncée par Lavoisier: en faisant un pas de plus, on découvrait la loi des proportions multiples, mais il ne l'a pas fait. Et la fixité, il n'a pas réussi non plus à en convaincre les autres (51).

This belief was based on the existence of a fixed relationship, and sometimes even a multiple one, between the metal and oxygen, as stated in Lavoisier's theory of acids and oxides. But is that sufficient evidence to constitute Lavoisier as the originator of the law of definite proportions?

Indeed, this thesis encounters a counter-example in the form of Berthollet: although a disciple of Lavoisier, Berthollet was nonetheless a dogged opponent of the law of fixed proportions. Never mind! Wurtz refused to be perturbed by this apparent paradox: Berthollet had not understood his master, or at least, the master had been unable to convince him. There remains a more serious drawback, however: if, like many of his contemporaries, Lavoisier had identified the existence of proportions, he never took the pain to specify it as a general law. Indeed, he was far from doing so, much further than Wenzel was, who at least made known a law of equivalents for acids and bases. Why then, is the name of Wenzel never even introduced?

This perfunctory manner of tracing everything back to Lavoisier was not devoid of problems. Another approach, more nuanced seemed more appropriate, and did not vex historical data. The conference on *La théorie des atomes dans la conception générale du monde,* whilst still centering upon Lavoisier, posed however the problem of continuity in post-Lavoisian research. Wurtz acknowledged the existence of lacuna in the Lavoisian system; and even admitted that in addition to a few defects, the system did contain some slight excesses, which the passage of time had in fact erased. But it was precisely this two-fold operation of filling in the gaps and of correction which supposedly led to the birth of atomism (52). Nonetheless, Wurtz was careful not to cast a slur on the memory of Lavoisier by attributing all these difficulties in the system to its perpetrators. It is they who committed a sin in thinking they could fill the gaps in Lavoisier's chemistry; who, by overladening it, forced it into error. Such was the case with Berzelius, who, wanting to complete the development of the scarcely defined theory of the radicals, got led astray:

Les routes que Lavoisier avait tracées dans ce domaine, il voulut les étendre vers le monde des produits formés sous l'influence de la vie; elles ont abouti à une impasse (53).

It was Berzelius alone, who was responsible for the mistakes, he alone who exceeded the limits and plunged into error. As for Lavoisier, he emerged unscathed from the whole affair, and his triumph was greater than ever before. For not only was his slate wiped clean, but the silences and lacuna of his system appeared to bear witness to his great sagacity. The creator's wisdom was even apparent in his mistakes. Mythology in chemistry once again made use of an old theological argument!

The memory of Lavoisier, then, is not necessarily connected with the concept of anti-atomism; fidelity to the founder can eventually be modified and enhanced by the introduction of a new concept. It was rather the religious component of the Lavoisian image which was most telling in the reluctance to accept atomism; for the cult contained dimensions of a political, at least sociological, character. The unswerving commitment to the founder genius encouraged a system of authority within the French chemistry community. Many disciples of the Lavoisian revolution thus became intellectual mandarins; J. B. Dumas and M. Berthelot were examples of this. And, since the organisation of the institutes of research permitted them to benefit from teaching posts in the most prestigious Parisian institutions, and to direct laboratories and scientific reviews, and even to occupy elevated political positions, they evidently could wield substantial power and hence enforce a certain scientific orthodoxy. New or imported ideas which could have threatened the established authorities were as a result, heavily censured; and young chemists, such as Laurent and Gerhardt, for example, saw their careers shattered as soon as they advanced non-conformist ideas. Hence, by taking shelter behind the revolutionary cult, French chemistry ended up by asserting its authority, but this at the expense of originality (54).

This investigation into the historical paths of a few chemists shows to what extent the history of science can serve as a refuge for all the religious or political values, exuded of practical science. If it is possible to detect beneath the surface of an objective description of the evolution of chemistry the ardent zeal of a devout, or the fervour of a patriot, it is perhaps because history is the privileged domain in which the imaginary dimension of science can thrive, and new religions can be born. It is here that the faith of modern times is located.

Notes

1. Daumas, M., *Lavoisier, théoricien et expérimentateur*, Paris, 1955; 'La chimie dans l'Encyclopedie et dans l'Encyclopedie méthodique', in *Revue d'histoire des sciences* 5 (1951) pp. 19–23.
2. Guerlac, H., Lavoisier: *The Crucial Year. The Background and Origin of His First experiments on Combustion in 1772*, Ithaca, Cornell University Press, 1961: *Antoine-Laurent Lavoisier. Chemist and Revolutionary*, New York, 1973; 'Lavoisier Antoine-Laurent', *Dictionary of Scientific Biography*, New York, 1973, VIII, pp. 66–91.
3. A quantitative analysis would reveal the full implications of this historical dimension. Here are a few examples: *Le Système des connaissances chimiques by Fourcroy*, Paris 1801, is arranged thus: the first part is theoretical, the second is historical, and only then are experiments and applications dealt with. Fourcroy differentiates so little chemistry from its history, that he defines the former in terms of the latter: In his article 'Chimie', published in the *Encyclopédie Méthodique*, he writes: 'La chimie se distingue des autres sciences plus par son histoire que par ses progrès'; a statement confirmed by the 478 pages of detailed historical analysis that followed. With Dumas, history is again at the forefront of the *Leçons sur la Philosophie chimique*, Paris, 1836, six lectures are devoted to history, as opposed to only five given over to contemporary chemistry. Berthelot, turned historian in two works, *Les origines de l'alchimie*, Paris 1885 and *La révolution chimique*, Lavoisier (Paris, 1890); but his works still devote a lot of space to history: *La synthèse chimique*, Paris, 1879, is set out in two parts: the first, 'historique de

la chimie organique', is 214 pages long, whereas the second, 'La chimie organique fondée sur la synthèse', numbers only 50 pages.

4. Guyton de Morveau L. B., *Dictionnaire de chimie de l'Encyclopédie Méthodique*, T. I. (1786), p. 628.
5. *Ibid.*, p. 633–634.
6. *Ibid.*, p. 634.
7. Fourcroy, article 'chimie', *op. cit.*, supra (4), T. III, p. 303.
8. Lavoisier, laboratory note dated 20 February 1772; cited by Berthelot in *La révolution chimique*, Lavoisier, Paris 1890, p. 48.
9. Lavoisier, A., *Oeuvres* edited by J. B. Dumas and E. Grimaux, 1864, T. 2, p. 1–4–185; cf. also 'Sur la combustion en général', in *Oeuvres*, T. 2, p. 225.
10. *Ibid.*, p. 623; cf. also Dagognet, F., 'Lavoisier: Discours Préliminaire au Traité élementaire de chimie', in *Cahiers pour l'analyse*, 9 (1968) pp. 170–177; Anderson, W. C., *Between the Library and the Laboratory; The Language of Chemistry in 18th Century France*, P.H.D. 1979, Univ. Microfilms Intern.; McKie, D., *Antoine Lavoisier: Scientist, Economist, Social Reformer*, New York, 1952.
11. Lavoisier, A., *Oeuvres*, T. 2, p. 624.
12. *Ibid.*, T. 1, p. 12.
13. *Ibid.*, T. 2, p. 225.
14. *Ibid.*, T. 1, p. 12; Condillac, E., *La logique ou les premiers développements de l'art de penser*, Paris, 1768, p. 114; cf. also Rosenfeld, L., 'Condillac's Influence on French Scientific Thought', in *The Triumph of Culture: 19th Century Perspectives*, Toronto, 1972.
15. Lavoisier, A., *Oeuvres*, T. 1, p. 2.
16. Guyton de Morveau, L. B., Lavoisier, A., Berthollet, C., *Fourcroy, Méthode de nomenclature, Sur la nécessité de réformer la nomenclature de la chimie*, 1787, p. 16–17.
17. Macquer, J., Lettre à Guyton de Morveau du 4 janvier 1778; cited by Guyton, *op. cit.* (above 4), p. 626.
18. Comte, A., *Cours de philosophie positive*, 38ème leçon, 1835; ed. Hermann, Paris, 1975, T. I, p. 624.
19. Berthelot, M., *La révolution chimique, Lavoisier*, Paris, 1890, p. 79.
20. Guyton de Morveau, *op. cit.* (above 4), p. 629.
21. Priestley, J., quoted from R. E. Schofield, *Journal of Chemical Education* 53, 7, (1976) p. 409.
22. Dumas, J. B., *Leçons sur la philosophie chimique*, 1836; éd. culture et civilisation, Bruxelles, 1972, p. 110.
23. *Ibid.*, p. 112.
24. *Ibid.*, p. 157; my underlining.
25. *Ibid.*, p. 113.
26. *Ibid.*, p. 2.
27. *Ibid.*, p. 3.
28. *Ibid.*, p. 40–41.
29. *Ibid.*, p. 156.
30. See Kahane, E., *Lavoisier, Pages choisies*, Paris, éd. sociales, 1974, p. 72.
31. Berthelot, M., *op. cit.* (above 19), p. 53.
32. *Ibid.*, p. 23.

33. Wurtz, A., *Dictionnaire de chimie pure et appliquée, T. I*, Paris, 1869, p. 1.
34. Volhard, *La fondation de la chimie par Lavoisier, Kolbe, L'état de la chimie en France*, in *Berichte* 3 (1870), p. 873.
35. Mendéléev, D. I., *Principles of Chemistry*, London, 1891, preface.
36. Ostwald, W., *L'évolution d'une science, la chimie*, éd. fr. Paris, 1914, p. 21.
37. Duhem, P., *La chimie est-elle une science française?*, Paris, Hermann, 1916, p. 4.
38. *Ibid.*, p. 5; my underlining.
39. Dumas, J. B.; *op. cit.* (above 22), p. 159.
40. Berthelot, M.; *op. cit.* (above 19), p. 69.
41. *Ibid.*, p. 81.
42. Wurtz, A., *La théorie des atomes dans la conception générale du monde*, Paris, 1875, p. 10.
43. Berthelot, M.; *op. cit.* (above 19), p. 97.
44. Dalton, J., *A new System of Chemical Philosophy*, Part I, 1808; see also *J. Dalton and the progress of science*, Cardwell D.S.L., (ed.), Manchester Univ. Press, 1968.
45. Dumas, J. B.; *op. cit.* (above 22), p. 162.
46. *Ibid.*, p. 161.
47. *Ibid.*, p. 162.
48. *Ibid.*, p. 162.
49. Berthelot, M., *La synthèse chimique*, Paris, Alcan. 1897, pp. 1–2.
50. It must be remembered that Berthelot regarded the atomism based on the law of Avogadro-Ampère as 'un roman ingénieux et subtil', a pretentious system which only introduced cumbersome conventions of language. idem pp. 163–171.
51. Wurtz, A., *La théorie atomique*, 1864, 3° édit. 1883, p. 3.
52. Wurtz, A.; *op. cit.* (above 42), p. 12.
53. *Ibid.*, p. 22.
54. See Williams, L. P., 'Science Education, and the French Revolution', in *Isis* **XLIV** (1953) pp. 311–330; B. Bensaude-Vincent, 'Le mandarinat des chimistes francais du 19ème siècle', in *Bulletin de l'union des physiciens* (1979) pp. 383–392.

REDEFINITIONS OF A DISCIPLINE:
HISTORIES OF GEOLOGY AND GEOLOGICAL HISTORY

RACHEL LAUDAN

Center for the Study of Science in Society, and Department of History,
Virginia Polytechnic Institute and State University

1. Introduction

Periods of rapid theory change or 'revolutions' in science are apt to spur the scientists involved to write new histories of the discipline, and revolutions in geology are no exception. Two major episodes of historical writing by Anglo-Saxon geologists have been associated with revolutions in the discipline, namely Charles Lyell's uniformitarianism and recent plate tectonics (1). The most influential early nineteenth-century history of geology in English is Charles Lyell's introduction to his classic *Principles of Geology* (1830– 1833) (2). The *Principles* was the work that ushered in the 'uniformitarian-catastrophist' debates, and that was identified later by Kuhn as a geological paradigm. Lyell intended his history to form an integral part of the definition and articulation of the uniformitarian position which he thought was the sole means of making geology scientific. Uniformitarianism, as a geological tradition is thus inextricably bound up with Lyell's interpretation of the history of geology. In recent years, new histories and historical anthologies have documented the origins and triumphs of 'plate tectonic' theory, which has dominated geology since the mid-1960s. In order to structure their interpretation of this plate tectonic 'revolution', contemporary geologists have fastened on Kuhn's account of scientific change (albeit a dramatically transformed version of Kuhn's model as I shall show) (3).

To say that much history of science, particularly that written by scientists themselves, serves a legitimising or justificatory role is a truism, and one that certainly applies both to Lyell's history and to recent histories of plate tectonics (4). But granted that much of the history of geology, like the

79

Loren Graham, Wolf Lepenies, and Peter Weingart (eds.), Functions and Uses of Dis-
ciplinary Histories, Volume VII, 1983, 79–104.
Copyright © 1983 by D. Reidel Publishing Company.

history of any other science, has been used to justify either the actual, or the proposed geological practice of the period in which the history was written, just what kind of legitimation is wanted, and how in detail does the history function as justification? The central thesis of this paper is that both in the case of uniformitarianism and in the case of plate tectonics, history was used to confer scientific status on one particular conception of geology by re-defining the boundaries of the discipline (5). As we shall see, the changes that took place in geology around the time that these histories were written were not simply changes in the theories invoked to account for a static array of data, agreed upon by all to constitute the province of geology. Instead the very nature of the discipline itself was in question, the subject-matter that was regarded as central and the techniques for studying it changed, and in the process boundaries demarcating geology from other fields were redrawn. In each case, geologists in favor of the new conception of geology needed to justify their choice. The interaction of the redefinition of the disciplinary boundaries of geology, the need for justification that this redefinition produced, and the accompanying re-writing of history will form the focus of this paper.

However, besides the parallels between the two cases, there are also some very important distinctions. The remainder of this paper will address the similarities and differences in four related areas: first, the temporal relations between the rewriting of history and the revolution in the science; second, the role of history in redefining the boundaries of geology; third, philosophical and historiographic considerations in the definition of diciplinary boundaries; and fourth, the effect that the history had on the subsequent development of the discipline.

2. The Temporal Relations between the Re-writing of History and the Revolution in the Discipline

Although both the periods of historical writing were associated with revolutions in geology, the temporal relations between the revolution and the historical analysis were quite different in the two cases. Lyell wrote his history in order to set the stage for a revolution that he hoped to precipitate; the historians of plate tectonics wrote their histories *after* a revolution had already occurred in the science, in order to give even greater credence to the victorious theory. I shall call these two modes of writing history stipulative history and revisionist history.

2.1. *Lyell*

Turning to the first case study, it is important to understand why Lyell thought that there had to be a re-direction of geological thinking (or a revolution in the discipline) and also why he thought that history had such an important role to play in this re-direction. These attitudes of Lyell's were closely linked to his interpretation of eighteenth-century science. In Lyell's view, in the eighteenth century the earth had been studied by men who adopted one or another of two extreme positions, cosmogonical and geogonic respectively. Thus what in the nineteenth century came to be regarded as geology was, in the eighteenth century, parcelled out between two totally distinct activities between which only the glimmerings of a synthesis were perceived. Lyell wanted to stipulate changes in geology that would bring about this synthesis. This could only be done once geologists drew the correct morals from the earlier history of geology.

The cosmogonical tradition, at least in so far as it was concerned with the development of our unique planet, and not with eternal but cyclic worlds, could be traced back to the seventeenth century, when the replacement of Aristotle's concept of an eternal universe by the systems of Descartes and Newton opened the door to investigations of the origin and development of the cosmos in general, and hence of the earth in particular (6). A succession of "theories of the earth" was proposed, each of them a story of varying plausibility about the development of the earth from its first origins to its present habitable state. Descartes, Burnet, Whiston, Leibniz, Grew, Derham, and Buffon, to mention only some of the more prominent, laid out such systems, and controversy raged throughout the eighteenth century about their relative merits. The problem, as virtually everyone realised, was that these controversies were effectively unresolvable. The cosmogonies were necessarily constructed on the basis of the method of hypothesis, and therefore the sole empirical constraint on them was that they be consistent with contemporary knowledge about the earth. Since this was sketchy at best the constraint was rather easily satisfied. Most cosmogonists, it is true, also wanted their systems to satisfy another condition, namely they thought they should be consistent with the best available astronomy and physics, but since throughout much of the eighteenth century there was widespread disagreement about what constituted the best physical science, the additional constraint was of little help in choosing between rival systems. The fact that there seemed to be no rational way to decide between these different cosmogonies was worrying enough in itself to Lyell. But his worry was compounded by the fact that this lack of control gave license to those who wished to adopt a particular cosmogony because it was also consistent with the claims about the history of the earth put forward in the Old Testament (7). Thus cosmogony and theology became mutually reinforcing, and ever more compelling, while, Lyell believed, becoming increasingly insulated from empirical test. In Lyell's opinion, cosmogony was thereby rendered unscientific, for he believed that the testimony of the senses should be the warrant for the theory of the earth that we adopt, and not the authority vested by the clergy in the sacred writings of one or another primitive peoples. Particularly distasteful to Lyell, because most immediately threatening, were the claims about the origin and early history of the world contained in the initial chapters of *Genesis*. Not that Lyell was a modern atheist, or a thoroughgoing sceptic about the existence of a divine being. On the contrary, he, like James Hutton, the geologist he most admired, was wholeheartedly committed to a form of deism, and was quick to repudiate any charges of atheism, either against himself, or against Hutton (8). But as a deist, he saw the history of theology as a gradual sloughing off of primitive myths and unscientific cosmogonies, and their replacement by a less superstitious and more rational set of beliefs. In his opinion, Biblical criticism had shown convincingly the very mixed and primitive origins of many portions of the Old Testament. For geology to become entwined with a theology that gave credence to such outmoded beliefs was to serve the interests neither of religion nor of science. Lyell was acutely conscious of the battle to be fought, because entanglements between cosmogony and theology were still common in Britain, particularly at Oxford, where Lyell had first become seriously interested in geology as an undergraduate (9). In order to make geology scientific, Lyell came to the conclusion that it was necessary to find a principle of demarcation that would separate the systematic study of the earth from purported scriptural evidence; and he had to do this in an atmosphere in which most of his friends and colleagues were unconvinced of the urgency of the task, and in many cases were actively hostile to it.

Lyell knew quite well, of course, that there was an alternative approach to the study of the earth already available, and that the geognosists were well embarked on an avowedly inductive program, drawing on information from the natural history sciences of crystallography, mineralogy, chemistry and biological taxonomy. This tradition was most fully developed in Germany, where the long history of the mining academies at Freiberg and Chemnitz, and the lustre of Werner's reputation had ensured the collection of massive amounts of data about the mineral formations of the earth. In England, in part because of the different social, political and institutional framework, geognosists had not formed nearly such a coherent group in the eighteenth century, although gentlemen amateurs, collecting fossils and minerals for their 'cabinets', abounded (10). In 1807, a number of these men had banded together to form the Geological Society of London, with the explicit aim of putting geology on a scientific footing by gathering yet more facts, particularly about the arrangement of the strata of the British Isles (11). Theories were suspect and to be eschewed at all costs. Members were not recruited on the basis of their knowledge of the facts, and indeed a "want of systematical instruction" (12) was regarded as one of the surest ways of avoiding theoretical bias. But after a decade of this indiscriminate fact collecting had failed to produce any generalizable results, the newer members of the Society, including Lyell, began to feel that perhaps the founders had been mistaken about the route to scientific status. Legitimate theorising, as well as fact collection was required. Lyell urged that geologists should "entirely disavow the influence of that fashion, now too prevalent in this country, of discountenancing almost all geological speculation" (13). Geologists needed the systematicity of the cosmogonists, but not their speculative excesses, so disastrously susceptible to reconciliation with Scripture; and they needed to emulate the geognosists' dedication to expanding the empirical basis of the subject, while being readier to theorise. A re-direction of the discipline was desperately needed in Lyell's view. To this end, Lyell sat down to write his *Principles of Geology*, intended to "establish the principles of reasoning in the subject" (14).

This leads to my second question, namely why Lyell commenced the *Principles* with four chapters dealing with the history of the subject. In one sense, Lyell was following general practice by beginning his text with an historical introduction; almost all the cosmogonists had commenced their works with ritual (and usually highly derogatory) rehearsals of the systems of their predecessors. However Lyell's historical introduction was unusual in its length, its choice of topics, and its treatment of those topics. As such it played a much more important and subtle role in his presentation of his general argument than the customary perfunctory dismissal of predecessors in most cosmogonical texts. In particular Lyell was concerned to show how certain persistent methodological errors had led geologists in the past to blur the distinction between scientific enquiry into the history of the earth and other disciplines, particularly theology. Only a few geologists, in his view, had taken tentative steps in the direction of setting geology on the correct path between the cosmogonical and geognostic extremes. For Lyell, a knowledge of the origins and development of the study of the earth was not just antiquarian background, intended primarily to enhance his own status by denigrating his predecessors (although he was not averse to this), but a necessary prerequisite for the formulation of a strategy that would allow more rapid progress by learning from past errors. Certain contemporary errors could be exposed without offense to their perpetrators by discussion of historical analogues. The purpose of Lyell's history, then, was to help him stipulate the changes he believed should be made in the discipline of geology. In the following two sections we shall see what these were.

2.2. *Plate Tectonics*

In the case of plate tectonics, the temporal relations between the revolution in the science, and the writing of history were completely reversed, with the plate tectonic revolution coming before, not after the re-writing of history. The aim of the historians was not to stipulate change, but to revise history in light of recent events. During the 1950s and 1960s, a series of developments described below led most geologists to accept a novel comprehensive theory of the earth.

Plate tectonics was a new answer to one of the major questions of geology, namely the origin of the irregularities of the surface of the globe, such as continents, oceans, mountain chains, oceanic islands and so forth. Since the seventeenth century, and uninterruptedly through the Lyellian period, these features had been explained either as residual traces of events occurring during the formation and very early history of the globe (the cosmogonical approach), or as the result of vertical movements of the earth's crust, caused, for example, by changes in the earth's heat budget (an approach used by Lyell as well as by other schools of geologists and geophysicists). After the plate tectonic revolution, geologists ceased appealing to such explanations, and came to believe that these irregularities are largely the result of the lateral movement, and consequent jostling of a set of thin rigid plates which completely cover the earth. This was a very dramatic turnabout, and a brief excursion into its history is in order (15).

After World War II magnetometers sensitive enough to measure the 'remanent magnetism' (or fossil magnetism) of rocks of different ages were developed, primarily for the purpose of testing physical theories about the causes of the earth's magnetic field. To everyone's surprise, the direction of the earth's magnetic field appeared to have changed dramatically in the course of time. Various hypotheses to explain this result were proposed and tested, among them the possibility that the earth's pole had wandered, and even that the earth's field had not always been dipolar. Eventually by the end of the 1950's, a small but influential group of scientists had become convinced that at least part of the explanation was that the continents had moved relative to each other. Even so, given the arcane nature of the evidence and the difficulties of interpreting it, it is unlikely that most working geologists would have been convinced had not supporting evidence from oceanography been collected simultaneously.

Intensive oceanographic exploration had been going on since World War II. As in the case of paleomagnetism, the research produced results that conflicted with common sense intuitions. The geology of the ocean floors was quite unexpectedly unlike that of the continents. For example a worldwide system of 'mid-ocean ridges' (in fact enormous mountain chains) was discovered. These ridges had peculiar physical characteristics, such as median rift valleys in which the heat flow was unusually high, suggesting that they might be tensional features. At the beginning of the 1960's, among other explanatory hypotheses, Hess and others put forward the idea that the sea floors were 'spreading' away from these ridges, and a couple of years later a test of this hypothesis was put forward by Vine and Matthews. They predicted that the unusual patterns of magnetic anomalies that had been observed around the mid-ocean ridges were, in fact, the record of global magnetic reversals (another phenomenon detected by the paleomagnetists) that had occurred while lava was welling up, solidifying and moving apart from the tensional cracks along the mid-ocean ridges. The test was possible since by this juncture the global magnetic reversals had been dated on the continents using radioactive techniques. If the sea floor was spreading away from the rift, the magnetic anomalies should run parallel to the ridge, and be symmetrical on either side of it. After a couple of false starts, the predicted parallel strips of magnetic anomalies were found on both sides of one mid-ocean ridge system in 1965. Furthermore they were dated, and turned out to be quite consistent with the evidence from paleomagnetic reversals. The final piece of the puzzle was to link this oceanographic model of sea-floor spreading to a general tectonic model. Since the continents and ocean floors differ mineralogically, geologists had always assumed them to be structurally distinct as well. Perhaps, it was now suggested, this assumption was incorrect and the mineralogical differences were unimportant compared to the structural similarities. It was hypothesised that continents and oceans might be welded together in rigid 'plates' about one hundred kilometres thick, moving across the earth's surface. Created at the mid-ocean ridges by the cooling of the up-welling lava, the plates would move slowly apart, to be destroyed eventually at the contact with other plates by sinking into earthquake zones or by piling up into mountain chains. The idea was ingenious but lacked independent evidence, until J. Tuzo Wilson pointed out that if there really were mobile rigid plates moving about the surface of the earth, then there should be a third kind of junction between the plates, in addition to the mid-ocean ridges and "subduction zones" already mentioned, namely a previously undescribed type of fault which Wilson named a "transform" fault. If the plate tectonic hypothesis were correct, then the relative movement along a transform fault line would be in exactly the opposite direction to that predicted on any other theory of crustal behaviour. By the late 1960's, this prediction too had been confirmed. The theory known as plate tectonics now rapidly became, and remains the ruling geological orthodoxy.

By the early 1970s the scientists involved were already recounting the history of the revolution. Whereas Lyell had intended his history to help stipulate a revolution, these historians were attempting to make sense of a revolution that had already occurred. In particular, they had to explain why plate tectonics had displaced traditional geology, even though, as we shall see, the theory had been formulated by scientists with a disciplinary background outside mainstream geology, using new techniques, and employing the theory of continental drift, which was in considerable disrepute in the geological community. The rush of histories explaining the episode is impressive, many of them written by participants in the events. By 1973, both J. Tuzo Wilson and Allan Cox, who had been leading actors in the construction of plate tectonic theory, had produced anthologies of the classic articles as well as an interpretive historical framework. Anthony Hallam, one of the first to explore the implications of the new theory for palaeontology, and H. Takeuchi, S. Uyeda, and H. Kanamori who were active in Japanese discussions of the geophysical background to the revolution had produced historical monographs. Finally, Ursula Marvin, who though not involved in the revolution, was herself an earth scientist, had also produced a history (16). Other histories followed later, but for the purposes of this paper I shall concentrate on the interpretive framework offered by the authors already mentioned, hoping to obtain a clue about their aims as historians.

3. The Function of History in Redefining the Boundaries of Geology

In this section, I shall argue that one of the chief purposes of the historians discussed above was to establish (in Lyell's case), or justify (in the plate tectonic case) new disciplinary boundaries for the study of the earth (or geology). In doing so, of course they also redefined the relationship of geology to the other sciences. Such redefinitions may not have been their sole aim. In reading early histories of plate tectonics, for example, one gets an overpowering sense of the sheer excitement of the authors, and their need to communicate that excitement to the reader. But the concern with the demarcation of disciplinary boundaries is a major one.

3.1. *Lyell*

Throughout the historical introduction to the *Principles*, Lyell was quite explicit about his concerns with the demarcation of geological inquiry from other enterprises. "It was long", he said, "ere the distinct nature and legitimate objects of geology were fully recognized, and it was at first confounded with many other branches of inquiry, just as the limits of history, poetry and mythology were ill-defined in the infancy of civilization" (17). Lyell thought that such misconceptions continued until the recent past: he chastised Werner for regarding geology as "little other than a subordinate department of mineralogy", and Desmarest for confusing it with 'Physical Geography' (18). But Lyell reserved his greatest scorn for those who had confused geology and cosmogony — in his eyes almost all theorists who had studied the earth. Only Hutton had approached a correct conception of the subject, and this Lyell intended to build on this so as to show that "geology differs as widely from cosmogony, as speculations concerning the creation of man differ from history" (19). Just as history was distinct from, but dependent on a knowledge of the moral sciences of "ethics, politics, jurisprudence, the military art, [and] theology", geology was distinct from but dependent on the 'physical sciences' (20) (here opposed to the moral).

Moving to his historical survey of errors in the conception of the discipline, Lyell began in an unprecedented way with an entire chapter on the pre-Christian era, discussing particularly the interconnections between the study of the earth and different religious beliefs in India, Egypt, Greece, and Rome. Lyell claimed that the development of cosmogonies by 'rude nations' and "barbarous and uncultivated races" (21) was a common phenomenon, and one that left a legacy that became increasingly deleterious as society moved further from its primitive origins. "The superstitions of a savage tribe are transmitted through all the progressive stages of society", said Lyell "till they exert a powerful influence on the mind of the philosopher" (22). Unless forewarned, the latter might find "in the monuments of former change on the earth's surface, an apparent confirmation of tenets handed down through successive generations, from the rude hunter whose terrified imagination drew a false picture of those awful visitations and earthquakes, whereby the whole earth as known to him was simultaneously devastated" (23). Lyell had no need to draw an explicit parallel with contemporary efforts to find geological evidence for the Noachian deluge; the message would have been clear, if unpalatable, to all his contemporaries engaged in this effort. Past confusions between cosmogony and theology were still bedevilling the study of the earth.

Lyell devoted the following chapter to the period from the brief revival of learning among the Arabs in the tenth century to the end of the eighteenth century, excluding only those figures, particularly Hutton and Werner, whose influence on geology was still being strongly felt. Apart from discussing the usual figures, Lyell introduced a number of Italian geologists, such as Fracastoro, Scilla, Quirini, Vallisneri, Moro, Generelli, Targioni, Arduino, Fortis, and Testa, largely unknown to the Anglo-Saxon community then or now. His source was the historical introduction to Brocchi's *Conchologia Fossile Subappennina* (1814) a treatise that had been written for the rather different purpose of establishing that it was paleontology, and not mineralogy, that had led to the discovery that the ocean had once covered the tops of the highest mountains (24). Nonetheless Lyell was able to draw some morals from the history for his own purposes, although in doing so he sometimes altered Brocchi's emphasis to the point of misrepresentation. Aiming to establish that the use of fossils offered a promising approach to the study of the earth, less hypothetical than that used by the cosmogonists, but still theoretical, Lyell praised the struggles of many Italians to interpret the geological record. Fracastoro, for example, was commended for having argued that fossils were the remains of living beings, rather than the creation of a mysterious 'plastic force', and above all for having dismissed the possibility that all fossils could have been laid down by the Mosaic deluge. "His clear exposition of the evidence would have terminated the discussion for ever", concluded Lyell, "if the passions of mankind had not been enlisted in the dispute" (25). But despite this nascent geological tradition that avoided the perils of cosmogony, without falling into the geognosists' trap of avoiding all theory, its struggles to survive had not been very successful. "The clear and philosophical views of Fracastoro were disregarded, and the talent and argumentative powers of the learned were doomed for three centuries to be wasted in the discussion of these two simple and preliminary questions [the origin and placement of fossils]" (26). Meanwhile, the cosmogonists, like Burnet, Whiston, Woodward and Buffon "introduced purely hypothetical causes to account for natural phenomena" and therefore "retarded the progress of truth, diverting men from the investigation of the laws of sub-lunary nature, and inducing them to waste time in speculations on the power of comets to drag the waters of the ocean over the land — on the condensation of the vapours of their tails into water, and other matters equally edifying" (27). Those who, like Pallas and Saussure, inductively collected information, "did not pretend to have arrived at any general system" (28) without which Lyell thought geology would never achieve the status of a science. He concluded that the history of geology in the seventeenth and eighteenth centuries showed few indications of a correct and scientific conception of the discipline.

Lyell's final historical chapter was reserved for the Huttonian-Wernerian debates which he saw as essential background to the geology of his own day. Werner, the leading geognosist, could not be accused of having tangled with religion in an unjustifiable way, but when he allowed himself to theorise, he came dangerously close to cosmogony. He introduced not only "many imaginary causes supposed to have once effected great revolutions in the earth, and then to have become extinct, but new ones also were feigned to have come into play in modern times; and above all, that most violent instrument of change, the agency of subterranean heat" (29). By contrast, James Hutton, in his *Theory of the Earth* (1788 and 1795) (30) had wisely attempted "to dispense entirely with all hypothetical causes, and to explain the former changes of the earth's crust, by reference exclusively to natural agents" (31). Lyell was of the opinion that "too little progress had been made towards furnishing the necessary data to enable any philosopher, however great his genius to realize so noble a project" (32). The role of Newton on geology was thus still open for a geologist of a younger generation. Neither had Hutton used his own method as consistently as he should, so that his system's "greatest defect consisted in the undue influence attributed to subterranean heat, which was supposed necessary for the consolidation of all subterranean deposits", a cause that was clearly 'hypothetical' (33).

Nonetheless given the many merits of Hutton's position, Lyell felt it necessary to explain why others failed to perceive its advantages. This too had to do with confusion about the correct boundaries of geology. Hutton was unfortunate enough to publish at a time when "the mind of the English public ... was in a state of feverish excitement" (34) due to the political upheavals in France. Anti-clerical writers in France, like Voltaire, had used modern science "to diminish the influence of the clergy, by sapping the foundation of the Christian faith, and their success, and the consequences of the Revolution, had alarmed the most resolute minds" (35). Voltaire had seen geologists as the allies of the theologians, an understandable if unfortunate perception, given the prevalent conflation of cosmogony and scripture, and had therefore excluded geology from science and launched a vicious attack on even the well-founded beliefs of geologists. Hutton, who had divorced geology and Christian theology, had become widely regarded as belonging to the same socially and intellectually destructive tradition as Voltaire, and was consequently reviled as an atheist. The intellectual confusion resulted from the inability to distinguish the cosmogonies of the ancient world, with their postulation of eternal cycles, from Hutton's much more modest claim that the geologist could not detect traces of the beginning or end of the present world in the phenomena around him. Lyell, like Playfair and Hutton before him, believed that the earth had had a beginning and would have an end; these events were simply "not be brought about by the laws now existing" (36). Divorcing geology from cosmogony and from theology need not lead inexorably to atheism and social chaos.

The followers of Hutton and Werner had become engaged in a heated debate which Lyell, along with most of his contemporaries, thought had reached the point where "the two parties had been less occupied in searching for truth, than for such arguments as might strengthen their own cause, or serve to annoy their antagonists" (37). At such a juncture, Lyell agreed that the Geological Society was right to impose the "strictest neutrality, and the utmost indifference to the systems of Werner and Hutton" (38). For a period he thought this exaggeration of the antitheoretical stance of the geognosists had been appropriate for geologists. Now however Lyell's reader was in a position to ask whether the time had not arrived to stipulate a conception of geology that would incorporate the best features of both cosmogony and geognosy, and weld these formerly separate enterprises together in a new conception of the subject.

3.2. *Plate Tectonics*

The redefinition of the traditional boundaries in earth science following the acceptance of plate tectonics was also marked. The progress of this redefinition and the role played by history can be traced in the writings of J. Tuzo Wilson. A distinguished man in the field, with a reputation as a gadfly, stimulating his colleagues with a constant stream of new ideas, Wilson, who had been trained in both physics and geology, had long been concerned about the status of the geological sciences. Writing in 1953, well before the plate tectonic revolution, in an anthology intended to summarise and synthesise the state of knowledge in the earth sciences, Wilson began his contribution by briefly characterising the history of the discipline in terms of a dichotomy that should by now be familiar. As Wilson saw it, two distinct groups, separated by a 'great barrier' (39), were involved in the study of the earth's crust; the astronomers and physicists on the one hand, and the geologists, geographers and geodosists on the other. Not only did they look at different features of the earth using very different methods, but "the whole philosophy of their approach was different" (40). In a tone that suggested where his sympathies ultimately lay, Wilson praised the field men "for their assiduity, care and often courage in collecting a monumental volume of data about those detailed surface features which are exposed for them to see" (41), but regretted that by the very nature of their disciplinary orientation, they were constrained to be "more concerned with surface effects than with the nature and causes of the deep and fundamental processes" (42). The physicists, who had struggled to understand such processes had failed, "unable to analyze or make use of the field data", and able to reach more agreement "upon the nature of the nuclear processes which heat the sun and characterize the atoms of different elements" than about "those slow movements within the earth which have generated its powerful magnetic field, developed its mountains, and given structure to its crust" (43). Like Lyell a century and a half earlier, Wilson thought that a divided approach to the study of the earth was most unproductive, and again like Lyell, Wilson was optimistic that the situation would soon change. Recently developed methods of exploring the ocean bottoms, and of eliciting more information about the interior of the earth held out great hope. Fifteen years later, writing an article under similar auspices for the American Philosophical Society, Wilson could proclaim that the revolution in geology was well under way, and that the earth sciences were becoming organized around the synthesising concept of a form of continental drift (soon to be called plate tectonics) (44).

The plate tectonic revolution had its origins outside geology as it was generally understood in the mid-twentieth century. As Wilson put it "The majority of the members of geological surveys and departments of geology were not expecting any such revolution. All those organizations were concentrating on limited objectives. They were so absorbed in improving techniques, in amassing data and in planning computer codes by which to store the information that they forgot that other sciences have simplified their problems by discovering principles" (45). As we have seen, the fields of inquiry that generated the plate tectonic revolution were paleomagnetism and oceanography. Paleomagnetism was a branch of geophysics, studied within physics departments. It was the effort to make some headway on the recalcitrant problem of the causes of the earth's magnetic field that had led physicists to develop the sensitive magnetometers that could detect remanent magnetism. Oceanography too, was the province of scientists from different disciplines including physicists, chemists and biologists, and traditional geologists were not foremost in the discoveries that were made.

As a result of the success of the physicists and oceanographers in forging the plate tectonic revolution, the concerns and emphasis of the discipline came to look very different after the revolution. Whereas in the 1950s and 1960s stratigraphy still formed the central focus for all the other subdisciplines of geology, it has now been displaced from that position. Instead the theory of plate tectonics is regarded as the point around which the other earth sciences are organized. Paleontology and stratigraphy have declined in importance, and geology's links to the biological sciences, although still strong, are now overshadowed by its links to the physical sciences. What was, in the 1950s, as the earlier discussion by Wilson has shown, a parallel but non-overlapping enterprise carried out by physicists and field men has now become much more unified, but with the geophysicists clearly in the ascendancy. Oceanography, which used to be rather uncharitably regarded by traditional geologists as the province of those with more money than sense, has now become so dominant that a recent edition of *Science* included a plea for continental geology as an area desperately in need of more support.

To summarise this section, let me reiterate that in both examples of the re-writing of geological history that I have examined, the re-writing accompanied changes in the boundaries of the discipline. The specific connection was quite different in the two cases however. Lyell wanted to stipulate how the study of the earth should be reformed by taking the best features of the cosmogonic and geogonic traditions. Wilson and the other historians of plate tectonics were faced with the problem of revising geologists' conception of their discipline in the wake of unplanned and adventitious changes that had already occurred.

4. Philosophic and Historiographic Considerations in the Redefinition of Geological Boundaries

Whether stipulating the future course of geology or justifying changes of direction that had already occurred, all the historians under discussion felt the need for some conceptual background for their claims. They seemed to feel that the statements they were making about the redefinition of the boundaries of geology were more likely to be acceptable if they were seen in a wider framework of what was believed to be acceptable science. In order to find such a framework they turned either to the philosophy of science or to the historiography of science.

4.1. *Lyell*

Lyell's redefinition of the boundaries of geology was quite explicitly spurred by philosophical motives. Running throughout the *Principles* was a sustained argument for the adoption of a new methodology of geology. In particular, Lyell urged that geologists adopt the *vera causa* method, already highly esteemed in many of the other sciences, in order to ensure that geology, like these more prestigious sciences, would become truly scientific (45). He proposed that this methodology be used to demarcate those parts of geology that were truly scientific from the speculative excesses of the cosmogonists and the fact-grubbing of the geognosists. Thus Lyell's methodology, often characterised as 'uniformitarianism' or 'actualism', was in fact simply the importation into geology of the *vera causa* principle. This principle, often traced back to the first of Newton's influential 'rules of reasoning', was thought by many — the influential John Herschel among them — to represent the richest and most flexible methodology that also gave epistemically warranted results. The *vera causa* principle was ideal for Lyell's purposes, since by the beginning of the nineteenth century it was not only highly respectable, but, in its usual interpretation it did rule out those aspects of cosmogony and geognosy that Lyell found undesirable. The principle was generally taken to stipulate that if the scientist wished to hypothesise about unobservable causes that produced the effects to be explained, then he should limit himself to those causes that had already been observed acting in other circumstances, and that were known to be adequate to produce the effect in question. Such a principle clearly warranted the search for causes and was thus much less restrictive than the geognostic tradition. Equally, the principle rendered cosmogonies illegitimate, since these invoked causes acting in the very remote past that were quite unlike any observed at present. Lyell directed the geologist's attention instead to observable, and hence in most cases present-day causes, and following the lead of some the earlier Italian geologists and James Hutton, argued that these should constitute geologist's explanatory repertoire.

Returning to Lyell's use of history for a moment, it should now be clear that Lyell wanted his readers to draw the moral that the study of the earth had been misconceived in the past; that the two groups that had studied the earth had adopted the wrong methodologies; that the adoption of one of these methodologies (the method of hypothesis) had led them to include within the province of geology inappropriate cosmogonical problems and to give too much weight to the Scriptures which also claimed to address cosmogonical problems; and that the adoption of the other methodology (strict induction) had the equally unfortunate result of excluding even legitimate theorising so that geology failed to be a causal science. Furthermore Lyell wanted his readers to share his own conviction that hints about a better methodology could be found in certain earlier geologists, particularly Hutton, who had adopted a methodology closer to that that Lyell believed was the dominant method in the successful sciences of the day. Having followed the history, Lyell's reader was supposed to recognise that a methodological revolution was necessary in his discipline. The adoption of the correct methodology would mean that a new synthesis was created, welded out of what was most valuable in the two disparate traditions of cosmogony and geognosy.

4.2. *Plate Tectonics*

Historiographical considerations played a similar justificatory role in the reinterpretation of the history of geology after the triumph of plate tectonics. There was consensus among scientist-historians that Kuhn's *Structure of Scientific Revolutions* was directly relevant to the explanation of what had happened, and an examination of the way in which these authors interpreted Kuhn tells us a great deal about their motives in writing history. Wilson's historiography is particularly revealing, and although he never wrote more than short historical outlines, his framework appears to have been adopted for most of the subsequent history that has been written.

Rather than urge that geologists adopt a new methodology as Lyell had done, Wilson attempted to show that plate tectonics followed the developmental patterns observed in other sciences. Believing that these had been correctly identified and analysed by Kuhn, Wilson chose to describe recent events in geology as a Kuhnian revolution (46). Three of the first four historians to write on the subject echoed his words. In 1973, Ursula Marvin claimed that "the story of continental drift as a geologic concept, with its slow, tentative beginnings and violent controversy, followed by the spectacular band-wagon effect which has swept up the majority of earth scientists, bears out in dramatic fashion a thesis developed by Thomas S. Kuhn (47). In the same year, Allan Cox remarked in the introduction to his anthology that the development of plate tectonics "fits the pattern of Kuhn's scientific revolutions surprisingly well" (48). Anthony Hallam, although rather more critical of a Kuhnian analysis than the former authors, nonetheless concluded that "the earth sciences do indeed appear to have undergone a revolution in the Kuhnian sense" (49). Only the Japanese authors, who wrote the fourth of these early histories failed to use such terminology (50).

Wilson believed that the Kuhnian model identified four stages that typified the development of any advanced science. He also thought that these were evident in the history of plate tectonics. In the first stage, "most branches of science develope[d] out of the practical experience of such men as miners, seafarers, farmers, and foundrymen" (51). Such knowledge is "no more than a codification of the knowledge accumulated over several generations" (52), and hence, since it is grounded in practice, it is only natural that it works well and is useful in everyday life. This explained why there was much reliable information embodied in pre-plate-tectonic geology. Nonetheless, despite the seeming success of much proto-science, it is only the first step in the ascent to true science. The second stage Wilson believed to have been identified by "historians of science – notably T. S. Kuhn – [who] have pointed out that, as the quantity of knowledge increases, each branch of science reaches a stage in which theoreticians reinterpret the lore of practical men into new and subtler formulations" (53). Continuing to draw on Kuhn, Wilson cites Copernican astronomy and Lavoisieran chemistry as exemplifying this trend.

In other articles, Wilson includes discoveries and observations, as well as new ideas, as sources of change. Once this new discovery, observation or idea is in the public domain, it triggers the third stage since it "reveal[s] contradictions and introduce[s] problems which the old theory could not resolve" (54). This stage is essentially one of confusion and ferment, and in geology, Wilson thought, it occurred around 1953, when new techniques of geophysical exploration had overthrown cherished notions about the nature of the earth's crust.

Wilson also went to some pains to emphasise that the revolutionary discovery, observation, or idea was not advanced by insiders or experts in a discipline, but by "rebels, outsiders and interlopers from other fields of science who suggested the need for a revolution and produced the evidence" (55). The originators of the plate tectonic revolution, Wilson reminded his readers, were men "with a broad training, including an unusually good grasp of physics, and an interest in worldwide problems rather than small areas" (56). The fourth and final stage was the post-revolutionary period of normal science, when consensus was reached about the correct principles on which the revolutionary science should be based. Wilson stressed that there was continuity of a kind between pre- and post-revolutionary science. Referring to plate tectonics, he claimed that "the new beliefs do not invalidate past observations", and that in this respect the revolution was similar to the Copernican, Darwinian and Einsteinian revolutions, in all of which there were "great developments without the abandonment of older observations" (57).

While Wilson's account of scientific (and geological) change may not be unappealing, incorrect or incoherent, it noticeably lacks many of the features that have excited commentators about Kuhn's model. Wilson stresses cumulativity rather than incommensurability over the course of the revolution; he makes no mention of differences in values before and after the revolution; certainly he identifies no paradigms if paradigm is understood as exemplar; his account of pre-paradigmatic sciences bears little or no resemblance to Kuhn's; he places no emphasis on the sea of anomalies in which any theoretical science wallows; and, he is by and large unconcerned about the strict boundaries of normal science except for his point about revolutions being generated by outsiders to the discipline. Since Wilson pays scant attention to those features of the Kuhnian model that have excited most interest, we now have to ask why he found the model so relevant.

I believe that Wilson saw two related advantages to be gained by adopting a Kuhnian historiographic framework: first, he saw Kuhn's concept of a revolution as a way of demarcating proto-science and mature science. Anxious to show that geology need not be "forever destined to be a poor relation" (58), Wilson identified a revolution as a necessary, and even as a sufficient condition for establishing the scientific status of a discipline. The fact that, on a Kuhnian view, there can be a series of revolutions in a given discipline went unregarded. Wilson, like the other scientist-historians, acted as if revolutions in a discipline were a once-for-all event, separating the confusions of a theoretically incoherent investigation bound to the world of commonsense from the 'mopping-up' operations of a 'mature science' (59). In support of this interpretation, it is significant that none of the historians under consideration refers to previous episodes in the history of geology as revolutionary. For example, Wilson, who is given to listing revolutions identified by Kuhn in other disciplines, never mentions Lyell as precipitating an earlier revolution in the subject, even though Kuhn himself describes the *Principles of Geology* as paradigmatic (60). Rather these early historians of plate tectonics all emphasis that, by undergoing a revolution, the earth sciences may be presumed to have passed through the same stages of historical development as the more established sciences, and in doing so, they too have moved from being proto-sciences to mature sciences.

Second, Wilson's analysis of Kuhn (and to some extent that of the other historians) offers a rationale for the new disciplinary emphasis that emerged in the course of the revolution. Obviously an historical account, such as Kuhn's, that, whatever the author's intentions, was taken to show that progress in science tended to come from outsiders to the discipline, supplied a rationale for the changes that had taken place in the discipline of geology. Equally appealing in this connection was Kuhn's insistence that a revolution necessarily brought in its wake a pedagogical reform, with a need for the rewriting of text-books and a revision of the history of the subject (61). Both Wilson and Cox introduced Kuhn in their introductions to anthologies of the classic papers of plate tectonics intended to serve as texts, and Wilson, in particular, was an active campaigner in the cause of curriculum reform in geology.

5. The Effects of the Re-writing of History on the Development of Disciplines

The effect of the re-writing of history on the subsequent development of geology in these two cases is extremely difficult to judge, as we cannot turn to the counter-factual case of the development of the discipline without the re-writing of history. We have no way of knowing what might have happened in the science had the history *not* been re-written. Obviously all the historians in question believed that it was worth taking part of their valuable research time to write histories, and we have examined some of their aims in the preceding three sections. In this section I will draw what conclusions I can about their effectiveness.

5.1. *Lyell*

That the effect of Lyell's history was widespread is indubitable. The *Principles* was reprinted, revised and translated throughout the nineteenth century, with the historical introduction continuing to hold the same prominent place. Generations of geologists, particularly in the British Isles, were raised on the work. Its historiographic framework was unchallenged until the wave of writing by professional historians of science in the 1960s and 1970s. What is less easy to isolate is the extent to which this history influenced geological practice. Not that this practice did not change around the time that Lyell was writing the *Principles*. Cosmogony did become less important, and stratigraphical paleontology, of the sort that Lyell admired, became the accepted modus operandi of geologists. But there were signs that these changes were already underway, and whether they would have taken place regardless of Lyell's historical excursions, or whether the latter accelerated and directed the pace of change are questions that cannot be answered at this point. Indeed, somewhat ironically, it may even be the case that Lyell's historiography had more impact than his substantive proposals about geology. The historiography clearly stood unchallenged for something like a century, and certainly shaped geologists' conceptions of their discipline, reinforcing the idea, for example, that any interaction of geology with cosmogony was suspect. Lyell's substantive ideas gained few adherents, Darwin, Babbage and Herschel being the prominent examples of those sympathetic to Lyellian geology; even these men were quick to modify many of the specific theories.

Thus my intuition, though it is hard to test rigorously, is that Lyell's historiography did shape the direction of geology over the next century, and
that interestingly it had a more lasting impact than his geological theories, or
even his methodological strictures.

5.2. *Plate Tectonics*

The impact of the new histories of plate tectonics is, of course, even more
difficult to assess. My suspicion, however, from talking to geologists and
geology students is that we see a somewhat different pattern from the Lyellian
case. The history of the revolution still stands and is influential, but the
conceptual framework that originally justified it (in this case, Kuhn's historiography) is largely ignored and abandoned. Textbooks of geology continue
to give account of the history of the discipline that largely accords with
the one worked out in the wake of the revolution. They do not, in general,
spend much time on Kuhn's theory of scientific change, let alone on Wilson's
version of it. This is perhaps unsurprising as, unlike Lyell who used his
understanding of philosophy of science to construct his history of science
and to stipulate changes in the discipline, Wilson only used his understanding
of Kuhn as a post-hoc justification for events that had already taken place.
But only here time will tell the ultimate impact and interpretation of the
revolution.

6. Conclusion

Two of the major episodes of historical writing by geologists have been
associated with upheavals in the discipline. In one case that I examine,
namely Lyell's historical introduction to the *Principles of Geology*, the
history was intended to hasten that revolution, by demonstrating to readers
that progress in geology had been slowed by the adoption of the wrong
methodology (or methodologies) and by preparing readers to accept the
recommendation that geologists adopt the methodology that Lyell thought
characterised successful science. In the other case, namely the early histories
of plate tectonics, the re-writing of the history occurred as an aftermath of
a revolution that had already taken place. Here the aims of the historian were
two-fold, first to show that, like the more established sciences, geology had

passed through stages of historical development that guaranteed its maturity as a science, and second, to show that the new direction taken by the discipline was not peculiar to the plate tectonic revolution, but was a feature common to scientific revolutions. Thus in both cases, history played a legitimising role, showing that geology was a true member of the community of scientific disciplines, even though the criteria for establishing that membership differed in the two cases. That such uses of history are not uncommon in science is demonstrated by other cases presented in this volume.

Acknowledgement

I am grateful to Harold Burstyn, Arthur Donovan, Thomas Dunlap, Henry Frankel, Larry Laudan, David Oldroyd and Peter Weingart for comments on an earlier version of this paper.

Notes

1. The third major episode of historical writing by geologists that took place around the turn of the twentieth century seems to be for the most part an extension of Lyellian historiography. See Frank Dawson Adams, *The Birth and Development of the Geological Sciences*, Baltimore: Williams and Wilkins, 1938, and Sir Archibald Geikie, *The Founders of Geology*, 2nd ed., London: Macmillan, 1895. An interesting analysis of Geikie's work is given by D. R. Oldroyd, 'Sir Archibald Geikie (1835–1924), Geologist, Romantic, Aesthete, and Historian of Geology: The Problem of Whig Historiography of Science', *Annals of Science* 37 (1980), 441–462.
2. Charles Lyell, *Principles of Geology: Being an Attempt to Explain the Former Changes of the Earth's Surface by Reference to Causes now in Operation*, London: John Murray, 1830–33, 3 vols., hereafter referred to as *Principles*. Accounts of Lyell's history of geology are given by Martin Rudwick, 'The Strategy of Lyell's Principles of Geology', *Isis* 61 (1970), 4–33; Roy Porter, 'Charles Lyell and the Principles of the History of Geology', *British Journal for the History of Science* 9 (1976), 91–103; Paul J. McCartney, 'Charles Lyell and G. B. Brocchi: A Study in Comparative Historiography', *British Journal for the History of Science* 9 (1976), 175–189; and Alexander M. Ospovat, 'The Distortion of Werner in Lyell's Principles of Geology', *British Journal for the History of Science* 9 (1976), 190–198.
3. See A. Cox (ed.), *Plate Tectonics and Geomagnetic Reversals*, San Francisco: Freeman, 1973; A. A. Hallam, *A Revolution in the Earth Sciences: From Continental Drift to Plate Tectonics*, Oxford: Clarendon, 1973; U. B. Marvin, *Continental Drift: The Evolution of a Concept*, Washington, D.C.: Smithsonian Institution Press, 1973; H. Takeuchi, S. Uyeda, and H. Kanamori, *Debate about the Earth:*

Approach to Geophysics through Analysis of Continental Drift, San Francisco: Freeman, 1967; and J. Tuzo Wilson, 'Static or Mobile Earth – the Current Scientific Revolution', *American Philosophical Society Proceedings* 112 (1968), 309–320; 'A Revolution in Earth Science', *Geotimes* 13 (1968), 10–16; *Continental Drift*, San Francisco: Freeman, 1970; *Continents Adrift and Continents Aground*, San Francisco: Freeman, 1976.

4. Such an approach to history is often denigrated as 'Whig historiography', a term originally coined by Herbert Butterfield, *The Whig Interpretation of History*, London, 1931, reprinted Harmondsworth, 1973. For a convincing defense of the approach, see David Hull, 'In Defense of Presentism', *History and Theory* 18 (1979), 1–15.

5. For a theoretical, rather than historical account of these shifts see Rachel Laudan, 'Tensions in the Concept of Geology: Natural History or Natural Philosophy?' (Forthcoming).

6. Kathleen Collier, *Cosmogonies of Our Fathers: Some Theories of the Seventeenth and Eighteenth Centuries*, New York: Columbia University Press, 1934 and David Kubrin, *Providence and the Mechanical Philosophy: The Creation and Dissolution of the World in Newtonian Thought*, Cornell University Ph.D dissertation, 1968.

7. The classic account of the interpenetration of geology and religion in the early nineteenth century is in C. C. Gillispie, *Genesis and Geology*, Cambridge, Mass: Harvard University Press, 1951, although Gillispie does not consider Lyell's deism. See also M. J. S. Rudwick, 'Charles Lyell, F. R. S. (1797–1875) and his London Lectures on Geology (1832–3)', *Notes and Records of the Royal Society of London* 29 (1975), 231–62.

8. This point is insufficiently recognized by Porter who frequently refers to Lyell as a Christian, *op. cit.*, note 2.

9. Willim Buckland's inaugural lecture *Vindicae Geologicae*, Oxford, 1821, is a striking example of this mode of geological theorising.

10. An excellent account of this movement is given in Roy Porter, *The Making of Geology*, Cambridge: Cambridge University Press, 1979.

11. See M. J. S. Rudwick, 'The Foundation of the Geological Society of London: Its Scheme for Co-operative Research and Its Struggle for Independence', *British Journal for the History of Science* 1 (1963), 325–355, and R. Laudan, 'Ideas and Organizations: The Case of the Geological Society of London', *Isis* 68 (1977), 527–538.

12. W. H. Fitton in his review of 'Transactions of the Geological Society, Vol. III', *Edinburgh Review* 29 (1817), 70.

13. C. Lyell, 'Review of *Memoir on the Geology of Central France* . . . by G. P. Scrope F. R. S., London, 1827', *Quarterly Review* 36 (1827), 440–1.

14. *Principles*, Vol. 1, frontespiece.

15. Apart from the authors just mentioned, the following works discuss the history of plate tectonics: Henry Frankel, 'The Development, Reception and Acceptance of the Vine-Matthews-Morley Hypothesis', forthcoming *Historical Studies in the Physical Sciences*; Rachel Laudan, 'The Method of Multiple Working Hypotheses and the Discovery of Plate Tectonic Theory in Geology', in Thomas Nickles (ed.), *Scientific Discovery: Case Studies*, Dordrecht: Reidel, 1980, 331–343; and 'The Recent Revolution in Geology and Kuhn's Theory of Scientific Change', in Gary Gutting (ed.), *Paradigms and Revolutions, An Interdisciplinary Approach to Kuhn,*

South Bend: Notre Dame University Press, 1980, 284–296; D. P. McKenzie, 'Plate Tectonics and Its Relationship to the Evolution of Ideas in the Geological Sciences', *Daedalus* **106** (1977), 97–124; and S. Uyeda, *The New View of the Earth: Moving Continents and Moving Oceans*, San Francisco: Freeman, 1978. I am very conscious of the problems of trying to give an account of the history of geology independent of the interpretations of the scholars I am studying in this paper.

16. For these references, see note 3.
17. *Principles*, Vol. 1, 4.
18. *Principles*, Vol. 1, 4.
19. *Principles*, Vol. 1, 4.
20. *Principles*, Vol. 1, 2.
21. *Principles*, Vol. 1, 8.
22. *Principles*, Vol. 1, 8.
23. *Principles*, Vol. 1, 9.
24. McCartney, *op. cit.*, note 2.
25. *Principles*, Vol. 1, 23–24.
26. *Principles*, Vol. 1, 24.
27. *Principles*, Vol. 1, 39.
28. *Principles*, Vol. 1, 54.
29. *Principles*, Vol. 1, 58.
30. James Hutton, 'Theory of the Earth, or an Investigation of the Laws Observable in the Composition, Dissolution, and Restoration of Land upon the Globe', *Transactions of the Royal Society of Edinburgh* **1** (1788) and *Theory of the Earth, with Proofs and Illustrations*, Edinburgh, 1795.
31. *Principles*, Vol. 1, 61.
32. *Principles*, Vol. 1, 61.
33. *Principles*, Vol. 1, 63.
34. *Principles*, Vol. 1, 65.
35. *Principles*, Vol. 1, 65.
36. *Principles*, Vol. 1, 65.
37. *Principles*, Vol. 1, 71.
38. *Principles*, Vol. 1, 71.
39. J. Tuzo Wilson, 'The Development and Structure of the Crust', in Gerard P. Kuiper (ed.), *The Earth as a Planet*, Chicago: University of Chicago Press, 1954, 138.
40. *Ibid.*, 139.
41. *Ibid.*
42. *Ibid.*
43. *Ibid.*, 138.
44. Wilson, *American Philosophical Society Proceedings*, 1968a, *op. cit.*, note 3.
45. Wilson, *Geotimes*, 1968, *op. cit.*, note 3.
46. See R. Laudan, 'The Role of Methodology in Lyell's Geology', *Studies in History and Philosophy of Science* (1982), forthcoming, and M. Ruse, 'Charles Lyell and the Philosophers of Science', *British Journal for the History of Science* **9** (1976), 121–131; *The Darwinian Revolution: Science Red in Tooth and Claw*, Chicago: Chicago University Press, 1979, 59–63.
46. Wilson, *Geotimes* (1968), *op. cit.*, note 3, 12.

47. Marvin, *op. cit.*, note 3, 189.
48. Cox, *op. cit.*, note 3, 5.
49. Hallam, *op. cit.*, note 3, 108.
50. Presumably the reason for this was that Kuhn's work had not gained the currency in Japan that it enjoyed in English speaking countries. For a criticism of the Kuhnian analysis, see David Kitts, 'Continental Drift and Scientific Revolution', *American Association of Petroleum Geologists Bulletin* 58 (1974), 2490–2496, reprinted in D. B. Kitts, *The Structure of Geology*, Dallas: Southern Methodist University Press, 1977.
51. Wilson (1970), *op. cit.*, note 3, unpaginated preface.
52. *Ibid.*
53. *Ibid.*
54. J. Tuzo Wilson, 'Overdue: Another Scientific Revolution', *Nature* 265 (1977), 196.
55. *Ibid.*, 196.
56. Wilson, *Geotimes* (1968), *op. cit.*, note 3, 12.
57. Wilson (1976), *op. cit.*, note 3, unpaginated preface.
58. Wilson, *Geotimes* (1968), *op. cit.*, footnote 3, 12.
59. *Ibid.*
60. Thomas Kuhn, *The Structure of Scientific Revolutions*, 2nd ed., Chicago: University of Chicago Press, 1970, 10.
61. Wilson's 1968 articles in *Geotimes* is largely devoted to this issue.

THE ROLE OF MEDICAL HISTORY IN THE HISTORY
OF MEDICINE IN GERMANY

ROLF WINAU

Freie Universität Berlin

"Under the mild sun of gentle recommendations advanced by the Wissen-schaftsrat" (1), during the early 1960s medical history as a subject was established in the universities of the Federal Republic of Germany, and institutes for the history of medicine were founded. This move reflected a newly awakened interest in an old discipline.

Until then medical history had served many widely different ends within medical science as a whole; it had experienced both high and low moments, including early flowering periods and other times of uncompromising rejection. If we try to divide the history of medical history as a subject into periods according to the role it was allotted within medical science, four phases of different length and different importance may be distinguished. During the first, which extended from antiquity well into the nineteenth century, medical history was looked upon as a means of providing reasons and justifications. The scientific character of contemporary medicine was assured by the appeal to ancient and medieval authorities.

During the second phase, i.e. when medical science, around the middle of the nineteenth century, became firmly based on the sciences, medical history was, from outside, allotted a role which it neither could vindicate for itself nor assume successfully. That assigned role was to provide a counterbalance to materialism in medicine.

The third phase was marked by an antiquarian interest of physicians in their own past. It began at the end of the last century and, in some places, has continued to the present day. The fourth phase set in in the 1920s, and its features are becoming increasingly prominent in the picture of today's medical history. This present phase is characterized by the attempt to regard medical history as an important constituent of general history and to emphasize its links with social and cultural history.

Loren Graham, Wolf Lepenies, and Peter Weingart (eds.), Functions and Uses of Disciplinary Histories, Volume VII, 1983, 105–117.
Copyright © 1983 *by D. Reidel Publishing Company.*

1. As the Old Masters Rightly Said

The distinctive feature of the first phase of medical history is the fact that at first no line is drawn between contemporary medicine and medical science in the past. In Greek and Roman medicine, this past is so much part of the present that it enters, as a matter of course, into the discussion of contemporary medical problems. Authors like Celsus or Pliny for instance feel no need to dwell on the historical development of medicine. The teachings of physicians (and philosophers, who often dealt with problems of physiology) who had died centuries ago were so widely known and accepted that they were discussed "the same way in which we nowadays discuss the work of contemporary authors or those belonging to the immediate past in the introductory chapter to a medical study" (2).

Yet even in antiquity there is a noticeable tendency to call authorities of the past as witnesses for one's own beliefs. The beginnings of this practice can be discerned in the Hippocratic treatise 'On Ancient Medicine'. There the hypotheses growing out of a newfangled medical science are contrasted with the straight path of ancient healing, on which future doctors are to advance. In this treatise (written presumably around 380 B.C.) justification is, for the first time, derived from an appeal to past medical practice (3). The case of Hippocrates himself offers an example. Hippocrates was, in the eyes of his contemporaries, a famous and outstanding physician, but apart from him there were others, equally outstanding. To the physicians and medical writers of the Rome of the first and second centuries A.D. he had become the Father of Medicine, whose words could be quoted as authoritative when one wished to prove one's own opinion. References to Hippocrates crop up again and again in the treatises of Galen, where the medical knowledge of antiquity has been brought into systematical order. Galen's achievement was impressive, his writings – preserved only in part – fill 22 tomes in the latest edition (which, incidentally, is bilingual: the original Greek accompanied by its Latin translation!).

Galen's teachings became the guideline of medical practice, not only during late antiquity, but also wherever medicine was practiced in the Byzantine empire, in Islamic countries, and in Western Europe during the Middle Ages. These teachings were abridged and simplified, they fossilized into rigid dogma, and thus the authority of the past became the one and only justification of medical practice. I need not stress how severely progress was hampered by this attitude.

The discovery of pulmonary circulation by Ibn-an-Nafīs provides a very instructive example. If, as in this case, a discovery was made that contradicted Galenic dogma, the physician had to try to remove the contradiction by sleight of hand. In his commentary of the *Anatomy* of Avicenna, who sought to combine the teachings of Galen and the theories of Aristotle, Ibn-an-Nafīs incidentally discusses the role of the heart. In his account he largely adheres to Galenic dogma and the role it assigned to the blood; however, he assumes that the necessary mixing of animal blood and pneuma does not take place in the left ventricle but in the lungs, to which, he claims, the blood is conveyed by a vascular system. And although this hypothesis glaringly contradicts approved tenets, Ibn-an-Nafīs recoils from contradicting Galen openly. "Our discussion, then", he says, "has been rooted almost entirely in the teachings of the divine Galen, apart from a few minor points where, in our opinion, the Galenic text has been disturbed by copyists' mistakes" (4).

Similarly, when at occasional dissections during the late Middle Ages discrepancies were observed between the teachings of Galen and what clearly lay before everybody's eyes, people would rather put these discrepancies down to a change in the anatomy of the human body during the last millenium than to a mistake of the great Galen.

Medieval medicine is characterized by its appeal to past authorities as well as the precedence of history over observable fact. Even when Andreas Vesalius, around the middle of the sixteenth century, exposed Galen's anatomy as based on the dissection of animal, not human cadavers — in contrast with his own studies founded on human corpses —, he was not able to detract from the influence of Galen and Avicenna. Moreover, Vesalius himself was so much caught up in those ancient doctrines that he rated them higher than his own observations. According to Galen, a very small amount of blood had to pass from the left to the right ventricle. Vesalius states in his description of the heart: "The surface (of the septum) is covered by a kind of small pits which reach deep down into the carneous substance. Each of these pits leads from the right to the left ventricle. However, they are scarcely visible, and we are forced to admire the art of the creator by which the blood, through invisible pores, flows from the right to the left ventricle" (5).

These quotations highlight the huge influence of ancient authorities, of medicine's history on the medicine of the day. Accordingly, no gulf separated historical medicine from contemporary medicine. Historical medicine continued to serve as the guiding principle and yardstick of all medical activity, although young anatomists held this kind of medicine up to ridicule: "Those people (i.e. the anatomists) are satisfied if something has been said by Galen, just as if they were disciples of Pythagoras. Some even nowadays (i.e. in 1559) swear by the anatomical doctrine of Galen and dare to claim that Galen had to be interpreted like the evangelist" (6).

While anatomy soon went its own ways and put the observation of nature into the place of old authorities, the position of ancient authorities did not change as far as clinical medicine was concerned. The appeal to Hippocrates and Galen remained, far into the eighteenth century, part of the stock-in-trade of the medical scientist.

Likewise, this attitude was a major influence on writers of textbooks of medical history, which started appearing in the early decades of the eighteenth century. John Freind wrote his *History of Physic* to demonstrate to his colleagues that much useful information for medical practice could be culled from history (7). A constant comparison of past and present can be made profitable for the progress of medical science. To this end, recent research and the knowledge enshrined in the writings of the old authorities are equally important. Tradition no longer is the absolute guideline of medical practice. Nevertheless, tradition continues to be looked upon as a yardstick against which modern medicine is measured.

Those were the years when medical history became a university subject, sometimes an independent one, sometimes one that was at least mentioned as part of a chairholder's duties. Around the middle of the nineteenth century more and more disciplines split off from the old range of courses taught by the professors of the Theory and Practice of Medicine, e.g., Surgery and Internal Medicine, Botany and Public Hygiene. Among the courses falling within the duties of the Chair for the Theory of Medicine, we often find, beside hygiene and pharmacology, Medical Encyclopedy, Methodology and History. Medical History had lost its place in contemporary medical practice and become a study of the past without any reference to the present.

2. A Counterbalance to Materialism

In 1834, the Chair for Medical History and Medical Encyclopedy and Methodology at the recently founded Berlin university was filled. Justus Friedrich Hecker became the first to hold the chair, after he had been professor extraordinary since 1822. This Berlin chair had been organized according to the pattern of traditional chairs for the Theory of Medicine. But time had passed over this traditional combination of disciplines. In a period when the sciences began to enter into the medical curriculum and soon developed into its growth sector, medical history met with no interest. Thus Hecker, in the second half of the 1840s, had scarcely any students. The number of students registered for his courses varied between 2 and 42 (8). And those who did attend his lectures were, without exception, alumni of the Pepinière, a training institution for military physicians, whose attendance was checked. When Hecker died in 1850, the faculty refused to fill the chair again. This corresponded with the wishes of the students who, in 1848, had successfully demanded that their examination in medical history be abolished.

In a report regarding the attitude of the medical faculty submitted by Johann Lukas Schönlein in his function as consultant of the Ministry of Religious, Educational and Medical Affairs, we read: "The faculty declares that even Hecker had a small audience for his historical lectures and concludes that the chair should remain vacant since the students have no penchant for historical lectures. I, however, can only see this as convincing proof of the bad mettle and lack of academic spirit among the great majority of medical students in this university. The duty of the authorities should be to combat these tendencies and not to support them" (9). But the faculty remained firm; the vacancy was filled, provisionally, by Christian Gottfried Ehrenberg. Ehrenberg was a recognized natural historian but had neither ability nor wish to fill the position of a medical historian. "Since Hecker's death, the Chair for the History of Medicine in this university has stood empty. Nevertheless, the discipline occurred in the university calendar in a way which can almost be called ironical: it was the duty every term of an otherwise outstanding scholar, whose clearly defined field of research had no link at all and nothing in common with medical history, to make an announcement which, in its very form, could be considered an oddity and which had no consequences –

a fact which probably met with the greatest gratification from the professor concerned, who had to fulfill this unpleasant duty" (10).

The background to this commentary was that Ehrenberg, through 35 semesters, regularly announced a lecture on 'The History of Medicine', but it was scheduled to take place from 1—2 o'clock p.m., and indeed he never had to give this lecture.

Medical history continued as a university subject, in Berlin and elsewhere, if in name only. Faculty and students were agreed that this discipline did not fit with modern medicine. Thus until the beginning of this century the chair for the history of medicine was used, wrongly, to accommodate well-deserving scholars from other medical disciplines, or to get rid of unpopular professors. When, in 1902, Schweninger, the personal physician of Bismarck, without much ado was relieved of his position as head of the dermatology department of the Charité and transferred to the Chair for the History of Medicine and General Pathology and Therapy, a comment in Volume 1 of *Mitteilungen zur Geschichte der Medizin und Naturwissenschaften* read: "If the minister's intention is removing both Schweninger and the History of Medicine out of harm's way, this assignment must be deeply regretted" (11).

However, around the middle of the nineteenth century the Ministry had quite different ideas about the chair for the history of medicine. Although Schönlein, in his report, had complained about the lack of academic spirit among the students, he had supplied an argument to the Ministry which was unearthed again in 1863. Schönlein had warned about a return to the situation of 1848, "when the sovereign people of the auditorium, led by its tribune Virchow, had dared to decide about chairs and professors" (12).

In the eyes of the young physicians of the 1848 revolution, there was an inseparable link between their profession, medicine rooted in the sciences, and their political ideas. In the eyes of the Ministry, this modern medicine was nothing but straight materialism. Virchow in his obituary for August Hirsch, who had been made professor for the History of Medicine against the declared wishes of the faculty, stressed that this candidate had been chosen with the sole and express purpose of providing a counterbalance to the materialism of the faculty (13). Virchow called the choice of Hirsch for this purpose a "strange misunderstanding", since Hirsch had received his education in the same institutions as the materialists; Hirsch, according to

Virchow, neither was able nor willing to teach the students 'speculative philosophy' and 'orthodoxy'.

Virchow may have presented a one-sided view of the events of 1863 thirty years later, but surely his information cannot be completely wrong. Hirsch had disappointed the officials in the Ministry, he was part of the new movement. Nevertheless, this did not remain the only attempt by the state to take in medical history for its own purposes. In the Third Reich medical history was put under state pressure to spread 'orthodox views', just as in socialist countries.

3. Antiquarian Interest in the Past

During the period in which the sciences reigned unchallenged in the medical faculty, the interest of professors and students in medical history was extremely low. When, in 1863, Ehrenberg's opinion about the Ministry candidates for the chair was asked, he knew about the case of a Berlin Privat Docent for this subject. This man had, in 1861, ceased his work owing to a total lack of student interest, had become melancholic and changed to divinity (14). At the beginning of this century, Richard Koch was the only student present at Julius Pagel's lecture in Berlin. Looking back to those years he concluded, in 1928: "The students' attitude towards instruction in medical history is so reserved that it is no exaggeration to state that they reject it . . . On the whole the audience of medical historians is formed by individual specifically interested students. The mainstream of students passes by lectures on the history of medicine" (15).

In spite of this assessment Koch was not discouraged from founding an Institute for the History of Medicine in Frankfurt. The words I quoted are taken from his inaugural speech.

In the meantime, medical history had matured into an independent subject, although one without wider impact. Medical history was represented by amateurs whose main area of work was in some other medical discipline. The historical-critical method had become their tool for elucidating the history of the medical profession with the necessary amount of background knowledge. These enthusiasts eventually resuscitated the interest of physicians in the history of healing. In 1889, at the annual conference of German Scientists and Physicians, Theodor Puschmann demanded that the history of

medicine and the sciences be given proper attention; five years later, during
the society's meeting at Vienna, he succeeded in establishing a section for
medical geography, statistics and history. In 1896 medical history was represented again at the society's annual congress. The breakthrough came two
years later, at Düsseldorf, when Karl Sudhoff managed to establish a section
for 'The History of Medicine and the Sciences; Historical and Geographical
Nosology'. The special commemorative volume of articles on medical history
issued on this occasion and an exhibition on medical history stirred up wide
interest.

In 1901, a long time before the universities took up this newly awakened
interest, the Deutsche Gesellschaft für Geschichte der Medizin und der
Naturwissenschaften (German Society for the History of Medicine and
Sciences) was founded (16). The purpose of the society was defined as
follows: promotion of all endeavours relating to research into the history of
medicine and the sciences, spreading the idea of the importance of a thorough
study of the history of a particular discipline, and publication of research in
the history of science.

Medical history meant, during these first years of consolidation, mainly
history of medical science. The recently acquired tools of historical research
were to be used to study and portray the past. Making new sources available,
protecting and publishing known sources, communicating facts hitherto
unknown were the main themes of papers read at the annual conferences
of the German Society for the History of Medicine and Sciences, and of
publications. When, in 1907, Sudhoff founded the *Archiv für Geschichte der
Medizin*, he summed up programmatically these intentions (17). Until then,
medical history as a discipline had relied on chance. Importance had been
attached to whatever the enthusiastic student had turned up. The Archiv was
to publish "shorter medical texts, legal documents (including those relating
to the history of medical instruction and the medical profession), letters and
other biographic documents, furthermore, critical studies and source studies
of medical writings of certain periods, doctrines and personages, of therapeutic and hygienic measures inside and outside the medical profession, of
institutions for instruction and therapy, of nursing in the widest sense" (18).

This is a full summary of what the history of a discipline, qua history of
that discipline, comprises. Written by physicians for physicians their interest
in the history of their profession was to be awakened. Sudhoff was a country

doctor from Hochdahl near Düsseldorf. His accession to the Chair for the History of Medicine in Leipzig in 1905 did not change his attitudes. He was self-taught, an assiduous collector, but had received no formal training as a historian (19). Important as his studies were, they lacked connection with general and cultural history. Nevertheless, the approach to medical history shaped and exemplified by him remained through decades for many medical historians the only possible approach and this is, in part, still true today. The reason must be sought in the biographies of these medical historians. They were, in the first place, physicians with practices to run who became medical historians in their spare time.

Frequently the choice of the themes for their studies was determined by the area in which they had received specialist training. Thus, they proved excellent experts in the history of their particular medical field; the aim of their studies was to prove the accomplishments of their own speciality, to highlight its importance. Their work provided a wealth of data and facts for medical history which otherwise would have gone unknown and neglected until today. This kind of research is as necessary in our day as it was in the time of Sudhoff, but the medical historian cannot be allowed to stop at just supplying facts and figures. In that case he would be open to the kind of reproach voiced by the students active in the student movement of the late 1960s: "Medical history is an integral part of medical studies; however, its raison d'être should not be getting carried away, as some university teachers do, by turning the pages of the family album of our profession, but studying medical history as one — verifiable — area of social conflict" (20). This is at least as one-sided as concentrating on the family album of the profession since medical history is infinitely more than a mirror of social conflicts. But the critical voices make themselves heard. The criticism is justified.

Dirk Blasius, in 1976, gave the following evaluation of the position of medical history from the point of view of a social historian: "Medical history today is mainly characterized by its duties within medical training. It is pursued almost exclusively by physicians on the basis of their unreflected conception of medicine. Thus, this branch of learning often serves as an ideological prop for medicine, to neutralize criticism from outside the medical profession. History and geography are followed through the course of time and in this process data about various therapeutical methods are collected with stupendous acrimony" (21). Leaving aside the meaningless phrase about the ideological propup and the problem which sort of ideology Blasius may be referring to, and leaving further aside the naive belief that medical history could play a role in dealing with the criticism levelled at contemporary medical practice, Blasius' further statements should give the medical historian some food for thought.

4. Medical History as Social and Cultural History

The accumulation of a host of results from research into the history of medicine is a challenge for the medical historian to continue building on this foundation. After all, medical history is more than an acrimonious register of series of generations of physicians, more than an accurate and comprehensive bibliography of their works, more than collecting the data about the first successful surgical operation or the introduction of a particular surgical instrument. As early as 50 years ago, Paul Diepgen and Henry E. Sigerist, two major medical historians, pointed out that medical history is at the same time social and cultural history, that medical facts always have to be seen in context with the facts of political, cultural, economic history, of the history of religion and of art.

The duty of the physician may have remained unchanged, i.e. to cure and to prevent disease, but the foundations and means have changed just as much as ideas about the essence of illness.

The responsibilities of medical history in the training of future physicians are clearly defined, but in a way different from how Blasius represents it. In the rules for state registration, the themes of the course in medical history are defined as follows: "Cultural and social foundations in the history of medical thought, knowledge and practice; change of the concepts of disease and health." The subject catalogue of the federal examination authority, which was drawn up with the consent of the professors of medical history, specifies areas like 'Attitudes of society towards being sick', 'The development of medicine as a profession', 'Models of medical practice'. A long chapter is devoted to the problems of 'Disease and society'. 'Epidemic diseases', and 'The influence of industrialization on the causes of sickness and death' are parts of this chapter. These themes, however, can only be discussed profitably if put into relation with the history of medical thought, knowledge and practice. Therefore the problems of medical thinking (e.g. its dependence on experience, philosophy, tradition, or the sciences) the problem of what should be taught and how, the question of guidelines for medical practice, medical ethics and deontology are of equal importance (22).

These tasks surpass by far the postulates of Blasius. They may be seen, as Werner Conze put it, as social history in a wider sense, within which the social history of disease in a narrower sense is only one ingredient.

This takes up a lead which goes back to the time of Sigerist and Diepgen. What they began must now be continued. Medical history only makes sense if we see it in the context of general history, it must be taken as a constituent part of cultural history defined in such a way that it does not run on separate tracks parallel to social or economic history but overlaps. Or, to quote the words of Walter Artelt: "Certainly, the history of states and their rulers, of constitutions, of economies and wars must be the supporting structure of a building of history, and, at the same time, its façade. But the history of sickness and health, of medical professions, the education and professional training of physicians, of prevention and cure, of the conceptions of life and disease, of epidemics and the fight against them, these do not form the back of this building but are part — judged from the point of view of the concerned, of man himself, no minor part — of its core" (23).

Consequently, medical history can only have its roots in meticulous historical research into the sources and an equally meticulous representation of the results. But medical history must be placed in the greater context of political, economic, social and cultural history as well as the history of ideas, to prevent it from degenerating into "turning the pages of the family album of the medical profession" and in order for it to become a medical and historical branch of learning on an equal footing with the others.

Medical history defined in this way could, above all, serve three purposes in its position in present-day academic life and within medical science: to provide insights, criticism, and a common denominator (24).

In addition to passing on facts, medical history can have the function of instructing medical thinking. A physician who wants to recognize and cure a disease has to think in coherent patterns of events. He must be able to recognize and structure conditions and consequences if he sees more in the human body than just a piece of clockwork whose parts have become faulty and can be repaired. The study of history can further this kind of thinking.

Historical awareness can lead to a critical reflection of one's own position.

If the framework and determinants of historical processes are understood correctly and historical attitudes are recognized as predetermined, this leads to perceiving the determining factors of one's own situation, which is more easily made out in its historical, cultural and social context. This is true of the physician's position, but also of the position of the patient and the position of both toward therapies and medical theories. Medical history can also help one to make a decision. The knowledge of historical patterns can influence one's own thinking, but not in such a way that history could offer, in an exemplary way, preformated decisions ready to be taken over. Learning from history does not mean copying historical events but analysing historical events and using such an analysis in one's own thinking.

There are several ways in which medical history plays an integrating role. At a time when medical science is splitting up more and more into specialities and subdivisions within these specialities, it is one of the few branches of medicine where the whole of medicine receives attention. Medical history can help one to understand the development of specialities, taking them back to the underlying common concept. Specialization in modern medicine has led to a retrenchment of the image of man and the concept of the body. Medical history can contribute to bringing back to physicians' minds the full picture of man in medicine. On the one hand, the medical historian can bring the results of social and cultural history to medical science and make them profitable for medical practice, e.g. for epidemiology. Collaboration with social, economic and cultural historians may further lead to an integration of all branches of historical research.

All these functions can only be taken up properly if history is recognized in its peculiarity and individuality. Where history is seen as a linear development leading straight to the present situation and is to serve only as an illumination of the present status, where history serves only as a vehicle for personal opinion in a historical garb, where history is used to adduce isolated facts to support one's own theories, there neither history nor medical history can play its role.

Acknowledgement

I gratefully acknowledge the assistance given by my colleague, Dr. K.-D. Fischer, in the preparation of the English version of this paper.

Notes

1. H. Schipperges, 'Ein Institut für Geschichte der Medizin an der Universität Heidelberg', *Ärztebl. Baden-Württemberg* **17** (1962), 249–251, p. 249.
2. E. Heischkel, 'Die Geschichte der Medizingeschichtschreibung', in W. Artelt, *Einführung in die Medizinhistorik*, Stuttgart 1949, pp. 202–237, p. 204.
3. Cf. Ch. Lichtenthaeler, *Chronologische und gedankliche Bezugssysteme in und um 'über die alte Medizin'*, Genf 1980.
4. G. Keil, A. M. Mokhtar, and H. J. Thies, 'Galenkritik bei Rhazes', *Med. Monatsschr.* **25** (1971), 559–563.
5. A. Vesal, *De humani corporis fabrica libri septem*, Basel 1543, p. 589.
6. R. Colombo, *De re anatomica*, Venedig 1559, p. 325.
7. J. Freind, *History of Physic from the Time of Galen to the Beginning of the 16th Century*, London 1725/26.
8. J. Klemperer, 'Der medizinhistorische Unterricht an der Berliner Universität von 1810 bis 1900', Diss. med. Göttingen 1965, p. 46.
9. *Ibid.*, p. 52.
10. L. Posner, 'Die Professur für Geschichte der Medizin an der Berliner Universität', *Allg. Med. Central-Ztg.* **32** (1863), Col. 220–223.
11. *Mitt. Gesch. Med. Naturwiss.* **1** (1902), 269f.
12. Klemperer, *op. cit.*, p. 52.
13. R. Virchow, 'August Hirsch', *Berliner klin. Wschr.* **31** (1894), 129f.
14. H. H. Eulner: 'Der Medizinhistoriker', *Medizinhist. J.* **3** (1968), 1–17, p. 7.
15. R. Koch, 'Die Geschichte der Medizin im Unterricht', *Arch. Gesch. Med.* **20** (1928), 1–6, p. 4.
16. Cf. R. Winau, *Deutsche Gesellschaft für Geschichte der Medizin, Naturwissenschaft und Technik 1901–1976*, Wiesbaden 1978 (= Beitr. Gesch. Wissensch. Tech. 15).
17. K. Sudhoff, 'Richtungen und Strebungen in der medizinischen Historik', *Arch. Gesch. Med.* **1** (1908), 1–11.
18. Sudhoff, *op. cit.*, p. 8.
19. Cf. G. Keil, 'Sudhoffs Sicht vom medizinischen Mittelalter', *Nachrichtenbl. Deutsch. Ges. Gesch. Med. Naturw. Techn.* **31** (1981), 94–129.
20. Kritische Universität, Provisorisches Verzeichnis der Studienveranstaltungen im Wintersemester 1967/68.
21. D. Blasius, 'Geschichte und Krankheit', *Geschichte und Gesellschaft* **2** (1976), 386–415, p. 390.
22. Cf. 'Gegenstandskatalog für den Ersten Abschnitt der Ärztlichen Prüfung', hrsg. v. IMMP, 2. Aufl. Mainz 1978, p. 105–108.
23. 'Antrittsrede des Hrn. Artelt', *Jb. Akad. Wissensch. Lit. Mainz*, Wiesbaden 1959, p. 88.
24. The following remarks are based on suggestions first voiced by R. Toellner during a Symposion in Berlin, 1973.

PART II

THE SOCIAL SCIENCES

ON MERTON'S "HISTORY" AND "SYSTEMATICS" OF
SOCIOLOGICAL THEORY*

ROBERT ALUN JONES

*Associate Professor of Sociology and Religious Studies, University of Illinois, Urbana,
Illinois 610801, U.S.A.*

Asked to assess the current state of the historiography of sociology, the pro-
historicist, anti-Whiggish historian of social science is (perhaps inevitably, and
surely ironically) tempted to indulge himself in precisely that sort of account
of linear progress from past sins to present salvation against which his historicist principles would otherwise inveigh. Where scholarly scruples intervene,
however, the redemptive struggle rather appears as frought with constant
backsliding, and milennarian optimism would be totally irresponsible.

Unfortunately, it was in a mood of such gloomy scrupulosity that I
approached the four questions put to the anthors of this volume (1). *Has
the historiography of sociology*, for example, *had any impact upon sociology
itself*? Sociology, like all emergent scientific disciplines, has generated a
largely mythological past which performs the important functions of legitimating present practice and reinforcing the solidarity of its practitioners (2).
But in the more specific sense of whether the post-Kuhnian historiography
of social science has altered the beliefs or practices of sociologists, the answer
is rather clearly that it has not. Inversely, *has the historiography of sociology
been influenced by the views of sociologists on the history of their discipline*?
As historians of sociology, we quite naturally – and, I think, quite rightly (3)
– focus on those figures who are, for whatever reason, of interest to current
sociological practitioners. But again, in the more specific sense of the influence
of sociological practice upon the *manner* in which these historical accounts
are rendered, I would have to say that this influence has been substantial,
but largely negative.

Again, *are there tendencies in sociology to promote "paradigmatic shifts"
through historical argument and insight*? In effect, this asks whether there

121

*Loren Graham, Wolf Lepenies, and Peter Weingart (eds.), Functions and Uses of Dis-
ciplinary Histories, Volume VII, 1983, 121–142.*

might soon appear a work comparable to Talcott Parsons' *Structure of
Social Action* (1937) — a study of four figures in the history of the social
sciences which had (arguably) paradigmatic consequences. Efforts toward
such a theoretical synthesis are of course constantly forthcoming, most
notably in Jeffrey Alexander's recent, 4-volume *Theoretical Logic in Sociology*. The more specific question we must ask of *these* works, however,
is whether they are genuinely "historical" — i.e., in the sense encouraged by
Kuhn. For surely Parsons' work was most theoretically influential precisely
where his intentions were least historical, and least influential precisely where
he adhered recognizably to the principles of sound historiography. Finally,
*how has this general problem changed since Kuhn and the development
of the post-Kuhnian sociology of science*? Very briefly, I don't think the
problem has changed at all, for at least two reasons: first, it is not clear to me
that the problems faced by historians of sociology and those involved in the
so-called "social study of science" are identical or even significantly similar;
and *second*, I think that the initial promise of the Kuhnian sociology of
science for historians of sociology was based on a misapprehension.

   In light of the received wisdom concerning Kuhn's impact on the social
sciences, however, these are rather dismal answers, and make for a paper
even shorter than the one the reader might prefer. If I might henceforth
indulge in a sort of apologia, therefore, I will explain *why* the answers to
these questions are so consistently disappointing — specifically, why the
entire project of applying Kuhn and the 'new history of science' to the
history of sociology has been largely misconceived. Mercifully, this is an
historical question, dealing as it must with the manner in which this application was effected.

   If not the earliest, certainly the most eloquent introduction of Kuhn to
the history of the social sciences was an article written in 1965 by George
Stocking: "The whig historian", Stocking's Butterfieldian indictment began,

reduces the mediating processes by which the totality of an historical past produces
the totality of its consequent future to a search for the origins of certain present
phenomena. He seeks out in the past phenomena which seem to resemble those of
concern in the present, and then moves forward in time by tracing lineages up to the
present in simple sequential movement. When this abridging procedure is charged with
a normative commitment to the phenomena whose origins are sought, the linear movement is 'progress' and those who seem to abet it are 'progressive'. The result is whiggish
history. Because it is informed by a normative commitment, its characteristic interpretive

mode is judgment rather than understanding, and history becomes the field for a dramatic struggle between children of light and children of darkness. Because it wrenches the
individual historical phenomenon from the complex network of its contemporary
context in order to see it in abstracted relationship to analogues in the present, it is
prone to anachronistic misinterpretation. Because it assumes in advance the progressive
character of historical change, it is less interested in the complex processes by which
change emerges than in agencies which direct it, whether they be great men, specific
deterministic forces, or the 'logic' of historical development itself. (Stocking, 1965:
3–4)

Such a "whiggish presentism", Stocking continued, is virtually built into the
history of science, and by extension, into the history of the social sciences;
for however disillusioned we may have become with the idea of progress
in other areas, most of us assume that the development of science is, in some
sense, a cumulative ever-upward progress in rationality — a claim which
Stocking was able to support with some stunning quotations from George
Sarton (4) — then the virtual doyen of all historians of science. There seem
to be good experiential grounds, Stocking thus added one year later, "for
arguing that the more a social scientific practitioner is committed to the
'scientism' of his discipline, the less likely he is to see it as an historical
growth conditioned in a variety of subtle ways by an intricate complexity
of contextual influences". To see the "history of theory" in these terms
is difficult for the advocate of the correctness of a given contemporary
theoretical point of view. Yet this, Stocking concluded, "is exactly what
the *historical* approach requires . . . " (Stocking, 1966: 286).

Stocking's explanation has made it easier to understand, though still
impossible to condone, some of the more disgraceful practices in the historiography of sociology. Most people who write the history of sociology, for
example, don't think of themselves as "historians" at all; rather they call
themselves "theorists", teach in departments of sociology rather than history,
and publish in sociology juournals rather than their historical counterparts.
Far from attempting to understand sociological knowledge as an historical
growth, conditioned by complex, contextual influences, these 'theorists'
rather view themselves as providing the *normative* framework within which
the more *empirical* study of society *ought* to take place; and ultimately they
regard themselves as the guardians of a sacred canon of "classic texts" whose
pages yield timeless truths of continuing relevance to their contemporaries.
Within such a perspective, the concerted effort to reconstruct the historical

setting of such texts is viewed, not merely as trivial, but as potentially dangerous; for the argument that such texts can be understood only within the broader social and intellectual context of *their own* time contains, however implicitly, the suggestion that they might lack such timeless truths altogether; and this, in turn, undermines the *traditional* justification for the investigation itself (5). The result is that the so-called "history of sociology theory" has frequently been less a serious scholarly pursuit than, as a clever friend has put it, that activity which fills the years between *genuine* achievement and retirement. (Collini, 1978: 47)

Some of the difficulties of this peculiar "historiography" may be illustrated simply by examining some of the statements which sociological theorists have made concerning a particularly distinguished member of their sacred canon — i.e., Durkheim's *Elementary Forms of the Religious Life* (Durkheim, 1912) (6). The *primary* difficulty here is familiar to anyone who has read Kuhn: i.e., that the theorist, committed to present "truths", and ignoring the (always trivial and occasionally dangerous) context, quickly reduces the task of *reading* the *Elementary Forms* to one of "finding" within it Durkheim's "contribution" to those ideas, themes, or problems currently regarded as constitutive of the discipline. Depending upon which theorist we read, for example, we find that Durkheim has contributed variously, substantially, and contradictorally, to the structural-functionalist, symbolic-interactionist, or neo-Marxist schools of sociological thought. Where Durkheim's own arguments fail to make this clear, scattered and isolated remarks are conjoined to form his "doctrine" on the mandatory theme; where his terminology is "obscure" or "confused", more modern language is substituted to "clarify" his true position; where he still falls short, Durkheim is credited with having "anticipated", or at least "adumbrated" the obligatory statement; and finally, where despite such heroic efforts on his behalf, Durkheim still "fails" to enunciate the compulsory ideas, this failure in turn becomes the occasion for some withering retrospective criticism, as well as condescending explanations of what he would have said if he had said the things which he, so inexplicably, did not say.

The obvious difficulties of such statements should surely have been avoidable after the appearance of the *Structure of Scientific Revolutions* (Kuhn, 1962). For whatever else Kuhn did, his lesson for the historian of social science, as Stocking pointed out almost immediately, was that we should see scientific knowledge as a set of arguments made in response to their own, quite specific questions; that we should understand the 'reasonableness' of points of view now superseded; that we should see historical change as a complex process of emergence rather than a simple linear sequence – in short, that we should understand the science of a given period in its own terms (see Stocking, 1968: 8). The fact that Kuhn rather clearly *did not* have this effect provokes three very brief observations.

First, the "lesson" referred to above could easily have been learned much earlier from a variety of other sources. It is noteworthy, for example, that when Stocking introduced Kuhn to the historiography of social science in 1965 and 1966, he used the classic, historicist terminology of Herbert Butterfield, R. G. Collingwood, and Marc Bloch, of works written more than forty years ago (7) and thoroughly familiar to intellectual historians if not to sociologists. Such familiarity, however, would surely have bred contempt, for in sociology the term "historicism" evokes at least two rather negative connotations – i.e., idealist metaphysics (e.g., Collingwood) and a non-generalizing concern for the particularities of time and place – both of which seem to threaten the *sociological* enterprise itself.

Second, Kuhn himself appeared untainted by such associations – i.e., a former graduate student in theoretical physics, Junior Fellow at Harvard, author of a widely respected book on the Copernican Revolution and, not insignificantly, Fellow of the Center for Advanced Studies in the Behavioral Sciences at Stanford. Not only was there no sociologist foolish enough to pursue Kuhn into the intricacies of the history and philosophy of science – more to the point, his impeccable scientific credentials suggested that there was no need. This impression is reinforced, incidently, when one re-reads the *Structure of Scientific Revolutions* almost 20 years after the fact. The book focuses almost entirely on the internal development of natural science to the neglect, if not exclusion, of the role of technological, socio-economic, and intellectual context, not to mention the influence of specific national traditions, or the late, lamented Weber thesis. Its language, moreover, is determinedly nomothetic, and its historicist implications thus considerably muted. Finally, the book says little about the social sciences and nothing about their history (8).

Third, if Kuhn's own work was thus "imperfectly historicist", neither was sociology, as an academic discipline, institutionally equipped to support the type of research embodied in Stocking's injunctions; and here we see for the first time the sharp distinction which must be made between Kuhn's eager reception in the sociology of science, and his rather limited influence on the historiography of sociology. For Kuhn's work not only brought a new and highly prestigious form of institutional behavior within the grasp of sociological practitioners; more important, it did so in a manner which could be fully accommodated within the already existing structure of dominant sociological concerns – e.g., the study of status hierarchies, communication networks, occupations and organizations, professionalization, and of course, the use of advanced statistical techniques. The historiography of social science encouraged by Stocking, on the other hand, presumed a considerable breadth of knowledge of economic, political, and social as well as intellectual history; a reading knowledge of the relevant foreign languages; and at least some understanding of the principles of the philosophy of social science. This perhaps explains an observation made by Geoff Hawthorn (1976: 5) – i.e., that the one thoroughly Kuhnian account of sociology's past, written by Robert Friedrichs (1970) deals almost exclusively with its American, and thus highly institutionalized and professionalized form. And it also explains why the best work in the history of sociology is being written, not by sociologists, but by historians.

Nonetheless, it remains true that most works in the history of sociology are written by sociologists, about sociologists, and for sociologists; and also that this situation will persist indefinitely (9). Moreover, the tendencies which provoke this prediction were already implicit within that particular agency whereby sociologists were first introduced to the so-called "new history of science", of which Kuhn was but an illustrious representative – specifically, Robert Merton's 1967 article, "On the 'History' and 'Systematics' of Sociological Theory" (10).

I

As early as 1957, Merton had argued that the entirely different functions of the history and systematics of sociological theory were "obvious enough to be embarrassing" – after all, "schools of medicine do not confuse the history of medicine with current medical knowledge, nor do departments of biology identify the history of biology with the viable theory now employed in guiding and interpreting biological research" (Merton, 1957: 4). Yet *sociologists*, Merton complained, produce neither history nor systematics, but rather a "poorly thought-out hybrid" which results in a "parochial, almost Pickwickian conception of the history of sociological theory as a collection of critical summaries of past theories spiced with short biographies of major theorists" (Merton, 1967: 2). And the irony, Merton added, is that sociologists persist in this despite the emergence of that 'new history of science' (here Merton mentions not only Kuhn but Everett Mendelsohn, Charles Gillispie, Derek Price, and others) which, unlike our ludicrous hybrid, is not designed for, or even concerned with, the currently operating theory, methods, or techniques of science itself.

That a distinction between the "history" and "systematics" of sociological theory *exists*, of course, may be heartily endorsed; the difficulties for Merton's account rather arise when one asks for the *criterion* by which the distinction might be maintained. In 1957, Merton had rather tentatively suggested that the "systematics" of theory "represents the highly selective accumulation of those small parts of earlier theory which have thus far survived the tests of empirical research", while "history" would include "the far greater mass of conceptions which fell to bits when confronted with empirical test. It includes also the false starts, the archaic doctrines, and the fruitless errors of the past" (Merton, 1957: 5). And in 1967, he added that a "genuinely historical" account of sociological theory "must extend beyond a chronologically ordered set of critical synopses of doctrine" to "the interplay between theory and such matters as the original origins and statuses of its exponents, the changing social organization of sociology, the changes that diffusion brings to ideas, and their relations to the environing social and cultural structure" (Merton, 1967: 34). The *history* of sociological theory would thus include not only false doctrine but the larger historical context within which such doctrine emerged, while the *systematics* of theory would be restricted to those parts of earlier theory which have received empirical support.

This distinction does have a curious appeal, for a truly historical account of past sociological thought is likely to be more inclusive, and sociologists (e.g. Parsons) have frequently applied the distinction in this way (11). Nonetheless, it is a distinction which no historian would be wise to accept; for surely the inclusiveness of an account of past ideas is an *effect* of its being

historical, not the criterion by which it becomes so. Consider the statements
about the *Elementary Forms* referred to earlier: we would hardly say that
such statements *would cease* being historical once the propositions to which
they referred received empirical warrant; nor would we say that they *became*
historical the moment they were falsified. Moreover, such a distinction would
ignore the fact that a large number of our statements about the *Elementary
Forms*, and some of the most interesting ones, refer not to 'propositions'
at all, but to passages equally meaningful, though less receptive to criteria
of truth and falsity. Historical statements, therefore, are inclusive because
they are historical, not historical because they are inclusive. And what *is*
distinctive about such statements, I would argue, is that they refer to actions
which have been performed or events which have occurred in the *past*; for
it is this reference, and the enormous difficulties of historical confirmation
which arise therefrom, which has required an autonomous academic discipline
(Murphey, 1973: 6; Jones, 1977: 291; Jones, 1981: 460–462).

II

This distinction becomes crucial when we turn to the *second* section of
Merton's paper, which is a lengthy discussion of "continuities" and "discontinuities" in the history of sociological theory. Here Merton refers to the
"occupational hazard" of the historian as one of claiming to find a "continuity" between past ideas where it does *not* exist, or of failing to find it where
it *does*, with the probability of error decidedly greater in the former case as
a consequence of some naive, pre-Kuhnian notions of incremental scientific
progress. For while the problem of identifying *real* continuities is always
great, it is exacerbated where historians ignore the complex interplay between
ideas and social structure, place the alleged link between earlier and later
ideas on center-stage, and confine themselves to distinguishing the extent
of similarity between earlier and later ideas — the range of differences being
embraced by terms like pre-discovery, rediscovery, anticipation and adumbration. What follows from these preliminary observations, however, is
surprisingly uncritical, both as an interpretation of Kuhn and as an application of Kuhn's view to the history of sociological theory; for in Merton's
view, this "occupational hazard" may be avoided simply by specifying those
conditions under which the historian might say, *with greater confidence*,

that a *genuine* prediscovery, rediscovery, anticipation or adumbration has occurred. Thus, where "substantively identical or functionally equivalent ideas" are set forth, by "two or more scientists, each unaware of the other's work", within the span of a few years, we refer to "simultaneous independent discoveries"; where longer periods separate them, the later is a "rediscovery" and the earlier a "prediscovery" (Kuhn, 1967: 9–10); where there is "somewhat less of a resemblence, in which earlier formulations overlap the later ones but do not focus upon or draw out the same set of implications", we have an "anticipation"; and where there is an "even smaller resemblance, in which earlier formulations have, quite literally, merely fore-shadowed later ones", we may speak confidently of an "adumbration" (Kuhn, 1967: 13).

To my historical sensibilities, the application of *this* lanquage to the history of *sociological* theory sounds rather curious. The term "discovery", for example, is particularly infelictous, and thus it's note worthy that this section of Merton's essay draws its most ingenius examples from the history of the *natural* sciences. *Second*, the reduction of the problem of historical continuity to one of determining the "substantive identity" or "functional equivalence" of earlier and later abstractions seems to ignore one of the more prominent arguments of the later Wittgenstein – very briefly, that the *meaning* of any statement to the effect that Marx and Durkheim, for example, held "the same idea" must ultimately depend upon the context within which that statement is uttered, and thus upon the rule to which it refers (12). *Third*, Merton's focus on the question of "continuity" itself seems rather ill-fitted to Kuhn's most famous argument – i.e., that much of the history of science, much of the time, is simply not "continuous" at all. Merton attempts to deflect this criticism with the observation that, according to Kuhn, most scientists, most of the time, are engaged not in "revolutionary" but rather in "normal" science – i.e., the development, by cumulative increments, of that knowledge which is based upon shared paradigms (Merton, 1967: 13). This is a reasonable interpretation, both of Kuhn and of natural scientific practice; but it surely has no relevance whatever to the historiography of sociology where, as Merton himself admits elsewhere (Merton, 1967: 34–35), examples of the cumulative tradition are still rare.

The best way to illustrate the difficulties of Merton's argument, however, is simply to apply it to a specific case. Consider, therefore, the classic

statements on primitative religion provided by three writers whom, with
stunning originality, I have labeled A, B, and C:

Writer A: It seems certain, that according to the natural progress of human thought, the
ignorant multitude must first entertain some groveling and familiar notion of superior
powers, before they stretch their conception to that perfect Being, who bestowed
order on the whole frame of nature. We may as reasonably imagine, that men inhabited
palaces before huts and cottages, or studied geometry before agriculture; as assert that
the Deity appeared to them a pure spirit, omniscient, omnipotent, and omnipresent,
before he was apprehended to be a powerful, though limited being, with human passions
and appetites, limbs and organs. The mind rises gradually, from inferior to superior:
By abstracting from what is imperfect, it forms an idea of perfection: And slowly
distinguishing the noble parts of its own frame from the grosser, it learns to transfer
only the former, much elevated and refined, to its divinity.

Writer B: It is important that we should realize to ourselves with some definiteness the
primitive view of the universe in which this conception [of the gods], arose, and in
which it has its natural place. It dates from a time when men had not learned to draw
sharp distinctions between the nature of one thing and another. Savages, we know,
are not only incapable of separating in thought between phenomenal and noumenal
existence, but habitually ignore the distinctions, which to us seem obvious, between
organic and inorganic nature, or within the former region between animals and plants.
Arguing, altogether by analogy, and concluding from the known to the unknown with
the freedom of men who do not know the difference between the imagination and the
reason, they ascribe to all material objects a life analogous to that which their own self-
consciousness reveals to them.

Writer C: ... the idea of the supernatural, as we understand it, dates only from today; in
fact, it presupposes the contrary idea, of which it is the negation; but this idea is not at
all primitive. In order to say that certain things are supernatural, it is necessary to have
the sentiment that a *natural order of things* exists, that is to say, that the phenomena of
the universe are bound together by necessary relations, called laws. When this principle
has once been admitted, all that is contrary to these laws must necessarily appear to be
outside of nature, and consequently, of reason; for what is natural in this sense of the
word, is also rational, these necessary relations only expressing the manner in which
things are logically related. But this idea of universal determinism is of recent origin;
even the greatest thinkers of classical antiquity never succeeded in becoming fully
conscious of it.

These statements are by no means identical; the first was written sometime
between 1749 and 1751, the second in 1889, and the third in 1912. But there
are obvious similarities. All three, for example, emphasize the irrationality
of primitive religion, its origin in emotion and sentiment rather than reason; and each views the subsequent evolution of religion as one of gradual

enlightenment whereby the nature and significance of numerous religious conceptions are rendered increasingly transparent. In doing so, A, B, and C seem to have more in common with one another, and with the subsequent history of sociology, than with their contemporaries; so that if the statements are not "substantively identical" or even "functionally equivalent", there is at least some "resemblance", "overlap", or, at the very least, "foreshadowing". Told that A and B were countrymen; that B was thoroughly aware of A, and that C was extremely preoccupied (if not obsessed) with both A and B, we would surely be tempted to say that A adumbrated B, that B anticipated C, while C was eventually to discover the sociological explanation for religion. That is not to say that Merton has or even would say such a thing (13); my point is rather that an historian could quite easily produce such an account without violating any of the injunctions contained in Merton's essay.

The difficulties for such an approach, however, arise where we ask what A, B, and C were *doing* in the three statements in question. I suggested, for example, that these were "classic statements on primitive religion"; but in fact, the word 'religion' itself means something different in each of these passages. A, for example, is concerned exclusively with "natural" religion, which has its foundations in human nature; B speaks rather of "positive" religion, as it is revealed to man, by God, through his prophetic emissaries; while C defines religion as an orientation toward sacred objects. The belief in the sacredness of such objects, however, is regarded by the skeptic, A, as a superstitious perversion of "true" religion; while B, a devout Calvinist and vehemently anti-Catholic, denies that the belief in such objects is primitive, and thus, that it plays any essential role in religion whatsoever.

Again, the "gradual enlightenment" referred to by A is the result of experience and the association of ideas, is characterized by a decline of superstition and enthusiasm, and culminates in a limited if rational belief in something analogous to a Designing Mind. B, however, is precisely the sort of religious "enthusiast" derided by A; he thus denies that reason is a sufficient warrant for such a belief, partially as a consequence of the fact that he lives in a world already inhabited and altered by A (not to mention Kant, as B's statement implies); but regardless of this, B regards the belief in a Designer as itself insufficient to the notion of "God", whose personal, moral character must rather be revealed through miraculous intervention. A, of course, has written a famous essay denying, not that miracles occur, but that they can ever provide the basis for religious belief; but this creates no problem for B, for whom the word "miracle" itself no longer means what it meant to A, or even will mean to C (i.e., for both A & C, a breach of natural law), but rather something comparable to what we would call "providence". For B, a frequent visitor to Germany, has adopted fashionably non-propositional notions of progressive revelation ("Heilsgeschichte"), and regards history itself as supernatural or "miraculous".

Again, for A, the pre-scientific irrationality of primitive religion has its foundation in human nature. B, however, refers the same observation to differences of *race*, thus invoking Victorian notions about the sensuous, non-rational mentality of Semitic peoples generally; this explanation does not recommend itself to C, however, who is an agnostic Alsatian Jew. But neither does C argue that religion is based on human nature; rather, human nature, including human reason, is founded on religion, religion itself being a representation of society, a notion which, though referred to B, is not in fact B's notion at all.

Finally, we must question the reliability of the statements themselves. B is the exception here, for he almost always says what he means, and has been tried (quite successfully) for heresy as a consequence. The foremost authority on C, however, warns us that C's style is frequently figurative, distorts his meaning, and conceals its significance. And the case of A is altogether notorious. Not only does he frequently and deliberately say what he does not mean (the passage read earlier, for example, was utterly disingenuous); but as virtually every expert on A now confirms, there are points at which he doesn't even mean what he says when he says what he means (14).

I want to emphasize that what is at stake here is not a mere difference of interpretation. Disagreements over what A, B, and C "meant" will surely persist indefinitely; but the fact that *some* interpretations are manifestly superior to *others* affirms the existence of common standards to which we might and in fact do, appeal. What is involved *here*, on the contrary, are differences over the role of history itself, over the questions we might put to the past, and thus over the answers we might expect in return. The hypothetical adherent of Merton's methodological injunctions is concerned with the existence or non-existence of "continuity" between A, B, and C, a question to be settled by an appeal to the *ostensive similarity* of their utterances. Referring to my earlier point, I see no way to make that question, or the language in which its answers are embodied, yield anything which we might recognize as an account of past social actions; and thus I have rather asked what A, B, and C were *doing* in saying what they said, a question to be settled through an appeal to their *intentions* (see Jones, 1977: 295–7)

III

The context for this appeal can be established through an examination of the *third* section of Merton's essay — a discussion of the peculiar location of sociology "between" the sciences and the humanities, and the implications of this location for its disciplinary history. The fact that the natural sciences have a tradition of selective accumulation of knowledge, according to Merton, means that the contributions of earlier works are, in some sense, incorporated in present knowledge; this results in a division of labor in which the study of Copernicus, Galileo, or Newton may be left to the historian of science, while scientists themselves concentrate on the advancement of current knowledge in their own fields. The humanities, on the other hand, according to Merton, make no such claim to a tradition of cumulative knowledge — philosophers, for example, thus regard the works of Aristotle, Aquinas and Hegel as part of the direct experience of succeeding generations of practitioners, and assume their relevance to ongoing practice. Sociologists, predictably, are caught in between, and are thus subject to cross-pressures in their orientation towards the past. Like *scientists*, they frequently claim to work within a cumulative tradition; but like *philosophers*, they are in fact reluctant to abandon first-hand acquaintance with the classic works of the past; and thus a familiarity with Marx, Durkheim, and Weber is presumed to be a part of their working knowledge.

There are several objections which might be entered here, not least to the observation that "humanists" make no claim to a tradition of cumulative knowledge. The most serious objection, however, arises from a recent, powerful, and sustained attack that has been made upon the very case which Merton takes as paradigmatic of the "humanistic" orientation toward the past — i.e., the thoroughly unhistorical assumption of modern philosophers that Aristotle, Aquinas, and Hegel are in some sense "contemporaries", both of ourselves and one another, participants in a single debate with a relatively unchanging subject-matter. For at least fifteen years, Alasdair MacIntyre, Quentin Skinner, John Dunn and others (15) have repeatedly warned philosophers that the result of this "timeless debate" is a totally artificial abstraction of ideas from their social milieu, which grants thought a wholly false independence from the rest of the culture. We receive, *not* Aristotle, Aquinas, and Hegel, but fragments stripped of their context, and thus of their original meaning and significance. The point, as I shall argue below, is not simply that this is bad history; it also engenders bad *philosophy* and by implication, bad *sociology*, for its result is precisely that conceptual incoherence and linguistic chaos which characterizes modern philosophical and sociological debate.

IV

First, however, I must return to Merton's *fourth* and final discussion, of the functions of "classical" (16) sociological theory for sociology itself. I should emphasize that Merton's concern *here* is exclusively with "systematic" sociological theory, not with the role of the classics within the "history" of theory, nor with the role of the history of theory within sociology – both interesting questions, but neither of which are raised in Merton's essay. Analyzing the pattern of citations in current sociological literature, therefore, Merton suggests that the *reading* of the classics has been useful in at least *four* distinct ways: (1) precisely because the more scientific tradition of "obliteration by incorporation" is still rare in sociology, there remains "unretrieved sociological knowledge" in the classics which can still be used as new points of departure for future research; (2) in the classics, theorists frequently discover ideas which they themselves have independently developed, producing a sort of "dialogue" between the living and the dead, in which the theorist's idea acquires renewed merit through its discovery in the work of an illustrrious predecessor; (3) the similar discovery of a classic denial of a theorist's ideas frequently leads to a profitable reformulation; and (4) an understanding of the manner in which the classic writers formulated *their* problems, and constructed *their* theoretical solutions, can provide models for the theorist's *own* formulations and constructions in the present. Finally, Merton adds that each of these four functions may be augmented by frequently re-reading the classics; for each time we approach a classic text, we do so with a new experiential background, which leads us to "understand" the work in a new way.

That the reading (and re-reading) of the classics performs these important functions is obvious. As emphasized above, however, Merton's discussion here is exclusively concerned with the "systematics" of sociological theory, and this invites two additional observations. First, it appears that the pattern of citations of the sociological literature to which Merton appeals is at least as consistent with my own distinction between "history" and "systematics" as it is with Merton's. If (as I have argued) the distinguishing feature of a genuinely "historical" account of such classics is its emphasis upon the recovery of their authors' intentions, for example, we should expect such an emphasis to be lacking in its "systematic" counterpart; and indeed, none of the four functions in question requires or even respects such an emphasis. In fact, Merton says quite explicitly that the utility of such readings and re-readings of the classics would be seriously compromised by a failure to distinguish *that* activity from "the scholastic practice of commentary and exegesis" (Merton, 1967: 37). Similarly, if (as Merton seems at the very least to imply) the distinguishing feature of the "systematics" of theory is its "highly selective accumulation of those small parts of earlier theory which have thus far survived the tests of empirical research" (Merton, 1957: 5), we should expect that the role of the classics in 'systematics' should reflect this concern for the empirical validity of the propositions which these classics allegedly contain. The fact that the four functions in question rather clearly *do not* reflect such a concern adds weight to our earlier conclusion – i.e., that Merton was quite right to urge such a distinction, but wrong in his definition of its respective terms.

My second observation concerns what is arguably the most glaring omission in Merton's entire argument – i.e., the lack of any discussion whatever of the putative value of the authentic "history" of theory for its "systematic" counterpart. The omission is curious, for one of Merton's arguments for the distinction itself is that, once clearly separated, "history" and "systematics" might interact to great effect on some other, higher plane (Merton, 1967: 3); and it is dangerous, for it seems to imply that Merton himself is unclear on what this effect might be. How might this hiatus be filled?

Alasdair MacIntyre has recently observed that the most striking feature of contemporary moral utterance is that so much of it is used to express disagreements, and also that these disagreements have three, quite peculiar, characteristics. *First*, they seem to be interminable, not only in the (undeniable) sense that they go on and on, but in the more alarming sense that they seem incapable (and are understood by their participants *to be incapable*) of reaching any conclusion whatever. Participants' arguments may be logically valid, in the sense that conclusions follow from premises; but the rival premises seem to be such that we have no rational means of weighing the claims of one against the other. And it is the recognition of this seemingly arbitrary, non-rational decision as to premises, MacIntyre suggests, which produces the rather shrill and assertive tone of modern moral discourse. The *second* characteristic, utterly ironic in light of the first, is that such arguments are constantly embodied in expressions whose distinctive function in our language is to make some sort of appeal to objective, impersonal, rational standards. The *terms* of the debate thus imply claims which the *tone* of the debate belies. And a *third* peculiar feature of these arguments is that each is typically conjoined with an appeal to that particular intellectual tradition (be it Marxian, Kantian, utilitarian, or whatever) of which the argument in question is, allegedly, a coherent part. It is MacIntyre's argument, however, that these are not appeals to authentic "traditions" at all, but rather, to the mere fragmentary survivals of those earlier traditions, which have been extracted from, and thus deprived of, those cultural contexts which rendered them meaningful and understandable in the first place; and as such, these conceptual survivals arrive in the present in a state of utter and complete intellectual chaos (see MacIntyre, 1981: 6–11, passim).

MacIntyre's description, of course, will be familiar to anyone who has attended presentations of the Theory Section of the American Sociological Association – e.g., debates not only interminable, but understood to be inevitably so; conclusions drawn logically from premises, themselves drawn non-logically, and thus incommensurable; the appeal to objective standards of rationality, in the most shrill and assertive manner; and the constant (if implicit) claim to speak for some distinguished intellectual tradition, of which mere fragments and vestiges survive. The problem, therefore, is not that sociologists no longer "read the classics"; indeed, if we are to believe the editorials of the Theory Section's Newsletters, there has been far too much reading of the classics, though for the wrong reason – i.e., in the search for ready-made answers to questions which the classic writers themselves never asked, let alone answered (17). The problem is rather that we have lost all sense of belonging to a common intellectual tradition, of speaking a common language, of arguing in the context of commonly-accepted standards of rationality.

Here, then, is a role for *history*. For one means to overcoming conceptual disorder and ideological incoherence is simply to restore our concepts and ideas to the social, historical, and linguistic contexts within which they once made sense. Ideas, after all, are not simply rationalizations or epiphenomenal reflections of more concrete social actions; rather, they are social actions themselves, literally constituted by the real conditions, needs, intentions, and purposes for which they were constructed. To treat ideas, on the contrary, as arbitrary and purely contingent, to strip them of the contexts within which their meaning and significance originally inhered, is surely to lead the discipline by a short route to conceptual chaos. This is not to say that sociologists ought not to read (and re-read) the classics for the reasons given by Merton, or for other heuristic, non-historical purposes; nor is it to say that the classics, in this setting, might not have a "meaning" for *us* which is different from that intended by their authors (18). But it *is* to insist, in a manner similar to Merton, that these activities be clearly distinguished from those which are genuinely *historical*; that there are limits on the extent to which an idea drawn from, say, Hume's *Dialogues*, stripped of the intentions and purposes for which it was uttered, and deprived of the conventions of eighteenth century Scottish Calvinism within which it was meaningful, can any longer be said to be "Hume's idea"; and finally, that the claim to speak for Hume, implicit within any account of the *Dialogues*, must take account of the action *he* was performing, of what *he* was doing in saying what he said, in terms which might reasonably have made sense to *him* and *his* contemporaries. Ironically, this promises the most "sociological" history of sociological thought; but meanwhile, that field remains a bag of tricks we play upon the dead.

Notes

*   In addition to many valuable comments made at the presentation of this paper at the conference in preparation of this volume itself, an early draft has been read by Jeffrey Alexander, Lewis A. Coser, William Form, Joan Huber, Guenther Roth, and Quentin Skinner; but while I have profited greatly from some of their critical remarks, responsibility for the conclusions herein is entirely my own.

1. These questions were raised in a letter from the editors announcing the Bielefeld Conference in preparation of this volume.

2. On this point, see my ethnographic parody, 'Myth and Symbol Among the Nacirema Tsigoloicos: A Fragment', *The American Sociologist* XV, No. 4 (November, 1980).

3. The alternative, suggested by Herbert Butterfield and other opponents of "whig" history, is to make our decisions about what deserves to be studied and what is best ignored by applying only those criteria of significance which were current and accepted during the historical period under investigation (Butterfield, 1973: 28). This over-zealous historicism would create at least two difficulties: first, it is unlikely that any historical period exhibits the sort of consensus on "what matters" which this injunction presumes; and second, even if some did, the passive endorsement of such judgements would yield some rather absurd historical accounts. See the examples cited in Skinner (1974: 284) and Jones, 1977. This rather obvious point is important, for it emphasises the fact that *some* of our judgements, however 'historicist' our intentions, *must* be based on our own, *present* criteria of what is rational and important.

4. The history of science, Sarton argued, is "the only history which can illustrate the progress of mankind", because "the acquisition and systematization of positive knowledge are the only human activities which are truly cumulative and progressive". See *The Study of the History of Science*. Cambridge, Mass., 1936, p. 5. Again, Sarton described the history of mathematics as "an endless series of victories of the human mind, victories without counterbalancing failures, that is, without dishonorable and humiliating ones, and without atrocities". *The Study of the History of Mathematics*. Cambridge, Mass., 1936, p. 13. Both cited in Stocking (1968: 6, 313).

5. These remarks were suggested to me by some observations on the history of political theory made by Quentin Skinner (1979: 11–13). The suggestion that the same observations might be made concerning the history of sociological theory is entirely my own. See also Jones (1981: 453).

6. For a considerably more detailed critique of such statements, with perhaps excessive citations, see Jones (1977: 284–9).

7. The works referred to include Butterfield's *The Whig Interpretation of History* (1913), Collingwood's *Autobiography* (1939), and Bloch's *The Historian's Craft* (1941).

8. See the remarks by Stocking (1968: 7) to the effect that, at the very least, Kuhn's work was 'imperfectly historicist'.

9. Sociologists are clearly reluctant to leave the writing of the history of their discipline to professional historians. See the evidence on this and other points in Jones and Kronus (1976).

10. Merton's 1967 article was itself an enlargement of an introductory section of his *Social Theory and Social Structure* (1957); and that section was in turn an enlargement of points made in a 1948 discussion of a paper by Talcott Parsons (see references).

11. See Parsons' remark that *The Structure of Social Action* "was not meant in the

first instance to be a study in intellectual history", for he limited himself to "a rather narrow sector within its time period and, except for background purposes, excluded previous contributions" (Parson, 1968: xiii). But in fact, Parsons was always rather elusive on the extent to which that work was (nor was not) an exer- in the history of ideas. Several pages before the statement cited above, for exam- ple, he referred to *The Structure* as "an empirical study in the analysis of social thought", in which the writings under scrutiny were "as truly documents as are manorial court rolls of the Middle Ages, and as such, present problems of under- standing and interpretation" (Parson, 1968: vii) – a claim rather ill-fitted to the arguments which follow (see Jones, 1977: 289–90).

12. The classic statement of this argument is found in Wittgenstein's *Philosophical Investigations* (1953); and the more popular presentation is Peter Winch's *The Idea of a Social Science* (Winch, 1958: 26–31).

13. It is important to make a distinction between Merton's own practice and the potential consequences of an uncritical acceptance of some of his methodological injunctions. This paper is concerned with the latter rather than the former. Any scholar familiar with the historiography of classical social theory will recognize that Merton himself has been among the most circumspect and sophisticated interpreters of the European sociological tradition, and it was doubtless to maintain the standards for such interpretations that the essay discussed herein was written. I am grateful to Wolf Lepenies for bringing this to my attention.

14. The passages of "writers A, B, and C", respectively, are taken from David Hume's *The Natural History of Religion* (Hume, 1749–51: 34), William Robertson Smith's *Lectures on the Religion of the Semites* (Smith, 1889: 85–86), and Emile Durk- heim's *Les Formes élémentaires de la vie religieuse* (Durkheim, 1912: 41). The discussion which follows – i.e., of what Hume, Smith, and Durkheim "were doing" – is drawn from sources which will be familiar to most students of the early scien- tific study of religion. On the potentially misleading statements of Durkheim's and Hume's "texts", however, the reader may wish to consult Lukes (1972: 4) and Smith (1935: 95), respectively.

15. The most prominent works of the three authors mentioned include MacIntyre's *A Short History of Ethics* (1966) and *After Virtue* (1981); Skinner's 'Meaning and Understanding in the History of Ideas' (1969), and *The Foundations of Modern Political Thought* (1978); and Dunn's 'The Identity of the History of Ideas' (1968) and *The Political Thought of John Locke* (1969). Efforts to introduce this critique into the historiography of sociological theory have included Geoffrey Hawthorn's "Introduction" to *Enlightenment and Despair* (1976: 1–7); Stefan Collini's "Soci- ology and Idealism in Britain, 1880–1920" (1978) and *Liberalism and Sociology* (1979); and my own "On understanding a Sociological Classic" (1977) and "On Quentin Skinner" (1981).

16. It is particularly disturbing that the "history of sociology" has frequently been assumed to be synonymous with the history of "great men" and "great books". One of the signal virtues of Merton's essay, therefore, was its criticism of this con- fusion, and its extension of the history of sociology beyond the "classics" to the important studies on the history of social *Research* conducted by Nathan Glazer, Paul Lazarsfeld, and Anthony Oberschall (Merton, 1967: 7). While I heartily endorse his extension, my own research deals with questions raised by (though

not limited to) such "classics;" thus I have been particularly interested in this fourth section of Merton's essay. Again, I am indebted to Wolf Lepenies for evoking this comment.

17. See the ASA Theory Section's Newsletters, Volume IV, Nos. 1 and 2 (Spring-Summer and Fall-Winter, 1981). The Newsletters also report another event indicative of the condition I describe. In 1979, the Theory Section established an annual prize for the best paper on sociological theory appearing within the previous two years, setting "no limits" as to "substance", "style of argument", "mode of concern", or "disciplinary boundaries" (Newsletter, Vol. III, No. 1, Fall, 1979). But (or perhaps thus), in 1981, the five theorists composing the Theory Prize Committee charged with selecting a worthy recipient were unable to conclude their deliberations successfully – in part because they were unable to agree upon what "theory" meant in this context.

18. This is a caveat which has been entered before, but apparently needs to be entered again. See, for example, Skinner: "I see no impropriety in speaking of a work having a meaning for me which the writer could not have intended. Nor does my thesis conflict with this possibility. I have been concerned only with the converse point that whatever a writer is *doing in* writing what he writes must be relevant interpretation, and thus with the claim that *amongst* the interpreter's tasks must be the recovery of the writer's intentions *in* writing what he writes" (Skinner, 1972: 405; see also Jones, 1977: 291; 1978: 176). I am grateful to Guenther Roth and Lewis Coser for insisting, (the latter rather forcefully!), upon this point.

References

Bloch, Marc: 1941, *The Historian's Craft*, P. Putnam (tr.), New York: Random House, 1953.

Butterfield, Herbert: 1931, *The Whig Interpretation of History*, Harmondsworth, Eng.: Penguin, 1973.

Collingwood, R. G.: 1939, *An Autobiography*, Oxford: Oxford University Press, 1970.

Collini, Stefan: 1978, 'Sociology and Idealism in Britain, 1880–1920', *European Journal of Sociology* **XIX**, pp. 3–50.

Collini, Stefan: 1979, *Liberalism and Sociology: L. T. Hobhouse and Political Argument in England, 1880–1914*. Cambridge: Cambridge Univ. Press.

Dunn, John: 1968, 'The Identity of the History of Ideas', *Journal of the Royal Institute of Philosophy* **XLIII**, No. 164 (April), pp. 85–104.

Dunn, John: 1969, *The Political Thought of John Locke*, Cambridge: Cambridge Univ. Press.

Durkheim, Emile: 1912, *Les Formes élémentaires de la vie religieuse*. J. W. Swain (tr.), *The Elementary Forms of the Religious Life*, New York: Macmillan, 1915.

Friedrichs, Robert W.: 1970, *A Sociology of Sociology*, New York: The Free Press.

Hawthorn, Geoffrey: 1966, *Enlightenment and Despair: A History of Sociology*, Cambridge: Cambridge Univ. Press.

Hume, David: 1749–51, *The Natural History of Religion*, reprinted in R. Wollheim (ed.), *Hume on Religion*, New York: World Pub. Co., 1963, pp. 31–98.

Jones, Robert Alun: 1977, 'On Understanding a Sociological Classic', *American Journal of Sociology* **LXXXIII**, No. 2 (September), pp. 279–319.

Jones, Robert Alun: 1978, 'Subjectivity, Objectivity, and Historicity: A Reply to Johnson', *American Journal of Sociology* **LXXXIV**, No. 1 (July), pp. 175–81.

Jones, Robert Alun: 1981, 'On Quentin Skinner', *American Journal of Sociology* **LXXXVIII**, No. 2, pp. 453–67.

Jones, Robert Alun and Kronus, Sidney: 1976, 'Professional Sociologists and the History of Sociology: A Survey of Recent Opinion', *Journal of the History of the Behavioral Sciences* **XII**, No. 1 (January).

Kuhn, Thomas: 1962, *The Structure of Scientific Revolutions*, Chicago: University of Chicago Press.

Lukes, Steven: 1972, *Emile Durkheim*, New York: Harper and Row.

MacIntyre, Alasdair: 1966, *A Short History of Ethics*, New York: Macmillan.

MacIntyre, Alasdair: 1981, *After Virtue: A Study in Moral Theory*, Notre Dame, Ind.: Univ. of Notre Dame Press.

Merton, Robert K.: 1948, 'Discussion of 'The Position of Sociological Theory', by Talcott Parsons', *American Sociological Review* **XIII**, No. 2 (April), pp. 164–68.

Merton, Robert K.: 1957, *Social Theory and Social Structure*, New York: The Free Press.

Merton, Robert K.: 1967, 'On the 'History' and 'Systematics' of Sociological Theory', in *On Theoretical Sociology*, New York: Free Press, pp. 1–37.

Parsons, Talcott: 1937, *The Structure of Social Action*, 2 vols. New York: Free Press, 1968.

Skinner, Quentin: 1969, 'Meaning and Understanding in the History of Ideas', *History and Theory* **VIII**, pp. 3–35.

Skinner, Quentin: 1972, 'Motives, Intentions and the Interpretation of Texts', *New Literary History* **III** (Winter), pp. 393–408.

Skinner, Quentin: 1974, 'Some Problems in the Analysis of Political Thought and Action', *Political Theory* **II**, No. 3 (August), pp. 277–303.

Skinner, Quentin: 1978, *The Foundations of Modern Political Thought*, 2 vols. Cambridge: Cambridge Univ. Press.

Skinner, Quentin: 1979, 'Intellectual History and the History of Political Thought', *Newsletter of the Intellectual History Group* No. 1 (Spring), pp. 11–13.

Smith, Norman Kemp: 1935, 'Introduction' to David Hume's *Dialogues Concerning Natural Religion*, Oxford: Oxford Univ. Press, pp. 1–96.

Smith, William Robertson: 1889, *Lectures on the Religion of the Semites*. 2nd edition, 1894. New York: Schocken, 1972.

Stocking, George W., Jr.: 1965, 'On the Limits of 'Presentism' and 'Historicism' in the Historiography of the Behavioral Sciences', *Journal of the History of the Behavioral Sciences* **I**, pp. 211–18, reprinted in Stocking's *Race, Culture, and Evolution: Essays in the History of Anthropology*, New York: Free Press, 1968. Pp. 1–12.

Stocking, George W., Jr.: 1966, 'The History of Anthropology: Where, Whence, Whither?' *Journal of the History of the Behavioral Sciences* **II**, No. 4 (October), pp. 281–90.

Stocking, George W., Jr.: 1968, *Race, Culture, and Evolution: Essays in the History of Anthropology*. New York: Free Press.

Winch, Peter: 1958, *The Idea of a Social Science and Its Relation to Philosophy*, London: Routledge and Kegan Paul.
Wittgenstein, Ludwig: 1953, *Philosophical Investigations*, G. E. M. Anscombe (tr.), New York: Macmillan.

THE SELF-PRESENTATION OF A DISCIPLINE: HISTORY OF PSYCHOLOGY IN THE UNITED STATES BETWEEN PEDAGOGY AND SCHOLARSHIP

MITCHELL G. ASH

Psychological Institute of Mainz University, F.R.G.

1. Introduction

Criticism of scholarship in the history of psychology from historians and philosophers of science is certainly not new. In 1966, for example, Robert M. Young characterized the field as "an avocation with very uneven standards", limited primarily to biographies of great psychologists, extended reviews of the literature and the uncritical chronicling of the rise of scientific psychology, based on a narrowly preconceived model of scientific development (1). Recent criticism has renewed all of these charges, particularly the last. Walter Weimer, a psychologist interested in the philosophy of science, accuses the writers of historical textbooks of 'crypto-justificationism', of describing the 'evolution' of their discipline as a continuously progressive path to the present. Weimer sees a close connection here between the history of psychology as traditionally written and the operationalist version of logical empiricism, the dominant philosophy of science in American psychology since the 1940s. In his view, both theorists and historians of psychology have continued to subscribe to a view of science which is "unbelievably out of date", if not "the blackest of metatheoretical lies" (2).

Perhaps more surprising than these accusations has been the response to them. In a review of Weimer's book, James Blight, a specialist in the history of psychology, states that Weimer's criticism is true but misdirected. Recent scholarship in the field, Blight claims, is free from justificationist bias; but as far as textbook histories go, such work has always been and always will be ideological. Citing Thomas Kuhn's characterization of 'textbook history', Blight asserts that its function has always been to purvey "the reigning

143

Loren Graham, Wolf Lepenies, and Peter Weingart (eds.), Functions and Uses of Disciplinary Histories, Volume VII, 1983, 143–189.

paradigmatic ideology", to show that the current state of the discipline exhibits "a high level of certainty, valid methods of inquiry and rapid, continous progress" (3).

Whether or not this assertion reflects the view of most historians of psychology, Blight's distinction between scholarship and 'textbook history' raises an important issue. According to Wolf Lepenies, disciplines rely in part upon their historiography to demonstrate both their descent from an ancient tradition of knowledge and their claim to scientific legitimacy and institutional standing in the present, as measured against currently dominant disciplines (4). We could call these two kinds of externally directed self-presentation, two ways in which a discipline presents itself to the members of other disciplines, to relevant sources of financial and institutional support, and to the educated public. Similar claims may also be directed internally, for such legitimating demonstrations can be important sources of self-assurance to the members of the discipline themselves. As Ulfried Geuter shows for Germany in his contribution to this volume, another form of internally directed self-presentation is the use of history as an auxiliary stage for inner-disciplinary conflicts.

The phrase 'textbook history' indicates, however, that internally directed legitimation strategies may also be aimed at beginning or more advanced students in a discipline; we might call this pedagogical self-presentation, to distinguish it from the others. This function of the history of disciplines has been particularly important in the history of psychology as practiced in the United States. Two-thirds of the world's psychologists live in that country; it is also the only nation in which the history of psychology is an institutionally organized subspecialty of the discipline. As this paper will show, the establishment of that subspecialty was supported to an important extent by the requirements of pedagogical self-presentation. However, these imperatives have changed over time, according to the social structure of the discipline and its situation in society; and both the style and the content of textbook history have changed with them. In the first half of the paper I will present some of the earlier stages of this history. The establishment of the subfield will then be set in its social and intellectual context. That process went hand in hand with the emergence of systematic scholarship in the history of psychology on a scale previously unknown, scholarship that has thoroughly outdated the work criticized by both Young and Weimer. At the same time, it has yielded results that may not be compatible with any form of textbook history. After presenting some of these results, I will ask, in conclusion, whether they can be integrated with the aims of textbook history in their current form, or whether those aims themselves are changing.

2. The Emergence of Textbook History: Sociohistorical Background

In Germany, the land of its original institutionalization, experimental psychology was differentiated in a number of respects from its parent disciplines, physiology and philosophy, by 1910. However, for a variety of reasons having to do mainly with the institutional structure and the social role of the German universities, the discipline remained formally affiliated with philosophy. Experimenting psychologists were thus required to compete for professorships with specialists in philosophical pedagogy as well as representatives of the more strictly philosophical specialties until the 1940s. In the United States, the institutionalization of psychology as an independent discipline proceeded much more rapidly; by the turn of the century there were more psychological laboratories in that country than there were universities in Germany. The establishment of the field benefitted greatly from the rise of the American university, with which it coincided; some of its leading figures became university presidents. However, numerous laboratories were also founded in liberal-arts colleges; and the dilemmas of legitimation were equally complex in both kinds of institution (5).

In the nineteenth century American college, philosophy and psychology were often taught by the college president, who was frequently an ordained Protestant minister. The courses tended to emphasize moral philosophy; for the aim was to use philosophy to form character, to produce educated people imbued with the injunction to be useful to society. Such training was not necessarily opposed to scientific endeavor. Rather, many of these educators promulgated Scottish common-sense realism and a Baconian, inductivist ideal of science, and tried to combine the latest findings from the German laboratories with their moral teachings (6). It was on the basis of this background that many of the first American laboratory psychologists chose to work in the field. Though they eagerly went to Germany to learn experimental technique, they did not forget the traditional injunction to be useful. This is shown most clearly in the cases of G. Stanley Hall, William

James and James Mark Baldwin. All of these men carried out extensive empirical research; however, they also tried to show that their results did not undermine either philosophy or religion, but offered instead a way of reconciling the demands of conscience and the kind of science demanded by the theory of evolution (7).

Though people such as Baldwin and James supported laboratory research, institutionalization was pushed forward most aggressively by others, such as Edward Lee Thorndike and James McKeen Cattell. These men, whom the historian Dorothy Ross calls 'the professional generation' to distinguish them from more genteel, 'traditional' philosopher-psychologists, had more interest in measuring and experimenting for its own sake than in either history or philosophy. However, the 'professionals', too, had a strong interest in demonstrating the potential social value of their work, particularly in education. In this they expressed the belief, widespread among the emergent middle classes during the so-called Progressive era, that science and technology could help combat the threat of social disorder posed by urbanization and industrialization. Social usefulness was also a strong selling point with both college and university presidents who had the power to establish new profes-sorships, departments and laboratories, and with the businessmen who sat on the boards of trustees that appointed the presidents (8). However, though they trumpeted the potential applications of their work, the vast majority of experimenting psychologists did so from within academia. In a 1929 survey of the field, James McKeen Cattell characterized psychologists as "the most academic of all scientific workers". Of the 307 members of the American Psychological Association in 1916 — a ten-fold increase over the 31 of the founding year, 1892 — 84% held the Ph.D., and 88.6% (272) were employed as university or college teachers (9).

It may be suggested that the first histories of psychology published in the United States helped to establish the discipline in its academic setting by demonstrating that the new science was a worthy heir to Scottish com-mon sense or Baconian philosophy, or at least that it was not incompatible with that tradition. James Mark Baldwin, for example, wrote his *History of Psychology* in 1913, after he had resigned his professorship at Johns Hopkins University and had begun to turn his attention increasingly to logic and epistemology. George Sidney Brett's three-volume history, the first volume of which was published in 1912, was devoted almost entirely to the history of philosophical psychology; only the final two chapters of the last volume treated experimental work. However, professors who wished to include history in their college survey courses probably used the histories by Max Dessoir and Otto Klemm, which appeared in English translation in 1912 and 1914, respectively, shortly after their publication in German. As a supplement to these books, Benjamin Rand published a collection of texts indicatively titled *The Classical Psychologists* in 1912. Of all these texts, the only one devoted primarily to the new experimental psychology was G. Stanley Hall's anecdotal account, *The Founders of Modern Psychology*, also published in 1912 (10).

By the 1920s, however, the situation had begun to change. The potential importance of applied psychology in both education and industry had been vigorously promoted at least since the turn of the century, but a turning point was reached with the use of intelligence tests to classify more than two million American soldiers during the First World War. In 1920 51.5% of the members of the American Psychological Association indicated that their work was mainly in applied psychology, while only 48.5% were working in experimental research (11). These figures soon changed, as psychologists employed by the military returned to their teaching positions; but it was nonetheless evident that with the army intelligence tests psychology had achieved a previously unknown level of public notice and acceptance. Psychologists seemed to have achieved the longed-for status of expert, with control over esoteric but apparently exact and recognizably useful knowledge.

Recent research indicates that the army intelligence tests were not as successful in their stated purpose as they were in promoting psychology. It was not entirely clear that the psychologists knew what it was they were testing, or that the instruments they used were as adequate to the task of classifying soldiers, many of whom were illiterate in English, as they may have been in an academic setting (12). Attempts to patent and sell or distribute psychological tests on a mass scale were also problematic, as the early difficulties of Cattell's 'Psychological Corporation' showed. Increasing recognition of these weaknesses, and of the amenability of the tests to social bias, led to public reaction against both the testing movement and applied psychology in general, which began even before the Depression raised these issues in a different way. Nonetheless, the social demand for apparently objective classification instruments continued, especially in the schools; for educators shared the psychologists' assumption that the abilities assessed and graded by these instruments — their own pencil-and-paper skills — really were the same as 'intelligence' (13).

3. The Problems of Progress I: Writing Psychology's 'Scientific' History

This was the situation in which the first full-length histories of experimental, or scientific psychology appeared, three of them in the same year, 1929 (14). The chronological coincidence may have been due in part to market requirements, since no text in the field had been published for fifteen years. However, the most important of these, Edwin G. Boring's *A History of Experimental Psychology*, was the product of a specific intellectual and institutional situation, which requires some specification.

Boring was one of the leading representatives of yet a third group of psychologists, in addition to the 'traditionalists' and 'militants' already described. This was the coterie of self-styled devotees of 'pure' experimental psychology assembled around Edward Bradford Titchener, for more than thirty years professor of psychology at Cornell University. In one sense they were 'professionals', since they opposed any subordination of psychology to philosophical concerns. On the other hand, however, they also opposed the direct application of scientific psychology to social problems, because this meant the confusion of psychological science — the carefully controlled, introspective study of the contents of consciousness — with 'technology'. It was Titchener and his followers who led the inner-disciplinary opposition to early behaviorism, which continued throughout the 1920s (15). Boring in particular took an important role in resisting the advance of applied psychology, as well. He chaired the committee which introduced the category of 'associate' membership in the American Psychological Association in 1925. This reserved full membership for holders of the Ph.D. with published research (16).

At Harvard University, his own base of operations, Boring had a somewhat different battle to fight; for Harvard was the last major university in which psychology was still affiliated with philosophy in a common department. The philosophers, who were in the majority, shared Boring's opposition to applied science. But they could not agree with his view of experimentation as an end in itself, because they still considered psychology to be a propaedeutic to philosophy — epistemology by another name, as one of their number described it (17). Boring engaged in a decade-long struggle for autonomy, which he finally won in 1932. As one historian has convincingly argued, his monumental *History* was thus an attempt both to reassert experimentalist hegemony in the discipline as a whole, and to show his philosopher colleagues that although philosophy had once been important to psychology's development, it had long since served its purpose (18).

Boring prefaced his work with the assertion that "A psychological sophistication that contains no component of historical orientation seems to me to be no sophistication at all". He made clear the sort of 'historical orientation' he meant in his very first sentence, where he modified Hermann Ebbinghaus' dictum to say that "in general the histories of psychology have emphasized its long past at the expense of its short *scientific* history" (19). The contrast to presentations like Brett's is nearly complete. Except for two pages on Aristotle, there was little treatment of ancient and none at all of medieval thought on the mind. Instead the book began with a disquisition on the rise of modern science. However, it proceeded from there not to the doctrines of Descartes and of British empiricism, but to a discussion of sensory physiology in the nineteenth century: the philosophical background came in part two. By doing violence to chronology in this way, Boring signalled the double purpose just described. He aligned his field with a neighboring discipline of recognized scientific status, and gave this alignment precedence over the metaphysical and epistemological allegiances in which both were rooted.

It was not only the scientific status of physiology with which Boring sought to identify, but also the ideal of cumulative progress which he saw expressed in that discipline's history. He presented the development of the physiology of the nervous system, especially the series of discoveries leading up to Helmholtz's measurement of the speed of nervous transmission, as "a paradigm of scientific progress". Important as it was, Helmholtz's achievement came, Boring noted, "just as psychology was getting ready to declare its immediate [*sic!*] independence of both philosophy and physiology". It "would almost inevitably have occurred under some agency in the 1850s — or at least in the 1860s — if Helmholtz had not been there to have the simple insight". As he put it in an essay of 1927, originality in science consists "not in the enunciation of any new principle, but in the selection and collocation

of certain old ones which gather force when brought thus into relation . . . ".
Scientific progress is a continuous 'stream' of evolution, which only appears
irregular when viewed for short periods; we would understand it better if we
could 'dehumanize' it (20).

This heroically humble conception of scientific development was not
unique to Boring. It was widely shared at the time, not only by scientists but
also by the founders of another fledgling discipline, the history of science.
Such views could be quite inspiring to younger scientists, and thus serve an
important socializing function. B. F. Skinner, who began graduate study at
Harvard in the late 1920s, recalls responding in this way when he read the
work of George Sarton and Ernst Mach's history of mechanics, and heard
the lectures of the chemist L. J. Henderson on the history of science, which
communicated much the same vision (21).

Boring's *History*, too, had pedagogical origins. He wrote it in part from
the notes to the '200-lecture' course in systematic psychology, which he had
developed at Clark University in 1921 and 1922, and polished at Harvard;
that course drew heavily in its turn upon the similar series which Titchener
gave at Cornell (22). In Boring's hands, however, the stream of progress
took on a peculiar form. Although he had advocated 'dehumanizing' the
history of science, he presented the history of experimental psychology
from 1860 to 1910 as a linear succession of ideas and methods from Fechner
and Helmholtz, especially the latter, to Helmholtz's long-time assistant
Wilhelm Wundt, thence to Wundt's student Titchener, and thus by implication
to Titchener's acolyte, Edwin G. Boring. This version of linear continuity
resulted in a number of striking omissions. Boring's limitation of his history
to psychology "as Wundt defined it — the study of the conscious, normal
human adult mind" as found in the laboratory — led to the treatment of
much of French psychology, based as it was largely on medical models, and
much of comparative and child psychology as 'peripheral' (23). The existence
of an autonomous Anglo-American tradition based largely upon Scottish
common-sense realism, then integrated with psychophysiology and evolutionary theory, was acknowledged only briefly. While he excluded some
things, Boring included others. Though he claimed to have written a history
of experimental psychology alone, he appropriated mental testing, and its
apparent success, into the narrative with little ado and even less critical
discussion of the socially biased assumptions about 'intelligence' that had

been built into the tests. Similarly ignored was the context of the rest of psychology's history. The careers of individual researchers and theorists receive full attention, but the larger social and political situations in which these biographies took on meaning went largely analysed.

Boring justified the inclusion of biographical material with the assertion that persons have indeed been important in history, for better and for worse. "Authority has often carried the day", as in the naming of the doctrine of specific sense energies for Johannes Müller, although it had been outlined two decades earlier by Charles Bell (24). True as this statement was, it seemed to contradict Boring's emphasis on continuity. This becomes more understandable when we see that he meant to use biography to reinforce the notion of continuous progress. The stream continues to flow, so long as the great men of science see themselves, and are themselves seen, as its continuators.

The results to which such a concept of scientific development could lead are revealed quite clearly by Boring's confrontation with an approach to psychology based on a different conception, Gestalt psychology. Boring's initial reception of Gestalt theory was positive. As he wrote to one of the Gestalt theorists, Kurt Koffka, in 1925, rumor had it that he had become a Gestalt psychologist himself. Though he declined the label, he did not mind the rumors; for the experimental work to which the new theory was leading made "eminently good scientific sense" (25). Apparently Boring saw in Gestalt theory some hope of support for his and Titchener's opposition to behaviorism. Koffka had vigorously attacked that theory as early as 1921, defending the right of cognitive experience — "inner behavior", as he then called it — to be part of the subject matter of psychology alongside 'outer behavior' (26).

However, by the time Wolfgang Köhler's book *Gestalt Psychology* appeared, in 1929, Boring's attitude had hardened. Although Köhler did not mention Titchener's — or Boring's — name, he attacked Titchener's approach to psychology in such a way as to place it on the same plane as behaviorism. The one reduced the perceptual world of structures and wholes to a collection of sensations, artifacts of the laboratory; the other reduced the functioning, adapting organism to a collection of reflexes in an equally arbitrary way. Analysis is necessary in science, Köhler wrote, but it is important to select appropriate, natural units from which to begin. "The right psychological formula is therefore: *constellation of stimuli – organization – response to the products of organization*" (27). With this it was clear that Gestalt theory could not be a suitable ally to the Titchener-Boring tradition, for it rejected the entire concept of science on which that tradition rested. In a brief note in response to the book, Boring expressed his views on the progress of science more bluntly than ever before, and placed his response to Gestalt psychology in this context.

Specifically, Boring accused Köhler of attacking doctrines which no one, including Titchener, had seriously held for two decades. "Gestalt psychology cultivates a fictitious opposition in the interests of its own self-preservation". This was the sign of an intellectual movement, and "I do not like movements".

The progress of thought is gradual, and the enunciation of a 'new' critical principle in science is never more than an event that follows naturally upon its antecedents and leads presently to unforeseen consequents . . . Science is a dynamic whole; it is not made up of schools where some are right and some are wrong; it is made up of the thoughts and activities of persons, all of whom affect each other, and no one of whom remains very long unchanged.

A movement is always negative; it is characterized in part by its opposition to some other older view . . . in its negativism, a movement seeks to give itself a separate individuality by setting itself off discretely from the immediate past. Thus movements . . . picture, falsely, a continuous upward trend as a series of abrupt steps.

There can not be the least doubt that *Gestalt* psychology represents an important positive advance within psychology. It seems to me that there is no less doubt that it exaggerates both the magnitude of the advance and its dependence upon a certain small group of persons. It is not clear that psychology might not have come the same way, only a little more slowly, had there been no *Gestalt* psychologists (28).

In response to this, Koffka wrote Boring to protest that "the Gestalt *movement* has been created not by the Gestalt psychologists but by their opponents". It was not their propaganda, as Boring alleged, but "the intrinsic beauty and fruitfulness" of the new approach that they wished to share with other scientists. "We didn't start a movement, we hoped to get rid of a number of problems that had been debated for a long time without any apparent progress." The fact that many psychologists continued to resist the Gestalt viewpoint showed only

that your theory of perfect continuity in the progress of science is not true. My idea of scientific progress is that certain problems arise at certain times in various places, and that several people have new ideas, in the strict sense of the word new. Metaphorically speaking, that each of them makes a small leap. Very often, and I suppose usually for a long time, these leaps are not high enough and therefore fail to raise the general level of science, which goes on as though these leaps had never been made. . . . Sometimes it happens that somebody succeeds in making a leap high enough; then the scientific situation is really changed and then the historian can always find other leaps going in the same direction and can construct a picture of continuity which is post factum and, as I see it, inadequate (29).

Koffka's denial of polemical intent was somewhat disingenuous; the notion of wanting to share something of "intrinsic beauty and fruitfulness", which is nonetheless not universally accepted, is characteristic of the prophet's pose. The entire style of self-presentation which the Gestalt theorists cultivated did not match well with the emerging professional style in American psychology, one of theoretically agnostic 'contributions' to the literature, which presupposed the concept of scientific progress that Boring advocated. Boring's answer was clear. 'I can see readily', he wrote, "that my emersion [*sic*] in history may have given me an exaggerated view of continuity. There are steps, and the question becomes largely a matter of how big the steps are thought to be . . . I cannot get away from the belief that most steps are rather small" (30).

On the historiographical side of this debate, the winner was obviously Boring, at least for a time. In his *Sensation and Perception in the History of Experimental Psychology* (1942), and in the second edition of his *History* (1950), he presented a picture of the history of Gestalt psychology which was essentially a magnified and enriched version of the view he had expressed in 1930. The primary emphasis fell upon the idea that nothing in Gestalt theory was new. Of the total of forty-one pages which Boring devoted to Gestalt psychology in the second edition of his *History*, eighteen were concerned in one way or another with its 'antecedents', including six pages on 'form qualities' from an earlier chapter. Everything from the epistemological perspective of Gestalt theory — the psychological reality of perceived wholes as logically and genetically prior to congeries of sensations — to its supporting methodological standpoint — heuristic phenomenalism, the acceptance in evidence of the psychologically given as such — to its approach to the mind-body problem — psychophysical isomorphism — had been proposed before by others, especially Christian von Ehrenfels and William James. The research areas promoted by the Gestalt theorists, for example the so-called perceptual constancies, had all been developing for decades. Here Boring added a new twist to his conception of scientific development — the *Zeitgeist*, here defined as the totality of ideas available for communication among scientists at a given time. After a description of research along methodological lines similar in some ways to that of Gestalt theory, but conducted in a different laboratory at the same time, he concluded that "phenomenology was in the air . . . [Max] Wertheimer's insight of 1910 was the sort of event which was required by the times" (31).

However, when he summarized the results of the enormous literature generated by Gestalt psychology in its forty years of existence up to that time, Boring had to recognize that the result was, "all in all, a new chapter in psychology. Not all the items in it are new. . . . But the whole chapter is a new structure which is more than the sum of its parts." It was the Gestalt theorists who had drawn the full implications of these various methodological and research trends, insisted upon the necessary categorical changes, and thus restructured the discussion of entire areas of research in perception. Thus the constancies had been known and studied before, "but the recognition of their full significance is new. . . . By studying these researches you see the continuity of science; yet, when you stand away to get the perspective, you see that the new systematic setting of Gestalt psychology gave the facts a significance they had not had before." In his discussion of Max Wertheimer's paper on apparent motion, from which Gestalt psychology got its start, Boring went still further. Wertheimer's assertion that apparent motion is no different psychologically from real motion, and his proof that motion can be perceived without the perception of an object moving, became the starting points for an entire literature on the subject; "problems cannot be solved until they are discovered", Boring acknowledged (32). Yet Wertheimer's discovery or restructuring of the problem was directly dependent upon the epistemological perspective whose originality Boring had doubted. Clearly, all this was different from the mere 'selection and collocation' of older ideas. Boring had applied principles of Gestalt psychology in his account of its history.

Yet Boring managed, or attempted, to turn even these admissions into arguments for his view of science. Now that the change had been accomplished, he asserted, the movement was no longer needed. "Gestalt psychology has already passed its peak and is now dying of its own success by being absorbed into what is Psychology [*sic*]. If it already seems a little Americanized as compared with what it was in Berlin and Frankfurt, why that is only what should happen to the emigre who has to fit his basic values into a new culture" (33). Aside from the nationalistic arrogance in his equation of 'Psychology' with American psychology, Boring's statement was more a prediction than a fact. Today it is widely recognized that Gestalt psychology has largely retained its character as a self-contained school, with a small but devoted following, influencing the mainstream of American psychology in important ways, but not from within. More disturbing still for advocates of continuous progress is the fact that many of the qualitative relationships the Gestalt theorists discovered − in particular the so-called 'Gestalt laws', tendencies of the visual field to become organized spontaneously in specifiable ways − have not been easy to define operationally; but they are too important to ignore. They tend to lead an anomalous existence in textbooks of perception: their existence and their descriptive fruitfulness are acknowledged; but the theoretical problems they raise remain unsolved (34).

4. The Problems of Progress II: The Transition Away from Linear Continuity

The embarrassing existence, and persistence, of competing schools in a discipline with pretensions to natural-scientific status was dealt with less dogmatically by other authors of the period than by Boring; but the hope of continuous progress, and the attempt to present the discipline's history in this light persisted. A good example of this is the second most important history after Boring's, Gardner Murphy's *Historical Introduction to Modern Psychology* (1929). Murphy, somewhat younger than Boring, was trained at Columbia University in the more intellectually open, not to say eclectic, functionalist perspective of Robert S. Woodworth. There, and at New York University, where he then taught, psychology's independence of philosophy was taken for granted, and links to both education and medicine encouraged. However, as the title of his book indicated, Murphy's purpose was pedagogical; and he, too, emphasized pure over applied science. He sought "to present in rough chronological order the conquest by scientific method of one research field after another", deliberately excluded philosophical forms of psychology and problems of epistemology and value theory, and admitted applied psychology only when it had demonstrably led to "new psychological principles" (35). Where it proved impossible to exclude philosophy, as in the case of psychology in Germany at that time, he solved the problem by relegating the topic to a special section authored by a German-trained colleague, Heinrich Klüver.

Murphy showed more awareness of the role of general historical and cultural conditions in the history of science and of psychology than Boring did. Examples include references to the role of the voyages of discovery and the commercial revolution in the rise of modern science, and the significance of the German university and the inclusive conception of *Wissenschaft* in German thought about cognition. In the second edition (1949), Murphy added many more such examples. He noted that personality theory had emerged primarily from the exigencies of clinical work, that pressure from military sources during the Second World War for knowledge of the psychology of enemy peoples had been an important stimulus for the rise of culture and personality studies, and that the problem of insufficient personnel for the care of psychologically disturbed military men contributed to the establishment of clinical psychology (36).

It was especially in the second edition of Murphy's text that the contradiction between the ideal of linear progress and the fact of psychology's division into a multitude of competing schools and specialties emerged most clearly. Murphy did his best to retain a chronological framework, but admitted that he had had to rewrite the portions of the book dealing with the period after 1910, adding a second section on schools and a third on selected specialties to the first, chronologically organized section. Murphy could present new specialties as additional examples of "the conquest by scientific method of one research field after another", despite his recognition of the role of social and political pressure in their emergence. He could not do this with the schools. His treatment of Gestalt psychology is indicative of the problems this raised.

Though Murphy, like Boring, pointed to the philosophical and psychological antecedents of Gestalt theory, he did not find it useful to spend much time on such matters. Instead, he concentrated upon that which set Gestalt psychology apart from its predecessors, above all the attempt to go beyond declarations of principle and to treat the psychological experience of wholes and structures in a manner that could lead to further research. In addition, Murphy revealed his sensitivity to the role of 'social forces' in the history of science by linking the reception of Gestalt theory to the transfer of the Gestalt theorists and many of their students to America. During the 1930s, he said, one could find "dozens" of younger psychologists, especially on the east coast of the United States, for whom the categories of Gestalt theory made a difference in their research, and 'literally hundreds' of clinical and educational practitioners who were willing to mix Gestalt ideas eclectically with notions from behaviorism and psychoanalysis for their own, practical purposes. It was in this way that Gestalt psychology became "a vital new phase of Ameican psychology".

As a result, "every nook and cranny of psychology has been invaded with the concept of structure, or system or interdependence". However, though Gestalt theory had been 'gratefully received', it was not seen as the only solution to psychological problems. Instead, attempts have been made to show that "both piecemeal and organized responses occur". Murphy admitted that such eclecticism was not theoretically satisfying; the 'impasse' between the advocates of proceeding from larger to smaller units and the proponents of the opposite route had become *'the* fundamental issue' in both biological and psychological thinking. Perhaps, he said, the problem was unsolvable, due to "a fundamental difference in temperament" (37).

By recognizing the influence of social and political factors on the development of specialties and on the reception of theories in psychology, Murphy had acknowledged at least implicitly that allusions to the progress of science alone could not entirely account for its history. And in his treatment of one important school of thought in psychology, he had to admit that the metaphor of 'cycles of opinion' or 'swings of the pendulum' might be more accurate than any notion of linear progress. In his attempt to resolve the dilemma, Murphy voiced a hope which anticipated the wishes of many contemporary textbook writers:

The complexity of contemporary psychology suggests that its understanding may well require the use of that *genetic* method which it has itself repeatedly demanded in recent years. Whatever difficulties there may be in finding unity in the various psychological disciplines, there is at least one unity to which we can cling for orientation and perspective, for appreciation and synthesis; and this is the tranquil unity of history (38).

Murphy apparently hoped to demonstrate a venerable tradition for psychology, and at the same time to apply the notion of a common past as a tranquilizing drug to soothe tensions and make it possible for science to go on, "while the warfare of ideologies continues both inside and outside the laboratories and clinics . . . " (39).

Similar hopes were voiced by the writers of a new genre of textbooks which emerged in the 1930s, in which the reality of 'schools of psychology' was faced directly. The most popular of these was Robert S. Woodworth's *Contemporary Schools of Psychology* (1931). Taking a self-consciously "middle of the road" position, Woodworth claimed to see a kind of unity in diversity. Each school has noticed an aspect of psychology that is worth emphasizing, and "probably all" of them "are here to stay". It would be wise, therefore, to define the discipline broadly enough to include them all. Most sophisticated in its optimism, however, was the view of Edna Heidbredder. In her 1933 text, entitled *Seven Psychologies*, she acknowledged that psychology "has not yet made its great discovery". The mere Baconian gathering of facts had proven insufficient, and the field was now "assembling resources for a longer and harder struggle than at first seemed necessary". In this situation, it was useful to recognize that "science has not grown by following the method Bacon described — that is, by the steady amassing of data and the emergence of generalizations . . . More often than not, the insight precedes the systematic evidence, is tested rather than suggested by it". Competing systems and schools thus offer "tools for the acquisition of fact"; for all theory "runs ahead of the facts". By structuring the discussion, setting limits upon the kinds of material accepted, and offering rules of procedure for further research, they provide a necessary and convenient "scaffolding" for the construction of psychology's theoretical edifice. Once the building was complete, she hoped, the scaffolding could be removed (40).

Since the schools exist, these authors seemed to say, at least students should know about them. Apparently there was a demand for this kind of orientation; Woodworth's *Contemporary Schools of Psychology* reached eight editions by 1951. In a 1950 survey of 330 institutions offering under-graduate instruction in psychology, 13.9% listed at least one course in 'systems and schools', while 8.8% listed a course in 'history'. Of the fifty-four course titles listed more than once, these two ranked fourteenth and eighteenth, respectively, in frequency. Most interesting was that the course offerings were strongly concentrated in larger, academically oriented institutions; the percentages for the universities surveyed were 49.9 for 'systems and schools' and 45.6 for 'history'. Thus, nearly half of university departments offered undergraduate instruction in both topics. The figures for colleges of arts and sciences were 27.3 and 7.3, respectively, and those for practically oriented institutions, such as business schools, were lower still (41). When the size of the department permitted it, then, "the tranquil unity of history" seems to have been a desirable quality, at least in the academic sector of American psychology. When the books by Boring, Murphy and Woodworth were issued in revised editions between 1949 and 1951, there was a significant market for them; and when the history of psychology later became an organized specialty, there was a constituency for it.

5. 'A Neglected Area' Becomes a Specialty

The expansion of psychology both as an academic discipline and as a practical profession continued in the 1950s and accelerated in the 1960s. Growth outside the academic sector was more rapid, but the general expansion of higher education and the need to provide trained personnel for the expanding profession led to growth within in the academic sector, as well. In both areas the leading field at first was clinical psychology. The institutionalization of clinical training in the universities after the Second World War, against academic resistance, occurred under pressure from government funding agencies, especially the Veterans' Administration and (later) the National Institute of Mental Health. This shift in the discipline's relation to the federal and state governments was characteristic of the social sciences in general. In the 1960s, the fastest-growing fields were social and educational psychology, due in part to increased government funding for social programs connected with the 'war on poverty' (42).

These changes were accompanied by significant shifts in the intellectual landscape of the discipline. In experimental psychology, 'cognitivism', particularly approaches based on linguistics and on information theory, challenged the dominance of behavioristic learning theory; and a range of self-styled humanistic psychologies, many connected with various psychotherapies, rose in protest against both behaviorism and psychoanalysis, in some cases against academic psychology in general. Both the increasing availability of employment for trained psychologists outside the universities and the emergence of new lines of thought and work inside them were reflected in the organizational history of the American Psychological Association. The

Association is organized into 'Divisions' representing both academic and applied specialties. In 1949 there were twenty of these; by 1979 there were 40, with 85% of the increase occurring after 1960 (43). One of the first of the new divisions, Division 26, founded in 1966, represented the history of psychology.

The founding of Division 26 was part of a broader institutionalization process which lasted throughout the 1960s. The leadership of the 'History of Psychology Group', from which later organizations developed, reflected in part the leading role of clinical psychology in the discipline's postwar expansion. Its organizer, and the first president of Division 26, was Robert I. Watson, Sr., then director of the graduate program in clinical psychology at the University of Chicago. Among the co-organizers were a historian specializing in the history of psychoanalysis and a professor of psychiatry interested in the history of that discipline. Encouraged by the interest in the group's newsletter, Watson founded the *Journal of the History of the Behavioral Sciences* in 1965; in the same year, two other group members, both psychologists, founded the Archives of the History of American Psychology at the University of Akron in Akron, Ohio. After Watson moved to the University of New Hampshire, he established a graduate program for the training of scholars in the new specialty in 1967. Princeton University was the site of the first meeting of Cheiron: Society for the History of the Social and Behavioral Sciences, in 1969. Though Cheiron's organizers were mainly members of the original 'History of Psychology Group', and the organization remains dominated by psychologists, its membership overlaps only partially with that of Division 26; and there is significant representation from historians of science and from social scientists, especially sociologists and anthropologists. With the founding of Cheiron, the organization of "a community of specialists", as Watson described it, was complete (44).

On the face of it, there was no reason why the 'History of Psychology Group' could not have remained an informal gathering for a longer period. As Watson later recalled, when discussion began about the possibility of divisional organization within the A.P.A., there was opposition at first; for the advantages of informality seemed obvious. A younger member of the group decided the issue with the remark that formalization would make his interest in history seem more 'authentic' and "established as an accepted part of psychology" (45). The acceptance of this reasoning reflected on the one hand the existing, highly bureaucratized structure of the discipline, and on the other the anxieties which life in such a 'reputational organization' can evoke. Apparently younger workers feared criticism for spending time with such scholarly matters, instead of doing research more in line with the self-image of the discipline.

Once the decision to organize was taken, however, the constituency for it proved to be strong enough to ensure survival. Membership in Division 26 grew from 211 in 1966 to 459 in 1979. The latter figure remained a tiny fraction – 1.03% – of the total membership of the Association in that year, but identification with the specialty was, and is, strong. The members must vote *en bloc* to retain a seat on the Association's Council, and they do (46). It is questionable, however, whether this constituency should be called "a community of specialists", if specialized research is meant. Indirect evidence indicates that this is a teaching, not a research specialty. Of 393 colleges and universities responding to a survey taken in 1970, 290, or 74%, offered at least one course called 'History and Systems', 'Systems and Theories', or a similar name; the membership of Division 26 at the time was slightly more than 320. Enrollment in these courses expanded from 8,174 in 1966 to 13,522 in 1971; this was an increase of 65%, half again as much as the increase in total college and university enrollment in the same period (47).

This growing textbook market was soon served in a variety of ways: by reissues of older texts, such as those by Murphy, Woodworth and Flügel, in revised editions; by brief outline histories; and by full-length textbooks. Most of these appeared between 1964 and 1975, and some have since gone into several editions. These have been supplemented by sourcebooks, and by collections of secondary articles (48). Some of these books clearly reflect the use of history in inner-disciplinary conflict. Erwin A. Esper's *History of Psychology* (1964), for example, may be seen as a rear-guard action by an older defender of operationalist behaviorism. He wrote, he said, to "trace the sources of our protocol sentences", in particular to trace the ancestry of behaviorism as part of the continuous development of "a natural science of man", in which the "mentalism" of Titchener was merely "an interruption", and Gestalt psychology a sign of "faddism" (49).

The majority, however, were and are textbooks in the classic American mold. Their authors, less tendentiously limited than Boring, have tried to offer more or less comprehensive coverage of the development of psychological theory and research, past and present. This inclusiveness is based less upon a unified, analytical conception of either history or of psychology than upon the requirements of the market, the necessity of attracting as many 'adoptions' — purchases for classroom use — as possible. The hope behind these efforts was expressed succinctly by Josef Brožek at a summer institute for college teachers that he and Watson organized in 1968 — that history could offer a 'vertical synthesis' of a field threatening to become the prey of centrifugal forces (50).

The same view has since been expressed by many others. In a recent essay, Michael Wertheimer calls it "the justification for the inclusion of history of psychology courses in many undergraduate psychology curricula" (51). One textbook author, addressing his student readers directly, puts it this way:

the history of psychology is probably the only course in the psychology department curriculum that can help you to integrate the numerous areas and issues that compose modern psychology and recognize the interrelations among the various facts and theories. The framework that binds these different forms and approaches of contemporary psychology is the historical development of the field ... only by exploring its origins can the diversity of modern psychology become clear; its history explains its present status (52).

Clearly, the hope expressed by Gardner Murphy in 1949 is still alive. However, if such a claim is to be something other than a tautology — what happened, happened — and if the resulting texts are to be something other than chrono-logical catch-alls, or "systems and theories" texts in chronological clothing, then phrases such as 'historical development' and 'history explains' must have some sort of content. The belief that history can provide a 'vertical synthesis' of any discipline presupposes an organizing principle beyond chronology alone.

6. From Linear to Static Continuity: History as Ahistory

One plausible route to such a synthesis might have been a reaffirmation of the ideal of linear progress. However, the reasons Robert Watson offered to make the study and teaching of history attractive to psychologists had the effect of undermining that ideal. In his first article directed to that end, in 1960, Watson called the history of psychology 'a neglected area', pointing to the nearly complete absence of historical articles in major psychological journals.

Drawing upon George Sarton's history of science, he cited the thought of medieval Arab and Jewish thinkers, such as Maimonides, as sources of long neglected ideas about the mind that could be made useful in the present. "As yet", he said, "we have not looked back on the past from the perspective of today finding values for the present from the past. Old material is still to be seen in a new perspective." He stated the assumption behind such remarks clearly in a speech made in 1962: "it is true that a species, once extinct, cannot be resurrected. With ideas we are more fortunate; we can play Nature and revive an idea at will, and give it a second chance" (53).

Watson insisted that the history of science is cumulative; this is one of its great advantages over other kinds of history. But this does not mean that all that is potentially valuable survives into the present. Science is continually developed, and in the new theoretical contexts thus created, ideas or facts from the past may take on new relevance. The example Watson cited was the recent expansion of psychology into applied fields, particularly clinical work, his own specialty. The addition of these areas meant the incorporation of other pasts, especially aspects of the history of medicine, into "our past." Watson was careful to exclude any essential reform in the past of experimental psychology. This was "the solid core of our history, presumably less changed in this re-examination". Nonetheless, specialists in the history of psychology are needed. "If the history of psychology is to be rewritten in the light of contemporary interests, then in each age there must be those who sift the material again to bring out its value for that particular age. The selectivity of our interests demands this rewriting with every generation" (54).

Watson claimed to have this Sysiphian conception of the historian's role from George Sarton. Sarton, however, had referred to the way in which new theories may change the value placed upon older facts; the changes brought about in a discipline by the addition of new specialties, as in Watson's example, may not be the same as these wrought by the development of theory in an already established specialty. The only way that such parallels could hold was to assume the essential continuity of psychology as a subject over time, which is what Watson in fact did. Men had thought about the issues we now discuss under the heading of 'personality' since the time of Homer, he pointed out. With this he had removed all boundaries. Every realm of human thought could be sifted for its 'psychological' content, and that content appropriated more or less at will into the history of the discipline, as present interests dictate. This was no longer an evolutionary continuity of cumulative progress, but a static continuity of themes, or 'persistent problems', as Robert MacLeod later called them, along which curves of progress might move, but within which there could also be recurrent cycles of opinion of the kind to which Murphy had pointed (55).

Watson made it clear that history ought not to be "limited to a mere chronology of events or biographical chitchat", and recognized that "psychological contributions are embedded in the social context from which they emerge". But the idea of persistent problems tended to exclude any direct, critical examination of why specialties like clinical psychology emerged and entered the discipline when they did. Such events cannot be a matter of improved knowledge alone, if the issues involved have always existed. But Watson offered no way of approaching these issues systematically within his framework. As befit a trained clinician, his ultimate justification for the introduction of the new specialty was therapeutic. The influence of history is as inescapable and determinative as that of early childhood experience:

> History cannot be denied; the choice is between making it a conscious determinant of our behavior as psychologists, or allowing it to influence us unawares. There is no other alternative. Denying history has stultifying consequences. An unarticulated view of the past results in being passively subject to it. Narrow provincial, class and regional prejudices then substitute for a historically founded background (56).

The model of progress invoked here is not linear, either; it is that of the patient on the way to recovery. Perhaps Watson thought of the discipline as having a divided personality, which only historical therapy could heal. That, at least, was the logic of his position; and in the 1960s, as operationalist orthodoxy had begun to decline and specialization to increase, the diagnosis might well have been apposite. But he did not make it, at least not in this form.

An expression both of Watson's heritage as a clinician and of his essentially static view of history was his doctrine of 'prescriptivism'. He developed this approach in direct response to Thomas Kuhn's claim that disciplines such as psychology are pre-paradigmatic. He accepted this claim on its face, offering as evidence the persistence of schools and of national differences in psychological thinking; and he attempted to construct a conceptual framework for dealing with such disciplines. The result was a table of eighteen pairs of categorical parameters, ranging from 'Mechanism' and 'Vitalism' to

'Objectivism' and 'Subjectivism'. In Watson's view, such 'isms' function not as logical axioms or rational directives for theorizing, but as orienting or attitudinal 'prescriptions', which are normative in the sense that "they tell us how the psychological scientist must or should behave". He thought that theories could be rated by assigning them values along these parameters on a point scale. Applied to recent American psychology, 'prescriptivism' yielded a subtle, layered characterization. The combination of Determinism (versus Indeterminism), Naturalism (versus Supernaturalism), Physicalism (versus Mentalism) and Monism (versus Dualism) was, according to Watson, an unchallenged part of the definition of psychology in the United States, while Functionalism (versus Structuralism), Objectivism (versus Subjectivism), 'Quantitativism' (versus 'Qualitativism'), Environmentalism (versus Hereditarianism) and 'Nomotheticism' (versus 'Idiographicism') are dominant prescriptions, for which there exist opposing, minority prescriptions (57).

There is much that is interesting in 'prescriptivism'. The idea that the various 'isms' are prescriptive injunctions rather than logical presuppositions or guides to thought might well reflect the way in which doctrines like naturalism and determinism have actually operated in history more accurately than philosophies of science centered exclusively around rationality. Yet it is unclear just how such an approach can account for change and development in the meaning and use of categories over time. The category "Mentalism", for example, could be applied to the thought of Plato, Socrates, Aristotle, various medieval philosophers, Kant, Wilhelm Wundt and Gestalt psychology; but it would be absurd to say that the designation meant the same thing in each case. Clearly the substantive, analytical use of these categories presupposed adequate definitions for them, a task not always easily solved even by trained philosophers.

Although Watson called his approach "a social psychology of the past", the use of paired parameters was taken from the personality inventories which are the stock in trade of the clinical or consulting psychologist. The notion of ratable parameters suffered under the same weaknesses here as it did in personality theory. All that can actually be concluded with such a method is that a high rating on one set of parameters is correlated with a low or high rating on another set. The idea that certain connections might be more intimate than this, rationally or emotionally, cannot be accounted for in this way. Nor can the method explain why specific combinations of prescriptions occur in particular times and places. The best one could do would be to rate a number of theories from a given period and then say that it was 'an age of' naturalism, or determinism. This would be little more than another way of invoking Boring's reified *Zeitgeist* by another name. The essentially ahistorical character of Watson's measuring device reflected the similarly ahistorical presuppositions of the discipline from which he had adapted it.

Watson insisted that his table of prescriptions was more than a classificatory device: "these prescriptions were and are part of the intellectual equipment of psychologists", he asserted (58). In fact, however, it was best understood as a convenient way of arranging material for pedagogical presentation. 'Prescriptivism' has been taken seriously by historians of psychology primarily in the pedagogical field. The validity of the parameters has been tested not upon the theories they were intended to describe, but on teachers and students engaged in studying those ideas.

In one test, Alfred Fuchs and Charles Kawash obtained ratings of five theoretical orientations – behaviorism, psychoanalysis, Titchenerian structuralism, functionalism, and Gestalt psychology – from sixty-eight members of Division 26. Using the list of categories singly, not as sets of paired opposites, they found that judges were able to rate the schools on a seven-point scale "with a satisfactory degree of reliability". Apparently they assumed that this alone sufficed to support the claim that the results were also accurate descriptions of the schools themselves. But they made no control measurements, such as, for example, asking the judges to rate unidentified statements from the systems in question. There was thus no way of counteracting the suspicion that the characteristics found were those which had already been assigned to the schools in question by generations of textbooks, and passed on by the members of Division 26 with or without knowledge of the primary sources. Fuchs and Kawash admitted the "possibility that the emphases only reflect current attitudes toward the schools", but contended that this was a danger in any kind of historical assessment (59).

Others have attempted to use prescriptive dimensions as a form of pedagogical quality control, again with ambiguous results. Two leading textbook writers, Melvin Marx and William Hillix, asked graduate students to rate the schools just named. Though ratings agreed for most of the schools, those for Gestalt psychology did not. Watson had said that the parameters Molarism (versus molecularism), Subjectivism and Nativism (versus empiricism) were 'salient' for Gestalt theory. Marx and Hillix selected Molarism, Centralism (versus peripheralism) and Qualitativism, while their students chose Molarism, Qualitativism and Irrationalism, the parameters their teachers would have selected for psychoanalysis (60). Similar tests were subsequently carried out by Abraham S. Luchins, a proponent of Gestalt psychology, with students in his psychology courses. Students were offered the test twice, once before and once after studying the theoretical and research work of the Gestalt psychologists from primary sources. The second time they selected many of the same terms as before, but selection of one of the terms originally paired by Watson did not involve rejection of its 'opposite'. Luchins not only questioned the advisability of using paired opposites, but implied that the rating system in general was at best too rough, and at worst only perpetuated the stereotypes of textbook writers, thus "keeping the students from understanding Gestalt psychology" (61).

Evidently, proper pedagogical application of Watson's 'prescriptivism' required not only that the parameters be adequate descriptions of their objects, but also that teachers and students be adequately informed about both — requirements for which there was no control in the method itself. The method became particularly questionable when it was applied to Gestalt psychology, an approach which sought to radically revise such stereotypical parameters. In this case, at least, there was no substitute for study of the primary sources.

7. The Shift in Scholarship: Forms of Critical History

Whatever the problems of Watson's perspective on the history of psychology, it was largely through the groups he helped to organize that the topic ceased to be a 'neglected area'. Two quantitative indicators may give at least a rough picture of the extent and the character of the publications which have since appeared. A survey of article listings in the standard psychological reference work, *Psychological Abstracts*, for selected years from 1960 to 1980 yields the results displayed in table one. These figures do not represent a complete count of historical articles on the history of psychology, even for the years indicated; articles which appeared in historical or sociological journals, for example, were not abstracted. Nonetheless, the upward character of the trend is clear enough.

It is also clear that the *Journal of the History of the Behavioral Sciences* is not the only outlet for this growing literature. In fact, subtracting the number of articles in that journal, which varied from year to year, yields a smoother curve. Other journals, most notably the *American Psychologist*, organ of the American Psychological Association, have opened their pages increasingly to historical papers. It cannot be said, however, that the discipline is about to become 'historical', as has been claimed in a different sense for sociology. The share of historical articles in the total output increased only until 1970, and has since remained static. This will no doubt change when the indexes for 1981 and 1982 register the flood of Wundt and other centennial literature that appeared in 1980 and 1981.

TABLE I

Articles on historical topics for selected sample years, 1960–1980*

Year	Psychoanalysis	General psychology (Incl. Clinical)	Psychiatry	Total	%
1960				15	0.18
1965	11 (1)	37 (14)		48 (15)	0.29
1970	13 (1)	49 (28)	22 (4)	84 (33)	0.38
1975	18 (1)	45 (17)	13	76 (18)	0.30
1980	24	44 (13)	13	81 (13)	0.30

Remarks:

The figures were obtained by scanning the rubrics 'History and Biography', 'Theory and Systems' and 'General' for the years 1960, 1965, and 1970, and the rubric 'History and Philosophies and Theories' for the years 1975 and 1980. This was supplemented by pursuing the listings under the index heading 'History of Psychology' for each year.

Of articles listed under 'Theories and Systems', only those were included which treated historical aspects – e.g., systematic articles about Freud, but not articles about the current state of psychoanalysis. In all cases the text of the abstract, not the title, was the guide to selection.

Only English-language articles in American or Canadian journals were counted; however, 'per cent' is the percentage of all abstracts for the given year, regardless of language. Obituaries were not counted.

The numbers in parentheses refer to articles published in the *Journal of the History of the Behavioral Sciences*.

* *Source: Psychological Abstracts*, Vols. 34, 39, 44, 53/54, 63/64.

At least as significant as the number of contributions is their interdisciplinary distribution, particularly the level of participation by historians and historians of science. One indicator of this is a survey taken by the author of the affiliation of contributors to the *Journal of the History of the Behavioral Sciences* for the years 1977 through1981. Of the 121 articles dealing with the history of psychology published in these years − 73.4% of the total − 74, or 61.2%, are by psychologists, and 47, or 38.8%, by non-psychologists; of the latter, 24 are by historians or historians of science. Members of these disciplines have also contributed a high proportion, probably the bulk of the monograph literature in the field. One recent account lists a total of 36 'representative' dissertations in the history of psychology since 1960, without pretending to be complete; of the sixteen of these that have appeared in book form, fourteen are by historians or historians of science. If we add to this the series of biographical and bibliographical reference works, guides to archival sources and the like which have appeared since the early 1970s, it is clear that a substantial body of publications and scholarly apparatus is now available for the specialist in the history of psychology (62).

Three recent trends from this literature will be discussed here. All are located within psychology, at least in a technical sense, and all have specific inner-disciplinary roots and goals. Though representatives of only two of the three trends invoke the term, we can describe them as forms of critical historiography; for their implications are critical for and of the history of the discipline as traditionally practiced and purveyed.

The earliest trend chronologically is the reassessment of the founding father of experimental psychology, Wilhelm Wundt, that resulted when scholars began to reread his work in the original. They discovered a philosopher and scientist quite different from the one portrayed in standard histories. In an article summarizing the results of this research up to 1975, Arthur Blumenthal, a cognitive psychologist specializing in psycholinguistics, listed a number of conventional textbook characterizations of Wundt which had turned out to be false. In many such accounts, he contended, Wundt is presented as philosophically a dualist, methodologically an introspectionist, and systematically an elementaristic classifier of psychic 'contents' who denied the role of an active agent in psychical life.

In fact, as Blumenthal showed, Wundt called his system 'voluntarism'; and the volitional and motivational processes he assembled under the rubric of 'apperception', including attention, were "a central, primary theme in Wundt's psychology". Examination of Wundt in the original showed that his psychology was as much one of 'process' as of 'content'. He expressly rejected the billiard-ball conception of mental 'elements', employing instead the concept of 'creative synthesis'. The real source of the textbook view of Wundt, Blumenthal claimed, was Edward Bradford Titchener. Uninterested himself in volitional processes, which were inconsistent with his own, neopositivist philosophy of science, Titchener simply dropped them from his system, and from his account of Wundt's system, as well. Titchener made Wundt appear to be a Lockean empiricist; in fact, Blumenthal claimed, his thought owed much more to the German idealist tradition (63).

Blumenthal's purpose in reassessing Wundt was not exclusively historical. He pointed to six current trends in psychology, especially in cognitive theory, "that could be viewed as reconstructions of Wundtian psychology in modern clothing". Wundt's emphasis on volition, for example, resembled modern work on 'cognitive control'; his treatment of the range of limits of attention resembled contemporary research on the role of selective attention in human information processing; and his theoretical work on the higher mental processes, particularly language, reminded Blumenthal of Chomskian psycholinguistics. Blumenthal even substituted terminology from Wundt's textbooks for current jargon, and noted the wide application currently being made of reaction-time measurements of the kind originally used in Wundt's laboratory. The inferences about 'information-processing' made from these measurements, he said, follow much the same logic Wundt employed for his own theorizing. "Strange as it may seem", he concluded, "Wundt may be more easily understood today than he could have been just a few years ago", precisely because of "the current milieu of cognitive psychology" (64).

Blumenthal's approach is vulnerable to a *tu quoque* rebuttal. He, too, has appropriated his own founding father, selecting the aspects of Wundt's system that make him seem more attractive to current science in a manner little different from that of Boring. However, when he claimed that Wundt's methods and even his terminology could all be applied today, he engaged in an implicit but nonetheless radical critique of precisely the scientists he sought to flatter. The implication, perhaps unintended, was that cognitive science has made no real progress in one hundred years, but has only reinvented the wheel. Thus it is not surprising that this aspect of Blumenthal's critique has been received with scepticism. But his reassessment of Wundt, coming as it did just before the centennial rites, marked the beginning of an important shift in psychology's view of its history.

Subsequent research has led to a nearly complete revision of Boring's account, not only of Wundt, but of much of nineteenth-century psychological thinking. In his desire to write a neopositivist psychologist's, and not a historian's history, the revisionists claimed, Boring failed to clarify the real philosophical basis of Wundt's system, particularly his doctrines of apperception and the immanent teleology of psychical life, which are rooted in the thought of Leibniz. As Kurt Danziger argued, there were not one but 'two traditions of psychology', one Leibnizian, of which Wundt was one of many inheritors, and one Lockean, in which Titchener had been steeped at Oxford before he studied with Wundt. Titchener, Danziger suggested, constructed a unitary line of succession from one tradition to the other in order to trade on Wundt's reputation; and Boring carried on this distortion in order to inherit the mantle of the great (65). But there was more to this than a question of two scientific reputations. As Blumenthal alleged in a later essay, only a few of Wundt's numerous American students understood the master's system. Most of them brought rather different, inductivist and pragmatic philosophical presuppositions with them to Leipzig. They took from Wundt only the experimental techniques, not the theoretical framework in which they were embedded. Thus, the psychology that was institution-alized in America bore only a superficial resemblance to that of the founding father (66).

Additional research by historians of science has undermined Boring's line of continuity from the other end. R. Steven Turner has shown, for example, that Hermann Helmholtz was anything but the proto-positivist Boring made him out to be. His mechanistic assumptions about nervous transmission were accompanied by a philosophy of mind drawn to an importart extent from the idealist Fichte. This dualism was not carried forward, but rejected by Wundt in favor of a psychologistic monism. Both were ignored or upended by the following generation of experimenting psychologists in Germany, which found more phenomenological methods and neopositivist concepts of science more congenial (67). Other scholars, particularly David Leary, have pointed to additional lines of philosophical thinking, ignored or misunder-stood by Boring, that fed into the conceptual development of scientific psychology (68). The critical implications of all this are clear. American psychologists, the revisionists claim, used Wundt's techniques for their own, more narrowly pragmatic purposes, and ignored or failed to understand their philosophical and systematic underpinnings. Historians of psychology, themselves students of these positivist repudiators of Wundt, helped them to cover their tracks by depicting a positivist Wundt, or by arrogantly declaring the aspects of Wundt's system that did not fit the new mold to be irrelevant. The continuous ascent Boring and others constructed from philosophical superstition to experimental science turns out to be more like a zig-zag from one kind of scientific philosophy to another.

Much of this new scholarship is based on the study or restudy of primary sources. To prepare their students for work of this kind is the aim of William Woodward and David Leary, Robert Watson's successors as co-directors of the graduate program in the history and theory of psychology at the University of New Hampshire. Woodward states that the program will contribute to the writing of "a critical historiography of psychology." However, he does not mean social criticism, but "a critical approach to knowledge – involving the pursuit of limited goals in keeping with modern historical scholarship". Leary and Woodward received their doctorates in intellectual history and history of science, respectively; in the graduate seminars at New Hampshire, their students carry out carefully guided library research with the aim of producing publishable articles, in a manner no different from that of history or history of science seminars. Woodward joins Thomas Kuhn in criticizing older histories of science and of psychology as 'Whig history', and calls for a more sophisticated appreciation of the contexts of scientific discovery. However, the New Hampshire program is clearly not intended to radically alter psychology, but to help it to enrich its knowledge of itself by professionalizing its historiography. The resulting historical studies "typically reveal a complex interaction over time of biographical, social and intellectual factors; by analogy, the student comes away with a truer sense of the development of his own professional identity". The hope is that 'critical history' will lead to "an expansion of his methodological horizon" and "increased sophistication about the tradition he belongs to" for other psychologists, as well (69).

Students from the New Hampshire program seem to have developed especially keen eyes for the interaction between philosophical presuppositions and psychological theory. Richard High, for example, has pointed to the origins of William James' perceptual realism in the proto-phenomenological philosophy of the Englishman Shadworth Hodgson, thus helping to end the exclusive preoccupation with the German-American nexus in the history of psychology once criticized by Robert Young. Lawrence Smith has published a subtle, detailed analysis of the relations between leading theories in experimental psychology and neorealist and logical positivist philosophy in the first half of this century. Work of this kind is a salutary corrective to a narrow, disciplinary view in which only the "psychological" aspects of older theories are selected for treatment, without regard to their intellectual contexts (70).

But here, too, as in the reassessment of Wundt, the true implications have been critical in a more fundamental sense. As Smith's work reveals, psychology attained scientific stability in the 1930s and 1940s only by adopting specific philosophical principles and methodological assumptions, particularly operationalism. If this is so, however, then the discipline's theoretical credentials must be questioned or revised when the philosophy becomes outmoded or is refuted. Just this implication has been drawn by David Leary and Stephan Toulmin. Psychologists, they claim, have subscribed to a "cult of empiricism"; they continue to hold onto logical positivist 'physicalism' and operationalism "in a manner that can only be called wish-fulfilling or fetishistic", long after the philosophical advocates of these views have pulled back from or completely rejected their most extreme positions. Psychology's best hope, they maintain, is to loosen such rigidities and return to the original source of psychological knowledge, 'experience' (71).

The critical side of this message is substantially the same as that of Walter Weimer, cited at the beginning of this paper. However, such an analysis raises the question of why psychologists continued to hold such an ideology of science for so long. Words like 'fetishistic' and 'cult' alone are hardly satisfactory explanations. They concede the argument too easily to those who would contend that there is no rational explanation for psychology's history, or that the only alternative to scientific rationality is irrationality. Perhaps the answer lies elsewhere, not in the intellectual but in the social context of psychology. This, at least, is the argument of a different group of critical historians.

This rather different kind of critical history came out of the political and intellectual ferment of the 1960 and 1970s. Compared with the work that emerged from the German student movement, much of the American 'radical psychology' of this period was ahistorical, in that it did not single out the historical development of psychology for particular criticism (72). However, historically oriented criticism was by no means absent. Much of it focused upon history's sins of omission, the exclusion of the contributions of non-white and women psychologists. However, it was not always clear whether an *ad hominem* argument was meant — because traditional history has been written by white males, it was therefore racist and sexist — or whether a more fundamental critique of both the discipline and its history was also intended (73). In the end, this work has been absorbed rather easily into mainstream scholarship. The traditional definition of a 'contribution' was left untouched, and the idea that history can be written in an additive fashion, as a collection of 'contributions', remained unquestioned.

Others have used a historical approach to attack the intellectual and social structures of the discipline more directly. Much of this work might be called 'ideology detection'. Though such a line of thinking could easily function as weaponry in inner-disciplinary battles, it is a reversible weapon, and has therefore been used most often by outsiders. Thus sociologists Hilary Rose and Stephan Rose have pointed to the ways in which neurobiology expresses and supports racism, publishing in a new journal for cognitive psychology, while political theorist Susan Buck-Morss has pointed to sources of ideology in cognitive psychology itself, especially in the work of Piaget (74). By far the favorite object of attack has been intelligence testing, the technique with which the discipline first attained public acceptance. In so far as such criticism has dealt with the histography of psychology at all, however, the sins excoriated have again been sins of omission. The accusation, largely justified, has been that standard histories simply gloss over or completely ignore the use of testing to support race and class bias, when they do not proclaim testing as a scientific success story (75).

The situation is different for the work of an informal group of 'critical historians' within the Cheiron society itself. Like the other critics, their goal is to show the ways in which psychology has served as an instrument of domination in particular times and places. However, the leading members of the group are social psychologists, and much of their work is a response to the intellectual and political crises that field has undergone in the 1960s and 1970s. On the one hand, the liberal consensus which had dominated the field since the 1940s — the hope of improving society by detecting and eliminating sources of social conflict – was severely shaken by the racial disturbances of the 1960s. On the other hand, the heavy involvement of social psychologists in the ameliorative social programs of the 1960s, which were created in part to deal with those disturbances, did not produce the intended results with the expected speed. The response of these critical historians has been to reconstruct the history of their specialty. Lorenz Finison has concentrated upon the political history of American psychology, especially organized psychology's attempts to deal with the employment crisis brought about by the Depression, and with the group of radical psychologists which came together in the "Society for the Psychological Study of Social Issues". He thus reminded social psychologists that the liberal consensus was not all there was to social psychology's past; its beginnings as a specialty had actually been marked by a different sort of political commitment (76).

The Kansas social psychologist Franz Samelson made the critique of historiography explicit in a 1974 essay. For him, psychology's history consists of a tightly held set of 'origin myths', idols of the tribe steadfastly maintained to fulfill the requirements of recognition and status. Gordon Allport's standard account of the history of social psychology, for example, proclaimed Auguste Comte as the discipline's founding father. In order to do this, however, he proceeded rather selectively, remembering Comte's positivism and his proclamation of *science morale*, but ignoring Comte's rejection of most of the defining features of modern behavioral science, including specialized research, probability theory and individualism. Allport also repressed Comte's assertion that *science morale* was not a mere method but a 'true anthropology', only a step in the way to the religion of humanity, which would change not only science but society as well. Only by stressing the methodological aspects of positivism and driving the ideological component underground did his successors obtain what Comte could not – "acceptance by the temporal powers, admission into the academy". Only then could social psychologists look back with pride upon their founding father. Citing Thomas Kuhn's critique of traditional history of science as "largely a by-product of pedagogy", Samelson recommended that historians of the field take note of recent research in the history of science and cease writing 'Whig history' (77).

Samelson continued this exposure of "origin myths" in his research on intelligence testing, social psychology and the origins of behaviorism. In his work on the army intelligence tests, already cited, he used extensive archival research to show that neither the role of psychologists in the passage of restrictive immigration legislation, harped upon by critics, nor the effectiveness of the tests themselves, insisted upon by apologists, was as unambiguous as previously thought. The tests were not a scientific triumph; nor was their use a matter of "the ideological intrusion of nativist, racist and illiberal prejudices . . . into an otherwise objective, value-free (and liberal) discipline". This view is common to the defenders of the tests, but also widely held by their critics, who often seem to think that the influence of the social context is confined to the past. Many of the testers saw themselves as progressive liberals; and once the immigration legislation was passed, psychologists shifted soon enough from the goal of keeping out unwanted peoples to that of smoothing out conflicts among the groups that were there (78).

What persisted was the belief in the validity of the tests; but their acceptance into the liberal consensus of social psychology, despite criticism, meant the equation of reality with measurability. This

transformed the idea of intelligence, itself a descendant of the idea of reason, from an amorphous, creative force to an 'objective', yet clearly value-laden dimension of individual differences consisting essentially, or 'operationally' of getting the right answer on more or less clever little problems. This narrowed and concretized idea of intelligence has permeated our social existence and become part of our social heritage; it has even been absorbed by most critics, who might question specific aspects of the tests, the assumption of inheritance and other technical details ... From this perspective, the contribution of intelligence testing was only a small part of the effort to rationalize and bureaucratize the world, to make human beings more manageable (79).

Samelson's critical knife cut deep. While worshipping the cult of method, psychologists had "opportunistically" taken the ideas to be cast into empirical form from the environment, "without carefully scrutinizing their substance, origins and implications". Put in this way, his critique could apply to all of the social sciences, and not only to them. However, his was, in the end, an attack upon the fundamental premise of scientific psychology in this century:

Theoretical preferences for behavior genetics, behaviorism, or 'cognitive theories' may not make all that much difference except in generating esoteric controversies, as long as the shared goal of the 'new' psychology remains, as it has been in this century, the prediction and (social) control of its subjects (80).

Given this line of argument, it was only consistent that Samelson also attacked the 'origin myths' surrounding environmentalist behaviorism, as well as hereditarian positions on intelligence testing. He and a colleague, Ben Harris, took another look at the famous studies made by John B. Watson of the child 'Little Albert', reported in textbooks to this day as the first scientific conditioning studies on human beings. After reviewing the films Watson made of the experiments and comparing them with his published reports and then again with textbook accounts, Samelson and Harris maintained that the experiments were in no sense classic, or even very carefully conducted; much less were they sufficient support for the vast conclusions Watson drew from them, and subsequent textbook writers drew from Watson. Samelson saw a similar urge to manipulate results to confirm cherished beliefs in the case of the British tester Cyril Burt, who fudged the data of his twin studies on a grand scale, less out of deliberate dishonesty than in the belief that the theory had to be right, regardless of what the data said. True, it could not be shown that either Watson or the textbook writers had manipulated their data in the same egregious manner as Burt. Nonetheless there was evidently a strong need to proclaim an ideology of "prediction and control", and to organize both scientific findings and historical accounts around it (81).

According to these critical historians, then, the function of psychology in the past has been the production not of science, but of saleable ideology. The implication, openly stated by Samelson, was "that the shared assumptions and problem definitions of today's psychologists and/or the social consequences of their work also incorporate fundamental ideological biases". The question must be raised, however, whether the cult of method is merely a means to an end. Though the critical historians sometimes cite Marx and the Frankfurt school, it cannot be said that their work is explicitly shaped by any theory of society, or of scientific development. They do not show as much systematic concern as their German counterparts for the changes in socioeconomic structure which lie behind the events they describe. The logical conclusion of their position is an extreme relativism, or social determinism, which would deny the possibility of scientific status to psychology altogether. They have been careful to avoid taking this step, and also to avoid taking a dogmatically Marxist position; but the reductionistic implications of the 'manipulation' model are nonetheless obvious. By confining themselves to relatively clear-cut cases, the critical historians may have made life somewhat easy for themselves. Though they are obviously aware of them, their approach has not yet done sufficient justice to the mediating structures that intervene between science and society, particularly the social and institutional situations in which science is produced. Several papers given at the 1982 meeting of the Cheiron society focus upon such situations.

These structures are also the central concern of the Toronto psychologist Kurt Danziger. His participation in the reassessment of Wundt, already cited, is part of a larger study of the institutionalization of psychology in both Europe and the United States. On a macrostructural level, Danziger treats the institutionalization of psychology in the universities as part of a long struggle for a "monopoly over the production of psychological knowledge", similar to the academic professionalization of other disciplines. However, he recognizes that this process took different forms, closely related to the different social and political situations of the university in various countries. In Germany, where the universities were oriented primarily to training members of the bureaucracy and the so-called 'free professions', psychologists were unable or unwilling at first to demonstrate a unique social function that would have brought state support; they therefore remained affiliated with philosophy far longer than their American colleagues. The Americans, participating in an expanding university system with both a different internal organization and a different relationship to business and government, committed them-selves more rapidly and wholeheartedly to a technocratically oriented concept of science (82).

On the microstructural level, Danziger applies concepts from sociolin-guistics and role theory to the history and institutionalization of the experi-menter-subject relationship. Wundt's psychological experiment, for example, was not simply an adaptation of physiological and psychophysical techniques, but also a reproduction of the German academic environment, in which professor and student were seen as active collaborators in research. In this setting, the roles of experimenter and subject were ambiguous, even inter-changeable. The actual prototype of the modern, manipulative relationship, Danziger argues, is the experimentation with hypnotized subjects carried out in France under the aegis of a medical model of the *sujet* not as thinking subject, but as suffering patient. Once the institutionalization process was completed at both levels, Danziger contends, these structures took on a life and acquired a history of their own. But this does not mean that they became somehow separate from the societies in which they were embedded. To participate adequately in Wundt's experiments, for example, it was not necessary to be a trained psychologist; but it was important to be a member of the educated elite which shared the common assumptions about the world and the conduct of science that lay behind such forms of knowledge-generation (83).

Danziger's work is not yet complete, but its message is clear. In the institutional history of science, too, linear development cannot be assumed and then read backward from the present into the past. Instead, the emergence of both scientific ideas and of scientific roles is a complex process of social construction, embedded not only in traditions of thought but also in specific sociocultural contexts. The development of such constructions can only be understood by studying these contexts individually and in depth. But Danziger does not mean to advocate historicist relativism. The experimenter-subject relationship, for example, has been a significant issue in psychology for the past two decades. Danziger believes that the knowledge that there have been other ways of generating valid psychological knowledge, and the realization that current forms are not the products of ineluctable scientific progress, make it possible to think more freely about alternative models. Partly in order to accomplish this, Danziger and others have set up a doctoral program in the history of psychology at York University, Toronto; cooperation with specialists in the philosophy of the social sciences is planned.

Though he has criticized Boring's history, Danziger has not directly attacked other 'textbook histories'. But the implications of his work and that of the other critical historians are evident. Both scientific psychology and its textbook history have been subliminally and openly influenced by a complex hierarchy of intellectual and social determinants. Not only 'justificationist' history, but any purely intellectual history is incapable in principle of grasping these determinants. Both social and intellectual contexts must be reconstructed in their interrelation in order to gain adequate historical perspective. Danziger's attempt to develop such a reconstruction may lead to a genuinely critical history of psychology that would also be a contribution to both the sociology and the social history of science.

8. Conclusion: A Problematic Maturity

Despite the contraction now taking place in psychology and in the other social sciences as a result of the changed political and economic situation, the history of psychology in the United States shows no sign of disappearing. In fact, it is currently enjoying something of a boom. If we can believe the claims of specialists in the field, "the history of psychology has come into its own at last" (84). A pause for reflection, including historical reflection, seems indicated for many reasons. Psychology is currently experiencing a twofold crisis – a crisis of coherence as a discipline, and a crisis of confidence in its relation with society and the state. The discipline's self-selected centennial has provided an opportunity for its historians to participate in the reflection process.

Whether psychology's historians will be able to provide much help may be questioned; for the historiography of psychology, too, faces a two-fold challenge. On the one hand, a growing body of broadly informed scholarship has undermined the disciplinary triumphalism of earlier accounts. Institutional autonomy, this work shows, did not eliminate psychology's intellectual and methodological dependence upon philosophy and the natural sciences. These results might be easy enough to accept, in themselves; for they indicate that, with respect at least to the role of metaphysical commitments in scientific thought and practice, the history of psychology is little different from that of physics. On the other hand, additional work by equally well-informed, socially critical historians and psychologists has presented a picture of the discipline and its relation to society rather different from that conveyed in most textbooks. If they were accepted, these results would fundamentally challenge both the scientific competence and the social allegiance of psychologists. Though the critical emphases may be different in each case, these two challenges converge at two points: in their attack upon operationalism, and in their demand that both the linear and the static models of continuity be replaced with a historically sophisticated contextualism.

How has this demand been received? Can its acceptance be reconciled with the demand of the college textbook market for a pedagogically useful 'vertical synthesis'? It is too soon to give a clear answer to such questions; the reception of these results is only beginning. We can, however, take a brief look at three of the incorporation strategies that have been attempted thus far.

One strategy might be called that of adding a chapter, or immaculate incorporation. This is skillfully employed in *The First Century of Experimental Psychology*, edited by Eliot Hearst under the auspices of the Psychonomic

Society, the leading organization of research psychologists, in commemoration of the discipline's centennial. The editor calls the book "an experiment". Historians, he states, are generally not "productive experimentalists"; here, some of the latter are given a chance to reflect upon the history of their specialties. Perhaps the results will bring the two groups together, "to fight or collaborate" (85). This comment indicates clearly that the division of labor between scientists and historians that has long since occurred in the natural sciences has also taken place in psychology; but it also indicates a certain ambivalence about accepting it. The volume includes eleven chapters devoted to the histories of research specialties from learning and physiological psychology to perception and cognition, and a historical overview by the editor. In addition, there is a chapter by Richard Littman on 'The Social Context of Modern Psychology'. Relying in part on Danziger's work, Littman surveys clearly and competently the role of institutions like the German university and the concepts of science institutionalized there in the development of experimental psychology. However, there is little or no trace of this perspective in any of the other chapters. Apparently, for many research psychologists, history is only worth the trouble if it can be a self-portrait of the present projected into the past.

More frequent than the strategy of adding a chapter is the strategy of mixed incorporation, in which the role of cultural contexts is at least acknowledged, but that of social and institutional factors either ignored or only briefly and clumsily treated. In the most recent edition of his college text, for example, Duane Schultz cites some of the new literature on the intellectual contexts of psychology, and attempts to work the results into his account. The result is a less linear, but still 'evolutionary' view of history. The various schools of psychology are depicted as emerging from one another in an "orderly developmental pattern" of movement and counter-movement. Thus functionalism, behaviorism and Gestalt psychology all "evolve" in reaction to Titchenerian 'structuralism', psychoanalysis and behaviorism in turn "spawn" schools of their own, and humanistic psychology reacts in protest against them. However, the pattern remains largely one of ideas begetting ideas. The thought that the rise of these movements might have had as much to do with changes in intellectual or social settings as with the character of previous theory is acknowledged, with a bow to the *Zeitgeist*, but not seriously pursued. Thus, for example, when Schultz asks why

experimental physiology developed most extensively in Germany, his answer
is a reference to "the German temperament" for the patient collection and
ordering of facts (86).

Last but not least, there is a strategy we might call friendly incorporation,
exhibited in an article by Michael Wertheimer, a former president of Division 26, entitled 'Historical Research: Why?' Wertheimer acknowledges
that historians tend to concentrate more upon the "social, cultural and
political milieu" in their work, while psychologists prefer a history of ideas
approach. He suggests that the two ought to complement one another;
"research psychologists had better be aware of the social, intellectual and
political context of their current research, lest it be unduly influenced by
such extrinsic factors". Thus the study of history "can become the great
liberator, the means of removing ourselves from blind adherence to the subtle,
insidious and often powerful matters of course [*Selbstverständlichkeiten*]
that make up the *Zeitgeist* within which we work" (87).

Whether historical scholarship can be so easily functionalized, or socially
critical historiography so easily rendered harmless, may be questioned. Instead, the tension among producing scientists, textbook writers and teachers,
and historical scholars from inside and outside the discipline is likely to
persist. What is missing, as yet, is an equally productive tension between
philosophers and historians of psychology, similar to that obtaining between
historians and philosophers of science in general.

Acknowledgments

The writing of this paper has been supported in part by the German Research
Council Project 'Psychology in Exile', administered by the Johann-Gutenberg-
Universität, Mainz, under the direction of Prof. Werner D. Fröhlich. Requests
for reprints should be sent to the author at his private address, Wilmers-
dorferstrasse 152a, D-1000 Berlin 10, Germany.

The letters to and from E. G. Boring are cited by permission of the Harvard
University Archives, Clark A. Elliott, Associate Curator.

I would also like to thank Ulfried Geuter, Christiane Hartnack, Siegfried
Jaeger, and William Woodward, who read the manuscript and offered valuable
comments and suggestions for improvement.

Notes and References

1. Robert M. Young, 'Scholarship and the History of the Behavioral Sciences', *Hist. Sci.* 5 (1966), p. 18.
2. Walter B. Weimer, *Notes on the Methodology of Scientific Research*, Hillsdale: N.J., Erlbaum, 1979, esp. pp. 220, 223.
3. James G. Blight, 'Toward the Reconstruction of Psychology and its Historiography', *Jour. Hist. Behav. Sci.* 17 (1981), p. 137.
4. Wolf Lepenies, 'Problems of a Historical Study of Science', in Everett Mendelsohn, Peter Weingart and Richard Whitley (eds.), *The Social Production of Scientific Knowledge*, Sociology of the Sciences Yearbook, Vol. 1, Dordrecht, and Boston: Reidel, 1977, 55–67; see also 'Wissenschaftsgeschichte und Disziplingeschichte', *Geschichte und Gesellschaft* 4 (1978), 437–51.
5. The most comprehensive study of the institutionalization of American psychology to date is John M. O'Donnell, 'The Origins of Behaviorism: American Psychology, 1870–1920', Ph.D. dissertation, University of Pennsylvania, 1979. On the number and location of American psychology laboratories, see C. R. Garvey, 'List of American Psychology Laboratories', *Psychol. Bull.* 26 (1929), 652–60.
6. See, e.g., Theodore Dwight Bozeman, *Protestants in an Age of Science: The Baconian Ideal and Antebellum American Religious Thought*, Chapel Hill, University of North Carolina Press, 1977, and J. David Hoeveler, Jr., *James McCosh and the Scottish Intellectual Tradition: From Glasgow to Princeton*, Princeton: Princeton University Press, 1980.
7. On Hall, James and Baldwin, see Dorothy Ross, *G. Stanley Hall: The Psychologist as Prophet*, Chicago: University of Chicago Press, 1972; Robert J. Richards, 'The Personal Equation in Science,' unpublished MS, 1982; Robert N. Wozniak, 'Metaphysics and Science, Reason and Reality: The Intellectual Origins of Genetic Epistemology', in John Broughton and John Freeman-Moir (eds.), *The Cognitive Developmental Psychology of James Mark Baldwin*, New York: Ablex, 1982.
8. See esp. Dorothy Ross, 'The Development of the Social Sciences', in Alexandra Oleson and John Voss (eds.), *The Organization of Knowledge in Modern America, 1860–1920*, Baltimore: Johns Hopkins University Press, 1979, esp. pp. 113ff. Ross uses the term 'professional generation' to cover all of the figures just named, including Hall, James and Baldwin; I prefer the additional distinction made here. On Thorndike and Cattell see also Geraldine Joncich, *The Sane Positivist: A Biography of Edward Lee Thorndike*, Middletown, Ct.: Wesleyan University Press, 1968, and the editor's notes in Michael M. Sokal (ed.), *An Education in Psychology: James McKeen Cattell's Journal and Letters from Germany and England, 1880–1888*, Cambridge, Mass.: M.I.T. Press, 1980.
9. James McKeen Cattell, 'Psychology in America', *Science* 70 (1929), p. 340.
10. James Mark Baldwin, *A History of Psychology: A Sketch and an Interpretation*, 2 vols., New York: Putnam, 1913; George Sidney Brett, *A History of Psychology*, 3 vols., New York: Macmillan, 1912–1921; Max Dessoir, *Outlines of the History of Psychology*, New York: Macmillan, 1912; Otto Klemm, *A History of Psychology*, New York: Scribner, 1914; Benjamin Rand (ed.), *The Classical Psychologists: Selections Illustrating Psychology from Anaxagoras to Wundt* (New York, 1912),

repr. Gloucester, Mass.: Peter Smith, 1966; G. Stanley Hall, *The Founders of Modern Psychology*, New York: Appleton, 1912.

11. Lewis M. Terman, 'The Status of Applied Psychology in the United States', *Jour. App. Psychol.* **5** (1921), 1–4.

12. Franz Samelson, 'Putting Psychology on the Map: Ideology and Intelligence Testing', in Allan R. Buss (ed.), *Psychology in Social Context*, New York: Irvington, 1979, 103–68; cf. Thomas M. Camfield, 'The Professionalization of American Psychology, 1870–1917', *Jour. Hist. Behav. Sci.* **9** (1973), 66–75.

13. On the Psychological Corporation and public reaction to applied psychology, see Michael M. Sokal, 'The Origins of the Psychological Corporation', *Jour. Hist. Behav. Sci.* **17** (1981), 54–67. On public reaction to the testing movement in this period, see Hamilton Cravens, *The Triumph of Evolution: American Scientists and the Heredity-Environment Controversy, 1900–1941*, Philadelphia: University of Pennsylvania Press, 1978, Chapter 2.

14. Edwin G. Boring, *A History of Experimental Psychology*, New York: Appleton, 1929; Gardner Murphy, *Historical Introduction to Modern Psychology*, New York: Harcourt, Brace, 1929; Walter S. Pillsbury, *The History of Psychology*, New York: Norton, 1929.

15. On Titchener's methodological position, see Gernot Böhme, 'Cognitive Norms, Knowledge-Interests and the Constitution of the Scientific Object: A Case Study in the Functioning of Rules for Experimentation', in E. Mendelsohn, *et al.* (eds.), *op. cit.* (Note 4), 129–42. On the inner-disciplinary opposition to behaviorism, see Franz Samelson, 'Struggle for Scientific Authority: The Reception of Watson's Behaviorism, 1913–1921', *Jour. Hist. Behav. Sci.* **17** (1981), 399–425. The extra-disciplinary opposition took other forms; cf. John Burnham, 'The New Psychology: From Narcissism to Social Control', in John Braemer, Robert H. Bremner, and David Brody (eds.), *Change and Continuity in Twentieth Century America: The 1920s*, Columbus: Ohio State University Press, 1968, 351–98

16. Cf. Samuel Fernberger, 'The A.P.A.: An Historical Summary, 1892–1930', *Psychol. Bull.* **29** (1932), esp. pp. 9ff. For a general discussion of such monopolization processes in the development of disciplines, see Richard Whitley, 'The Establishment and Structure of the Sciences as Reputational Organizations', in Norbert Elias, Herminio Martins, and Richard Whitley (eds.), *Scientific Establishments and Hierarchies*, Sociology of the Sciences Yearbook, Vol. 6, Dordrecht, and Boston: Riedel, 1982, esp. pp. 317ff.

17. Clarence Irving Lewis, undated, handwritten reply to a letter from Edwin G. Boring, dated 13 November, 1930, Edwin G. Boring papers, Harvard University Archives, Cambridge, Mass., cited henceforth as 'Boring papers'. On the relationship of philosophy and psychology at Harvard in the 1920s, see also Bruce Kuklick, *The Rise of American Philosophy: Cambridge, Massachusetts, 1860–1930*, New Haven: Yale University Press, 1977, esp. Chapter 24.

18. John M. O'Donnell, 'The Crisis of Experimentation in the 1920s: E. G. Boring and his Uses of History', *American Psychologist* **34** (1979), 289–95.

19. Boring, *op. cit.* (Note 14), 2nd ed., New York, Appleton Century Crofts, 1950, p. ix. Unfortunately, the first edition of this book was not available to me at the time of writing; citations are therefore to the second edition.

20. Boring, *op. cit.*, pp. 43–44. See also E. G. Boring, 'The Problem of Originality in Science', (1927), in *History, Psychology and Science: Selected Papers*, Robert I.

Watson and Donald T. Campbell (eds.), New York: John Wiley, 1963, esp. pp. 54, 66.

21. B. F. Skinner, *The Shaping of a Behaviorist*, New York: Knopf, 1979, pp. 66ff. On the development of the history of science as a discipline, see Arnold Thackray, 'Scientific Ideas and Social Causation: An American Example', in E. G. Forbes (ed.), *Human Implications of Scientific Advance*, Proceedings of the XV. International Congress of the History of Science, Edinburgh: Edinburgh University Press, 1978, 78–87.

22. E. G. Boring, 'Psychologist at Large', in *Psychologist at Large: An Autobiography and Other Essays*, New York: Basic Books, 1961, esp. pp. 34, 47, 49.

23. Boring, *op. cit.* (Note 19), pp. x–xi.

24. *Ibid.*, pp. 80ff; cf. 'Originality in Science', *op. cit.* (Note 20), pp. 54ff.

25. E. G. Boring to Kurt Koffka, 17 November 1925, Boring papers.

26. Kurt Koffka, *The Growth of the Mind*, Robert M. Ogden (trans.), New York: Harcourt, Brace, 1925, pp. 7ff.

27. Wolfgang Köhler, *Gestalt Psychology*, New York: Liveright, 1929, pp. 179–80.

28. E. G. Boring, 'The 'Gestalt' Psychology and the 'Gestalt' Movement', *Amer. Jour. Psychol.* **42** (1930), esp. pp. 308–10. For an earlier indication of this position, see E. G. Boring, 'The Psychology of Controversy' (1929), in *History, Psychology and Science*, on p. 82.

29. Koffka to Boring, 22 April 1930, Boring papers.

30. Boring to Koffka, 23 April 1930, Boring papers. For a full account of the relations between Boring and the Gestalt theorists in this period, see Michael M. Sokal, 'The Gestalt Psychologists in Behaviorist America', *American Historical Review*, in press.

31. Boring, *op. cit.* (Note 19), p. 604.

32. *Ibid.*, pp. 612, 614. Cf. E. G. Boring, *Sensation and Perception in the History of Experimental Psychology*, New York: Appleton Century Crofts, 1942, pp. 610–11.

33. Boring, *op. cit.* (Note 19), p. 600.

34. Abraham S. Luchins and Edith H. Luchins, 'The Place of Gestalt Theory in American Psychology: A Case Study', in Suitbert Ertel, Lily Kemmler, and Michael Stadler (eds.), *Gestalttheorie in der modernen Psychologie*, Darmstadt: Steinkopff, 1975, 21–44; Mary Henle, 'The Influence of Gestalt Psychology in America', in Robert W. Rieber and Kurt Salzinger (eds.), *Psychology: Theoretical and Historical Perspectives*, New York: Academic Press, 1980, 177–90. On the unresolved problems raised by Gestalt psychology, see Julian Hochberg, 'Organization and the Gestalt Tradition', in Edward C. Cartarette and Morton P. Friedman (eds.), *Handbook of Perception*, Vol. 1, *Historical and Philosophical Roots of Perception*, New York: Academic Press, 1974, 179–210.

35. Gardner Murphy, *op. cit.* (Note 14), rev. ed., New York, Harcourt Brace, 1949, p. xii.

36. *Ibid.*, esp. pp. 12–13, 22ff, 73f, 418, 422, 428.

37. *Ibid.*, esp. pp. 284, 292ff, 444f.

38. *Ibid.*, p. 3.

39. *Ibid.*, p. 446.

40. Robert S. Woodworth, *Contemporary Schools of Psychology*, New York: Ronald Press, 1931, esp. pp. 16, 213; Edna Heidbredder, *Seven Psychologies*, New York: Appleton, 1933, pp. 13ff, 425ff.

41. Fillmore H. Sanford and Edwin A. Fleishman, 'A Survey of Undergraduate Psychology Courses in American Colleges and Universities', *American Psychologist* 5 (1950), 33–37.

42. On the role of political factors in the institutionalization of clinical psychology, see David Bakan, 'Politics and American Psychology', in Robert W. Rieber and Kurt Salzinger (eds.), *op. cit.* (Note 34), esp. pp. 133f. On subsequent developments, see, e.g., Irving Louis Horowitz and James Everett Katz, *Social Science and Public Policy in the United States*, New York: Praeger, 1975, esp. 77ff, 171.

    On the relative growth of specialties in psychology since the 1950s, see K. Bättig, 'Thematische Gliederung der psychologischen Fachliteratur 1958–1974', *Psychologie* 35 (1976), 212–17, cited in Hans Thomae, *Psychologie in der modernen Gesellschaft*, Hamburg: Hoffmann and Campe, 1977, pp. 178ff.

43. The situation in sociology in the 1960s was apparently similar; see the essay by Whitley, *op. cit.* (Note 16), esp. p. 346.

44. This account follows Watson's own: Robert I. Watson, Sr., 'The History of Psychology as a Specialty: A Personal View of its First Fifteen Years', *Jour. Hist. Behav. Sci.* 11 (1975), 5–14.

45. *Ibid.*, p. 9.

46. Cf. Watson, *Ibid.*, and the Newsletter of Division 26 of the American Psychological Association, 11: 4, 1979.

47. Robert G. Riedel, 'The Current Status of the History and Systems of Psychology Courses in American Colleges and Universities', *Jour. Hist. Behav. Sci.* 10 (1971), 410–12. For a discussion of history of psychology courses in Canada, see A. Bryan Lavar, 'The History of Psychology in Canada', *Jour. Hist. Behav. Sci.* 13 (1977), 243–51.

48. Reissues of older texts are: Robert S. Woodworth and Mary R. Sheehan, *Contemporary Schools of Psychology*, New York: Ronald Press, 1964; John C. Flugel and J. West, *A Hundred Years of Psychology*, New York: International Universities Press, 1970; and Gardner Murphy and J. K. Kowach, *Historical Introduction to Modern Psychology*, rev. ed., New York: Harcourt Brace Jovanovich, 1972. Outline histories include: Patrick Capretta, *A History of Psychology in Outline*, New York: Dell, 1967; Gardner Murphy, *Psychological Thought from Pythagoras to Freud: An Informal Introduction*, New York: Harcourt Brace, 1968; Robert Thomson, *The Pelican History of Psychology*, Harmondsworth and Baltimore: Penguin Books, 1968; Michael Wertheimer, *A Brief History of Psychology*, New York: Holt, Rinehart, & Winston, 1970, rev. ed., 1979; and Frank J. Bruno, *The Story of Psychology*, New York: Holt, Rinehart, & Winston, 1972. Full-length texts are: Robert I. Watson, Sr., *The Great Psychologists: Aristotle to Freud*, Philadelphia: Lippincott, 1963, 4th ed., 1977; George A. Miller, *Psychology: The Science of Mental Life*, New York: Harper & Row, 1962, 2nd ed. (with Robert Buckhout) 1973; Henrik Misiak and Virginia Staudt Sexton, *History of Psychology: An Overview*, New York: Grunne & Stratton, 1966; Duane Schultz, *A History of Modern Psychology*, New York: Academic Press, 1969, 3rd ed., 1981; Richard Lowry, *The Evolution of Psychological Theory: 1650 to the Present*, Chicago: Aldine, 1971; William S. Sahakian, *History and Systems of Psychology*, New York: Schenkman, 1975; Daniel N. Robinson, *An Intellectual History of Psychology*, New York: Macmillan, 1976; Thomas H. Leahey, *A History of Psychology: Main*

Currents in Psychological Thought, Englewood Cliffs, N.J.: Prentice-Hall, 1980. Sourcebooks include Thorne Shipley (ed.), *Classics in Psychology*, New York: Philosophical Library, 1961; Richard J. Herrnstein and E. G. Boring (eds.), *A Sourcebook in the History of Psychology*, Cambridge, Mass.: Harvard University Press, 1965; Solomon Diamond (ed.), *The Roots of Psychology: A Sourcebook in the History of Ideas*, New York: Basic Books, 1974; and Robert I. Watson, Sr., *Basic Writings in the History of Psychology*, New York: Oxford University Press, 1979.

49. Erwin A. Esper, *A History of Psychology*, Philadelphia: Saunders, 1964, pp. v—vi, 7—8.

50. Josef Brožek, Robert I. Watson, and Barbara Ross, 'A Summer Institute on the History of Psychology: Part I', *Jour. Hist. Behav. Sci.* 5 (1969), 307—19.

51. Michael Wertheimer, 'Historical Research: Why?', in Josef Brožek and Ludwig J. Pongratz (eds.), *Historiography of Modern Psychology*, Toronto: Hogrefe, 1980, pp. 16—17. For other justifications for courses on the history of psychology, see the contributions to the symposium on the subject in *Teaching of Psychology* 6 (1979); for comparison with the other social sciences, see Maurice Finocchiaro, *et al.*, 'A Symposium on the Use of History in the Social Sciences', *Jour. Hist. Behav. Sci.* 18 (1982).

52. Duane Schultz, *A History of Modern Psychology* (*op. cit.*, Note 48), p. 5.

53. Robert I. Watson, 'The History of Psychology: A Neglected Area', *American Psychologist* 15 (1960), p. 254; 'The Role and Use of History in the Psychology Curriculum', *Jour. Hist. Behav. Sci.* 2 (1966), 64—69, esp. p. 66.

54. Watson, *loc. cit.*

55. Cf. Robert Brodie MacLeod, *The Persistent Problems of Psychology*, Pittsburgh: Duquesne University Press, 1975.

56. Watson, *op. cit.* (Note 53), pp. 254, 64, resp.

57. Watson, 'Psychology: A Prescriptive Science', *American Psychologist* 22, 1967, esp. p. 436.

58. *Ibid.*, p. 438.

59. Alfred H. Fuchs and George F. Kawash, 'Prescriptive Dimensions for Five Schools of Psychology', *Jour. Hist. Behav. Sci.* 10 (1974), 352—66.

60. Melvin Marx and William Hillix, *Systems and Theories of Psychology*, 2nd ed., New York: McGraw-Hill, 1973, pp. 68—75, 236—37; cf. R. W. Coan, 'Dimensions of Psychological Theory', *American Psychologist* 23 (1968), 715—22.

61. Abraham S. Luchins and Edith H. Luchins, 'On the Inapplicability of Dichotomous Prescriptive Terms to Characterize Gestalt Psychology', *Gestalt Theory* 3 (1981), 5—19, esp. p. 16; cf. 'Prescriptive Dimensions of Gestalt Psychology', *Methodology and Science* 11 (1978), 14—33.

62. William R. Woodward, 'Toward a Critical History of Psychology', in Josef Brožek and Ludwig Pongratz (eds.), *op. cit.* (Note 51), 29—67, esp. pp. 41—43, 57. I have updated Woodward's listing to take account of recent publications.

63. Arthur L. Blumenthal, 'A Reappraisal of Wilhelm Wundt', *American Psychologist* 30 (1975), 1081—86.

64. *Ibid.*, pp. 1084, 1087.

65. Kurt Danziger, 'Wundt and the Two Traditions of Psychology', in Robert W. Rieber (ed.), *Wilhelm Wundt and the Making of a Scientific Psychology*, New York:

Plenum Press, 1980, 73–88. For a different view see Ryan D. Tweney and Stephen A. Yachanin, 'Titchener's Wundt', in Wolfgang G. Bringmann and Ryan D. Tweney (eds.), *Wundt Studies*, Toronto: Hogrefe, 1980, 380–95.

66. Arthur L. Blumenthal, 'Wilhelm Wundt and Early American Psychology: A Clash of Two Cultures', in Rieber (ed.), *op. cit.* (Note 65), 117–36. For independent confirmation of this view, see R. G. A. Dolby, 'The Transmission of Two New Scientific Disciplines from Europe to North America in the Late Nineteenth Century', *Annals of Science* 34 (1977), 287–310.

67. R. Steven Turner, 'Hermann Helmholtz and the Empiricist Vision', *Jour. Hist. Behav. Sci.* 13 (1977), 48–58; 'Helmholtz, Sensory Physiology and the Disciplinary Differentiation of German Psychology', in William R. Woodward and Mitchell G. Ash (eds.), *The Problematic Science: Psychology in Nineteenth Century Thought*, New York: Praeger, 1982, 147–166.

68. David E. Leary, 'The Philosophical Development of the Conception of Psychology in Germany, 1780–1850', *Jour. Hist. Behav. Sci.* 14 (1978), 113–21; 'German Idealism and the Development of Psychology in the Nineteenth Century', *Jour. Hist. Phil.* 18 (1980), 299–317.

69. Woodward, *op. cit.* (Note 62), pp. 51–52.

70. Richard High, 'Shadworth Hodgson and William James's Formulation of Space Perception', *Jour. Hist. Behav. Sci.* 17 (1981), 466–85; Lawrence D. Smith, 'Psychology and Philosophy: Towards a Realignment, 1905–1935', *Jour. Hist. Behav. Sci.* 17 (1981), 28–37.

71. Stephen Toulmin and David E. Leary, 'The Cult of Empiricism in Psychology, and Beyond', in Sigmund Koch and David E. Leary (eds.), *A Century of Psychology as Science: Retrospectives and Assessments*, New York: McGraw-Hill, 1982.

72. See, e.g., Phil Brown (ed.), *Radical Psychology*, London: Tavistock, 1973; Benjamin M. Braginsky and Dorothea D. Braginsky, *Mainstream Psychology: A Critique*, New York: Holt, Rinehart, & Winston, 1974.

73. Robert V. Guthrie, *Even the Rat Was White: A Historical View of Psychology*, New York: Harper & Row, 1976; Vincent P. Franklin, 'Black Social Scientists and the Mental Testing Movement, 1920–1940', in Reginald L. Jones (ed.), *Black Psychology*, 2nd ed., New York: Harper & Row, 1980, 201–15; Maxine D. Bernstein and Nancy Felipe Russo, 'The History of Psychology Revisited, or up with our Foremothers', *American Psychologist* 29 (1974), 130–34; Stephanie Shields, "Ms. Pilgrim's Progress: The Contribution of Leta Stetter Hollingworth to the Psychology of Women', *American Psychologist* 30 (1975), 852–57; Laurel Furomoto, 'Mary Whiton Calkins (1863–1930), Fourteenth President of the A.P.A.', *Jour. Hist. Behav. Sci.* 15 (1979), 346–56.

74. Hilary Rose and Stephan Rose, ''Do Not Adjust Your Mind – there is a Fault in Reality': Ideology in Neurobiology', *Cognition* 2 (1973), 479–502; Susan Buck-Morss, 'Socioeconomic Bias in Piaget's Theory: Implications for Cross-Cultural Studies', in Allan R. Buss (ed.), *op. cit.* (Note 12), 349–63.

75. See, e.g., Leon J. Kamin, *The Science and Politics of I.Q.*, Patomac, Md.: Lawrence Erlbaum, 1974, and Stephen J. Gould, *The Mismeasure of Man*, New York: Norton, 1981.

76. Lorenz J. Finison, 'Psychologists and Spain: A Historical Note', *American Psychologist* 32 (1977), 1080–84; 'Unemployment, Politics and the History of Organized

Psychology', *American Psychologist* **31** (1976), 747–55; **33** (1978), 471–77; 'An Aspect of the Early History of the Society for the Psychological Study of Social Issues: Psychologists and Labor', *Jour. Hist. Behav. Sci.* **15** (1979), 29–37.

77. Franz Samelson, 'History, Origin Myths and Ideology: Comte's 'Discovery' of Social Psychology', *Jour. Theory Soc. Behav.* **4** (1974), 217–31, esp. pp. 222–23, 228.

78. Samelson, *op. cit.* (Note 12), p. 155.

79. *Ibid.*

80. Franz Samelson, 'On the Science and Politics of the I.Q.', *Social Research* **42** (1975), p. 487.

81. Ben Harris, 'What Ever Happened to Little Albert?' *American Psychologist* **34** (1979), 151–60; Franz Samelson, 'J. B. Watson's Little Albert, Cyril Burt's Twins, and the Need for a Critical Science', *American Psychologist* **35** (1980), 619–25.

82. Kurt Danziger, 'The Social Origins of Modern Psychology', in Buss (ed.), *op. cit.* (Note 12), 27–46. For abundant independent confirmation of this thesis for the case of Germany, see Mitchell G. Ash, 'Academic Politics in the History of Science: Experimental Psychology in Germany, 1879–1941', *Central European History* **13** (1980), 255–86; and 'Wilhelm Wundt and Oswald Külpe on the Institutional Status of Psychology: An Academic Controversy in Historical Context', in Bringmann and Tweney (eds.), *op. cit.* (Note 65), 396–421.

83. Kurt Danziger, 'Wundt's Psychological Experiment in the Light of His Philosophy of Science', *Psychol. Res.* **42** (1980), 109–22; 'The Historical Construction of Social Roles in the Psychological Experiment', invited address to the 89th convention of the American Psychological Association, Los Angeles, Calif., 26 August, 1981.

84. Robert W. Rieber, 'Preface' to Rieber and Salzinger, *op. cit.* (Note 34), p. xiii.

85. Eliot Hearst, 'One Hundred Years: Themes and Perspectives', in Eliot Hearst (ed.), *The First Century of Experimental Psychology*, Hillsdale, N.Y.: Lawrence Erlbaum, 1979, p. 8.

86. Schultz, *op. cit.* (Note 48), pp. 12, 14, 42.

87. Michael Wertheimer, *op. cit.* (Note 51), pp. 17, 18, 20. The term 'matters of course' (*Selbstverständlichkeiten*) comes from a book by Wolf Lepenies, *Das Ende der Naturgeschichte. Wandel kultureller Selbstverständlichkeiten in den Wissenschaften des 18. und 19. Jahrhunderts*, Frankfurt a.M.: Suhrkamp, 1978.

THE USES OF HISTORY FOR THE SHAPING OF A FIELD:
OBSERVATIONS ON GERMAN PSYCHOLOGY (1)

ULFRIED GEUTER

Free University of Berlin

In the United States an established and recognized university must have red brick walls covered with ivy. Even with your eyes closed you can tell that such a university has a certain dignified age, and this seems to guarantee scientific standards. For the sciences it seems too, that their age proves their intellectual maturity. Apparently the discipline of psychology must be at least a hundred years old to have its own history.

When in 1900 Hermann Ebbinghaus paid a short tribute to the closing century at the fourth international congress of psychology in Paris, he maintained that although it had sometimes been named the scientific or the historical century, it could also be called the 'century of psychology' (Ebbinghaus, 1901, p. 49). In 1933 Flugel wrote a book 'A Hundred Years of Psychology' which began with Herbart, leaving aside the ancient forerunners often treated by earlier historical accounts. The history of British psychology, written by Hearnshaw in 1964, covered the period from 1840 to 1940.

One hundred must be a magic figure indicating the maturity of a discipline and providing the justification to reflect about or to write its history. This became far more apparent when psychology celebrated its hundredth 'birthday' in 1979. The American Psychological Association declared 1979/80 "as the centennial year celebrating the founding of scientific psychology" (Ross, 1979, p. 203). The International Union of Psychologists held a centennial ceremony in the form of its XXIInd International Congress, which took place in 1980 at the birth-place in Leipzig where Wilhelm Wundt had brought the baby named Psychology into the world by establishing a small psychological laboratory at the university. But 1879 was not only claimed as the birth year of academic psychology. Volker Ebel, President of the Union of Professional Psychologists in Germany (who are organized separately

191

Loren Graham, Wolf Lepenies, and Peter Weingart (eds.), Functions and Uses of Disciplinary Histories, Volume VII, 1983, 191–228.
Copyright © 1983 by D. Reidel Publishing Company.

from the academicians), welcomed the year 1979 as the centenary of applied psychology (Ebel, 1978, p. 2), although Wundt had not applied psychology to practical tasks.

Perhaps even more than for the common members of the discipline, 1979 was important for its historians. The symposia in memory of Wilhelm Wundt at the XXIInd International Congress, placed first in the abstract guide, were only attended by a very small number of congress participants. But the very old woman Psychology was finally old enough to have its history as its own 'daughter-discipline' (2). The centennial provided great impetus for looking back into the history of the field. It brought many publications dealing with the history of psychology, e.g. the first volume on problems of method in the historiography of psychology (Brožek and Pongratz, 1980), in the German Democratic Republic a volume on history of psychology (Eckardt, 1979), and a great number of publications on Wundt, too numerous to be listed here.

Even when those engaged in the new research had other aims in mind than those of the leading representatives of the discipline, the centennial throws a light upon what seems to be a main function of historical accounts of their subject by psychologists up to now. History serves to institute a scientific tradition, to line up the ancestors in order to give prestige to the field and to fall into line with the established sciences, or to conceive oneself within a stream of scientific progress. A short look at the bibliography of the German-language psychological literature from 1942 onwards shows that most of the studies refer to this function. (See Table I) In the center of interest are, overwhelmingly, psychologists as persons. Obituaries, biographies, person-related studies and commemorative volumes account for more than 90% of the literature which the bibliography classifies under historical works. These are badly ordered in categories which only mirror the confusion as to what the history of psychology really is (3). If we asked why historical studies cluster in certain years, we would surely find as a main factor the anniversaries of important psychologists. (See Table I, Note 1)

I do not want to go into the details here; the table will offer proof for the statement that the implicit and common approach to the history of psychology is to commemorate its progenitors and to institute a tradition of 'great men' and their 'great ideas', an important factor for the disciplinary ego. (See Geuter, 1981, p. 826)

TABLE I
Quantitative analysis of German-language literature on the history of psychology

Source: 1942–1960: Wellek (1965)
1961–1964: Psychological Abstracts
1971–1978: Dambauer (1971 pp.)

Year	Sum of publi- cations	History of psychology, general	History of psychology, special branches	History of psychology, schools	Biographical accounts; obituaries	Psychology in different countries
1942	–					
1943	1				1	
1944	1				1	
1945	1				1	
1946	–					
1947	2				2	
1948	6				5	1
1949	3	1		1	1	
1950	6			1	5	
1951	4				3	1
1952	6				6	
1953	12				12	
1954	12	1		1	10	
1955	18				18	
1956	57	2	1		54 (1)	
1957	26				27	
1958	7				5	2
1959	16				16	
1960	23	1			21	1
1961 (2)	2		1	1		
1962	1		1			
1963	4	1		1	2	
1964	2				1	1
–						
1971	65	2			63 (3)	
1972	139	1			137	1
1973	115	1			114	
1974	130				129	1
1975	169				161	8
1976	162	1	1		153	7
1977	222	3			216	3
1978	277		2		270	5

Notes
1. This peak is due to the anniversaries of Kraepelin and Freud and the death of Oswald Kroh.
2. The figures of the Psychological Abstracts have only been mentioned as an example for 1961–1964 because little German-language literature is listed compared with the German-language bibliographies.
3. Since 1971 commemorative volumes have been included in the corresponding category of Dambauer but have been omitted here.

Since the work of Butterfield (1931) and Stocking (1965), it may not be surprising that forerunners are honoured more in terms of the sanctioning, anticipation or suspecting of present scientific ideas than in terms of their historically demonstrable significance; for it is always better for your own reputation to have been on the side of the winners in history. Thus the definition of the forerunners of the discipline becomes interesting. For instance the celebration of the year 1879 as the birth year of scientific psychology not only reflects the effort of a whole and self-contained field to present its great and old tradition; it also points to a certain concept of what is thought to be scientific in psychology. If the birth of psychology is seen in the placing of some laboratory instruments in a room at Leipzig university, then psychology is an experimental science, defined in terms of certain scientific methods and instruments and not as a certain set of research-problems or within a theoretical framework even if Wundt had not had this in mind. This has been sharply criticized by Alexandre Métraux (1980), who refuses to accept the identification of the scientific character of psychology with its material and institutional possibilities for making experiments, or the myth that the institutionalization of the Leipzig laboratory should be the sign of a theoretical development and the turning point from philosophical to scientific psychology. Métraux wonders why such a myth is so common among historians of psychology, and he argues that this construction of a long and autonomous tradition of research serves as a legitimation for a discipline which has so often been accused of not being independent of philosophy. In fact, legitimation of scientific autonomy seems to have been an important impetus for the construction of a history of psychology by psychologists themselves, and this not only recently. We can find history of psychology claiming independence for the discipline right from the time of its first academic institutionalization. It may be pure chance that exactly in 1879 Hermann Siebeck of Zurich published a history of psychology, in which he wanted to contribute to the separation of psychology from philosophy.

However, opinion is divided as to who are the winners in history, and this is why there is an everlasting quarrel about the evaluation of the forerunners of the field. Thus around the Centennial of Psychology we find not only celebrations of the discipline but also a dispute about the scientific heritage of Wundt. The East German psychologist Hans Hiebsch (1979, p. 6) presents

Wundt as the 'founder of *experimental* psychology' in a state in which psychology has had to stand its own methodological and theoretical ground for years against the universal pretensions of Marxist-Leninist theory of science. On the other hand, Carl F. Graumann, an advocate of phenomenological psychology, refers to a model of psychology in the early work of Wundt which Wundt unfortunately later forgot, but which could have led to an "evolutionary and historically oriented socio-psychology of conscious and of unconscious mental life and action" (Graumann, 1980, p. 81). In contrast to Hiebsch, Klaus Holzkamp of West Berlin, who has developed a 'Critical Psychology' based on Marxism, inherits from Wundt the 'Völkerpsychologie' (roughly translated as folk-psychology or ethnological psychology) as an independent, historical approach to human thinking especially preserved in 'Marxist-Leninist psychology'. (Holzkamp, 1980, p. 162)

The last two authors, like Kurt Danziger (1979; 1980) in Canada, run counter to the dominant attitude to Wundt's heritage. The different forms of inheritance point to a further function of history: approaching history to clarify and corroborate one's own standpoint in disciplinary controversies.

In an article on 'History of science and history of disciplines', Wolf Lepenies (1978) has dealt generally with the function of the history of disciplines for the disciplines. He asserts that the interest in histories of disciplines presupposes the existence of an academic system in which disciplines compete for identities and resources. He then states three functions of these histories: (1) to gain or reinforce legitimation by proving the ancient character of the discipline, (2) to strengthen identity by standing out against competing disciplines and by producing a mainstream of one's own discipline based on the model of highly prestigious disciplines, and (3) to test theories in the laboratory of history.

For psychology the first of these functions has already appeared in our outline of the centennial. The second one seems to me to be closely bound to the first. Legitimation is directed outward, strengthening of identity is directed inward; both result from the construction of a maturity and a mainstream as opposed to other disciplines. The third function can be found in the German historiography of psychology too, for instance in the work of Ludwig Pongratz (1967). For the treatment of the history of psychology in Germany by psychologists, a further function seems to me to be decisive: History is used to back up one's own standpoint in controversies on theory and method in the discipline. With respect to American historiography of psychology, this function has been impressively documented in the analysis of Edwin G. Boring's standard history of psychology by John O'Donnel (1979). Boring opposed the advance of applied and technological psychology by professional-political and scientific means, and his history of scientific psychology written as the history of an academic experimental science may be understood as a scientific flank attack (4).

It would be nothing new to state that the study of history always reflects contemporary concerns. Mac Leod (1977, p. 149) has called this a truism, and Samelson (1974, p. 228) has stated that "there is little question that the history of our science is shot through with elements of professional and political ideologies". But what those particular contemporary concerns and ideologies are which have shaped the study of the history of German psychology still needs to be investigated. I do not want to say that using history for the sake of the present is in any sense disreputable. History as 'l'art pour l'art' does not offer any knowledge. But what has to be asked is from which 'interest of knowledge' (Habermas) and how — and with what distortions — history is perceived. For, from a fixed viewpoint, one usually has only a limited field of vision.

What I would like to ask here is how particular problems from within the discipline motivated the disciplinary actors to take recourse to history, and how these problems led to a certain way of dealing with the history of the field. Of course, historical self-reflection is only one factor, and not the most important one at that, in the solution of disciplinary problems and controversies. For the shaping of the field other means are much more effective. But the use of history as an argument was and still is such a means.

The range of this use is rather widely reaching, from a historical remark in a footnote to an explicit book on the history of psychology. But prior to all the explicit thematization of the discipline's history is the implicit (or tacit) way of approaching it within the discipline, as found in the introduction of handbooks, in preliminaries, in biographies and obituaries, as well as in part in scientific treatises, however sometimes hidden (5). Inner-disciplinary purposes and needs seem to lead to different forms of using history. Some forms, like the historical note or introduction, may be to be found at all time. Above all the explicit thematization of history appears, however, to be mainly due to the need for clarity in phases of crisis.

For research on history of psychology Harald Grünwald (1979; 1980) has offered the program that phases should be studied in which the concepts of research have been positively explained; such phases are mainly phases of the formation of subdisciplines and phases of crises and controversies. For our question, this consideration seems to be fruitful too.

Here I want to discuss three such phases which provide some illuminating material. One is the time of the development of psychology as an independent discipline. In Germany this was one of the two flowering periods of books explicitly dealing with the history of psychology. As a second example I choose the methodological debate in German psychology during the Fifties. This debate was set against the background of the successful employment of the old psychology in the Nazi period, a period which did not fit well into the self-portrait of a discipline moving from progress to progress. I will examine here how the debate related to psychology in the Nazi period and how later evaluations of psychology in the Third Reich were still predetermined by the methodological standpoint of their authors. As a third situation I will take the 'crisis of relevance' (Seeger, 1977) in West German psychology, beginning in the Sixties. During this time we can find a second blossoming of explicit historical accounts. I will discuss how they reacted to this situation of massive change. The first and third example will mainly deal with explicit historical accounts of the history of psychology (6); a small, special chapter will refer to the question why the time between these two phases was a rather unproductive one of explicit historiography. The second example shows a case of history in marginal notes.

Psychology's Emancipation from Philosophy – The First Contours of an Independent History

It was during the last decades of nineteenth century that psychology started to establish its own methods, its own research problems and its own institutional forms of existence in the universities. But the pioneers could not agree about the new field. They were at one in the rejection of 'pure' philosophical speculation, and they were convinced that current problems of the theory of knowledge could be solved by empirical methods. Institutionally, and to some extent intellectually, however, psychology was still a subdiscipline of philosophy in the German universities. Between 1879 and 1908, the year in which Ebbinghaus published his 'Abriß der Psychologie' (which will be treated in the following), twelve psychological institutes, departments, or seminars were founded, but all of them attached to chairs of philosophy. Most of the protagonists of this institutionalization saw the experimental method as the *via regia* to the solution of the problems of psychological research. It was this situation which also produced psychology's first accounts of its history as that of an independent field.

In 1879 Hermann Siebeck wrote the first part of the first volume of his 'History of Psychology', the second part of which was to follow in 1883, although the whole work was not completed as planned. The aim of his presentation was "to show the growth of psychology within occidental thinking" (Siebeck, 1879, p. x). He begins the preface with the following words (7): "For a particular science the need for its own history is always greatest when it is about to enter a new phase of its development. It needs history above all in order to become aware of the realignment it is beginning to make and in order to ascertain the importance of the new step (approximately at least) on the basis of a comparison with the course of pertinent research hitherto. It further demands that history differentiate the really original from the only apparently new, and not least to decide the question to what extent it has followed the true path of a science with the corresponding results, and how the new turn relates to this aspect of the consideration with respect to subject-matter and method" (p. vii/viii). For Siebeck, this turning point of psychological research, 'perhaps the most important one", is that psychology "starts to free itself from the frame of general philosophy like others before and to establish itself as a discipline in its own right ('Special-wissenschaft') beside others, with its own field of research and an independent method on the basis of and within copious material offered by inner and outer experience. Of course given the characteristic nature of its subject-matter it can never dispense with close connection and interaction with work on real philosophical problems" (p. viii). In a situation of an optimistic outlook on the future, his retrospective glance would surely meet with interest.

Some object to seeing the history of science as a history of prefaces; but at scientific turning points such as this one prefaces give a very good indication of intentions, because they put things more bluntly than in times of 'normal science'. And such a time was the time when psychology liberated itself from philosophy, and into which I cannot go in more detail here (see Ash, 1980; 1981; Ebert, 1966).

I have quoted Siebeck so extensively because it becomes evident here that the history of psychology had been written to establish it as a discipline ('Specialwissenschaft') which is independent from, though still connected with, philosophy. Now it is interesting that the empirical question of nineteenth century psychophysics which is, for example, to be found in the work of Gustav Theodor Fechner — the correlation of physical stimulus and subjective sensations — serves as a foil to the question Siebeck uses to screen the history of philosophy from the pre-Socratics to Thomas Aquinas. His topic in analyzing the history of philosophy is the mind-body-problem. For him the development of psychological thinking (mainly by Aristotle) is connected with overcoming dualism. This is not surprising if one bears in mind that the monistic viewpoint of psycho-physical parallelism was widespread among experimental psychologists at the end of nineteenth century. Hence Siebeck not only tries to demonstrate that the central problem of psychology has always existed as a part of philosophy — which would have been sufficient reason to legitimize psychology — but by his presentation the reader will come to know psychology as the modern science which can solve this basic philosophical problem.

Let us now turn to a second history of psychology, first published in 1894 by Max Dessoir, a pupil of Dilthey, who regarded psychology as the basis of philosophy. Here, too, only the first volume appeared, covering the time up to the eighteenth century, and not the second volume which had been planned (see Dessoir, 1947). Dessoir lets psychology's history start in earnest with Leibniz, because for Leibniz a world-view would have to be based on an understanding of soul, and then psychology would become identical with philosophy (Dessoir, 1902, p. 33ff). I want to emphasize two points distinguishing this history of psychology from later ones. According to Dessoir, psychology has three roots: ideas of the animation of the body, religious ideas, and observations on the character of man. Psychology thus has three parts: a descriptive and explanatory empirical psychology on the model of natural science — the 'Seelenphysik' (physics of the mind); a psychosophy — the 'Seelentheologie' (theology of the mind); and a psychognosis — the 'Seelenkunst' (psychological art) of practical psychology (see

Dessoir, 1902; 1911). The second remarkable point is that psychognosis (which includes knowledge of men (Menschenkunde), knowledge of character (Charakterkunde), the system of temperaments (Temperamentslehre), physiognomy, and even occultism, i.e. questions of cosmic influences on individuals, the dreams, the magnetism, etc.) has a place in Dessoir's history of psychology. These two peculiarities refer to the second determinant of historical presentations of psychology mentioned above: the position of the author on the subject-matter and method of the field. At least at the time when the first edition of Dessoir's 'A History of Recent German Psychology' appeared, he was engaged in scientific research on occult phenomena, and for this reason had founded with others the Berlin 'Society for Experimental Psychology' (see Kurzweg, 1976). Dessoir, himself an aesthetician and philosopher, did not belong to the 'invisible college' of those experimentalists who put their stamp on psychology's outlook during its first decades.

Psychognosis did not fit into the landscape of an upcoming discipline entering the halls of the university, and thus this area did not play any role within the histories of experimentalists as Herman Ebbinghaus and Otto Klemm presented below.

The attempt to establish psychology as an independent discipline was connected with internal quarrels about the scientific form of psychology. In 1894 Dilthey (1924) had challenged experimental psychology in his 'Ideas Concerning a Descriptive and Analytical Psychology'. Also well known is the controversy between Wundt and the Würzburg School on the universality of the experimental method. Histories of psychology were increasingly seen as partial works within these quarrels. In 1901 the philosopher Eduard v. Hartmann used the subtitle 'History of German Psychology in the Second Half of Nineteenth Century' for his book 'Modern Psychology'. He was mainly interested in the principal points of controversies of modern psychology which he chose highly selectively, following his own doctrine that psychology's subject-matter is the unconscious and that physiological questions should be left to the natural sciences. The points are: "First, the significance and range of the unconscious and its genetic relation to conscious phenomena, second, the relationship between sensation and emotion and between emotion and volition (Wille)..., third, the significance, scope and validity of psychophysical parallelism" (v. Hartmann, 1901, p. 7). For v. Hartmann, history is the struggle for a correct basic approach to psychology, whose subject matter is, according to him, "the relation between a given conscious and a supposed unconscious" (p. 30) while the meaning of the conscious remains the subject matter of the theory of knowledge.

It should be mentioned that in the history of psychology written by the Berlin professor of philosophy Friedrich Harms psychology is a subordinate discipline of philosophy (Pongratz, 1980, p. 77). As psychology institutionally was part of philosophy at the universities, its history had existed only as an aspect of the history of philosophy, even if the order of things was structured in such a new way that it could appear as though psychology had always existed as an aspect of scientific thought in the occident.

But this opinion was not shared by all of the experimental psychologists. With the work of Ebbinghaus and Klemm they made themselves heard on questions of the history of psychology. Ebbinghaus did not write a special history of psychology, but the historical chapter in his 'Abriß der Psychologie' (Compendium of psychology) first published in 1908 was written to set out contemporary scientific psychology. This marked a confident approach by experimental psychologists to the history of their science (8).

The introductory sentence of this chapter has become legendary. Klemm (1911) referred to the phrase in his 'History of Psychology', and by quoting this sentence Boring began the preface to the first edition of his 'A History of Experimental Psychology' in 1929. In Boring's translation "Psychology has a long past, but only a short history". Boring adds: " . . . but in general the historians of psychology have emphasized its long past at the expense of its short *scientific* history" (Boring, 1950, p. ix, my emphasis (U.G.)).

Distinguishing between a past and a history, or as Lepenies (1978) has put it, between a pre-history and a history seems to be a hallmark of self-confident histories of disciplines. Here the history of psychology is not part of the history of philosophy, as with Harms and others, but an independent one. For Ebbinghaus the history from Aristotle to the nineteenth century is worth no more than a sentence – during that time the structure of psychology had stayed the same. Only in the 'recent past' does he see a 'development' of psychology (Ebbinghaus, 1912, p. 9). The progress of psychology was made possible by the progress of the natural sciences. The extent to which he prefers the natural scientific experiment to philosophical thinking may be shown by the following, highly polemical passage: "When in 1829 E. H. Weber – inspired by apparently petty curiosity – wanted to know with what fineness two separate touches at different points of the skin can be distinguished, and later with what exactness we are able to tell the difference between two weights laid on our hand; or when he considered how he could examine the perception mediated by muscles when lifting a weight separately from the perception mediated by skin, more real progress was made for psychology than by all the distinctions, definitions and classifications from the time of Aristotle to Hobbes" (p. 18).

A second quotation will show how Ebbinghaus saw the position of psychology: "Psychology has undergone a transformation in the textbooks and at the rostrums; moreover, more nurseries have grown for it in the form of psychological laboratories, which express best the total shift of its style of working. At the same time, it has started to become an independent and self-sufficient science. It used to serve other interests only . . . . For most people it was a branch or a servant of philosophy . . . . For others practical purposes stood in the foreground . . . ". But now one had "started to study psychology for its own sake as a science requiring ones undivided attention" (p. 22/3) (9).

For Ebbinghaus psychology was a science of laws ('Gesetzeswissenschaft'). By its experimental methods all areas of mental life even the higher ones could be approached. Thus the 'real hallmark' of the history of psychology in nineteenth century was the development of its methods (Ebbinghaus, 1901, p. 50), and therefore its history was reduced to the natural scientific forerunners. Franz Samelson (1974), examining Allport's idea of the origin of social psychology in the work of Comte, coined the term 'origin myth'. One could speak of such a disciplinary origin myth in the work of Ebbinghaus, which is still prevalent in psychology today. (See above, and the critique of Métraux, 1980)

Because of the familiarity and the role of the famous Ebbinghaus sentence as a mythical initiation phrase among psychologists I have treated Ebbinghaus first as the outstanding example of a self-confident experimentalist's approach to the history of psychology. However, Wundt had expressed a similar view on questions of history and methods of psychology in 1862 in the introduction to his 'Contributions to a Theory of Sensory Perception'. At this time the experimental method of physiology for Wundt was still the central method for psychological research, a method which had just started to be applied to psychological questions. Since for Wundt the progress of science was bound to the progress of its methods, he some forty years before had come to the same conclusion as Ebbinghaus: "One could say about psychology with better reason what Kant once said of logic: since Aristotle it had not made the slightest headway" (Wundt, 1976, p. 119). Wundt further stated what is to be found in similar words in Ebbinghaus' book, that you can learn more from statistical inquiries for psychology than from all the philosophers except Aristotle (p. 133).

Not as radical as Ebbinghaus, but also written from the viewpoint of an experimental approach, is the 'History of Psychology' by Otto Klemm (1911). He starts his introduction by quoting the legendary Ebbinghaus sentence, and continues in the same vein that a fruitful development of psychology is to be ascertained only in the recent past. For Klemm, the real history of psychology is only the short history of experimental psychology. The recourse to history is justified by maintaining that the basic concepts of psychology and the ideas included therein have their own history. Klemm, a private tutor of philosophy at Leipzig, is not fully consistent. On the one hand he speaks about 'pre-scientific concepts' when treating the psychology of capabilities ('Vermögenspsychologie') (p. 44 ff.) and calls a 'new psychology' that of the middle of the nineteenth century, whereas Dessoir (1911) let the 'new period' of psychology last from Descartes to the German psychology of capabilities at the end of the eighteenth century and the 'newest period' start with Kant. On the other hand Klemm writes that Aristotle "for the first time had marked off psychology as an independent science" (Klemm, 1911, p. 25). He also distinguishes between pre-history and history in the various problem areas. For example the prehistory of associationist psychology starts with Parmenides and its history with Hume and Ch. Wolff (p. 90 ff.). Without naming Dessoir, Klemm distances himself from him by discounting the occult sciences as unimportant for the history of psychology (p. 3), or by carping at the profane psychologists of the character- or temperament-doctrine like Juan Huarte or the physiognomists (p. 58 ff.), whom Dessoir had evaluated in the same way as others.

Klemm writes the history of a discipline which has gained its first contours. This is shown by the fact that he writes history as an issue oriented history — a history of the growth of those problems with which contemporary scientific psychology is concerned. Of course, this means that those approaches to psychological questions are ignored which did not gain admission to 'scientific'

psychology, but which are not less interesting for historiography (see Obermeit, 1980). Klemm pursues the history of the discipline in a strict sense
as the history of an 'independent science of experience' ('selbständige Erfah-
rungswissenschaft'), which seeks by its 'historical evidence' to prevent misun-
derstandings among older sister-disciplines (p. 11). This discipline has its
own supertemporal subject-matter — consciousness which distinguishes it
from philosophy and the natural sciences (p. 175).

Finally, for Klemm the theories of the newer psychology are already
ripe for a historical account, we thus find in the third part of his book an
overview of theories of visual and auditory sensation, of spatial perception,
and of matters of feeling and volition (p. 278ff). Even the psychological
methods of measurement are worth a historical presentation, though Klemm
concedes that they do not have a real history (p. 222). Looking at Klemm's
book, it becomes clear that history of psychology is written in order to
emphasize the claim for an independent disciplinary existence of psychology,
and at the same time in order to aid the breakthrough of new approaches
in the field.

The 'Lean Years'

Pongratz (1980) has referred to the fifty 'lean years' in the historiography
of German psychology. He noted that between 1911 and 1963 only two
publications "dealing systematically with the history of psychology were
written in German" (p. 82), one by Richard Müller-Freienfels which appeared
first in an English translation in 1935, and the other one by Paul von Schiller
which came out in German in 1948 but had first appeared in Hungarian in
1940, which Pongratz does not mention. Müller-Freienfels wrote his book
after losing his post as professor at the Pedagogical Academy at Stettin in
1934, being transferred to the post of a master at a secondary school and
then working at a college of economics. Müller-Freienfels then could no
longer take part in the life of the discipline, neither intellectually nor institutionally (10).

In fact it is astonishing that between the second decade of this century
and the Sixties no other German-language historical books on psychology
appeared. According to the thesis that doing disciplinary history is a form
of dealing with situations of scientific realignment in the discipline, one

might have expected a rush of historical treatises at the end of the Twenties when psychology in Germany was strongly hit by its own crisis (11).

In the United States the first important historical books on psychology came out during the late Twenties and the early Thirties, in part connected with the struggle of academic psychology against the rapid advance of professional psychology (12). I must leave the question open why there was not a similar development in Germany, but I may make some observations. In Germany, the crisis of academic psychology was not a crisis of competition against applied psychology, and not solely a crisis of its methodological and theoretical concepts, but a crisis of its academic existence. Moreover, psychotechnics was also struck by a crisis (see Jaeger and Staeuble, 1981). Academic psychology reacted with a comprehensive strategy of legitimizing itself as both a philosophically and practically useful discipline (see Kundgebung ... , 1930). In any case, the Twenties were a time of competing schools in German psychology. An attempt at integration (like that of Karl Bühler, 1927) was probably more desired for the presentation of the discipline than an outline of the history of psychology as an homogeneously developed science. But one could also consider it as a sign of a certain inner consolidation that in the Twenties many books on contemporary psychology came out mainly portraying the different schools, systems and fields of application. Pongratz (1980, p. 83) has quoted these books; those of Messer (1927) and Saupe (1928) should also be mentioned.

Let us continue with the 'lean years'. During the first part of the Third Reich works on the history of psychology may not have appeared because most psychologists were in a mood to tackle the coming tasks with all energy (Geuter, 1979), while some of them (if they did not emigrate) felt insecure about what the future was to bring. Later this period became a successful one with regard to professional politics. In the German army psychology became a profession with its own career system for the first time, in the universities it gained more professorships, and the *Diplom-Prüfungsordnung* of 1941 brought the academic recognition of psychology as a subject of study in its own right and its final institutional separation from philosophy (13). I would therefore disagree with Pongratz, who argued that the lack of studies on the history of psychology during the 'lean years' was due to the competition of the schools, a decline of the discipline during the Nazi period, and a preoccupation with the present in times of war. This last factor does not seem to have been too pervasive, since literary works of this time did not lack historical themes.

Snubbing the Other Side — Uses of an Undebated History after the Nazi Period

One may expect that in the post-war period the political circumstances of the employment of psychology in the Third Reich and the impact of the dismissal of Jewish professors would have led to a debate on history of psychology under the Nazis. But this did not happen. Psychologists cut themselves off from this experience, first to make professional progress with the field as a whole, and later to use history only to support their own particular viewpoints in inner-disciplinary controversies (14).

On the one hand we find also in this period the use of history to raise the status of the discipline. One technique was the overestimation of psychology's importance in retrospect, even as a victim (15). For that purpose Albert Wellek (1960) invented a call of highest Nazi authorities in 1937 to abolish psychology, which could neither be found in the records nor be testified to by any other psychologist of that period in the courst of numerous interviews (16). If the Nazis had wanted to ban psychology, then it must have had an anti-National-Socialistic substance. This is what Wellek imputes and what Wolfgang Metzger (1965, p. 112) asserts by writing: "it is characteristic of autocratic systems that they are, without exception, full of distrust and aversion against this science". Later, Metzger (1979) claimed of Gestalt psychology that it is incompatible with Nazi ideology, although during the Nazi period he had himself tried to show its compatibility (17). Another example of the overestimation of German psychology as a whole is the article by Wellek (1964) on the influence of the German emigration on American psychology. Here, Wellek sketches American psychology as though all its important theoretical developments were the result of the contributions of German emigrants. He concludes: "American psychology would not be what it is and could not become what it promises to become without the humus of German emigration" (p. 261). The history of psychology seems to serve as an instrument for raising national prestige, too. It is the same when Dessoir (1894) starts with Leibniz as the first great psychologist — and a German one.

But psychology in the Third Reich was not used mainly to add to the credit of the field as a whole. It was used more as a welcome opportunity to push through one's own position in inner-scientific controversies by use of comparisons and insinuations. Characteristic for this is the methodological debate ('Methodenstreit') of the Fifties. In that time we do not find any explicit historical accounts of psychology, but a debate in which a recourse to history serves the function of snubbing the scientific opponent.

The opportunity provided by the Wehrmacht to prove the usefulness of psychology, especially in the selection of officer candidates, had united the rival German psychological schools around a common 'paradigm': the paradigm of characterological diagnostics. Characterology had focused more on the general personal qualities of man and on the dominant traits of his character than on his different functions, using situational and interpretational methods in diagnostics. Theoretically psychologists shared the basic approach of 'Ganzheits-psychology' at this time, which had emphasized the original 'holisticness' of a person. In the Fifties, however, the needs of school and industry called for more economical methods of selecting candidates and predicting achievement (see Schmid and Wacker, 1978; Maikowski *et al.*, 1976). In addition to this, the intellectual and political climate was more favorable for the adoption of American thinking than for the revival of an older German irrationalistic psychology. Hence, with the so-called 'Methoden-streit' a new discussion of methodological fundamentals began. Should 'Ganzheits-Psychology', characterology, and the diagnostics of expression be maintained, or the American standards of measuring and predicting science and objective testing be followed? According to Stocking (1965, p. 215) such a discussion of scientific fundamentals leads to "historiography simply extend(ing) the arena of competition" among the competing schools. In the 'Methodenstreit' the antagonists turned to the psychology of the Third Reich for arguments to back up their own position within the debate. For instance, instead of discussing the problem of having worked for an army which had served the expansive aims of Nazism, the evaluation of Wehrmacht psychology was dominated by the question whether its methods should remain a method-ological guideline for psychological diagnostics or not.

In 1954, Max Simoneit, the former director of German Wehrmacht psychology, heavily attacked test diagnostics and defended characterological diagnostics and methods of studying the human expression by arguing that

these methods had proven their value in the Wehrmacht (Simoneit, 1954).
For Simoneit the war had been the 'heyday' of the practical proof of German
psychology. In the next issue of the journal in which Simoneit had placed
his attack, the *Psychologische Rundschau*, the Swiss psychologist Richard
Meili defended test diagnostics against Simoneit, accusing him of not evaluating diagnostics critically, but of appealing to the ideas of a decade before. In a
footnote Meili (1954) hinted that it would be strange to play German psychology of that time off against the present one. That it was not psychology
during the Nazi period as a whole but only the methods of Wehrmacht
psychology which became the subject of debate in the early Fifties throws
light upon the uses to which history was put. The only question was whether
the methods of Wehrmacht psychology should be further used or not. And
the different evaluations were determined by the position of the author
in the methodological debate itself. We can see this in the main controversy
between Peter R. Hofstätter and Albert Wellek, too.

Hofstätter, himself a former Wehrmacht psychologist who was trained
by Bühler before 1938, started his polemic on the purpose and method of
psychology from Washington, where he taught between 1949 and 1956.
Hofstätter's position was that psychology, as an empirical science, should
make predictions which can be proven true or false and should use mathematics in its methods (Hofstätter, 1953). He trims up his polemic against
irrationalistic German psychology with a subtle insinuation about psychology
in the Nazi period: "The pure gaze (of intuition), whose goal is evidence of
the essential shape (of personality), can lead to the solipsism of delusion"
(p. 146, additions in brackets are mine, U.G. (19)). His opponent, Wellek, is
no less polemical for his part, and uses the history of the Third Reich, as
well. For him American psychology was the psychology of an homunculus,
the psychology of a mechanistic machine-man which experiments without
theorizing. In contrast, the old German psychology had been much more
generous in questions of method. He refers to the good old times: "In 1940
things seem to be clear. In fact, according to the definitions of Krueger and
Lersch (who accepted experiment as one method among others, U.G.) the
German situation of the early Forties is exhaustively described. In the middle
of the most terrible of all wars, comfortingly, we are at least in our own
house of our own science in the state of greatest methodological peace-
fullness" (Wellek, 1959, p. 6). And in the last sentence of his lecture at the

Bonn Congress of the German Society for Psychology in 1957, he appealed for a return to the state of disciplined methodological freedom which psychologists had reached during the Second World War (*op. cit.*, p. 29).

It was in 1960 that the question of the connection between psychological theories and Nazi ideology was first publicly, if cautiously, raised by Ferdinand Merz. He did this by including one and a half pages about psychology under the Nazis in a thirteen-page review of a book by Burkart Holzner (undated) on "American and German psychology". Merz argued that the book, a dissertation written under the supervision of Friedrich Sander, a member of the Leipzig School of Ganzheits-psychology, confused 'Weltanschauung' and science, and that precisely this had been the mistake of German psychology under the Nazis. Merz belonged, together with Erwin Roth and Klaus Foppa, to a circle of young scientists in Würzburg who discussed the differences between American and German psychology with an American visiting professor, Russell. In his critique he supports an 'American' position and therefore opposes in the main the opponents in the 'Methodenstreit', namely the Leipzig Ganzheits-psychology. It is only their attitude towards the Third Reich which was considered, not that of other schools. Nor is the function of those parts of military and occupational psychology considered which had already oriented themselves more to 'American' quantitative standards than to 'German' psychology during World War II. The conflict between the different psychological orientations led to Merz's rather restricted view of psychology in Nazi Germany. His aim was to strike a blow against Ganzheits-psychology. The academic psychologists reacted accordingly. They did not see Merz's polemic as the starting point for a discussion on psychology and National Socialism, but were content to leave it to Wellek to reply on behalf of the Leipzig school. In his reply Wellek (1960) does not go into the reasons why certain schools of psychology could 'mix' with Nazism. Instead he accuses other psychologists such as Narziß Ach and C. G. Jung of Nazi affinities, and tries to cast a better light on Ganzheits-psychology. Merz had quoted a comment by Sander that Ganzheits-psychology and Nazi ideology were in agreement. Here Wellek tries to pull the wool over the eyes of post-war psychologists not familiar with the material by playing down Sander's support of Nazism — which had in fact gone as far as providing a Ganzheits-psychological legitimation for the 'elimination' of the Jews. Wellek's statement thus contains typical elements of an approach to the history of the field which regards it only under the aspect of providing arguments for the strengthening and justification of one's own position in actual disciplinary controversies.

This approach remained typical for statements on psychology during the Nazi period in the psychological literature of the following years. Thus Klaus Eyferth in 1967 identifies the progress of psychology with a 'scientific' as opposed to a 'humanistic' orientation (20). The flowering of the mathematization of psychology was shown by the fact that in recent years some chairs of psychology had been reestablished at the Technical Universities. What Eyferth does not mention is that most of them had already existed in the Third Reich, a period which Eyferth had accused two paragraphs earlier (under the label 'second quarter of our century') of being the dark ages of the 'humanistic' orientation.

Theo Hermann (1966) maintains that psychotechnics was able to survive under the Nazis because it followed the path of 'objective' methods without adopting Nazi ideology, and does not ask if there was another reason that these methods were respected as useful and were not persecuted by the rulers. Thus he reduces the question about the relation of psychology and National Socialism to that of the penetration of psychological theory by Nazi ideology. Adler and Rosemeier (1970) see the decrease of 'scientific' methods in the Thirties as a sign of the decline of German psychology. For all these authors the guideline of progress or regress is whether the modern positivistic methodological viewpoint is shared or not. A pro-Nazi stance is identified with a 'humanistic' orientation and a non-Nazi one with a 'scientific' one.

In the Fifties and Sixties psychology did not have the problem of emancipating the field as a whole from the old mother philosophy. It had already reached adolescence. But it did not yet have the identity to be sure of where to go, and it did not want to be reminded of where it came from. In addition its transatlantic brother was showing his modern mathematical muscles. In this situation psychologists went back to history, but in only a limited way — to help decide whether to continue on the same path or to go in a new direction, but without actually discussing the problems of the juvenile stage in general. Apparently, there was no more need to create a tradition for the whole discipline by presenting its history in full. The first book after 1911 dealing with the history of psychology was written by Wilhelm Hehlmann in 1963 (21).

Reorientation in the Crisis of the Sixties – The Student Movement and the New History of Psychology

The situation changed in the late Sixties when psychology underwent a new crisis, which Seeger (1977) has called the crisis of its social relevance. This crisis was international in scope; in the following I will, however, concentrate on the peculiarities of the German situation.

The situation of psychology in the German universities during that time was mainly governed by three factors: the diversification of theories, the increasing demands of practical tasks, especially in the field of educational reform, and the boom in the number of students, which was exceptionally large in psychology (see Maikowski *et al.*, 1976). The students gave an additional impulse to psychology to turn to practical demands; for their goal was to become practicising psychologists, not scientists. Meanwhile, mathematically formalized psychology had gained some successes on the academic scene, but in the Sixties it became clearer and clearer that the new psychology was not practically relevant, either (*op. cit.*, p. 268ff.).

In 1967, before the crisis of relevance led to an open discussion and before the student movement attacked academic psychology, Pongratz had brought out an issue-oriented history of psychology which aimed to reintegrate the diversifying theoretical approaches to psychology into a well-rounded system. As he wrote in 1980 about his own book, he viewed "the history of a science as an essential component of the concern with the foundations ('Grundlagenforschung') of the particular science" (Pongratz, 1980, p. 86). In this 'History of the problems of psychology' he focusses on the question of psychology's subject matter. By means of an historical analysis he tries to make a contribution to overcoming restricted conceptions of psychology's subject matter, as the exclusive concentration on a special aspect of the mental life of a person, like consciousness (Wundt), the unconscious (depth psychology), 'experience' (German academic psychology), and behavior (objective psychology). Pongratz calls for a comprehensive conception of psychology's subject matter as the mental life of the person. He wants to use history as a think tank for testing psychological theories. This function of the history of psychology is explicitly stressed by Ernst G. Wehner (1973, p. 216). In a situation in which psychology tries to create a homogeneous theoretical system he writes "the history of psychology is called to its most distinguished task — to participate in the project of scientific psychology by systematically analyzing its developmental process" (22).

In the late Sixties and the early Seventies, Pongratz and Wehner, both at the University of Würzburg, remained the only exponents of the traditional sort of historical research on and in psychology. The unease about the discipline, which Stocking (1978) has cited as a reason for going back to questions of history, including the history of one's own discipline (in his case ethnology), was mainly formulated and perhaps mainly felt by outsiders and critics. Among the established members of the discipline, the critique of the student movement of the irrelevance of psychological research for practical requirements was taken up above all by the Berlin professor Klaus Holzkamp in 1970. One of his main points was that psychological research should have to show its wider relevance, too (Holzkamp, 1972).

I think that the crisis of relevance, which I could only sketch very roughly, and the political impetus of the student-movement are the main reasons for the following increase of historical studies in psychology during the late Sixties and the Seventies. The argument of Pongratz (1980, p. 84) that the increase is a reflection of the blossomming of psychological research in that period seems to me superficial, because no new plants flowered, but the old ones only brought forth large numbers of the old flowers, and one or two weird offshoots. In what follows I will sketch some important and widely discussed studies, focussing on their disciplinary concerns.

The history of psychology became a subject for the student rebels and their successors, who couched their critique in historical research on the ideological character of psychology and its function in the capitalist system. At the Tübingen Congress of the German Society for Psychology in 1968, at which the famous specialist in the psychology of learning and education Franz Weinert stated that all the years of research into learning had not brought any advancement of real human learning processes, a group of circa 20 students occupied the podium during a symposium, and one of them read out 27 theses demanding psychological theories which were not only fit for rats but were socially relevant, a psychology which did not perpetuate ideology and domination. The political guidance of 'big science' and the Vietnam war had so clearly shown the dependency of science on social factors that the critics wanted to know to what extent these factors had shaped the character of psychological theories as well as the function of professional psychologists in society. The historical studies done in the years following the student movement focussed on these two problems.

The development of a new psychology presupposed the critique and unmasking of the old one. That this critique and unmasking was primarily done historically seems to be due to the fact that the members of the student movement studied Marx in order to come to terms theoretically with bourgeois science. The orientation to Marx meant that both the critique of and the search for a new conception for psychology were guided by certain understandings about historical-materialistic method. Thus the international discussion on the relevance of psychology took specific form in Germany.

The call for historical investigations was thus stated very explicitly, and was based on a specific view of science. When Klaus-Jürgen Bruder and Irmingard Staeuble began to uncover the genesis of psychological categories in their early studies, they claimed that they could do for psychology what Marx had done for political economy, i.e. to lay the foundations for a truly scientific psychology by proving the historical relativity of the categories of bourgeois psychology.

According to Bruder (1973), the structure of psychology's subject matter and methods corresponds to the tasks required by the capitalist production process. Analyzing the twofold starting point of psychology in psychophysics and psychotechnics, Bruder reconstructed the social conditions which demanded the adjustment of human behavior, and at the same time constituted the categories of psychology as the science of that adjustment. Staeuble (1972) investigated the early history of American social psychology and showed that theoretical considerations were given up in favor of technological social research. The unity of theoretical fundamentals was replaced by the unity of methods. Social psychology thus gave up the claim of explaining social conflicts scientifically, and reduced itself to the treatment of their symptoms.

In a paper on history and anthropology, Lepenies (1975) has remarked that the history of a discipline may serve the end of 'historization', i.e. to consider the historical nature of the discipline's subject. How psychology could be historized was the central question of debate at the Psychological Institute in Berlin. A programmatic statement on this question, a book on the theory of perception entitled 'Sensory Knowledge' ('Sinnliche Erkenntnis'), was published by Holzkamp in 1973. With it he aimed to found a new psychological school, and in this he was successful. In the beginning Holzkamp criticizes the common historiography of psychology; in the following parts, however, history of psychology no longer plays any role in his argumentation. The reason is that Holzkamp conceives an historical analysis in psychology in a certain way, as the investigation of the development of specifically human capacities from prehuman natural history via original society to class society. Holzkamp's attempt to historize the subject of psychology paradoxically had the opposite effect. He preserves the ahistorical character of psychology's subjects, such as 'perception', 'learning' and so on, as natural capacities which are only overlaid more or less by social historical development. The subjects of research are the human capacities in their 'having become' ('Gewordensein'), rather than the specific historical character of the problems of human subjectivity in their coming and going. By arguing that the historical analysis of the development of psychology must be based on an analysis of the knowledge psychology can possibly gain ('potentieller Erkenntnischarakter'), he quickly switches from history of psychology to its subject matters. Thus for Holzkamp the history of psychology served only as an introduction as in many other textbooks, and remained as usual a field in which to demonstrate the inadequacies and troubles of former scientists. But there is one little difference: Holzkamp later pretentiously went so far as to define new periods of psychology's history: the period of pre-scientific psychology (condemned as arbitrary in its theories and only to be evaluated in its relevance by Critical Psychology) and the period of 'Critical Psychology' as a discipline ('Einzelwissenschaft') and a part of scientific socialism (Holzkamp, 1977, p. 95).

What Holzkamp had only pretended to do (to extend the historical method to the subject *and* its science (see Holzkamp, 1973, p. 44)) was done in a book by Siegfried Jaeger and Irmingard Staeuble (1978) called 'The Social Genesis of Psychology'. In it they investigate the question why certain aspects of 'empirical subjectivity' had become so problematic in specific areas of bourgeois society in the eighteenth and nineteenth century that a specific discipline – psychology – developed to confront these problems. Psychology is thus analyzed as one special practical and theoretical attempt to solve problems produced by the society in its historical development. The main problems demanding psychological answers were the subjectivity and identity of the bourgeois and the qualification of human labor. Psychology was only one way to approach social problems. What appears as a psychological problem on the surface could be shown by historical analysis to have social causes. The central problems reflected in psychology were actually problems of the realization of given social forms of individuality. But psychology dealt only with particular aspects of these problems, without comprehending its own questions as socially produced, and without having a theoretical framework for this. Jaeger and Staeuble's historical analysis thus runs counter to the conventional departmentalization of the social sciences. At this point its inner-disciplinary purpose is revealed. The theory of the forms of individuality is taken from the French Marxist Lucien Sève. Using this theory, the history of the genesis of psychological problems and of psychology is then reexamined, in order to base psychology on a broader theory of social relations, and thus to redefine its inner structure according to the problems of empirical subjectivity in the realization of forms of individuality in bourgeois society (23).

Besides the question of the theoretical and ideological status of psychology, the second problem raised by the student movement was the role and function of psychology as a practical and professional instrument for dealing with social problems. Students were looking for a revolutionary perspective as intellectuals, and the Holzkamp-group asserted that the solution was the development and application of a critical and emancipatory psychology. Against this other psychologists at the Berlin institute stressed the institutional constraints on psychological work outside the university. They criticized the overestimation of the capacity of psychology to reform society, and maintained that psychologists inevitably had to serve the ruling class (Mattes, 1972). In the context of this controversy they went back into history to show that the self-assessment of psychologists — that they served the people — was a self-deception. Rainer Maikowski, Peter Mattes, and Gerhard Rott (1976) investigated the history of academic, educational, and industrial psychology in West Germany from 1945 up to the Seventies in order to demonstrate that the subject matter of psychology is not an ahistorical individual. On the contrary psychology is concerned with the ideological reflection and institutional treatment of social problems.

Some work done at other West German institutes also stressed the social function of practical psychology, mainly in diagnostics. In the center of the book by Rudolf Schmid (1977) on the history of intelligence-tests and achievement-tests stands the question of the social need for these instruments. He focuses mainly on the relation between economic development and the development of diagnostical tools — sometimes more drawing parallels than analyzing. Subject of his inquiry is the early development of psychological tests at the end of the nineteenth and the beginning of the twentieth century, especially its roots in psychiatric and pedagogical problems. However, the book is not only to be seen as an exposé of the social dependency of psychology. Above all it seems to have been an anticyclic book within the test-euphoria of the Sixties and early Seventies. It aims at the adoption of a new dimension in the evaluation of psychological tests, the dimension of its social function. History is thus used to push psychology away from its uncritical belief in tests.

Grünwald (1979) investigates the history of psychological diagnostics for a similar reason. He tends to see psychology as a science of the human subject, but test-diagnostics treats man as an object. Diagnostics should subjectivise examiner and examinee and conceive the situation of psychological diagnostics as a situation of interaction.

The old achievement-oriented diagnostics were no longer suitable for the psychological tasks of the Seventies, which were more oriented towards clinical questions. New diagnostics were required, but the old ones were still defended by the established academic community. This adherence to established methods and procedures of research by academic groups may have been a starting point for Grünwald's analysis, just as the experience that certain controversies in diagnostics like the race-intelligence-controversy were not to be decided by scientific research, because the opposing positions were based on prescientific beliefs. Hence it is not surprising that Grünwald picks up the theory of Kuhn and stresses the scientific community as the main level of historical analysis in psychology. His purpose is to break up the established concepts of psychological diagnostics. He tries to do this by demonstrating the historical process of the establishment of these concepts, thus showing their historical relativity.

It may have been the same experience which made a leading figure of West German psychology, Hans Thomae (1977), a professor at the University of Bonn, write a social history of psychology. According to Thomae the social determinants of psychology are mainly to be found in the activities of groups within the discipline and in the processes between these groups.

By stressing this point of analysis Thomae was also reacting to oversimplifications of the relation between economic processes and psychology in the Marxist critiques. In contrast to this, Thomae emphasizes the plurality of the forms of relation between science and society. This corresponds with his own position towards psychology itself. Thomae maintains that psychology can only be defined as a pluralistic system with manifold approaches: he thus stands in opposition to all the intolerant schools and movements in psychology which he analyses as shaping the history of the field. It seems that Thomae does not have his own castle in psychology, and so his stress upon group processes as main social determinants in the history of psychology may be understood as a polemic against the lords and rulers by a scientist who fights his own theoretical battles without a large posse of retainers. The fact that the factors determining the history of psychology are a bit disordered in Thomae's book, and that he tries to clear up the social role of science by the *casuistic* method (p. 204) corresponds to his method of personality research (Thomae, 1968) and to what he writes of as the political confession of being a liberal (pp. 190–91) and a pluralist, and his wish to maintain theoretical and methodological pluralism in psychology (see, e.g., p. 164). The differentiation of problems is the main function of psychology (p. 250) and thus the community should be wary of the simplifiers. It is interesting to note that Thomae does not mention Kuhn or any other historian or theoretician of science. His experience and inquiries alone seem to have been sufficient to bring Thomae to this thesis.

In the same year as Thomae published his book Falk Seeger (1977) brought out a study of the crisis of psychology and the corresponding debates in the United States in which he pleads, unlike Thomae, for the adoption of the new concept of an integrating theory of action to overcome the crisis. According to Seeger the crisis is mainly a crisis of the relation between science and society, a crisis of the social usefulness of psychology. To back up his argument he (among other things) goes back to the history of crisis-debates. Seeger does not adopt the theory of Kuhn (which he discusses fully) because he thinks that after the phase of predominance by behaviorism psychology should overcome mutually excluding paradigms and find a way to an integrative model.

It is not the aim of this contribution to present a comprehensive overview of all the research done recently on the history of psychology in Germany.

I leave aside other work which could be analyzed as a way of facing theoretical and professional problems or the problems of the discipline's political stance (Bruder, 1978; Geuter, 1979, 1980c; Graumann, 1980; Mattes, 1979, 1980). The portrayal of some literature may have been sufficient to show that since the student movement and the crisis of relevance ways of writing the history of psychology reflect different views on the critique or the further development of the discipline. History is mainly put for developing scientific alternatives in psychology, even if the two aiming points of critique of the early works of this last period are still alive. The theoretical and methodological crisis of psychology has not come to an end. It is to be expected that the situation will give rise to more reflections on the history of the discipline, as well as to more historically oriented attempts to answer the scientific questions of psychology themselves (24).

As the field is now established, its legitimation as a whole gives way to the problem of legitimizing subdisciplines. Here the genre of the historical chapter can be found, which Kuhn (1978, p. 169) speaks of as the main form of history of science over a long period; it is possible that we will have more and more 'sub-histories' in the future.

It can happen that history will soon be a teaching subject to give students some orientation within the jungle of concepts and branches of psychology, as Ash (25) shows for the American scene. Last year the first German introduction to psychology was published which chooses the history of psychology as its starting point. Here Wehner (1980) states that by studying historical derivations students have the chance to enter the process of contemporary research (p. 11). The use of history as an introduction leads psychology back to the old example of philosophy, the history of which was always a relevant part of its teaching and research.

Today, however, not only the history of the field but the theory of science is used as a shopping centre of ideas. *Le dernier cri* is self-service in Thomas Kuhn's shop. Recently Hans Westmeyer (1981) accused psychologists of using the theory of Kuhn to legitimize their 'cognitive' revolution against behaviorism without settling whether this theory can be used for psychology or not. As Westmeyer focusses on his disciplinary opponents, I want to mention another example not quoted by him which clearly shows the normative function — not to say the fashionable use — of the concept of paradigms. Rudinger (1979) holds that developmental psychology should be changed —

which is the trend anyway — towards a new model of life-span-development. Instead of experimental child psychology we have developmental psychology, instead of laboratory experiments we have analysis of socioecological conditions, instead of univariate, multi-variate research — and all this is summarized in the call: "changes of paradigms have to be made in order to explain changes (in the development of individuals, U.G.) over a longer period" (p. 163). In the introduction to the 'Year-book for developmental psychology' where Rudinger's paper is published, the editor Rauh sees a change of paradigm as a result of the discussions on the concept of development (Rauh, 1979, p. 14). It may be that it raises one's self-esteem not to take part in a 'normal' concept-change, but in a scientific revolution leading to a change of the 'paradigm'.

History of psychology is practised because the discipline needs it. Therefore it took off as a branch of psychology and not as part of the history of science. The study of the different uses of history in German psychology now leads to the impression that these uses change according to the development of the discipline. Of course the three examples studied are hard to compare, because they do not cover the whole development of German psychology, and because the use of history in all three examples is rather different in content as well as in form. Nonetheless it is my impression that particular disciplinary conditions led to specific uses. Around the turn of the century, history of psychology served mainly to define psychology's relation to philosophy and to crystallize the subject matter of the whole field. We can relate this to the first and second function of history of disciplines named by Lepenies. But also the function of supporting one's inner-disciplinary position by history appeared. During the methodological debate, after the discipline had been established as an independent academic field, and when an open controversy on basic methods had arisen, history was only used here and there mainly to back up arguments within the debate. Then its function was to carry certain concepts against inner-disciplinary opponents. In the crisis of relevance beginning in the Sixties, when psychology had lost its clearcut character and was widening its field to problems of social and therapeutic help, many historical studies were done by psychologists swimming against the mainstream. History then served to support a general critique of established psychology and to aid in the search for alternatives (26).

In addition to this one could ask if the aforesaid aims of history relate to different reference groups. Thus in our first example the wider philosophical community seems to be the target group of the studies; in our second example, history was referred to only for insiders; and the reference group of the critical studies of our third example were mainly students looking for a critical stance to the traditions of their subject.

The way of historical self-reflection within psychology seems mainly to be determined by certain limited disciplinary concerns, by the problems facing the whole discipline and by internal controversies. History is used to stake out the field and to give it a specific orientation, although many authors do not reveal how they (re-)arrange the past for the sake of the future (or may not even be aware that they are doing this). The history of psychology provides the chance to understand oneself within a historical process of social and scientific development, to examine one's own position, to relativize it against the background of historical experiences, and to see the determinants of what one is actually doing. But this chance will be lost if the plans for the future predetermine the findings in the past, or worse, if the plans for the future lead to a superficial use of history to support competition with others.

Stating that history is used in psychology for some restricted aims of the discipline leads to the question "whether social scientists engaged in current controversies, given the legitimatory pressure prevalent among all social sciences compared to the natural sciences, are able to deal in any objective way with the history of their field, or whether their inevitable 'presentism' precludes this option" (27). Within the natural sciences there are certain areas in which science has closed explanations. Theories are proved by scientific experiments, and some of them are definitely rejected when new results show their falseness. However, within the social sciences theories do not have a natural process of aging. You cannot say that Marx or Weber or Wertheimer or Watson are out of date. Faced with new problems, social scientists therefore often go on a haul through history to catch ideas. In psychology one might doubt if there has been any progress in theories or merely a refinement of instruments (see Holzkamp, 1977, p. 6f.). It seems to me that herein lies a structural cause for a certain arbitrariness of the social sciences in their recourse to historical antecedents. A lot of new ideas are created only by historical borrowings. This leads to a situation in which the history of the discipline and the history of its findings can never be written for all times, but must continually be reconsidered as the relevance of its various actors changes.

But this may only be a part of the explanation. The problem is not only one of the self-reflection of disciplines. The critique of psychology in the student movement was due to political attitudes and purposes. Critique of one's field of study was a way to defining one's position in society. This leads to a further consideration.

In the discipline of history, basic concepts are also changed according to the development of the political climate. Perhaps the general relation of men to history is shaped by contemporary problems. The recourse to history is a common way of mastering a crisis of political or national identity, and the evaluation of the political history of a people mainly reflects the stance of an author to contemporary political problems. It is a fact and maybe a necessity that history is used in the solution of current problems. But the interests which are served are not always declared, or easy to ascertain.

Notes

1. The author wishes to thank Richard Holmes and Mitchell G. Ash for their helpful stylistic corrections. Thanks are also due to Irmingard Staeuble, Siegfried Jaeger, Mitchell G. Ash, Wolf Lepenies, and the members of the colloquium on problems and methods of research in the history of psychology at the Free University of Berlin for their valuable comments on a preliminary version. – The manuscript was completed in late 1981.
2. No doubt in the United States the history of psychology had long ceased to be a 'neglected area', as R. I. Watson had put it in 1960. In 1965 the first issue of the *Journal of the History of the Behavioral Sciences* came out, in the same year the governing body of the APA approved the formation of the Division 26, History of Psychology (Ross, 1979). In 1967 the history of psychology was included in the doctoral program of the University of New Hampshire, and in 1969 the first meeting of Cheiron, the *International Society for the History of the Behavioral and Social Sciences* was held. Nonetheless the centennial gave a great credit to the new field.
3. Table I cannot present a really exact account of German-speaking literature in the historiography of psychology. But the figures may show tendencies.
   The categories used in the bibliographies are highly problematic, mirroring the confusion about the nature of history of psychology.
   In the bibliography of Wellek, Section I, 3 is entitled 'Historisches und Biographisches' (Historical and Biographical Accounts). Only the entries of this section have been counted although historical studies on psychology are sometimes listed within other sections too, e.g. Section I, 2 'Systematik, Methode, Gesamtdarstellungen' (systematics, methods, general accounts). Within Section I, 3 reflections

of psychologists on general historical matters have been registered too; these
have been left out here.

The Psychological Abstracts are ordered in the following way:

1960 – History and Biography (incl. obituaries)
     – Theories and Systems
1961 – Obituaries and Biography
     – History and Systems
1962 – Obituaries
  to – History and Biography
1965 – Theory and Systems
1966 – Obituaries
  to – History (incl. Biographies)
1970 – Theory and Systems

The categories used by Dambauer are the following:

1971 pp. – A 10 – History of psychology
                  (a) General accounts
                  (b) Biographically oriented literature
         – A 11 – Psychology in different countries (within this category his-
                  torical studies are to be found)
1975 pp. – A 3 – History of psychology
                – Biographically oriented literature
         – A 4 – Psychology in different countries
         – A 2 – Commemorative volumes and obituaries
1977 pp. – B   – History of psychology
                  1. General accounts
                  2. Biographically oriented literature
                  (a) Commemorative volumes
                  (b) Literature on individual persons

What is reported under the different categories is sometimes very arbitrary.
For instance, under the label 'biographically oriented literature' are listed works
on theories of named authors too, or studies on Aristotelian thought, on Kant,
Plutarch etc. The name of Freud in the title of a study on the concept of labor by
Freud or the name of Eysenck in a study on the 'Eysenck Personality Inventory'
are reason to pigeonhole them into the division of history. Even editions of articles
of prominent psychologists have been included here. On the other hand, historical
literature of a more general type like the dissertation of Kurzweg (1976) is subsumed in the section 'biographically oriented literature' perhaps only because the
name of Dessoir is mentioned in the subtitle.

So I may recommend to read the figures with a certain amount of caution.

4. See the contribution of Mitchell G. Ash in this volume.
5. If I speak about the use of history I mean this whole range, even if I cannot treat
   it all in this study. I will especially focus the explicit historical contributions, but
   not attempt to give a comprehensive survey of all the German ones.

   This study refers only to uses of history documented in the literature. Apart
   from this it also has a use within teaching. The function may be similar. I remember
   our standard course in developmental psychology at the University of Bonn which
   started with a few hours on the history of this branch. The overview left the impression that the field had natural and specific demarcations.

6. A review of German-language works in the history of psychology reporting the different approaches can be found in Pongratz (1980) and Geuter (1981). Pongratz stresses the older works, omitting the newer especially the critical ones including Thomae; I have stressed these and left out the older contributions surveyed in this paper. Pongratz does not touch upon the function of history of psychology in disciplinary development; he only orders the different forms of presentation.

7. All translations from German are my own.

8. Some of the appraisals of this chapter had already been presented by Ebbinghaus at the fourth international congress of psychology in 1900. In part they are word for word the same (see Ebbinghaus, 1901).

9. See also Ebbinghaus, 1901, p. 58.

10. As this study focusses on the role of historical treatises in the disciplinary development of German psychology, this is a further reason that the book (as well as the book of the Hungarian Paul von Schiller) has not been included in this investigation.

11. For instance, in the Netherlands a history of psychology was published in 1929 whose function is explained by van Hoorn (1976, pp. 310–11) as follows:
   "How can one explain the fact that J. van Dael's *History of Empirical Psychology* (1929) appeared in the same year as Boring's first edition of his magnum opus? I think that it was the disturbing plurality of psychology's development in the first quarter of this century that made van Dael decide to give at least an overview of the different opinions. For this purpose he chose a historical approach."

12. See note 4.

13. The institutional and professional development of German psychology will be described more fully in my forthcoming dissertation.

14. An earlier and less extensive version of this chapter was part of a paper presented at the XIIth Annual Meeting of Cheiron (Geuter, 1980b). For a more detailed account of the institutional and professional constraints on the discussion of psychology in the Nazi period in post-war West Germany see Geuter (1980a).

15. For an example in Sociology see the statement on the development of German sociology by Lepsius (1979) and the critique of Schelsky (1980).

16. See my collection of interviews with 39 contemporary psychologists in: Institut für Zeitgeschichte, München, ZS/A 37, esp. pp. 73, 86, 187, and 193.

17. See esp. Wolfgang Metzger, 'Der Auftrag der Psychologie in der Auseinandersetzung mit dem Geist des Westens', *Volk im Werden*, 1942, **10**, pp. 133–144.

18. For a more detailed account of 'Ganzheits-psychology' see Geuter (1980c).

19. Because of its innuendoes we quote here the German original: "Die reine Schau, die in der Evidenz einer Wesensgestalt ihr Ziel findet, kann in den Solipsismus des Wahns führen".

20. I will use these terms to characterize the debate about a 'naturwissenschaftliche' or 'geisteswissenschaftliche' orientation of German psychology. There are some similarities between the old 'geisteswissenschaftliche' psychology and the modern 'humanistic psychology', but they are not identical.

21. Hehlmann had compromised himself during the Nazi regime, had had to leave the university after the war, and then worked in the Brockhaus publishing house, which edited the great German encyclopaedia. His work may be seen primarily as a book for the educated public and not for specialists.

22. The German text leaves open the question whether the history of psychology

should try to show or to develop the scientific character of psychology. The original reads as follows: " ... ist Psychologiegeschichte zu ihrer vornehmsten Arbeit aufgerufen, nämlich derjenigen, durch eine systematische Analyse des Entwicklungsprozesses der Psychologie mitzuwirken am Projekt ihrer Wissenschaftlichkeit".

23. Unfortunately, the disciplinary opponents of this book are located only within the narrow scope of discussions on the definition of psychology's subject matter. In this book the authors did not try to go into the discussions of the historians of science as well, and did not confront the wider problem of the change to modern science. This may mean that it will receive insufficient attention from both psychologists and historians of science.

24. There are some indications for such a tendency. Information which reached me at the end of 1981 may be added here: The council of the German society for Psychology has called for papers for its congress in September, 1982 with the following remark: particularly welcome will be contributions including the historical foundation of one's research problem and method, not in order to show what it was like in the past, but to reveal positions which still shape contemporary research.
    It seems that a relativization of research problems and methods is intended for the sake of a new orientation.

25. See note 4.

26. That even the heavy critique by the students of 'bourgeois' psychology was tangled up with actual disciplinary developments can be seen in their treatment of psychology in the Third Reich. See Geuter (1980 a).

27. I have taken this question with some corrections from a paper of 1980 (b).

References

Adler, M. and Rosemeier, H. P.: 1970, 'Analyse der in der deutschen Psychologie benützten Methoden', *Archiv für Psychologie* **122**, 327–338.

Ash, M. G.: 1980, 'Wilhelm Wundt and Oswald Külpe on the Institutional Status of Psychology: An Academic Controversy in Historical Context', in W. G. Bringmann and R. D. Tweney (eds.), *Wundt Studies/Wundt Studien*. Toronto, pp. 396–421.

Ash, M. G.: 1981, 'Academic Politics in the History of Science: Experimental Psychology in Germany before and after 1914', *Central European History* **14**, 255–286.

Boring, E. G.: 1950, 'A History of Experimental Psychology', New York.

Brožek, J. and Pongratz, L. J. (eds.): 1980, 'Historiography of Modern Psychology', Toronto.

Bruder, K. -J.: 1973, 'Entwurf der Kritik der bürgerlichen Psychologie', in K. -J. Bruder (ed.), *Kritik der bürgerlichen Psychologie*. Frankfurt/M., pp. 92–217.

Bruder, K. -J.: 1978, 'Propaganda der sozialen Kontrolle. Über Skinners 'Radical Behaviorism' ', *Psychologie- und Gesellschaftskritik* **2** (4), 37–57.

Bühler, K.: 1978, 'Die Krise der Psychologie', Frankfurt/M./Berlin/Wien (1927).

Butterfield, H.: 1963, 'The Whig Interpretation of History', London (1931). (Quoted by Stocking, 1965)

Dambauer, J. (ed.): 1971ff., 'Bibliographie der deutschsprachigen psychologischen Literatur', Frankfurt/M.

Danziger, K.: 1979, 'The Positivist Repudiation of Wundt', *Journal of the History of the Behavioral Sciences* 15, 205–230.

Danziger, K.: 1980, 'Wundt as Methodologist', Paper presented at the XXIInd International Congress of Psychology, Leipzig.

Dessoir, M.: 1902, 'Geschichte der neueren deutschen Psychologie', Berlin.

Dessoir, M.: 1911, 'Abriß einer Geschichte der Psychologie', Heidelberg.

Dessoir, M.: 1947, 'Buch der Erinnerung', Stuttgart.

Dilthey, W.: 1924, 'Ideen über eine beschreibende und zergliedernde Psychologie', in *Gesammelte Schriften*, Vol. V. Leipzig/Berlin, pp. 139–140 (1894).

Ebbinghaus, H.: 1901, 'Die Psychologie jetzt und vor hundert Jahren', in P. Janet (ed.), *IVe Congrès International de Psychologie*, Tenu à Paris 1900. Paris, pp. 49–60.

Ebbinghaus, H.: 4/1912, 'Abriß der Psychologie', Leipzig (1908).

Ebel, V.: 1978, 'Zur Situation der Anwender von Psychologie in der BRD. Grußwort des Präsidenten des BdP zum 19. internat. Kongreß für Ang. Psychol. in München, 1978', in Berufsverband Deutscher Psychologen (ed.), *Psychologengesetz oder ein neuer Beruf?* München, pp. 1–2.

Ebert, M.: 1966, 'Die Bedeutung der Philosophie für die Entwicklung der Psychologie zur Einzelwissenschaft', Phil. Diss., München.

Eckardt, G. (ed.): 1979, 'Zur Geschichte der Psychologie', Berlin.

Eyferth, K.: 1967, 'Die Errichtung eines psychologischen Lehrstuhls an der Technischen Hochschule Darmstadt. *Darmstädter Hochschulnachrichten* 5 (1), 7–10.

Flugel, J. C.: undated, 'Probleme und Ergebnisse der Psychologie. Hundert Jahre psychologischer Forschung', Stuttgart, n.d. (engl. 1933).

Geuter, U.: 1979, 'Der Leipziger Kongreß der Deutschen Gesellschaft für Psychologie 1933 – Ausrichtung, Anbieten und Arrangement einer Wissenschaft im nationalsozialistischen Staat', *Psychologie- und Gesellschaftskritik* 3 (4), 6–25.

Geuter, U.: 1980a, 'Institutionelle und professionelle Schranken der Nachkriegsauseinandersetzungen über die Psychologie im Nationalsozialismus', *Psychologie- und Gesellschaftskritik* 4 (1/2), 5–39. Revised English-language summary: 'Constraints on the Discussion of History: German Post-War Treatment of Psychology under the Nazis'. Paper presented at the 12th Annual Meeting of Cheiron, Brunswick 1980b.

Geuter, U.: 1980c, 'Die Zerstörung wissenschaftlicher Vernunft. Felix Krueger und die Leipziger Schule der Ganzheitspsychologie', *Psychologie heute* 7 (4), 35–43.

Geuter, U.: 1981, 'Psychologiegeschichte', in G. Rexilius und S. Grubitzsch (eds.), *Handbuch psychologischer Grundbegriffe*, Reinbek, pp. 824–838.

Graumann, C. F.: 1980, 'Experiment, Statistik, Geschichte. Wundts erstes Heidelberger Programm einer Psychologie', *Psychologische Rundschau* 31, 73–83.

Grünwald, H.: 1979, 'Der soziale Charakter von Konzeptionen psychologischer Diagnostik. Eine Untersuchung zu Inhalt, Entstehung und Konkurrenz von Diagnostikkonzeptionen', Phil. Diss., München.

Grünwald, H.: 'Über die Vernachlässigung der Psychologiegeschichtsschreibung und wie und zu welchem besseren Ende Historiographie der Psychologie betrieben werden sollte', in W. Michaelis (ed.), *Bericht über den 32. Kongreß der Deutschen Gesellschaft für Psychologie in Zürich 1980*, Göttingen, Toronto, Zürich, pp. 139–145.

Hartmann, E. v.: 1901, 'Die moderne Psychologie. Eine kritische Geschichte der deutschen Psychologie in der zweiten Hälfte des neunzehnten Jahrhunderts', Leipzig.

Hearnshaw, L. S.: 1964, 'A Short History of British Psychology, 1840–1940', London.

Hehlmann, W.: 1963, 'Geschichte der Psychologie', Stuttgart.

Herrmann, T.: 1966, 'Zur Geschichte der Berufseignungsdiagnostik', *Archiv für die gesamte Psychologie* 118, 253–278.

Hiebsch, H.: 1979, 'Wilhelm Wundt und die Anfänge der experimentellen Psychologie – Zur Hundertjahrfeier des ersten Psychologischen Laboratoriums der Welt in Leipzig', *Probleme und Ergebnisse der Psychologie* (No. 71), 5–18.

Hofstätter, P. R.: 1953, 'Psychologie und Mathematik', *Studium Generale* 6, 652–662.

Holzkamp, K.: 1972, 'Kritische Psychologie', Frankfurt/M.

Holzkamp, K.: 1973, 'Sinnliche Erkenntnis. Historischer Ursprung und gesellschaftliche Funktion der Wahrnehmung', Frankfurt/M.

Holzkamp, K.: 1977, 'Die Überwindung der wissenschaftlichen Beliebigkeit psychologischer Theorien durch die Kritische Psychologie', *Zeitschrift für Sozialpsychologie* 8, 1–22 and 78–97.

Holzkamp, K.: 1980, 'Zu Wundts Kritik an der experimentellen Erforschung des Denkens', *Forum Kritische Psychologie* (No. 6) (= Argument-Sonderband, 49), 156–165.

Holzner, B.: undated, 'Amerikanische und deutsche Psychologie', Würzburg (1959).

Hoorn, W. van: 1976, 'Netherlands', in V. S. Sexton and H. Misiak (eds.), *Psychology around the World*. Monterey, Cal., pp. 293–316.

Jaeger, S. and Staeuble, I.: 1978, 'Die gesellschaftliche Genese der Psychologie', Frankfurt/M., New York.

Jaeger, S. and Staeuble, I.: 1981, 'Die Psychotechnik und ihre gesellschaftlichen Entwicklungsbedingungen', in Die *Psychologie des 20. Jahrhunderts*, Vol. XIII, Zürich, pp. 53–95.

Klemm, O.: 1911, 'Geschichte der Psychologie', Leipzig, Berlin.

Kuhn, T. S.: 1978, 'Die Entstehung des Neuen'. Frankfurt/M.

'Kundgebung der Deutschen Gesellschaft für Psychologie: Über die Pflege der Psychologie an den deutschen Hochschulen', 1930, in H. Volkelt (ed.), *Bericht über den XI. Kongreß der Gesellschaft für experimentelle Psychologie in Wien 1929*, Jena, pp. VII–X.

Kurzweg, A.: 1976, 'Die Geschichte der Berliner "Gesellschaft für Experimental-Psychologie" mit besonderer Berücksichtigung ihrer Ausgangssituation und des Wirkens von Max Dessoir', Med. Diss., Berlin.

Lepenies, W.: 1975, 'Geschichte und Anthropologie', *Geschichte und Gesellschaft* 1, 325–343.

Lepenies, W.: 1978, 'Wissenschaftsgeschichte und Disziplingeschichte', *Geschichte und Gesellschaft* 4, 437–451.

Lepsius, R.: 1979, 'Die Entwicklung der Soziologie nach dem Zweiten Weltkrieg 1945 bis 1967', *Kölner Zeitschrift für Soziologie und Sozialpsychologie, Sonderheft* 21, 25–70.

MacLeod, R.: 1977, 'Changing Perspectives in the Social History of Science', in I. Spiegel-Rösing and D. de Sola Price (eds.), *Science, Technology, and Society*. London, Beverley Hills, pp. 149–195.

Maikowski, R., Mattes, P., and Rott, G.: 1976, 'Psychologie und ihre Praxis. Materialien zur Geschichte und Funktion einer Einzelwissenschaft in der Bundesrepublik', Frankfurt/M.

Mattes, P.: 1972, 'Entwicklung der Berufstätigkeit von Psychologen in der BRD', in

Psychologie als historische Wissenschaft, Pressedienst Wissenschaft, Freie Universität Berlin, 8, pp. 39–45.

Mattes, P.: 1979, 'Der Akademismus der Kritischen Psychologie. Hinweise auf ihre Entstehungsgeschichte', in T. Busch *et al., Zur Kritik der Kritischen Psychologie*. Berlin, 8, pp. 39–54.

Mattes, P.: 1980, 'Profession bei Fuß – Wehrmachtspsychologie nach 1945', *Psychologie- und Gesellschaftskritik* 4 (1/2), 40–46.

Meili, R.: 1954, 'Ein Zerrbild der Testpsychologie', *Psychologische Rundschau* 5, 81–86.

Messer, A.: 1927, 'Einführung in die Psychologie', Leipzig.

Métraux, A.: 1980, 'Wilhelm Wundt und die Institutionalisierung der Psychologie', *Psychologische Rundschau* 31, 84–98.

Metzger, W.: 1965, 'The Historical Background for National Trends in Psychology: German Psychology', *Journal of the History of the Behavioral Sciences* 1, 109–115.

Metzger, W.: 1979, 'Gestaltpsychologie – ein Ärgernis für die Nazis', *Psychologie heute* 6 (3), 84–85.

Müller-Freienfels, R.: 1935, 'The Evolution of Modern Psychology', New Haven.

Obermeit, W.: 1980, 'Das unsichtbare Ding, das Seele heißt'. Die Entdeckung der Psyche im bürgerlichen Zeitalter'. Frankfurt/M.

O'Donnell, J. M.: 1979, 'The Crisis of Experimentalism in the 1920s: E. G. Boring and his Uses of History', *American Psychologist* 34, 289–295.

Pongratz, L. J.: 1967, 'Problemgeschichte der Psychologie', Bern, München.

Pongratz, L. J.: 1980, 'German Historiography of Psychology, 1808–1972', in J. Brožek and L. J. Pongratz (eds.), *Historiography of Modern Psychology*. Toronto, pp. 74–89.

Rauh, H.: 1979, 'Der Wandel von der traditionellen zur modernen Entwicklungspsy- chologie', *Jahrbuch für Entwicklungspsychologie* 1, 9–23.

Ross, B., 1979, 'Psychology's Centennial Year', *Journal of the History of the Behavioral Sciences* 15, 203–204.

Rudinger, G.: 1979, 'Erfassung von Entwicklungsveränderungen im Lebenslauf', *Jahrbuch für Entwicklungspsychologie* 1, 157–214.

Samelson, F.: 1974, 'History, origin myth, and ideology: Comte's 'discovery' of social psychology', *Journal for the Theory of Social Behavior* 4, 217–231.

Saupe, E.: 1928, 'Einführung in die neuere Psychologie', Osterwieck.

Schelsky, H.: 1980, 'Zur Entstehungsgeschichte der bundesdeutschen Soziologie. Ein Brief an Rainer Lepsius'. *Kölner Zeitschrift für Soziologie und Sozialpsychologie* 32, 417–456.

Schiller, P. v.: 1948, 'Aufgabe der Psychologie', Wien, (Hungarian 1940).

Schmid, R.: 1977, 'Intelligenz- und Leistungsmessung. Geschichte und Funktion psy- chologischer Tests'. Frankfurt/M., New York.

Schmid, R. and Wacker, A.: 1978, 'Begabung und Intelligenz in Pädagogik und Psy- chologie – Darstellung und Analyse der Problemstellungen seit 1945', in R. Schmid (ed.) *Intelligenzforschung und pädagogische Praxis*, München, pp. 15–71.

Seeger, F.: 1977, 'Relevanz und Entwicklung der Psychologie', Darmstadt.

Siebeck, H.: 1961, 'Geschichte der Psychologie', Amsterdam, (reprint) (1879; 1883).

Simoneit, M.: 1954, 'Zur Kritik der Testdiagnostik', *Psychologische Rundschau* 5, 44–53.

Staeuble, I.: 1972, 'Politischer Ursprung und politische Funktionen der pragmatischen Sozialpsychologie', in: H. Nolte and I. Staeuble, *Zur Kritik der Sozialpsychologie*, München, pp. 7–65.

Thomae, H.: 1968, 'Das Individuum und seine Welt:. Göttingen.

Thomae, H.: 1977, 'Psychologie in der modernen Gesellschaft', Hamburg.

Watson, R. I.: 1960, 'The History of Psychology: A Neglected Area', *American Psychologist* 15, 251–255.

Wehner, E. G.: 1973, 'Ordnungsaspekte der Psychologiegeschichtsschreibung', in G. Reinert (ed.), *Bericht über den 27. Kongreß der Deutschen Gesellschaft für Psychologie*, Göttingen, pp. 206–218.

Wehner, E. G.: 1980, 'Einführung in die empirische Psychologie', Stuttgart, Berlin, Köln, Mainz.

Wellek, A.: 1959, 'Der Rückfall in die Methodenkrise der Psychologie und ihre Überwindung', Göttingen.

Wellek, A.: 1960, 'Deutsche Psychologie und Nationalsozialismus', *Psychologie und Praxis* 4, 177–182.

Wellek, A.: 1964, 'Der Einfluß der deutschen Emigration auf die Entwicklung der amerikanischen Psychologie', *Psychologische Rundschau* 15, 239–262.

Wellek, A. (ed.): 1965, 'Gesamtverzeichnis der deutschsprachigen psychologischen Literatur der Jahre 1942 bis 1960', Göttingen.

Westmeyer, H.: 1981, 'Zur Paradigmadiskussion in der Psychologie', in W. Michaelis (ed.), *Bericht über den 32. Kongreß der Deutschen Gesellschaft für Psychologie in Zürich 1980*, Göttingen, Toronto, Zürich, pp. 115–126.

Wundt, W.: 1976, 'Beiträge zur Theorie der Sinneswahrnehmung', in W. G. Bringmann (ed.), *The Origins of Psychology*, Vol. IV. New York, Amsterdam, pp. 109–205.

CULTURAL ANTHROPOLOGY AND THE PARADIGM-CONCEPT: A BRIEF HISTORY OF THEIR RECENT CONVERGENCE (1)

BOB SCHOLTE

University of Amsterdam

I

The purpose of this essay is two-fold: to trace the use (and perhaps mis-use) of the paradigm concept in contemporary anthropology and to delineate the anthropological contribution to redefining the notion of paradigm more adequately. Certain preliminary strictures must be kept in mind, however, in order to appreciate what this essay hopes to contribute and what it cannot achieve.

Firstly, this article is in part an intellectual-historical auto-biography. That is, an attempt to indicate and to assess the professional circumstances which led many critical anthropologists in the United States to be directly influenced by, or at least receptive to, Thomas Kuhn's *The Structure of Scientific Revolutions* when first published in 1962. The book's publication constituted a kind of conscious-raising event, even for those social scientists and others who did not explicitly use Kuhn's central metaphor: the concept of paradigm. As the one who initially introduced the term paradigm to the anthropological literature (2), I want to trace the specific circumstances which made me use the concept in the first place and why it became such a prominent term in the social scientific literature during the nineteenth-sixties and seventies. I am, in other words, looking back on the intellectual-historical circumstances of my own formative years, interpreting some of the professional developments of the past two decades retrospectively. I do so as one who was involved actively, albeit selectively, in a period of disciplinary crisis and who, like others, has gained a certain distance on the period in question and would like to come to an initial assessment of what occurred. I do not, of

Loren Graham, Wolf Lepenies, and Peter Weingart (eds.), *Functions and Uses of Disciplinary Histories, Volume VII*, 1983, 229–278.

course, pretend to represent an entire community of critical anthropologists, let alone an entire generation of social scientists (in my own case predominantly American) (3). Furthermore, I can well imagine that others might come to an entirely different assessment of the sixties and seventies, would draw other conclusions from our discipline's recent history, and are currently engaged in a variety of projects not directly related to the specific issues that preoccupied them in the previous two decades. That does not, however, preclude the possibility that continuities exist and should be explored. That is what I should like to begin doing here.

Secondly, this essay is programmatic. It is part and parcel of a much larger effort and represents by itself and in skeleton form only the beginning. I shall discuss existential, sociological, philosophical, and historical dimensions of the paradigm concept (both as used in anthropology and as anthropologically redefined), though much more would need to be concretely exemplified for a proper assessment of both the concept's use and its anthropological reformulation. The former topic would require a detailed social history of recent anthropology, while the latter suggests fruitful lines of inquiry that remain to be fully explored (4). Both topics are formidable and well beyond the limited scope of this essay (for similar overviews, see Lepenies, 1974 and 1981).

II

The initial appeal of Kuhn's notion of paradigm during the early sixties can be explained on several levels. Broadly viewed, it served as a means to articulate (though not to solve) the then current crisis in cultural anthropology. Let me right away point out that Kuhn's definition of the concept did not at first constitute a serious problem. On the contrary, precisely because the concept seemed 'overdetermined', i.e., apparently all-encompassing, it seemed 'universally' applicable to both the natural and the social sciences. Some have, indeed, questioned the applicability of Kuhn's ideas to the social sciences and have designated the latter as pre-paradigmatic in comparison with the authentic paradigms of the natural sciences (Kuhn himself seems unclear on the issue, cf. 1970: 207ff). But even if formally correct, this circumscription is − in my estimation − based on too literal a reading of Kuhn's book and fails to account for the actual reverberations that the paradigm concept had, rightly or wrongly, in the intellectual-historical climate of the sixties (especially in the social sciences!). With the benefit of hind-sight, it is too easy to claim that "social scientists uncritically ransacked Kuhn's theories and made indiscriminate and biased use of the concept of paradigm" (Llobera, 1976: 28) without at one and the same time explaining why so many social scientists responded positively to Kuhn's book in the first place.

Anthropologists did so for several reasons: most notably because Kuhn's history of the natural sciences served, by analogy to the social sciences, to relativize and to contextualize an 'established' anthropology with which many of us had become disenchanted (see Scholte, 1971). Through an 'anthropology of anthropology' (which seemed the most comprehensive intellectual-historical message of Kuhn's book), we were in a better position to evaluate our discipline as the intellectual symptom of an ethnocentric and imperialist culture or, ideally, as the empathetic and humane response to a crual and fragmented world in political and moral crisis.

There were other and more specific reasons why Kuhn's book should have appealed to cultural anthropologists. The sociological factors and historical processes Kuhn described and analyzed in the transition from a normal to a revolutionary disciplinary praxis seemed particularly well suited to the specific situation in which our generation found itself — both descriptively and normatively. Kuhn's book served to legitimize our 'radical' aspirations for a 'reinvented' anthropology (see Hymes, 1972) and to provide the conceptual equipment for criticizing the reactionary, dogmatic, and irrelevant anthropology we were (or thought we were) largely taught.

Kuhn's specific appeal must also have had something to do with the fact that his entire sensibility not only suited our existential circumstances and professional hopes, but that *The Structure of Scientific Revolutions* seemed so obviously anthropological in spirit. We may, of course, have been mistaken on both accounts. The notion of paradigm may imply a conservative rather than a revolutionary ideology or, for that matter, carry no clear prescriptive implications at all (see Feyerabend, 1979: 197ff). Kuhn himself is unclear on the ideological alternatives, apparently wanting to have his cake and eat it too. He considers the scientific enterprise as a whole paradoxical since "successful research demands a deep commitment to the *status quo*, [though] innovation remains at the heart of the enterprise" (Kuhn, 1972: 102). These conflicting values effect scientific socialization as well: "Though scientific development is particularly productive of consequential novelties, scientific education remains a relatively dogmatic initiation into preestablished problem-solving traditions that the student is neither invited nor equipped to evaluate" (Kuhn, 1972: 84–85).

Perhaps Kuhn was indeed more conservative than we recognized at the time (see also Martins, 1972 and Simmons and Stehr, 1981), but our felt response was in any event the opposite of what might be deduced from the liberal establishment's critiques (e.g., Kaplan and Manners, 1979) or, say, Bloor's contrast between Kuhn's conservative Romanticism and Popper's Enlightenment liberalism (Bloor 1976: 54ff; see also Wilson, 1977: 73). We actually saw the Popperians (Jarvie, Leach, Kaplan, and Manners in anthropology) as the establishmentarians par excellence and argued extensively with all of them (see Scholte, 1978 for a summary). We saw Kuhn's perspective, perhaps naively, as a legitimate means to shatter the restrictive syntax of the established order (Monod, 1970–1971: 1062).

As far as the anthropological spirit of *The Structure of Scientific Revolutions* is concerned, it certainly wasn't remotely anthropological or even sociological until the second edition, but we interpreted it as an anthropological study: as an ethno-history of the ethno-sciences (our own). Moreover, we read into Kuhn's approach a semiotic or linguistic dimension (the term paradigm is, after all, derived from linguistics) which only later became the explicit focus of Kuhn's own reassessment (see Kuhn, 1969 and 1970). This language-centered reading fitted in especially well with the American tradition of linguistic relativity, the burgeoning efforts to contextualize formal linguistics, the application of ethno-semantic methods to cultural domains (also called ethno-science!) and, finally, the inadequately understood but nonetheless felt arrival of the semiotic revolution. Specifically, Kuhn's notion of paradigm was used in an early and comparative study of linguistic traditions (Grace, 1969) and again, quite extensively, in a more recent and detailed history of American structuralism (Hymes and Fought, 1975) (5).

I have thus far given a rather impressionistic account of Kuhn's appeal. With the benefit of hind-sight, we may have been excessively enthusiastic (the critique of Kuhn had not as yet reached us) and perhaps somewhat naive (making Kuhn a cultural, language-centered anthropologist *malgré lui*). Nevertheless *The Structure of Scientific Revolutions* offered, so it seemed, a means for understanding anthropological traditions contextually: as more or less distinctive, multiple, and relative 'universes of discourse' (6). The anthropological ideal that had often been taught, despite the discipline's humanistic heritage, was that of a scientifically rigorous and syntagmatically formal discourse on a known or in principle knowable universe (7). Kuhn's more inclusive message seemed clear by comparison: universes of discourse (including science) are not only syntagmatic, but more essentially paradigmatic. They should not exclusively nor even primarily be considered syntactically (as an internally structured, logically related and historically progressive sequence), but above all in terms of their contextual meaning (semantics) and their specific use (pragmatics) [see Wilden, 1972 or Scholte, 1976]. Even the formal rules and ideal logic proper to a deductive scientific discourse are in the last analysis embedded in a natural language *in situ* (ordinary language is in this sense always the last meta-language). As Wellmer puts it: " . . . grammatical rules are necessarily more than *mere* grammatical rules; in as much as they govern a *praxis*, they are also rules of training in a social form of life" (Wellmer, 1969: 26—27). Similarly, Fabian (1979: 23) observes that any process of knowledge production, including formalism, takes place in an inter-subjective, processual, and communicative context and is therefore, by definition and in fact, practical and constitutive as well as formal. Formalism as such merely generates an illusionary competence (equating all true knowledge with scientific knowledge) and thereby obscures its actual and vested interests (sustaining academic careers, legitimizing the status quo, etc.).

To put all this in its historical context and in anthropologically familiar terms, Kuhn showed that scientific traditions were specific language games reflecting distinctive forms of life. This was an especially relevant insight for our generation since we also were (or thought we were) experimenting with alternative life-styles and their appropriate intellectual embodiment. The notion of paradigm was useful in this regard and could be applied to anthropological traditions, including the ones we were taught. This required a dual perspective that we anthropologists had readily and consistently applied to everyone's ethno-science *but* our own: The principles of context and comparison. As I formulated it in several working papers during the sixties, all anthropological *texts* are defined by their cultural *con*texts and every *logic* is at one and the same time an *ethno*-logic. Context-dependence is integral

to the proper understanding of anthropological traditions, even though
considered an embarrassment to formal analyses of scientific progress (compare Giddens, 1976: 105).

III

Still, the question remains: Why was Kuhn specifically singled out? The term
paradigm may have served as a convenient and timely device for contextu-
alizing and relativizing anthropological traditions, but the dual perspective
for doing so had, after all, been an integral part of the critical tradition from
Vico, Montaigne, Rousseau, and Marx onwards (see Lemaire, 1976 and 1980).
It is explicit in several 'classical' anthropological books and articles on cultural
relativism during the thirties, forties, and fifties (one thinks of Benedict,
Herskovits, Mead, Sapir and others). I think there are at least two additional
reasons why Kuhn's notion of paradigm — although perhaps not all that
different in spirit from such traditional concepts as 'pattern,' 'configuration,'
or even 'culture' itself — nevertheless allowed us to explicate what had thus
far remained largely implicit. First of all, the specific analysis Kuhn made of
paradigmatic change corresponded closely to the institutional situation of
cultural anthropology in the sixties. Secondly, our rendition of his analysis
legitimized the disciplinary importance of external sociopolitical developments to which we felt compelled to address ourselves at the time as citizens
and anthropologists (most notably the student revolution, the civil-rights
movement, and the Viet-Nam war protest). Traditional concepts of culture,
no matter how contextually sensitive and comparatively relativistic, had
failed to address precisely these kinds of historical developments. In fact,
they tended to obscure them: "In the discipline of anthropology, it is the
ambiguous and ill-defined term 'culture' that anthropologists who wish
to avoid political realities have conveniently hidden behind; and it is the
concept of culture, with its strong psychological and ideological emphasis,
that has recently opened the door to new forms of . . . ideology with which
to rationalize the status quo" (Leacock, 1980: 154) (8).

   Kuhn's analysis of the history of science demystified the ideology of
normal science which most of our mentors formally taught. That Kuhn
humanized a reified conception of the natural sciences was all the more
dramatic since we had been urged to model our own procedures on these very

sciences. We had been taught to consider the existential, social, historical, and philosophical mediation of the human sciences as mere residual factors that could and should be transcended by means of methodological rigor. In practice this abstract ideal seemed more like *rigor mortis* to many of us and certainly did not correspond to our actual functioning both inside the academy and in the outside world. Inside we were beginning to challenge institutional priorities (the absence of minorities and women from our faculties, the hierarchical structure of the academy as a whole) as well as the repressed and repressive metaphors of normal scientific discourse (e.g., harmony and equilibrium models that seemed beyond time and space, acculturation studies that obligingly 'forgot' colonialism, formal elegance at the express of substantive knowledge, etc.). Just as importantly, we began to question the (mis) use of such metaphors in policy recommendations regarding the Third-World (in developmental programs, applied anthropology, technological and economic aid). There were even explicit critiques phrased in terms of a disenchantment with normal science (emphasizing continuity, consensus, order, prediction, control) and an advocacy of revolutionary science (emphasizing discontinuity, dissensus, class-struggle, emancipation, independence (e.g., Bodenheimer, 1970).

The sixties were a time of political turmoil abroad as well as at home. As responsive and responsible anthropologists, how could we not question normal science when the so-called Third-World began to define its own historical destiny and when its peoples commenced to talk back at the social scientist (an unpleasant and inconvenient anomaly for those who had applied their structural-functional models to passive and silent natives in a colonial setting)? And how did science as usual respond, or rather, fail to respond to genocide and ethnocide — homicidal practices we saw (and still see) happening in South-East Asia or South and Central America, often with the direct participation of normal scientists? Not surprisingly, Wolf and Jorgensen felt compelled to wash our dirty-linen in public, to the consternation and displeasure of the 'true' professionals. They ominously concluded that "the grimmest lesson of all the events of the past years [is perhaps this:] ... many a naive anthropologist has become, wittingly or unwittingly, an informer" (Wolf and Jorgensen, 1970: 34). To rephrase this rude political awakening in terms provided by Kuhn, our notions of the trivial and important began to change. We judged normal science as professionally fragmented, specialized, and circumstantial and – above all – as morally partial, blind, even corrupt. Kuhn might call it a crisis in legitimacy (but no less political because of it, see Nowotny, 1979: 81) and one demanding a revolution or at least a reinvention of anthropology (see again Hymes, 1972).

As with the other social sciences, the most explicit symptom of the crisis in anthropology was the disenchantment with a value-free or neutral epistemology, one that in practice proved to be value-laden and ethno-centric. There was instead the desire to found a value-committed anthropology, one that would stand by the emancipatory aspirations of oppressed peoples rather than by the vested interests of the oppressor civilization. *The Structure of Scientific Revolutions* did not, admittedly, give us an alternative model for a normative anthropology (neo-Marxism served that function for several of us), but it did provide a meta-level recognition of the media*ted* status of cultural anthropology, one which also inhibited and/or encouraged its media*ting* possibilities.

It seemed clear that this meta-level recognition entailed two political options. One, anthropology might continue outside the academy where, so we rather naively thought, 'proof' would not be strictly identified with abstract reason, formal experiment, or predictive law and where human values, however problematic and ambiguous, could still be recognized and honored: that love is preferable to hate, peace to war, food to hunger, health to sickness. Many younger anthropologists did, in fact, leave graduate school for precisely these reasons (9).

The second alternative was the one the 'new Left Establishment' took: not to take anthropology out of the academy, but to try to make the academy more relevant and humane. That is, first of all to understand the discipline itself as an anthropological and cultural invention, subject to historical and social circumstances. Then, if possible, to make the profession more responsive to individuals both inside and outside its largely urban and Occidental confines. In the case of some of us (e.g., Diamond, Hymes, myself) this led directly to a renewed interest in the history and sociology of anthropology – both as an academic and, more dramatically, issue-oriented enterprise.

IV

In the sixties and seventies, Kuhn's notion of paradigm served to reorient the reflexive study of anthropological traditions along anthropological lines. In the eighties, when normal science seems once again to have hardened its paradigmatic arteries, it seems *à propos* to reverse the question and to ask what anthropologists might contribute to a reformulation or refinement of the paradigm concept. The two issues are, of course, related. In using Kuhn's notion of paradigmatic change to study the past and present circumstances of cultural anthropology, one encounters anthropological perspectives and issues (the semiotic one, for instance, or the rationality debate) which are either implicit or simply absent from Kuhn's own formulation or, indeed, from the sociological and philosophical literature which succeeded the publication of *The Structure of Scientific Revolutions*.

I shall divide my discussion into several dimensions: the existential, the sociological, the philosophical, and the historical. These divisions are in principle arbitrary, though their respective importance can probably be weighed historically. Thus, in the sixties and seventies, we were actively and personally engaged in radicalizing and reformulating our profession and the existential dimension loomed correspondingly large. In the eighties, looking back with a sense of distance (and perhaps nostalgia) and the 'wisdom' of middle-age (or is it political exhaustion and academic compromise?), the historical dimension gains in relative importance. In other words, our social circumstances have changed. Most of us now have vested interests of our own and are not likely to rock the academic boat (which has recently been battered by waves of economic and demographic decline). I would venture to guess that by the time we retire, philosophical reflection will seem the most promising and appropriate . . . .

V

The existential dimension of the paradigm concept involves the fundamental question of the continuity and/or discontinuity between human experience and scientific knowledge. In both the philosophical critique of Kuhn's work and the establishmentarian response to critical anthropology, the issue is often misrepresented (no doubt for rhetorical reasons) as an *ego*-logical instead of an *eco*-logical one (10). What is actually meant by using a paradigmatic perspective is based on the epistemological and dialectical realization that all scientific activity, anthropological praxis included, is part and parcel of the natural processes and human relations studied and that there is, by definition and in practice, an existential, inter-subjective, conditioned, and situated component to all sciencing.

The methodological dualism generated by a discontinuous epistemology (the one prevalent in positivism and characteristic of structuralism) does not so much enhance as diminish objectivity. In fact, repressing the subject is not objective at all. It is either a self-serving theoretical over-sight (see Feyerabend, 1978: 83) or a coercive means to compel submission and conformity to establishmentarian definitions of reality, reasonableness, realism, objectivity, truth, verification, practicality, common-sense, necessity, or whatever (compare Franck, 1979). As an epistemological position, methodological dualism (in contrast to dialectical reflexivity) is disastrous – philosophically *and* politically. In anthropological praxis, for instance, epistemological dualism reduces the ethnographic self to a solitary and privileged voyeur: a divinely constituting subject from whom emanates the ethnological designs of other cultures (see especially Bourdieu, 1977 or Sahlins, 1976). The ethnographer's constituted cultural patterns may become the static objects of further semiotic contemplations, reducing the actual cultures and peoples themselves to speechless units of anthropological analyses. In theory, such analyses permit any learned discourses whatever or, more specifically, abstract monologues guided by the historical needs and political interests of the dominant culture represented (intentionally or not) by the observer-analyst. To paraphrase Sartre, the questioned are thus absorbed by the question posed on behalf of the questioner (Sartre, 1963: 174). In other words, self-interest is uncritically disguised as methodological rigor.

The theoretical and practical considerations that attend epistemological continuity in contrast to methodological discontinuity are not my specific concern here (but see Scholte, 1971, 1972, 1976, or 1980). Let me simply stress that the constitutive role of the social scientist is, from a paradigmatic point of view, crucial to the actual determination of his or her scientific 'object' *and* to the *critical* understanding of any situated knowledge whatsoever. Any syntagmatic discourse considered paradigmatically demands a further question: Who defines significance (scientific, ideological, aesthetic, normative, or whatever) on whose behalf and at what expense? Who authorizes the discourse in question and/or who invests it with authority (truth-value, legitimacy, beauty, relevance)? These are precisely the kinds of questions that are neglected in the dualistic epistemologies of empiricism, positivism, structuralism, even Popperianism (see Law, 1975). And such an oversight makes all the difference in the world.

The anthropological perspective can, I believe, add a crucial dimension to the notion of paradigm here, one commensurate with the linguistic or semiotic turn taken by Kuhn himself. The anthropological contribution is at least three-fold: substantive, epistemological, and historical. Substantively, a paradigmatic approach to formal discourse compensates for the systematic neglect, in both the social and the natural sciences, of situating authoritative discourse (the scientific text and its specific object) in its concrete socio-historical context. In cultural anthropology, reification of professional discourse generates an abstract description and analysis of the 'real' or 'authentic' society in question (the object) which is then mistaken for an actual account and in-depth elucidation of that culture's authoritative history and behavior (see Asad, 1975, 1979 and Said, 1979). Not only does the anthropologist thereby circumvent and obscure the society's own criteria of authority (which would give the very idea of social legitimacy its indigenous authenticity), he or she also substitutes for a culture's *ethno*-logic the allegedly superior or transcending authority of the scientific logic proper to Western rationality.

Bourdieu calls this co-optative process the 'paralogism' underlying 'legalism' and he further points out that it is not only ethnocentric, but epistemologically faulty as well. The process "consists in implicitly placing in the consciousness of individual agents the theoretical knowledge which can only be constructed and conquered against practical experience; in other terms, it consists of conferring the value of an anthropological description upon a theoretical model constructed in order to account for practices. The theory of action as simple *execution* of a model (in the dual sense of norm and scientific construction) is one example among many of the imaginary anthropology engendered by objectivism when taking, as Marx put it, 'the things of logic for the logic of things' " (Bourdieu, 1973: 63) (11).

Being a syntagmatic discourse, this formal logic's epistemological dualism (the philosophy of discontinuity) is often semiotically marked. The specific grammar of science is ideally de-authorized grammar, that is, a discourse that prefers to hide its author and thereby to obscure the contingency of what is being said (see Gouldner, 1976). The cultural anthropological use of the impersonal third-person 'he' or 'she' in ethnographic description is a concrete

example; the exclusively monological rendition of field-work (an epistemological situation which is or ought to be dialogical per excellence) is another
(cf. Dwyer, 1979; or Tedlock, 1979). Syntagmatic discourse, in other words,
ignores the socio-linguistic extent to which the 'object' spoken about is
paradigmatically dependent on a situated speaker and his or her specific
language game. It thereby generates an illusionary objectivity whose actual
intentions must be deciphered from the text.

Historically, the epistemological reification of the formal grammar proper
to Western rationality reflects the unique authority and trans-cultural legitimacy we attribute to what is, in fact, the circumscribed logic of a specific
historical praxis (our own). As our exemplary paradigm, this disembodied
logos is presumed to be context-independent and to constitute all possible
knowledge. It is in that sense theological rather than scientific; or rather, it is
a rationalism that may be characterized as "a secularized form of the belief
in the power of the word of God" (Feyerabend, 1978: 20). The underlying
motives for this alleged transcendence can be traced historically. For instance,
in the history of anthropology, differing formal traditions variously domesti-
cate and encase the exotic and unknown for their own specific, historical,
scientific, ideological, or outright political purposes. The native (the scientific
'object') thus becomes culturally derivative: the artifact or the projection of
the intellectualization which was intended to comprehend him or her (see
Burridge, 1973: 234).

VI

The sociological dimension of Kuhn's perspective (or rather, its inadequacies)
has been commented upon extensively and I only want to add a few anthropological remarks here. The term 'paradigm' suited the historical circumstance
of cultural anthropology in the sixties in part because we explicitly sought
to relate intellectual traditions to life-styles (not only those of native others,
but in our own case as well). Kuhn had suggested such a relation for the
natural sciences (however inadequately) and we had other examples from
sociology (e.g., Marxism and the sociology of knowledge) and anthropology
(e.g., linguistic relativity, ethno-science). The task entailed, first of all, contextualization, that is, an ethnographic inquiry into the social organization
of ethnological theory. Among many of us, this effort immediately took a

critical turn (though it did not exclude more conventional studies, e.g., on the institutionalization of anthropology departments, see Darnell, 1971 and Gruber, 1975). There was a distinct sense that the culture of science was not necessarily nor even primarily the exclusive and privileged road to exalted and eternal truths, but that it was in actual practice one 'cultural habitus' (Bourdieu, 1967: 234) among others. Moreover, as a way of 'learning how to learn' (Bateson, 1972), science education was often experienced as inhibiting and alienating. Diamond expressed our specific situation succinctly: "The 'professional' anthropologist is an alien, although — perhaps because — he claims the whole of the Western tradition for his ancestry. Claiming everything, he is in danger of being nothing. Indeed, he is estranged three times over: first, in his own society . . . ; second, in the choice of his profession; and finally, in relation to those whom he studies" (Diamond, 1974: 94—95). We considered oversocialization in the then current paradigms as tantamount to dulling the critical faculties — especially in the face of the moral and political crises that surrounded us and the historical events in which many of us were taking an active part (12).

There was a related institutional dimension to the critique of scientific learning: the academy itself. Professionalism as taught there seemed democratic and universalistic in theory, but distinctly hierarchical and bureaucratic in practice. Many of us rejected the *soi-disant* liberal ideology of university establishments that were only beginning (and reluctantly at that) to address questions of co-optation, repression, sexism, racism, etc.

Whether we were right or wrong in every detail of our criticism of institutionalized anthropology as we encountered it is less significant, I think, than the radical relativism it generated. And this is again where Kuhn's *The Structure of Scientific Revolutions* came into play. Viewed paradigmatically, scientific logic is a socio- or ethno-logic among others. Scientific truth, in other words, is a conventional representation, not of the ultimately real, but of relative standards perpetuated by an academic community. The reified discourse of this language community is not distinctive because it reveals universal truths, but rather because it self-righteously and pompously hides its own competitive and alienating form of life behind an elaborate verbal facade.

Scientific ideals, institutionally concretized, seemed little more than an ideological consensus among largely male, white, middle-aged and middle-class cliques in which positional power often seemed vastly more decisive than so-called empirical demonstration (in which the very definition of the factual was in any event a political question) and where paradigmatic choices between different modes of scientific explanation were social processes rather than methodological decisions in which personal taste, class prejudice, sexual discrimination, or institutional coercion played at least as decisive a role as did the canons of scientific reason designed to obfuscate them.

In retrospect, we may have (mis) used the sociological dimension of the paradigm concept more like a hatchet than a tool. Still, twenty years later, the socio-political processes of academic life that we decried then seem as pervasive as ever. Perhaps they are simply inherent in the scientific enterprise considered as competitive activity: " ... the scientific field is the locus of a competitive struggle, in which the *specific* issue at stake is the monopoly of *scientific authority*, defined inseparately as technical capacity and social power, or, to put it in another way, the monopoly of *scientific competence*, in the sense of a particular agent's socially recognized capacity to speak and act legitimately (i.e. in an authorized and authoritative way) in scientific matters" (Bourdieu, 1975: 19). Nor are there any 'disinterested' interests (akin to Mannheim's free-floating intellectuals or Popper's proper British gentlemen) to mediate and to resolve such social and scientific power struggles: "In the scientific field as in the field of class relations, no arbitrating authority exists to legitimate legitimacy-giving authorities; claims to legitimacy draw their legitimacy from the relative strengths of the groups whose interests they express: inasmuch as the definition of the criteria of judgment and the principles of hierarchisation is itself at issue in the struggle, there are no good judges, because there is no judge who is not also a party to the dispute" (Bourdieu, 1975: 24–25).

Whether our critique of the anthropological establishment was correct or not, one thing now seems clear: we were not consistent. We never analyzed the New Left establishment in the same radically contextual terms that we readily applied to the Liberal establishment. Yet the same processes we condemned in the latter were evident among professional radicals: their exclusiveness, arrogance, competitiveness, even their conventionality and ethno-centrism (13). But however inconsistently or unilaterally applied in the past, the crucial issue raised remains: "We must be prepared to accept the fact that a representation is *eo ipso* implicated, intertwined, embedded, interwoven, with a great many other things besides the 'truth' which is itself a representation ... as inhabiting a common field of play defined for [the scholar], not by some inherent common subject-matter alone, but by some common history, tradition, universe of discourse" (Said, 1979: 272–273).

Such a paradigmatic definition of intellectual activity obviously challenged the ivory tower image of academic knowledge. Not only because the latter's 'disinterested' objectivity proved to be an ideological front for establish-mentarian interests or because professionalism was deemed trivial and irrelevant, if not outright dangerous, to our own political interests but – more encompassing – because all scientific paradigms entail theoretical *and* social commitments. As Kuhn put it in comparative and anthropologically congenial terms, an intellectual choice between differing paradigms entails "a choice between incompatible modes of community life" (Kuhn, 1962: 93). Or, to phrase it in terms prevalent in the sociology of science, the distinction between internal and external in the cultural analysis of scientific traditions is, if not arbitrary, at least a question of one's point of view to be assessed *a posteriori* and not to be posited *a priori* (compare to Barnes and Shapin, 1979: 9).

The sociological dimension of the paradigm concept was, as just indicated, congenial to the ethnological analysis of anthropological traditions. Yet Kuhn's own definition may not have been sociological enough. It certainly wasn't ethnographic or ethnological as such (14). To understand the natural and social sciences contextually and comparatively (which is what a paradigmatic analysis is or ought to be), an anthropological perspective is imperative. This is true even if one arrives at the historical conclusion, as does Joseph Needham (1969), that the scientific spirit in its ideal and universal form is a distinctly Occidental contribution. The anthropological argument holds, even more so, for the social sciences. They are at all times defined, perhaps even determined, by the social contexts in which they originate, exist, and develop. Again, the form and function of these sciences may have taken on distinctive characteristics in the West, but even a description and assessment of that distinctiveness requires a comparative analysis and judgment.

It should be noted in this connection that the sociology of science has repeatedly called for such comparative studies (e.g., Lepenies, 1981; or Mendelsohn, 1981), but this plea has remained largely programmatic rather than substantive. And if the latter, it "has hardly been used for anything else so far than to demonstrate the superiority of modern Western science" (Ben-David cited in Gebhardt, 1978: 42). The implicit (and illicit) assumption is that "the present level and form of sciencing in the most advanced Western lands needs to constitute the criterion for the life and form of science in all other times and climes" (Nelson, 1974: 15).

An interesting example of this curious combination of comparative and provincial sensibilities is the illustrious work of the aforementioned Joseph Needham. Note, for instance, the implications of the following reminder: "it should be clearly understood that Europe did not give rise to 'European' or 'Western' science, but to universally valid world science" (Needham, 1969a: 12–13). Needham clarifies his statement as follows: history progresses towards a 'modern universal science' (European in origin, in other words) which "will embrace all in the end" (Needham, 1969b: 52–53). I shall return to this seemingly gracious but nonetheless deceptive European *noblesse oblige* in the context of the rationality debate.

There are numerous ways in which the comparative anthropological dimension would enhance the notion of scientific paradigm. It would broaden our cultural horizons, for instance, to talk about ethno-science, ethno-technology, medicine, etc. instead of science *tout court* (see Lepenies, 1980). I shall limit myself to just one obvious anthropological contribution (one nontheless persistently overlooked by cultural anthropologists themselves! (15)): the cultural character of the social sciences. Since cultural origins are not supposed to play a significant role in the international ideology of the scientific enterprise any more than ethnic or religious factors, their purported influence has usually been relegated to the anecdotal level. It has been whispered, for example, that Malinowski's Trobrianders and Firth's Tikopia share many of the personal and cultural traits of their respective ethnographers. Or again, that Lévi-Strauss' natives are notoriously Cartesian and it is not surprising that structuralism should as a result rub Americans the wrong way or make little sense in 'plain' English to the British.

The specific question of nationality and science, however, goes much deeper than the idiosyncratic. The relation between the two may have a significant philosophical dimension, as I showed some time ago in the case of Anglo-American empiricism and French-Continental rationalism (Scholte, 1966). Here we are dealing not only with incommensurate epistemic paradigms, but with incommensurate cultural differences and "it looks as if the scientific idea of truth as that which is intersubjectively communicable and reproducible needs to be modified considerably due to [these] cultural differences" (Galtung, 1981: 835).

There are important historical considerations as well, as indicated by Clark's (1973) study comparing Cartesianism and the *'esprit géometrique'* with the philosophy of spontaneity and the *'esprit de finesse'* in the cultural origins and historical developments of French sociology. These philosophical and historical dimensions have distinct social and intellectual preconditions and consequences. This may in part be a question of the specific relation between cultural and intellectual style, or of different norms in weighing social, historical, and disciplinary factors in differing definitions of what constitute relevant questions and appropriate explanations (see Lemaire *et al.*, 1976). Comparatively little attention has been paid to these important topics (but see Galtung, 1981).

That such paradigmatic features as cultural genesis can have unexpected descriptive and analytic consequences may be briefly illustrated with a remarkable and humorous example from the history of anthropology. It concerns Leo Frobenius' distinction between Hamitic and Ethiopean cultures. This distinction became an integral part of Senghor's *Négritude* movement in twentieth-century African Nationalism. But as it turns out, Frobenius' 'hidden' inspiration for this mytho-poetic distinction apparently derived from his post World-War I reflections on the normative differences between French and German culture, especially their respective ideologies of womanhood (see Ita, 1973). Yet the ethnocentric genesis of Frobenius' curious hermeneutic did not prevent him from recently being hailed as a unique example of non-repressive, empathetic, and dialogical anthropology! (Watson-Franke and Watson, 1975: 259).

The reformulation of the social dimension of the paradigm concept in comparative terms is only one side of the Kuhnian coin, a more comprehensive definition of cultural context is the other. Here, too, the cultural anthropologist can make a distinct contribution. For example, he or she can do so in terms of the semiotic turn suggested by Kuhn himself. What I have in mind here is the often over-looked but intellectually significant fact that the scientific community is not merely a language community (or the social sciences, talking sciences, cf. Garfinkel *et al.*, 1981: 133), but more specifically, an elite society of academic *writers* — of men and women committed to a distinct and class-bound form of reflexivity and rationality, one proper to what Bernstein (1971) calls 'elaborate code' users.

The grammar of rationality specific to this culture of the written word is not eternal and universal, but social and historical. It is "the shared ideology of different secularized intelligentsia" and has always been "supportive of the special status interests and social position of the intelligentsia themselves" (Gouldner, 1976: 133). Moreover, it cannot go unnoticed among Third World peoples, that they are almost invariably spoken to, or written about, by this privileged class: one characterized by "a conspicuous consumption of syllables, clauses, prepositions, concomitant with their economic resources and the spacious quarters they inhabit" (Steiner, 1975: 33).

What are the specific features of written communication and how do they both contribute *and* detract from our understanding of nonwritten phenomena or, as in the case of traditional anthropology, peoples without writing? (16) Writing does allow for a certain distantiation, both temporally and spatially, which in turn facilitates reflection and criticism (which does *not*, however, imply that writing is therefore by definition a precondition for 'objectivity', 'rationality', or whatever!). Masterman's itemized enumeration of Kuhn's paradigm concept, for instance, would have been virtually impossible if *The Structure of Scientific Revolutions* had been an oral discourse (17).

We often forget that alphabetic writing and its attendant distantiation also distort; that they de-contextualize (the intellectual context of a written text is often presumed to be yet another written text), systematize, formalize, classify, simplify, constrain and thus arrest the ambiguity of speech (e.g., para-linguistic intonation) or the plenitude of verbal performance (e.g., aesthetic enactment). Alphabetic writing, in other words, is an intellectual sword that cuts both ways. It "represents not only a great progress in thought but also a great danger: the unilateral development of reason at the cost of sensibility" (Wald, 1975: 52). Alphabetic writing and that which is comprehended by means of the written word express both the specific virtues as well as the distinct limits of Western reason.

We write and translate, certainly in the social sciences, on behalf and about others. But just as importantly, we write for and translate in the direction of ourselves. That is why, historically, writing has so often been the ideological means of social oppression or of the legitimation of that

oppression. Cross-cultural translation has similarly functioned as the intellectual arm of political and economic conquest. As Diamond points out, imperialism's victims could not or can not read and write, while "the compulsive
rite of civilization is writing, and the compulsions of the official concept of
reality are both experienced and expressed in the exclusive mode of cognition
signified by writing." It is a motivated writing, moreover, on behalf of "the
civilized upper classes who, conceiving their positions as determined by God,
talent or technology, create the facts of history and the deterministic theories
which justify both the facts and their own pre-eminence" (Diamond, 1974: 2,
3–4).

Writing and translation in contemporary anthropology are by no means
exempt from Diamond's critique. They frequently provide the graphic and
coercive framework "by which a modern 'colored' man [or woman] is
chained irrevocably to the general truths formulated about his prototypical
linguistic, anthropological, and doctrinal forebears by a white European
scholar . . . " (Said, 1979: 237).

Socio-linguistic conventions (such as academic writing) are not only forms
of intellectual comprehension, but also entail a subsequent projection back
upon the objectified subject-matter and hence define the latter's cognitive
appropriation. For example, in the case of the so-called rationality debate
(to be discussed presently), one can and should ask whether the social preconditions and intellectual virtues we like to attribute to Western logic and
which are said to be latent or simply absent from primitive logic (18) are
not in essence the unconscious result of privileging the abstract, digital, and
de-contextualized logic embedded in, and generated by, the written code:
categories (hence generalizations), units (therefore differentiation) and
enumeration (thus prediction).

VII

The issue of rationality provides a convenient bridge to the philosophical
dimension of Kuhn's paradigm concept, again in terms of both its importance
to the historical development of critical anthropology and to the anthropological reformulation of that concept. The relation between reason and
science is an interesting one, both historically and structurally. It has been a

pivotal theme in the social science at least from the Enlightenment onwards and has once again taken center-stage in the various controversies surrounding Kuhn's paradigm concept, in the counter-critique to critical anthropology and, most recently, among the participants in the 'rationality debate' in social anthropology.

The historical persistence of the rationality theme is not surprising since the philosophical dimension, of which the rationality debate is a fruitful cross-disciplinary illustration, involves fundamental domain assumptions which are not always made explicit in the social sciences. They nonetheless form an integral part of virtually everything we do. Thus, the kind and degree of relation between science and reason we do or do not posit also defines the epistemological, ontological and normative continuities and/or discontinuities we do or do not posit between ourselves and those 'others' (our subjects or objects of study) whom we seek to comprehend, define, and judge. This effort, in turn, reflects back upon our self-understanding and makes a more informed understanding of others possible.

The paradigm concept allowed us, first of all, to make the philosophical dimension of anthropological praxis explicit both beyond and including the domain assumptions of the ruling paradigms: empiricism, positivism, structuralism. Such philosophical reflexivity had been resisted by traditional anthropology (see Murphy, 1971: 37). Explication proceeded, as in the case of the other dimensions discussed, by means of contextualization and relativization – both with critical intent. It became clear upon paradigmatic reflection, i.e., by placing anthropological texts in their socio-historical contexts, that ethnographic materials had always been described and ethnological analyses made within the culturally specific context of the philosophical cross-currents of European civilization.

Whether the 'non-civilized' savage was assessed as child-like or noble, he or she was in the last analysis made intelligible (and useful) in terms of a scientific meta-language originating in, sustained by, and congenial to Western preconceptions and interests. In the specific case of the rationality debate, both the contrast/inversion and the continuity/evolution views of the 'great transition' (from primitive to civilized, magic to science) are invariably phrased in terms of a unilateral *and* judgemental movement from 'them' to 'us' (see Horton, 1973). Whether this motivated chronology is assumed to be progressive or regressive (and there are numerous examples of both in past and contemporary anthropology) is intellectually less important than the more encompassing realization that any and all such evolutionary schemes are essentially ethno-centric, that is, normatively motivated and paradigmatically generated. Some anthropologists may make the natives as rational, even more so than themselves. Others prefer to keep them prerational or simply irrational. But virtually all anthropologists understand, analyze, and judge indigenous rationality as a version (the inverse or mirror image) of their own scientific and normative world-views.

Such ethnocentricity may inhere in the anthropological enterprise, even if and when critically understood. As Diamond has contended, the task of anthropology is to clarify the questions *we* bring to history: "In this anthro-pological 'experiment' which we initiate, it is not they who are the ultimate objects but ourselves . . . . We are engaged in a complex search for the subject in history, as the precondition for a minimal definition of humanity and, therefore, of self-knowledge as the ground for self-criticism" (Diamond, 1974: 100).

Self-criticism presupposes self-knowledge. Self-knowledge, in turn, entails a contrast (real of imagined) between ourselves and others. This contrasting image is intentional and motivated: "to find something out about ourselves rather than about others – and to find out who *we* are by distinguishing ourselves from who we are *not*" (Finnegan and Horton, 1973: 15). The ideological dangers of these projected comparisons are, of course, consider-able. In fact, the distinctive oppositions may be so unequivocally formulated as to meet up in their extremes: a critical image of Western society and an inverted one of primitive society (see Horton, 1973: 297). The romantic search for a lost paradise may thus generate a new ethno-philosophical myth: "the authenticity of difference" (Augé, 1979: 174; see also Amselle, 1979, Bourdieu, 1977, Goody, 1977).

The political implications of the philosophical dimension can be especially disconcerting. To the literal historical reality of genocide and ethnocide should be added another, more figurative, but equally destructive reality: epistemocide. It consists of the deliberate cooptation and subsequent reduc-tion of non-Western and non-scientific forms of knowledge and belief to the abstract framework of Western science and metaphysics. For all its liberal pretentions and humane protestations, epistemocide has always been an integral, if pre-conscious, part of the ethnographic gaze and the ethnological deconstructions of the anthropological establishment (see Cahiers de l'Institut d'Etudes du Développement [1975 and 1976] for concrete examples).

In the context of professional anthropology, primitive thought never simply 'is'. It is always being 'fiddled with'. It 'expresses', 'reveals', 'functions', or 'exhibits', but it never exists in its own right (see Feyerabend, 1978: 75ff). Perhaps cultural anthropologists couldn't or didn't dare 'say it as it was' because registering what really was would require more than a mimetic or copy theory of scientific verification. It demands an historical anthropology that does not leave unmentioned those very colonial powers that so deeply effected what was (and still is) and to which many anthropologists were indirectly indebted. Most anthropologists did not radically question colonialism. That "would [have been] tantamount to questioning the validity of their own position — so they contended themselves with registering what existed" (Magubane, 1971: 426; see also Leclerc, 1972; or Lewis, 1973).

These brief examples illustrate the more comprehensive awareness that the paradigm concept made possible. Cultural anthropology, to put it negatively, is the intellectual prisoner of the culturally specific, historically situated, socially motivated, and philosophically defined paradigms dominant at any given time within its own intellectual-historical boundaries. Or, to put it more positively, cultural anthropology in non-repressive circumstances might, as a dialectical and critical praxis, be "the metaphorical extension of our own cultural resources" (Barnes, 1973: 183; see also Barnes, 1974: 49. 57ff). In either event, cultural anthropology demands a radical reflexivity, not only logically, but ethno-logically. This concretely implies that the most serious source of misunderstanding the concepts of alien cultures is the inadequate mastery of the conceptual apparatus of our own society (see Barnes, 1972: 274). In order to appreciate magic, for instance, one must first of all properly understand science (though one could with equal plausibility argue that to understand science, an appreciation of magic is also desirable).

The paradigmatic realization that Western logic is the intellectual source of anthropological reason demands a contextually refined understanding of this ethno-logic and, comparatively reasoned, of its cultural relativity. Such a demand is, of course, more easily made than realized and it is not surprising that what is contextually relevant to the one (anthropologist, historian, philosopher, or whoever) is paradigmatically irrelevant to the other (see Gellner, 1970). There is, in addition, the problem of infinite regress: contextual determination *ad infinitum* at the expense of the actual topic at issue. The subject-matter threatens to disappear from view as we concentrate on our navels and our eye-sight progressively deteriorates as a consequence of a myopic obsession (see Gellner, 1975) (19).

I would counter as follows: Critical consciousness is itself a specific moment in the over-all history of consciousness. The concept of contextual determination is therefore doubly relative — both in terms of its actual content and the prior definition of what may or must be counted as contextually relevant. But this is no ethno-logical reason to abstain from reflexive critique. Nor, for that matter, is the danger of regress. Quite the contrary. The entire history of the social sciences consists of differentially weighed or discovered contexts not previously taken seriously or known. The ethnology of anthropological traditions simply extends these different insights (albeit intentionally and selectively) to the historical and cultural circumstances of its practitioners. To do otherwise would sustain the ethno-centric illusion that the Western intelligentsia is magically free from the very social determinants they prescribe for everyone else.

Anthropological traditions, then, must at all times be considered paradigmatically. They, too, represent more or less distinct socio-cultural and linguistic communities guided by differing, perhaps incommensurate, metaphors. And here, too, internal and syntagmatic criteria of description, explanation, and viability are supplemented by external and paradigmatic criteria of aesthetic preference, persuasive argument, political urgency, and market-place norms (especially when economic resources are scarce and competition for limited goods correspondingly fierce).

The aesthetic dimension, incidentally, is an especially interesting one, certainly from a semiotic point of view, and much neglected in the social sciences. As White (1973), among others, has shown, historical and by analogy social scientific events, data, descriptions, analyses, explanations, and theories are linguistically prefigured, that is, narratively (dramatically and poetically) structured. Such prefigurations are not simply 'added to' reality. Rather, they make any reality whatsoever intelligible and significant in the first place. From this perspective, social scientific traditions are symbolic forms that constitute rather than imitate the reality known (20).

The paradigmatic features that are to be considered relevant or irrelevant cannot be selected *a priori*; they must be discovered *a posteriori*. Criteria of their selection will in turn depend on paradigmatic judgements regarding existential relevance, social commitment, historical insight, and philosophical significance. Anthropological traditions are in this sense doubly and inescapably relative. They are not inherently good or bad, progressive or regressive, but become one or the other (or a combination of both) only from a particular point of view (see Feyerabend, 1978: 8). Neither in cultural anthropological activity itself nor on the meta-level of a critical ethnology of anthropological traditions are there transcendental means of circumventing the paradigmatic realization that "intelligibility takes many and various forms [and] ... that reality has no [single] key" (Winch, 1958: 102) (21).

Descriptive contextualization and comparative relativization can also enhance the anthropological reformulation of the paradigm concept itself. This has in part already been achieved in the sociology of science, e.g., through the descriptive emphasis on scientific behavior (see Lepenies, 1981) or the comparative perspective provided by Mary Douglas' work (most recently 1982). I here want to discuss the anthropological contribution in terms especially *à propos* to the philosophical dimension I am discussing. It concerns the problem of universal and relative truth — an issue implicit in much of this essay thus-far, a central theme in the theoretical controversies surrounding *The Structure of Scientific Revolutions* and, certainly, the critical anthropological and sociological literature, including the rationality debate.

Dell Hymes (1964: 21) once observed that cultural anthropology must stand or fall on the basis of an adequate concept of the concrete universal. I would add that his remark is applicable to all the social sciences and perhaps the natural sciences as well. Certainly in anthropology, the problem of the relation between the unique, irreducible, and 'radically other' on the one hand and the universal, reducible, and ultimately 'identical' on the other is especially acute. Contextualization and relativization carried far enough seem to leave no ontological ground in which to anchor epistemological procedure, let alone normative judgement. It is nevertheless my contention that relativism is and must at all times be the starting point of any reflexive analysis consistent with a paradigmatic perspective and that no transcendent truths can be *a priori* exempted from the context-dependent vicissitudes of time, place and circumstance.

I realize that this position is problematic, even on purely logical grounds (e.g., de Laguna, 1941: 232ff). But the logical dilemma pales in comparison with the *ethno*-logical necessity of grounding our logic (philosophical, social scientific, normative). Only if this anthropological requirement is met, is a subsequent reflection on ontological grounds, epistemological procedures, and evaluative judgements possible. If, on the contrary, we try to derive domain assumptions and norms simply from the logical imperatives of Western science or metaphysics, we invariably run the risk of arriving at an ethnocentric and pre-judgemental point of view. No doubt, cultural relativism entails an embarrassing, even contradictory, claim: "the knowledge of the impossibility of knowledge" (Geras, 1972: 80). But circumventing cultural relativism by means of a stipulated logical claim – the autonomy and universality of pure or syntagmatic knowledge – is the greater embarrassment and danger.

True, the social sciences – cultural anthropology among them – seem to require *a priori* assumptions, including comparative universals, to function at all (see Hollis, 1970 and 1972; or Lukes, 1970 and 1973). In that sense the social sciences not only discover putative universals, but actually premise their entire enterprise on their implicit existence. The specific reasons may be ontological (discovering the real presupposes its existence), epistemological (all translation requires a meta-language), or normative (the search for a common humanity). To give an example, the structuralist enterprise is ontologically, epistemologically and normatively anchored in the *a priori* continuity and discontinuity between the natural and the cultural. This universal relationship is said to transcend both its concrete ethnographic embodiment and ethnology's concrete historical circumstances (Foucault, 1966: 377ff.; for a critique see Scholte, 1980). Similarly, the rationality debate in the end boils down to the presupposed existence or non-existence of cross-culturally identifiable features of universal reason. Definitions range from common-sense and problem-solving to biological constants and unconscious universals in language.

The sociology and anthropology of science, it seems to me, must proceed in an inverse direction. They must assume that not only the definition of reason in the social sciences, but also concepts such as rationality and nature in the pure sciences, are culturally and historically mediated and therefore contextually relative rather than universally true (see Barnes and Shapin, 1979). Kuhn failed to be sufficiently radical on this point. Though *The*

Structure of Scientific Revolutions appeared to announce the disintegration of an exclusively cognitive justification of the natural sciences, Kuhn subsequently shies away from this conclusion. He considers the 'irrationality argument' (which is itself a misnomer) "not only absurd but vaguely obscene". "To suppose", he says, "that we possess criteria of rationality which are independent of our understanding of the essentials of the scientific process is to open the door to cloud-cuckoo land" (Kuhn, 1970: 264; see also Mendelsohn, 1977).

Kuhn also retains a cognitive definition of what constitutes the natural. Yet it is anthropologically and historically obvious that any definition of nature, including that of the sciences, is culturally mediated, e.g., Mary Douglas' comparisons between the 'body politick' and the body natural (1973) or Alfred Schmidt's study of Marx's concept of nature (1964). The epistemological implications of nature as a mediated phenomenon is especially significant: "if we change the paradigm of nature, we may have to change quite substantially our notion of scientific problems" (Skolimowski, 1974: 67).

The cultural definition of the natural is of more than academic interest since nature as a social category carries normative import — both in primitive societies and in their civilized counter-parts. Though Occidental science no longer views nature as a prescriptive force, the investigations of nature as an 'object' is not value-neutral. Not only because 'law and order' in nature can often enough function as a deterministic rationalization for 'law and order' in society (see Elias, 1974: 32 or Gran, 1974: 202), but also because in the 'business of science,' "the mastery of nature may itself be mastered" (Leiss, 1972: 23). As a result, "what we call Man's power over Nature turns out to be the power exercised by some men over other men with Nature as its instrument" (Lewis cited in Leiss, 1972: 195) (22).

The crucial paradigmatic question in both the social and natural sciences concerns the genesis and purpose of these purported universals. Their specific definition may simply be ethno-centric such as the digital logic of the structuralists or the common-sense of the 'realists'. More far-reaching still, the very tension between universal and particular, between scientific generality and historical specificity, may in large part derive from our own socio-cultural situation: a heritage of Judeo-Christian and Hellenic problems *we* bring to bear on historical, anthropological, and philosophical materials. To consider these problems universal and scientific rather than particular and historical is, from a non-Western point of view, yet another instance of Occidental intellectual imperialism.

It is often overlooked in scientific debates on truth and relativism that this problematic, as part and parcel of our cultural heritage, has normative implications and practical consequences that go well beyond the specific . historical confines of science as such. Though norms may be discussed within a professional context of syntagmatic 'is' and 'ought' (the traditional values of the scientific community), the meta-level question of the value of science, anthropologically viewed, should be placed within its widest possible cultural and comparative framework. This certainly holds for the ethno-centric definitions of universal rationality (scientific and ethno-scientific) mentioned above, especially since these abstract definitions often generate and support concrete political programs (23). Most inclusively, a paradigmatic critique may be required of any formal definition of reason, irrespective of its specific characteristics, which in theory posits itself *above* concrete human beings, but which *in situ* functions to manipulate the relations *between* human beings (Dickson, 1975: 36) (24). 'Transcendental' reason is objectivist ideology par excellence: "a rationality [which] does not understand itself as an historically produced discourse but as suprahistorical and supracultural, as the sacred, disembodied word: logos" (Gouldner, 1976: 50).

Cultural relativism, too, carries normative import. Paradigmatically viewed, it may be symptomatic of the bad faith of the conqueror: the leisurely intellectual tourist in a historical position of dominant power who can afford to be tolerant of any and all cultural 'oddities', secure in the self-assured knowledge of the inherent superiority of his own politics and cognitive customs (see Diamond 1974: 110). Within academic anthropology, cultural relativism may express the liberal bankruptcy of the established professional — expert at sustaining the studious tolerance of a scientific gaze but immune and impotent in the face of human suffering (see Wolff, 1972). This is precisely why in the sixties, cultural relativism no longer seemed morally and intellectually adequate to the changing circumstances in which that generation of anthropologists found themselves. Whereas cultural relativism had been the paragon of anthropological humanism to previous generations, we saw it as "subconsciously designed to preserve the *status quo*" (Jay, 1973: 79; see also Lemaire, 1976: 98ff).

For many cultural anthropologists professionally schooled during the turbulent yet hopeful sixties, neo-Marxism replaced cultural relativism as the practical and theoretical source for a more timely and relevant anthropology. But as I indicated at the beginning of this essay, not many of us applied a paradigmatic perspective to neo-Marxism with the same rigor and enthusiasm that we displayed in our critique of the anthropological establishment. An inconsistent position, no doubt, and one I would in part attribute to the over-all failure to explore the last dimension of the paradigm concept to which I now turn: the historical.

VIII

The socio-political events of the sixties and the then urgent question of cultural anthropology's proper and/or improper role in these events generated a quite sudden and dramatic interest in the history of the discipline. Thus, when I began studying anthropology in 1961, the only Anglo-American history of anthropology of any scope and completeness available was Robert Lowie's classic *The History of Ethnological Theory* (published in 1937!). By the end of the decade, Marvin Harris had published his monumental (and monumentally biased) *The Rise of Anthropological Theory* (1968) and George Stocking his judicious (and judiciously academic) *Race, Culture and Evolution* (1968). In the seventies, several American text-books in the history of anthropology appeared, among them Fred Voget's encyclopedic *The History of Ethnology* (1975) and John Honigman's spirited *The Development of Anthropological Ideas* (1976). In the eighties, finally, critical assessments of what the history of anthropology is or ought to be began to appear, e.g., Stanley Diamond's *Anthropology: Ancestors and Heirs* (1980) (25).

Anthropology's historical turn was motivated by a sense of disciplinary crisis: "What had gone wrong and how were we to proceed?" The mystification of science to which many of our mentors were prone proved no satisfactory answer whatsoever. Formal scientific praxis either rejected historical inquiry as simply irrelevant (see Timpanaro, 1975: 196), or it reified the historical past to vindicate its own superiority (see Dolby, 1972). Kuhn's reflections on the self-serving use of text-books in the natural sciences only served to remind us that in our own text-books the unilinear evolution of anthropological theory was never questioned while evolutionary theory in cultural anthropology was summarily dismissed. Most cultural anthropologists, like the historians of science prior to the publication of *The Structure of Scientific Revolutions*, seemed "to have accepted the historiography and the mythology of science as devised by the practicing scientists themselves" (Mendelsohn, 1977: 4). In fact, often being social scientists strenuously imitating the natural scientists, they often exhibited that proverbial bad taste of the enthusiast: they out-believed their model scientists in their absolute faith in cumulative knowledge.

It must also be remembered that many of us had been directly trained or indirectly exposed to a nineteen-fifties generation of 'up-and-coming' young Turks: ethno-scientists and computer methodologists who often spent more time with 'real' scientists in engineering and psychology departments than with their fellow anthropologists or 'soft-headed' humanists. Their nearly mystical devotion to the elegant logic of kinship structures did not so much express *'Geschichtsmüdigheit'* (Schmidt, 1971: 9) — after all, they were young then and had promising carreers to attend to — as utter indifference, even contempt, for what had preceded them. As a direct consequence, they exhibited an unwavering faith in their own brilliance, exclusiveness, and scientificity (26).

In the sixties meanwhile, many of their graduate students had begun to understand, or perhaps merely sense, that science in practice is never an abstract question of science as such (see Becker, 1979: 134 and, of course, the entire 'message' of *The Structure of Scientific Revolutions*). From a critical and historical perspective, today's science is likely to become tomorrow's ideology (see Goldman, 1966). In fact, had that not precisely happened to the 'end-of-ideology' social science of the fifties? Had it not lost its innocence and credibility in South America and Viet-Nam as a result of cooptation, service to governmental agencies and political interests?

Questions such as these (for details, see Scholte, 1971) motivated an interest in the history of anthropology. If not for the purpose of seeking a purer past, then certainly in terms of a goal Kuhn had formulated explicitly: How to rediscover the integrity of a scientific tradition in its own time? (Kuhn, 1962: 3). That, of course, was precisely our problem — not only historically, but normatively. We addressed it first of all in terms of the contextualization, relativization, and critique of the anthropological traditions of the immediate past and present.

There was, in retrospect, an obvious problem to which we did not adequately address ourselves at the time: the paradigmatic mediation of our own criteria of critique and evaluation. These were often New Left, neo-Marxist and, so it seemed in the sixties, not in any obvious need of further reflexive historical or anthropological grounding. Yet we should have realized that what is desired of history is given by history (Thompson, 1978: 137) and that this applied to ourselves as much as to those we, quite legitimately, criticized for writing one-dimensional histories on behalf of the mostly white, male, and rich interests which seemed to own the past and guide the future on behalf of their own greed (see Zinn, 1967: 181ff). Nevertheless this lack of self-critique hid an ethno-logical inconsistency which has surfaced in the eighties and to which I shall return presently.

The most important historical function of the paradigm concept when first introduced into cultural anthropology was to relativize anthropological traditions by means of their context-specific understanding. This had, again, a diacritical purpose: the awareness and assimilation of tradition, however important, is not equivalent to the continuity and acceptance of tradition (see Ahlers, 1970: 116). That was certainly our generation's attitude toward the then prevalent academic traditions in which we were socialized and educated as professional anthropologists. Hence the emphasis, among some critical anthropologists, on non-academic historical alternatives (see Diamond *et al.*, 1975). Most importantly, the historical relativization of anthropological traditions went beyond the specific presuppositions and results of any given anthropological discourse and raised in addition, as had Kuhn, the more fundamental issue: not merely the *history* of scientific traditions, but their irreducible *historicity*.

All scientific rationality is and should be considered as a conditioned rather than an unconditioned socio-cultural and historical achievement. Not merely error and illusion are culturally mediated and historically situated (as the sociology of knowledge had traditionally and safely suggested [see Larrain, 1979 or Stehr, 1981]), but objectivity and truth are similarly conditioned (as Kuhn, once again, had also implied, see Barnes, 1972). Description, analysis, comprehension, prediction, are historical, social and cultural events, more often than not political in nature.

The intimate connection between epistemology and politics was an especially significant issue. The historical relation between anthropological praxis and colonial domination became the subject of intensive scrutiny during the sixties (see Asad, 1973) and one finds, in contemporary anthropology, its muted echo in the rationality debate. Prejudgemental schemes still find their expression in Gellner's (1975) or even Horton's (1970) justifications of scientific progress in terms of the historical transition from context-bound (primitive) belief to context-free (civilized) science (27). Even critical neo-Marxists, who on the basis of their critique of Occidental reason ought to know better but do not, retain an evolutionary and ethno-centric bias when addressing the anthropological literature on comparative rationality (e.g., Eder, 1975; Habermas, 1976 and 1979; or Wellmer, 1980).

All such developmental schemes are in the last analysis bound by an explicit adherence to Western scientific and philosophical standards. They thereby also run the risk of a concommittant and conservative attachment to Western social and political forms. When anthropologically implemented, such developmental schemes do not in theory or in practice differ very much from any other form of intellectual imperialism (see Scholte, 1978). In the specific context of the rationality debate, the rise of industry, capitalism, and science, until quite recently entirely Western in nature, are seen as historical (even inevitable or ideal) models of how traditional societies became or should become modern *and* (therefore!) rational (for a critique, see Tambiah, 1973).

During the sixties, then, the paradigm concept served to resensitize a generation of cultural anthropologists to the historical dimension of their discipline. Such historical sensitivity had never been entirely absent, but it gained in both intensity and purposefulness during a decade in which the profession as a whole was in intellectual crisis. Distinctive about the use of the term paradigm and the attendant historization of anthropology was the self-referential application of anthropological concepts to the history of the discipline itself (28) and, as a result, the anthropologization of that history. Previous histories of the field (to the extent that there were any) had been exclusively syntagmatic (e.g., Lowie's previously mentioned standard history of pre-World-War II anthropology).

The mutual, or better dialectical, relation between history and anthropology is probably not unique to the critical tradition. It must have had other historical precedents and it certainly generated related theoretical developments. But irrespective of previous and/or related developments, I would suggest that the specific anthropological perspective implied by Kuhn's history of the natural sciences paved the way, perhaps indirectly, for a similar anthropologization of the history of anthropological traditions. This self-referential dimension is almost entirely absent from the early work of a man who is otherwise and quite properly credited with rejuvinating the history of anthropology: George Stocking Jr. Stocking's immensely valuable studies of anthropological traditions are in essence traditional, academic, and syntagmatic histories (compare to Kuhn's assessment, 1977: 112). They are, as a result, internal critiques proper to a historicist view point. There are few if any historical (or presentistic) critiques of anthropological ideologies along the lines of men as different as, say, Stanley Diamond or Marvin Harris (29). And the difference, in turn, indicates a fundamental transition from a syntagmatic to a paradigmatic point of view or, if you will, from an academic to a critical perspective on the history of anthropology. This development, finally, also makes the anthropological reformulation of the historical dimension of the paradigm concept plausible.

I should like to illustrate what I have in mind by briefly discussing the complex issue of cultural anthropology's European signature, especially its Judeo-Christian heritage. Since this is obviously far too vast a topic to be adequately dealt with here, I shall limit myself to some very brief suggestions. I hope the main historical point can nonetheless be made: There are meta-historical (and meta-anthropological) factors to consider in the proper understanding of anthropological (and social scientific) traditions. These factors serve to structure and guide the descriptive and explanatory discourse of such traditions. Though they are often syntagmatically marked (e.g., in terms of their narrative styles), they are invariably paradigmatic in origin: normative, ideological, aesthetic, even theological. There are, for example, the literary analyses of social scientific discourse by Löwith (1946), Hyman (1962), or White (1973). They clearly show how the narrative structures 'invented' by Marx, Darwin, Frazer, Freud, 'mirror' those employed in the Bible (30).

With regard to cultural anthropology's Judeo-Christian heritage, there is — first of all — the neglected historical question of "the way in which the Bible functioned as a kind of Kuhnian paradigm for research on the cultural, linguistic, and physical diversity of mankind" (Stocking, 1968: 71). Though the scholarly emphasis placed on the historical effect of ethnographic material on European Christendom is certainly important (e.g., Hazard, 1935), the obverse effect of Judeo-Christian categories in structuring comparative data is equally significant (see Hodgen, 1964). The intimate, if often hidden, relationship between theology and anthropology becomes all the more evident if one singles out the categories of space and time used in ethnographic description and subsequent analysis. Cultural anthropology has always been a reformer's science whose spatial and temporal categories are both theological and teleological (evolutionism is an obvious example). And they remain hierarchical and normative in their contemporary taxonomic and structuralist versions (see Burridge, 1973 and Fabian, 1980). Though secularized and stripped of their specific Judeo-Christian substance, these contemporary analytic devices continue to describe, order, and judge ethnographic materials in terms of spatio-temporal distance and/or proximity, including their respective progressive and/or regressive characteristics, that *we* attribute to the continuities and/or discontinuities between ourselves and others (see especially Fabian, 1980, Sahlins, 1976, and Said, 1979) (31).

The hidden influence of Judeo-Christian categories, even in secular form, on cultural anthropology cannot be detailed here. What should be mentioned, however, is that non-Western social scientists are aware and critical of this theological dimension of cultural anthropology and of Western science's normative import generally. This reaction is entirely understandible and justified. Not only because of the historical continuity between the Christian and Scientific missions, including their mutually reinforcing ideological role in legitimizing colonial policies (see Feyerabend, 1975: 216; Hsu, 1977: 807; Jaulin, 1970: 336ff and Mudimbe, 1973: 40), but also because the consumate attempt to transcend comparative history by means of universal categories (themselves historical) is a distinctly Judeo-Christian, Western *and* scientific passion (see Saran's [1975] especially eloquent critique). Within the confines of an Occidental preoccupation, native peoples are once again assigned their mediating, therapeutic and thus derivative role (see Burridge, 1973: 176ff, 193ff).

The Occidental *Weltanschauung*, however diverse its actual contents or concrete historical manifestations, is ultimately guided by universal (hence abstract) and teleological (hence judgemental) aims to be realized or realizable in history. Western theologians, scientists, and others argue *ad infinitum* about the specific nature of these ultimate aims, but the over-riding anthropological consideration is that all interested parties presuppose transcendental and prescriptive norms by means of which concrete and diverse historical societies may be described, analyzed, assessed, *and* influenced. To the non-Western 'beneficiaries' of these Occidental *idées fixes*, they must seem like so many exotic variations on an alien theme: Christ's Second Coming, the Proletarian Revolution, Rational Scientific Closure.

The different Western belief systems meet in their philosophic and pragmatic aims: their common telos is in theory trans-historical (formal, universal, and 'true' irrespective of time and place), in practice imperialistic (reductionistic, deterministic, intolerant of diversity and ambiguity). They claim to be historical (even relativistic), but their ultimate goal is theological, cosmological, or ideological closure. Historical and cultural events are mere contingent means toward a more encompassing and transcendental end (32).

We can trace the historical continuity between Christianity and Science (which does not preclude discontinuities [see White, 1896]). Secularization, for instance, entailed a clear conversation, but from one side of the intellectual coin to the other. Both theology and science retained their missionary zeal. In time, the social sciences replaced theology to become the new secular theology (whether radical or conservative politically) with a scientifically sanctioned program for 'delivering' the Third World (development and modernization). The intellectual hegemony of Occidental discourse was rarely if ever radically questioned, at least not at its roots (no more than cultural anthropology has ever seriously considered the genesis and implications of its own ethno-centricity). Historically, the theologian's faith in God (his own) was converted into the scientist's faith in Reason (his own) and the latter took the former's place as the Redeemer of History. The Judeo-Christian paradigm may have been transformed, but it was never abandoned.

A final observation: The emphasis I have placed on the intellectual arm of Western imperialism should not blind us to its political and economic effects nor to its institutional and academic consequences. For instance, in the international development of modern science, the hierarchical and stratified organizational structure of Western scientific establishments is especially detrimental to a corresponding development of the sciences in 'less developed' societies (see Malecki and Olszewski, 1972). As always, the deck is stacked in favor of the West and the cards are shuffled at the expense of the Rest. In emphasizing intellectual history rather than political praxis, I have tried to make a complementary point: That politics is also epistemological and, conversely, that epistemology is invariably political (see Scholte, 1976 and 1978 and Wilden, 1972). That is precisely what 'critical' rationalism persistantly obscures (see Law, 1975: 374).

IX

This brings me to a concluding observation I should like to make regarding the historical dimension of the paradigm concept. Critical anthropologists often looked toward Marxism (or, more accurately, to a variety of Marxisms part and parcel of the intellectual currency of the times) as a source of normative inspiration and a model for anthropological reconstruction. But we did not, in my estimation, sufficiently contextualize and thus radicalize the very Marxism that gave us (or should have given us) a paradigmatic insight into the cultural production of *any* anthropological knowledge whatsoever — *our own included* (33). After all, Marxism is the historical product of Western civilization (see Foucault, 1966: 261ff and especially Sahlins, 1976); it may be radical in its analysis of capitalism (and, as Lukacs suggested, should be limited to such analyses), but it nonetheless expresses an intellectual consensus (anthropologically viewed) with bourgeois rationalism (see Baudrillard, 1975, Bourdieu, 1977: 171ff, Fabian, 1980: 241, or Mudimbe, 1973: 123ff and especially Dumont, 1977 for a detailed textual analysis). Marxism shares the formal features of our Judeo-Christian discourse, including its missionary zeal (see Löwith, 1946 or Hyman, 1962). When universalized, often under the non-reflexive rubric of scientific naturalism, Marxism becomes a constitutive ideology — creating, like any other ethnocentrism, its object of study rather than comprehending it (see Sahlins, 1976). This obviously happens in the case of Soviet ethnology (see Diamond, 1975 or Ryle, 1975), but also in those neo-Marxist circles which share the former's evolutionary prejudices. The comparative framework, originally intended as a descriptive and analytic device, becomes expository, evaluative, and self-serving (see Said, 1979: 149ff).

X

The ethno-centric potential of Marxism brings me full circle. Critical anthropologists in the sixties gained a paradigmatic perspective on an anthropological establishment that had arrogantly and mistakenly presumed itself syntag-matically self-contained. Yet in the final analysis, they themselves presumed no less, perhaps more: that the natives would actually profit from their often involuted and scholastic arguments regarding the 'true' Marx and the 'proper' Marxism (see Feyerabend, 1978: 121). These leisured ruminations of the theory class in part expressed their own rather than the natives' alienation (see Braroe and Hicks, 1967 or Vidich, 1974). True, we were not blind to the imperialism of orthodoxy, Marxist or otherwise (see any number of articles in *Critique of Anthropology* or *Dialectical Anthropology*). And surely we should be especially guarded in our pronouncements on Marxism today when it has once again become fashionable for New Left intellectuals to flagellate themselves and to denounce their erstwhile radical sins (Susan Sontag's recent confession comes to mind). But such caution does not take away from the need to recognize the deadly potentiality of any ethnocentric dogma in whatever form or colour. We need not paint Marxism black to mourn the blood spilled in its name . . . .

In conclusion, it seems to me that there are few if any compelling options that would transcend the specific circumstances of the social sciences at any given time *and* be founded on trans-cultural values to which anthropology should at all times be committed. Admittedly, the political and moral cyni-cism that attends a thorough, consistent relativism also seems intellectually irresponsible and politically impotent. Horkheimer's warning must certainly be taken to heart, especially since it quite accurately describes the institu-tional compromise made by many intellectuals: "Well informed cynicism is only another mode of conformity. These people willingly embrace or force themselves to accept the rule of the stronger as the eternal norm" (Horkheimer, 1947: 113; see also Rose, 1979: 280ff; Rose and Rose, 1980 for radical critiques of intellectual relativism).

Perhaps I have simply phrased the question in terms that defy an answer. There is certainly no shortage of specific suggestions in the anthropological literature. They range from a critique of Western instrumental rationality and its socio-cultural embodiment (see Diamond, 1974 or Lemaire, 1976 and 1980) to an appreciation of the paradigm-breaking and paradigm-building capacities of non-Western cultures (see Fahim and Helmer, 1980). In between there is a profusion of concrete and urgent recommendations: from applied, developmental, medical, urban, and feminist anthropology (to name but a few obvious examples) to fashionable theoretical solutions – biogenetic, bio-social, historical, demographic, ecological, economic, symbolic, culturological, ... And through them all are inter-woven those socio-historical, political, and economic questions that define the cultural circumstance of the social scientific enterprise: the arms race, the ecological crisis, the inhumanity of power-politics, joblessness, hunger, sickness, oppression, and discrimination.

To these and other issues we shall have to continue to address ourselves as we have in the past, even though our specific contributions are bound to be contingent and circumstantial. This time-bound tension between anthropological understanding on the one hand and historical mediation on the other will no doubt remain. This need not, however, be disabling as such. As Merleau-Ponty observed more than three decades ago: "If history envelops us all, it is up to us to understand that whatever we can have of the truth is not to be obtained in spite of our historical situation but because of it. Considered superficially, history destroys all truth, though considered radically, it founds a new idea of truth. As long as I hold the ideal of an absolute spectator before me, of knowledge without a point of view, I can see my situation only as a principle of error. But having once recognized that through this situation I have become part of all action and all knowledge that can be meaningful for me, then my contact with the social in the finitude of my situation reveals itself as the origin of all truths, including that of science; and since we have an idea of truth, since we are in the truth and cannot escape it, then the only thing left for us to do is to define a truth within a situation. Knowledge will be founded upon the irrefutable fact that we are not in the situation as is the object in objective space, and that it is for us the principle of our curiosity, our research and interest in other situations as variants of ours, and in our own lives, illuminated by fellow men, as variants of the lives of others. Finally, it is that which unites us to the totality of human experience no less than that which separates us from it" (Merleau-Ponty, 1951: 501).

And the social scientist? The very least he or she can do (and it is preciously little given the awesome inequalities in political exchange and economic distribution) is to make audible and give a hearing to the suppressed voices of those who have been rendered virtually silent by the self-serving rhetoric of the West (see Horkheimer and Adorno, 1944: 23). Such an effort, like any other inter-subjective, communicative, processual, and discursive task is existentially motivated, socially conditioned, historically situated, and philosophically motivated. As a media*ting* activity, it requires a reflexive understanding of its media*ted* circumstances (including and especially its own elitism and the political inequality of its relationship to its 'objects' of study). It is certainly not sufficient to advocate an ostrich policy akin to Panoff's (1977: 154ff) who suggests that we not bother with the ethnocentrism of scientific discourse since discourse does not move the world in any event. Of course discourse does not move the world. But discourse can try to make explicit that which does. Nor will it do to simply decry 'external' ideologies and forms of activism generated by Left-Wing rhetoric from the United States, as does Dumont (1979: 786ff), because they distract him from doing normal science on the basis of such 'sound and durable' universals as hierarchical oppositions (!). It is precisely an attitude such as Dumont's which is immune to what may, in the last analysis, be central to an activity we grace with the term science: self-critique.

Notes

1. Special thanks to Willem de Blécourt, Johannes Fabian, Ton Lemaire, Wolf Lepenies, and Richard Whitley for their comments and observations. The responsibility for the final contents of this essay are my own.
2. I intend no self-serving remark here. I actually owe my 'discovery' of Thomas Kuhn to Dell Hymes.
3. The first decade of critical anthropology was largely, though by no means exclusively, an American affair. The passing of Belgian, British, Dutch and French colonial empires and their attendant emancipatory movements and struggles apparently did not have the same immediate effect on these countries' anthropological traditions that the Viet-Nam debacle had on the U.S. social sciences (e.g., Copans, 1970–1971: 1192). This changed significantly in the seventies, as evidenced by collections such as Asad's (1973) or journals such as *Critique of Anthropology* in England and books by Copans (1974) or Leclerc (1972) and debates in *Les Temps modernes* in France.
4. A promising beginning has indeed been made, notably in the sociology and history of science, cf. Barnes and Shapin, 1979 or Mendelsohn and Elkana, 1981.
5. The semiotic or linguistic context in which Kuhn's notion of paradigm was placed is of considerable significance. Though Kuhn had explicitly borrowed the concept from language teaching (Kuhn, 1977: xix), it initially had merely an exemplary and restricted sense. Paradigms are not theories or symbols: "Most fundamentally, they are concrete examples of scientific achievement, actual problems which scientists study with care and upon which they model their own work" (Kuhn, 1977: 351). Even the suggestive reference to Wittgenstein in *The Structure of*

Scientific Revolutions (Kuhn, 1962: 44) did not entail an elaboration of the semiotic dimension until the Second Edition (1970) and the publication of *The Essential Tension* (Kuhn, 1977: xxii—xxiii; 338ff). When I first used the term paradigm, I quite 'naturally' placed the concept in the context of the 'Unified Science Movement' of Pierce, Morris, and others in whose Encyclopedia *The Structure of Scientific Revolutions* was first published. This interpretation was further reinforced by the above-mentioned reference to Wittgenstein, the general influence of English language philosophy at the time, and — as far as anthropology is concerned — the importance of Peter Winch's *The Idea of a Social Science* (1958) and the ethnography of speech and communication (compare to Phillips, 1977: 90). Because of my initial association of Kuhn with semiotics, I have always contrasted the paradigmatic with the syntagmatic and have retained the difference in this essay. I have done so despite Kuhn's own preference for a more restrictive approach (Kuhn, 1977: xix) and his cautious remarks regarding the complementarity of internal and external approaches to the history of science (Kuhn, 1977: 112).

6. The term 'universe of discourse' had a more relativistic connotation when it gained currency in the early sixties than it has now in either symbolic anthropology or neo-Marxism (see Bauman, 1973). What it initially implied, at least for some of us, was that any discourse on the universe, including those symbolic forms which were said to mirror the universe, were themselves constitutive and context-specific universes of discourse.

7. The most sophisticated philosophical example of syntagmatic formalism and one that was to have a considerable influence on certain Marxist anthropologists is that of Louis Althusser (1965, 1968, 1971, and 1972; for sustained critiques, see George, 1969, Lefebvre, 1971 and especially Thompson, 1978). Comparisons between Kuhn (or Feyerabend!) and Althusser are, as far as I can tell, historically unfounded and theoretically indefensible (see Balckburn and Jones, 1972: 376ff for a far-fetched analogy).

8. The author mentions the culture of poverty and the dichotomy between traditional and modern cultures, but her point is applicable to all ethno-centric definitions of culture.

9. There were other and less idealistic reasons as well. But the loss of a laboratory and hence of 'pure' research opportunities which apparently led many biologists to turn to social action (see Mok and Westerdiep, 1974: 211) was not then, as it may be now, an explicit motive among cultural anthropologists (despite the rapid disappearance of their traditional 'objects' of study). More significant and troublesome was the unbearable discrepancy between the academic definition of professional anthropology on the one hand and the moral and political turmoil in the world on the other. Let me add that the specific reasons for continuing and/or discontinuing one's studies in the eighties may be quite different again.

10. See Scholte, 1978 and Kaplan and Manners, 1979 for contrasting overviews in the case of cultural anthropology; Ferguson (1973) for a summary of the conflict in the philosophy of science.

11. For comparable critiques of transformational linguistics, see Itkohnen, 1974 and Verhaar, 1966, 1971, and 1973.

12. It is a terrible shock to members of my generation to find that many students today

find 'nibbling' at the paradigmatic edges a superfluous exercise: a past luxury irrelevant to, and impractical in, today's ever-shrinking academic market-place.

13. And, I am sure, women social scientists can attest to the New Left's sexism, see Easlea (1981).

14. In the course of time, Kuhn seems to have completely retreated from what I would consider a properly paradigmatic perspective. In a 1971 article he chides historians of science for neglecting the internal history of the natural sciences, especially their technical core, and for mistakenly emphasizing the external factors in their development (see also Kuhn, 1977). Perhaps shaken by this critics' accusation that he is in fief with student radicals and religious maniacs (Lakatos, 1970; this accusation and analogy sounds very familiar to the critical anthropologist! [see Scholte, 1978]), he blames "the increasingly virulent anti-scientific climate" of the times for the excessive attention paid to extra-scientific factors (Kuhn, 1971: 300).

15. There are exceptions. For instance, Halpern and Hammel conclude their intellectual-historical observations on Yugoslavian social sciences with the following general statement: "As anthropologists turn increasingly to the study of complex societies, they are led to reflect on the role that social science plays in national ideologies and the ways in which the current state and development of social science reflects other cultural states and processes. Indeed such reflections can usefully be turned on our own society. One sees that it is much more appropriate to discard old notions of the distinction between 'science' and 'folklore' and to regard the social science of a particular society, however sophisticated and presumably objective, as an important part of its subjective ideology about itself and the world and thus a part of its own folk theory about the relations of man to society and of men to men" (Halpern and Hammel, 1969: 17).

16. On the sociological correlates to writing in 'hot' (civilized) societies and iconography in 'cold' (primitive) societies, see Wilden, 1972: 407ff.

17. See Goody (1977) from whom both the concrete example and the characterization of writing are distilled.

18. Natives are almost invariably understood in contrasting terms, that is, by what we do and they do not have (see Kehoe, 1981: 505).

19. Marcus is in part correct to claim that "it is not a question of breaking the hermeneutic circle, but how this circle is to be represented in a genre of writing which continues to have a priority concern with knowledge of the 'other' rather than of the 'self'" (Marcus, 1980: 508). The issue, however, is not one or the other, but of the dialectical and constitutive relation between them (see Dwyer 1979 or Tedlock 1979).

20. See also Boon, 1972 for an anthropological example and Hyman's, 1962 neglected classic or Gay's, 1974 study on narrative style and historical reconstruction.

21. Giddens (1976: 18) has tried to show "how it is possible, and important, to sustain a principle of relativity while rejecting relativism." Perhaps I do not sufficiently understand or appreciate his argument, but I remained unconvinced and disappointed.

22. Though beyond the scope and intent of this essay, a history of the use and especially misuse of biological and neurological paradigms in the social and human sciences would be most interesting and valuable (see *Radical Science Journal*) or H. & S. Rose (1976).

23. See especially Cahiers de l'Institut de l'Etudes du Développement (1975: 108ff) on the relation between scientific universalism and aid to 'underdeveloped' areas.
24. See Fabian 1980 and Said 1979 for anthropologically significant examples.
25. My example is American for two reasons: One, because I can speak about it from experience; two, the crisis in anthropology which generated this renewed interest in the history of the discipline was, initially, an American development (see also footnote three). Subsequently, British anthropologists made a major contribution (and continue to do so), as exemplified by Banaji's initial study (1970) and Llobera's recent work (1976, 1978, 1979, and 1980).
26. My rather harsh judgement is no doubt coloured by personal experiences at Stanford University in the early sixties. But the Magistrar Ludi mentality did not reign supreme only there, it was endemic to the ideology of the profession as a whole.
27. Of course not all the participants in the rationality debate share the positions advocated by Gellner or Horton. Winch does not and neither does Beatty. The British editor of an informative volume on the debate (Wilson, 1970) seems characteristically reasonable: " . . . the criteria of rationality in Western society may be properly applied more widely, even if does not establish them as *the* universally valid criteria of rationality" (Wilson, 1970: x). This reminds me of the Chinese proverb of the man who walks in the middle of the street and gets hit by traffic coming from both directions . . . .
28. Hallowell's classic essay (1965) must be singled out in this regard.
29. The latter combination — between the history of anthropology and the critique of ideology — can be fruitfully supplemented with a sociology of knowledge perspective, see Wolf, 1969.
30. These literary analyses are rich in specific textual detail and should be distinguished from the more global and accusative analogies between Judeo-Christian scholasticisms and social scientific discourse such as Delfendahl's (1971) critique of Lévi-Strauss.
31. The question of the role of spatio-temporal categories in cultural anthropology may be equally germane to the historical and comparative development of the natural sciences. According to Needham (1969: 284ff), the distinctive use of time and space is one of the defining characteristics of Occidental science.
32. A remarkably vulgar but by no means exclusive anthropological example is provided by Marvin Harris (1979). He considers science "a unique and precious contribution of Western civilisation" (27) as well as a "way of knowing that has a uniquely transcendant value for all human beings" (27). Questioning science in the name of relativism is "an intellectual crime against humanity" (28). We must therefore agree 'to submit' to science's "distinctive logical and empirical discipline" (35). *All* of us, including those stubborn natives who might erroneously think otherwise (36). Why? Because any logic other than scientific logic (as defined by Harris) is a 'bad bet' (57) given the 'cost-benefit options' (61) available. Different options are, in fact, of derivative importance: cultural and cognitive differences are, scientifically considered (that is, by Harris), 'mystifications' (256) which do not "honor the science of history" (256). Those who nevertheless prefer to respect these cultural and cognitive differences, thereby dishonor "the attempt to achieve a science of society" (235). The ethnocentrism and arrogance of Harris' 'bourgois rationalism' is made explicit and criticized accordingly by Paul and Rabinow (1976).

33. See Kahn and Llobera, 1981 for a similar oversight among French Marxist anthropologists.

Bibliography

Ahlers, Rolf: 1970, 'Is Technology Intrinsically Repressive?' *Continuum* 8 (1): 111–122.

Althusser, Louis: 1965, *For Marx*, New York: Vintage Books (1970).

Althusser, Louis: 1971, *Lenin and Philosophy and other Essays*, London: New Left Books.

Althusser, Louis: 1972, *Politics and History: Montesquieu, Rousseau, Hegel and Marx*, London: New Left Books.

Althusser, Louis and Etienne Balibar: 1968, *Reading Capital*, London: New Left Books (1970).

Amselle, Jean-Loup: 1979, *Le Sauvage à la mode*, Paris: Editions Le Sycomore.

Asad, Talal (ed.): 1973, *Anthropology and the Colonial Encounter*. London: Ithaca Press.

Asad, Talal: 1975, 'Anthropological Texts and Ideological Problems: An Analysis of Cohen On Arab Villages in Israel', *Economy and Society* 4 (3), 251–282.

Asad, Talal: 1979, 'Anthropology and the Analysis of Ideology', *Man* 14, 607–627.

Auge, Marc: 1979, *Symbole, Fonction, Histoire: Les intérrogations de l'anthropologie*, Paris: Hachette.

Banaji, Jairus: 1970, 'The Crisis of British Anthropology', *New Left Review* 64, 71–84.

Barnes, Barry: 1972, 'Sociological Explanation and Natural Science: A Kuhnian Reappraisal', *Archives of European Sociology* 13, 373–391.

Barnes, Barry (ed.): 1972, *Sociology of Science*, Middlesex: Penguin.

Barnes, Barry: 1974, *Scientific Knowledge and Sociological Theory*, London: Routledge & Kegan Paul.

Barnes, Barry: 1976, 'Natural Rationality: A Neglected Concept in the Social Sciences', *Philosophy of the Social Sciences* 6 (2), 115–126.

Barnes, Barry and Steven Shapin (eds.): 1979, *Natural Order: Historical Studies of Scientific Culture*, Beverly Hills/London: Sage Publications.

Bateson, Gregory: 1972, *Steps to an Ecology of Mind*, New York: Chandler Publishing Company.

Baudrillard, Jean: 1975, *The Mirror of Production*, St. Louis: Telos Press.

Bauman, Zygmunt: 1973, *Culture as Praxis*, London: Routledge & Kegan Paul.

Becker, Ernest: 1968, *The Structure of Evil: An Essay On the Unification of the Science of Man*, New York: Braziller.

Becker, Ernest: 1971, *The Lost Science of Man*, New York: Braziller.

Bernstein, Basil: 1971, *Class, Codes and Control*, 3 Vols. London: Routledge & Kegal Paul.

Blackburn, Robin and Gareth Stedman Jones: 1972, 'Louis Althusser and the Struggle for Marxism', in Dick Howard and Karl E. Klare (eds.), *The Unknown Dimension: European Marxism Since Lenin*, pp. 365–387. New York: Basic Books.

Bloor, David: 1976, *Knowledge and Social Imagery*, London: Routledge & Kegan Paul.

Bodenheimer, Susanne J.: 1970, 'The Ideology of Developmentalism: American Political Science's Paradigm-Surrogate for Latin-American Studies', *Berkeley Journal of Sociology* 15, 95–137.

Boon, James A.: 1972, *From Symbolism to Structuralism: Lévi-Strauss in a Literary Tradition*, Oxford: Blackwell's.
Bourdieu, Pierre: 1967, 'Systems of Education and Systems of Thought', *International Social Science Journal* 19 (3), 338–358.
Bourdieu, Pierre: 1973, 'The Three Forms of Theoretical Knowledge', *Social Science Information* 12 (1): 53–80.
Bourdieu, Pierre: 1975, 'The Specificity of the Scientific Field and the Social Conditions of the Progress of Reason', *Social Science Information* 14 (6), 19–47.
Bourdieu, Pierre: 1977, *Outline of a Theory of Practice*, Cambridge: University Press.
Braroe, Niels W. and George L. Hicks: 1967, 'Observations on the Mystique of Anthropology', *Sociological Quarterly* 8 (2), 173–186.
Burridge, Kenelm: 1973, *Encountering Aborigines: A Case Study*, New York: Pergamon.
Cahiers de l'Institut d'Études du Developpement: 1975, *Le Savoir et le faire: Relations interculturelles et développement*. Genève: CIED.
Cahiers de l'Institut d'Études du Developpement: 1975, *La Pluralité des mondes: Théories et pratiques du développement*, Genève: CIED.
Cahiers de l'Institut d'Études du Developpement: 1976, *L'Ambivalence de la production: Logiques communautaires et logique capitaliste*, Paris: P.U.F.
Clark, Terry N.: 1973, *Prophets and Patrons: The French University and the Emergence of the Social Sciences*, Cambridge: Harvard.
Copans, Jean: 1970–1971, 'Quelques réflections', *Les Temps modernes* 293–294: 1179–1193.
Copans, Jean (ed.): 1974, *Critiques et politiques de l'anthropologie*, Paris: Maspero.
Darnell, Regna: 1971, 'The Professionalization of American Anthropology: A Case Study in the Sociology of Knowledge', *Social Science Information* 10 (2), 83–103.
De Laguna, Grace: 1941, 'Cultural Relativism and Science', in *On Existence and the Human World*, pp. 232–262. New Haven: Yale (1966).
Delfendahl, Bernard: 1971, 'Critique de l'anthropologie savante: Claude Lévi-Strauss, homéliste et scolastique', *L'Homme et la société* 22, 211–235.
Diamond, Stanley: 1974, *In Search of the Primitive: A Critique of Civilization*, New Brunswick, N.J.: Transaction Books.
Diamond, Stanley: 1975, 'The Marxist Tradition As a Dialectical Anthropology', *Dialectical Anthropology* 1 (1), 1–5.
Diamond, Stanley (ed.): 1980, *Anthropology: Ancestors and Hiers*, The Hague: Mouton.
Diamond, Stanley, Bob Scholte, and Eric Wolf: 1975, 'Anti-Kaplan: Defining the Marxist Tradition', *American Anthropologist* 77 (4), 876–879.
Dickson, David: 1974, 'Technology and the Construction of Social Reality', *Radical Science Journal* 1, 29–50.
Dolby, R. G. A.: 1972, 'The Sociology of Knowledge in Natural Science', in Barry Barnes (ed.), *Sociology of Science*, pp. 309–320, Middlesex: Penguin.
Douglas, Mary: 1973, *Natural Symbols*, New York: Vintage Books.
Douglas, Mary (ed.): 1982, *Essays in the Sociology of Perception*, London: Routledge & Kegan Paul.
Dumont, Louis: 1977, *From Mandeville to Marx: The Genesis and Triumph of Economic Ideology*, Chicago: University Press.
Dumont, Louis: 1979, 'The Anthropological Community and Ideology', *Social Science Information* 18 (6): 785–817.

272   Bob Scholte

Dwyer, Kevin: 1979, 'The Dialogic of Ethnology', *Dialectical Anthropology* **4** (3), 205–224.

Easlea, Brian: 1981, *Science and Sexual Oppression*, London: Weidenfeld and Nicolson.

Eder, Klaus: 1975, *Die Entsehung vorkapitalistischer Klassengesellschaften: Ein Beitrag zur Konstruktion einer Theorie der Sozio-Kulturellen Evolution*, Starnberg: Max Planck Institut.

Elias, Norbert: 1974, 'The Sciences: Towards a Theory', in Richard Whitley (ed.), *Social Processes of Scientific Development*, pp. 21–42. London: Routledge & Kegal Paul.

Fabian, Johannes: 1979, 'Rule and Process: Thoughts On Ethnography as Communication', *Philosophy of the Social Sciences* **9** (1), 1–26.

Fabian, Johannes: 1980, *Time and the Other: Politics of Time in Anthropology*, New York: Columbia University Press (in press).

Fahim, Hussein and Katherine Helmer: 1980, 'Indigenous Anthropology in Non-Western Countries: A Further Elaboration', *Current Anthropology* **21** (5), 644–663.

Ferguson, Thomas: 1973, 'The Political Economy of Knowledge and the Changing Politics of the Philosophy of Science', *Telos* **15**, 124–137.

Feyerabend, Paul: 1970, 'Consolations for a Specialist', in Lakatos, Imre and Alan Musgrave (eds.), *Criticism and the Growth of Knowledge*, pp. 197–230. Cambridge: University Press.

Feyerabend, Paul: 1975, *Against Method*, London: New Left Books.

Feyerabend, Paul: 1978, *Science in a Free Society*, London: New Left Books.

Finnegan, Ruth & Robin Horton (eds.): 1973, *Modes of Thought: Essays on Thinking in Western and Non-Western Societies*, London: Faber & Faber.

Foucault, Michel: 1966, *The Order of Things: An Archaeology of the Human Sciences*, London: Tavistock (1970).

Franck, Robert, 1979, 'Knowledge and Opinions', in Helga Nowotny and Hilary Rose (eds.), *Counter-movements in the Sciences*, pp. 39–56. Dordrecht: Reidel.

Galtung, Johan: 1981, 'Structure, Culture, and Intellectual Style: An Essay Comparing Saxonic, Teutonic, Gallic and Nipponic Approaches', *Social Science Information* **20** (6), 817–856.

Garfinkel, Harold, Michael Lynch, and Eric Livingston: 1981, 'The Work of a Discovering Science Construed With Materials From the Optically Discovered Pulsar', *Philosophy of the Social Sciences* **11** (2), 131–158.

Gay, Peter: 1974, *Style in History*, New York: Basic Books.

Gebhardt, Eike: 1978, 'Residual Problems in the Sociology of Science – A Map For a New Field?' *International Journal of Sociology* **8** (1–2), 3–44.

Gellner, Ernest: 1970, 'Concepts and Society', in Bryan R. Wilson (ed.), *Rationality*, pp. 18–49. New York: Harper Torchbooks.

Gellner, Ernest: 1975, 'A Wittgensteinian Philosophy of (Or Against) the Social Sciences', *Philosophy of the Social Sciences* **5** (2), 173–199.

Gellner, Ernest: 1975, 'Ethnomethodology: The Re-Enchantment Industry or the California Way of Subjectivity', *Philosophy of the Social Sciences* **5** (4), 431–450.

George, François: 1969, 'Lire Althusser', *Les Temps modernes* **24** (295), 1921–1962.

Geras, Norman: 1972, 'Althusser's Marxism: An Account and Assessment', *New Left Review* **71**, 57–86.

Giddens, Anthony: 1976, *New Rules of Sociological Method: A Positive Critique of Interpretative Sociologies*, London: Hutchinson.

Goldman, Lucien: 1966, *The Human Sciences and Philosophy*, London: Cape (1969).
Goody, Jack: 1977, *The Domestication of the Savage Mind*, Cambridge: University Press.
Gouldner, Alvin W.: 1976, *The Dialectic of Ideology and Technology: The Origins, Grammar and Future of Ideology*, London: Macmillan.
Grace, George W.: 1969, 'Notes on the Philosophical Background of Current Linguistic Controversy', *Working Papers in Linguistics*, 1. Honolulu: University of Hawaii.
Gran, Thorvald: 1974, 'Elements from the Debate on Science in Society: A Study of Joseph Ben-David's Theory', in Richard Whitley (ed.), *Social Processes of Scientific Development*, pp. 195–209. London: Routledge & Kegan Paul.
Gruber, Jacob W.: 1975, 'Introduction', in Timothy H. H. Thoreson (ed.), *Toward A Science of Man: Essays in the History of Anthropology*, pp. 1–13. The Hague: Mouton.
Habermas, Jurgen: 1976, *Zur Rekonstruktion des Historischen Materialismus*, Frankfurt/ M: Suhrkamp.
Habermas, Jurgen: 1979, *Communication and the Evolution of Society*, London: Heinemann.
Hallowell, Irving A.: 1965, 'The History of Anthropology As an Anthropological Problem', *Journal of the History of the Behavioral Sciences* 1 (1), 24–38.
Halpern, Joel M. and Eugene A. Hammel: 1969, 'Observations on the Intellectual History of Ethnology and other Social Sciences in Yugoslavia', *Comparative Studies in Society and History* 11 (1), 17–26.
Harris, Marvin: 1968, *The Rise of Anthropological Theory: A History of Theories of Culture*, New York: Crowell.
Harris, Marvin: 1979, *Cultural Materialism: The Struggle for a Science of Culture*, New York: Vintage Books.
Hazard, Paul: 1935, *The European Mind: 1680–1715*, Middlesex: Penguin.
Hodgen, Margaret T.: 1964, *Early Anthropology in the Sixteenth and Seventeenth Centuries*, Philadelphia: University of Pennsylvania Press.
Hollis, Martin: 1970, 'The Limits of Irrationality', in Bryan R. Wilson (ed.), *Rationality*, pp. 214–220. New York: Harper Torchbooks.
Hollis, Martin: 1972, 'Witchcraft and Winchcraft', *Philosophy of the Social Sciences* 2 (2), 89–103.
Honigmann, John: 1976, *The Development of Anthropological Ideas*, Homewood, Ill.: The Dorsey Press.
Horkheimer, Max: 1947, *The Eclipse of Reason*, New York: Seabury Press (1974).
Horkheimer, Max and Theodor W. Adorno: 1944, *Dialectic of Enlightenment*, New York: Herder & Herder.
Horton, Robin: 1970, 'African Traditional Thought and Western Science', in Bryan Wilson (ed.), *Rationality*, pp. 131–171. New York: Harper Torchbooks.
Horton, Robin: 1973, 'Lévy-Bruhl, Durkheim and the Scientific Revolution', in Ruth Finnegan and Robin Horton (eds.), *Modes of Thought: Essays On Thinking in Western and Non-Western Societies*, pp. 249–305. London: Farber & Farber.
Horton, Robin: 1973, 'Paradox and Explanation: A reply to Mr. Skorupski I & II", *Philosophy of the Social Sciences* 3 (3 & 4), 231–256; 289–312.
Hsu, Francis L. K.: 1977, 'Role, Affect, and Anthropology', *American Anthropologist* 79 (4), 805–808.

Hyman, Stanley Edgar: 1962, *The Tangled Bank: Darwin, Marx, Frazer and Freud as Imaginative Writers*, New York: Atheneum.

Hymes, Dell H.: 1964, 'Directions in (Ethno-) Linguistic Theory', in A. K. Romney and R. G. D'Andrade (eds.), *Transcultural Studies in Cognition*, pp. 6–56. American Anthropologist 66, No. 3, pt. 2 (special issue).

Hymes, Dell H. (ed.): 1972, *Reinventing Anthropology*, New York: Pantheon.

Hymes, Dell H. and John Fought: 1975, *American Structuralism*, The Hague: Mouton (1981).

Ita, J. M.: 1973, 'Frobenius, Senghor and the Image of Africa', in Ruth Finnegan and Robin Horton (eds.), *Modes of Thought: Essays on Thinking in Western and Non-Western Societies*, pp. 306–336. London: Farber & Farber.

Itkonen, Esa: 1974, *Linguistics and Metascience*, Kokemäki: Societas Philosophica et Phaenomenologica Finlandiae (Studia Philosophica Turkuensia Fasc. 11).

Jay, Martin: 1973, *The Dialectical Imagination: A History of the Frankfurt School and the Institute of Social Research, 1923–1950*, Boston: Little, Brown & Co.

Jaulin, Robert: 1970, *La Paix blanche: Introduction à l'ethnocide*, Paris: du Seuil.

Kahn, Joel S. and Josep R. Llobera (eds.): 1981, *The Anthropology of Pre-Capitalist Societies*, London: Macmillan.

Kaplan, David and Robert A. Manners: 1979, 'Some Critical Observations on Scholte's Critical Anthropology', *Anthropology and Humanism Quarterly* 4 (1), 5–9.

Kehoe, Alice B.: 1981, 'Revisionist Anthropology: Aboriginal North America', *Current Anthropology* 22 (5), 503–517.

Kuhn, Thomas S.: 1962, *The Structure of Scientific Revolutions*, Chicago: University Press.

Kuhn, Thomas S.: 1969, 'Postscript', in *The Structure of Scientific Revolutions* (Second Edition). Chicago: University Press (1970).

Kuhn, Thomas S.: 1970, 'Reflections on My Critics', in Imre Lakatos and Alan Musgrave (eds.), *Criticism and the Growth of Knowledge*, pp. 231–278. Cambridge: University Press.

Kuhn, Thomas S.: 1971, 'The Relations Between History and the History of Science', in Paul Rabinow and William M. Sullivan (eds.), *Interpretative Social Science: A Reader*, pp. 267–300. Berkeley: University of California Press.

Kuhn, Thomas S.: 1972, 'Scientific Paradigms', in Barry Barnes (ed.), *Sociology of Science*, pp. 80–104. Middlesex: Penguin.

Kuhn, Thomas S.: 1977, *The Essential Tension: Selected Studies in Scientific Tradition and Change*, Chicago: University Press.

Lakatos, Imre: 1970, 'Falsification and the Methodology of Scientific Research Programmes', in Imre Lakatos and Alan Musgrave (eds.), *Criticism and the Growth of Knowledge*, pp. 91–195. Cambridge: University Press.

Larrain, Jorge: 1979, *The Concept of Ideology*, London: Hutchinson.

Law, John: 1975, 'Is Epistemology Redundant? A Sociological View', *Philosophy of the Social Sciences* 5 (3), 317–337.

Leacock, Eleanor: 1980, 'Politics, Theory, and Racism in the Study of Black Children', in Stanley Diamond (ed.), *Theory and Practice: Essays Presented to Gene Weltfish*, pp. 153–178. The Hague: Mouton.

Leclerc, Gerard: 1972, *Anthropology et Colonialisme: Essai sur l'histoire de l'Africanisme*, Paris: Fayard.

Lefebvre, Henri: 1971, *Au-delà du structuralisme*, Paris: Editions Anthropos.

Leiss, William: 1972, *The Domination of Nature*, New York: Braziller.

Lemaire, Ton: 1976, *Over de waarde van kulturen*, Baarn: Ambo.

Lemaire, Ton: 1980, *Het vertoog over de ongelijkheid van Jean-Jacques Rousseau*. Baarn: Ambo.

Lemaire, Gerald, Roy Macleod, Michael Mulkay, and Peter Weingart (eds.): 1976, *Perspectives on the Emergence of Scientific Disciplines*, The Hague: Mouton.

Lepenies, Wolf: 1974, 'History and Anthropology – A Historical Appraisal of the Current Contact Between the Disciplines', *Social Science Information*, 1976, **15** (2–3), 287–306.

Lepenies, Wolf: 1980, 'The Critique of Learning and Science and the Crisis of Orientation', *Social Science Information* **19** (1), 1–37.

Lepenies, Wolf, 1981, 'Anthropological Perspectives in the Sociology of Science', in Everett Mendelsohn and Y. Elkana (eds.), *Sciences and Cultures*, pp. 245–261. Dordrecht: Reidel.

Lewis, Diane: 1973, 'Anthropology and Colonialism', *Current Anthropology* **14** (5): 581–602.

Llobera, Josep R.: 1976, 'The History of Anthropology as a Problem', *Critique of Anthropology* **7**, 17–42.

Llobera, Josep R.: 1978, 'Epistemology: The End of an Illusion?' *Critique of Anthropology* **13**, 89–95.

Llobera, Josep R.: 1979, 'Newton, the Scientific Model, and Social Thought in the Enlightenment', *Dialectical Anthropology* **4** (2), 147–153.

Llobera, Josep R.: 1980, 'Durkheim, the Durkheimians and Their Collective Misrepresentation of Marx', *Social Science Information* **19** (2), 385–411.

Lowie, Robert H.: 1937, *The History of Ethnological Theory*, New York: Holt, Rinehart & Winston.

Lowith, Karl: 1946, *Meaning in History*, Chicago: University Press.

Lukes, Steven: 1970, 'Some Problems About Rationality', in Bryan Wilson (ed.), *Rationality*, pp. 172–193. New York: Harper Torchbooks.

Lukes, Steven: 1973, 'On the Social Determination of Truth', in Ruth Finnegan and Robin Horton (eds.), *Modes of Thought: Essays On Thinking in Western and Non-Western Societies*, pp. 230–248. London: Farber & Farber.

Magubane, Bernard: 1971, 'A Critical Look at Indices Used in the Study of Social Change in Colonial Africa', *Current Anthropology* **12** (4–5): 419–445.

Malecki, Ignacy, and Eugenuisz Olszeski: 1972, 'Regularities in the Development of Contemporary Science', in Barry Barnes (ed.), *Sociology of Science*, pp. 147–165. Middlesex: Penguin.

Marcus, George E.: 1980, 'Rhetoric and the Ethnographic Genre in Anthropological Research', *Current Anthropology* **21** (4), 507–510.

Martins, H.: 1972, 'The Kuhnian Revolution and Its Implications for Sociology', in A. H. Hanson *et al.* (eds.), *Imagination and Precision in Political Analysis: Essays in Honor of Peter Nettl*, London: Farber & Farber.

Mendelsohn, Everett: 1977, 'The Social Construction of Scientific Knowledge', in Everett Mendelsohn, Peter Weingart, and Richard Whitley (eds.), *The Social Production of Scientific Knowledge*, pp. 3–26. Dordrecht: Reidel.

Mendelsohn, Everett: 1981, 'Introduction', in Everett Mendelsohn and Y. Elkana (eds.), *Sciences and Cultures*, pp. vii–xii. Dordrecht: Reidel.

Mendelsohn, Everett and Y. Elkana (eds.): 1981, *Sciences and Cultures*, Dordrecht: Reidel.

Merleau-Ponty, Maurice: 1951, 'The Philosopher and Sociology', in Maurice Natanson (ed.), *Philosophy of the Social Sciences: A Reader*, pp. 487–505. New York: Random House.

Mok, Albert and Anne Westerdiep: 1974, 'Societal Influences on the Choice of Research Topics of Biologists', in Richard Whitley (ed.), *Social Processes of Scientific Development*, pp. 210–223. London: Routledge & Kegan Paul.

Monod, Jean: 1970–1971, 'Un Riche Cannibale: Ethno-récit', *Les Temps modernes*, 293–294: 1061–1120.

Mudimbe, V. Y.: 1973, *L'Autre face du royaume*, Dole: L'age de l'homme.

Murphy, Robert F.: 1971, *The Dialectics of Social Life: Alarms and Excursions in Anthropological Theory*, New York: Basic Books.

Needham, Joseph: 1969, *Within the Four Seas: The Dialogue of East and West*, London: George Allen & Unwin.

Needham, Joseph: 1969, *The Grand Titration: Science and Society in East and West*, London: George Allen & Unwin.

Nelson, Benjamin: 1974, 'On the Shoulders of the Giants of the Comparative Sociology of "Science" in Civilizational Perspective', in Richard Whitley (ed.), *Social Processes of Scientific Development*, pp. 13–20. London: Routledge & Kegan Paul.

Nowotny, Helga: 1979, 'Science and Its Critics: Reflections on Anti-Science', in Helga Nowotny and Hilary Rose (eds.), *Counter-movements in the Sciences*, pp. 1–26. Dordrecht: Reidel.

Panoff, Michel: 1977, *Ethnologie: le deuxième souffle*, Paris: Payot.

Phillips, Derek L.: 1977, *Wittgenstein and Scientific Knowledge: A Sociological Perspective*, London: Macmillan.

Paul, Robert and Paul Rabinow: 1976, 'Bourgeois Rationalism Revived', *Dialectical Anthropology* 1 (2), 121–134.

Rose, Hilary: 1979, 'Hyper-Reflexivity – A New Danger For the Counter-Movements', in Helga Nowotny and Hilary Rose (eds.), *Counter-movements in the Sciences*, pp. 277–289. Dordrecht: Reidel.

Rose, Hilary and Steven Rose: 1976, *The Radicalization of Science*, London: Macmillan.

Rose, Hilary and Steven Rose: 1976, *The Political Economy of Science*, London: Macmillan.

Rose, Hilary and Steven Rose: 1980, 'Against an Oversocialized Conception of Science', *Communication & Cognition* 13 (2–3), 269–283.

Ruyle, Eugene E.: 1975, 'Mode of Production and Mode of Exploitation: The Mechanical and the Dialectical', *Dialiectical Anthropology* 1 (1), 7–23.

Sahlins, Marshall: 1976, *Culture and Practical Reason*, Chicago: University Press.

Said, Edward W.: 1979, *Orientalism*, New York: Vintage Books.

Saran, A. K.: 1975, 'Some Reflections On Sociology in Crisis', in Tom Bottomore (ed.), *Crisis and Contention in Sociology*, pp. 85–122. London: Sage Publications.

Sartre, Jean-Paul: 1963, *Search for a Method*, New York: Vintage

Schmidt, Alfred: 1962, *The Concept of Nature in Marx*, London: Books (1971).

Schmidt, Alfred: 1971, *Geschichte und Struktur*, München: Hanser Verlag.

Scholte, Bob: 1966, 'Epistemic Paradigms: Some Problems in Cross-Cultural ...ch on Anthropological Theory and History', *American Anthropologist* 68 (5), 1255–1256.

Scholte, Bob: 1971, 'Discontents in Anthropology', *Social Research* 38 (4), 777–8...

Scholte, Bob: 1972, 'Toward a Reflexive and Critical Anthropology', in Dell Hy... (ed.), *Reinventing Anthropology*, pp. 430–457. New York: Pantheon.

Scholte, Bob: 1976, 'On the Function of Scientific Discourse', *American Anthropologist* 78 (1): 74–78.

Scholte, Bob: 1978, 'Critical Anthropology Since Its Reinvention', *Anthropology and Humanism Quarterly* 3 (1 & 2), 4–17.

Scholte, Bob: 1980, 'From Discourse to Silence: The Structuralist Impasse', in Stanley Diamond (ed.), *Towards a Marxist Anthropology*, pp. 31–67. The Hague: Mouton.

Scholte, Bob: 1980, 'Anthropological Traditions: Their Definitions', in Stanley Diamond (ed.), *Anthropology: Ancestors and Heirs*, pp. 53–87. The Hague: Mouton.

Simmons, Anthony and Nico Stehr: 1981, 'Language and the Growth of Knowledge in Sociology', *Social Science Information* 20 (4–5), 703–741.

Skolimowski, Henryk: 1974, 'The Scientific World View and the Illusions of Progress', *Social Research* 41 (1), 52–82.

Stehr, Nico: 1981, 'The Magic Triangle: In Defense of a General Sociology of Knowledge', *Philosophy of the Social Sciences* 11 (2), 225–229.

Steiner, George: 1975, *After Babel: Aspects of Language and Translation*, London: Oxford University Press.

Stocking, George W. Jr.: 1968, *Race, Culture and Evolution: Essays in the History of Anthropology*, New York: The Free Press.

Tambiah, S. J.: 1973, 'Form and Meaning of Magical Acts: A Point of View', in Ruth Finnegan and Robin Horton (eds.), *Modes of Thought. Essays On Thinking in Western and Non-Western Societies*, pp. 199–229. London: Farber & Farber.

Tedlock, Dennis: 1979, 'The Analogical Tradition and the Emergence of a Dialogical Anthropology', Harvey Lecture, University of New Mexico, March 20th.

Thompson, E. P.: 1978, *The Poverty of Theory and Other Essays*, London: Merlin Press.

Timpanaro, Sebastiono: 1970, *On Materialism*, London: New Left Books.

Verhaar, John W.: 1966, 'Method, Theory, and Phenomenology', in Paul L. Garvin (ed.), *Method and Theory in Linguistics*, New York: Humanities Press.

Verhaar, John W.: 1971, 'Philosophy and Linguistic Theory', *Language Sciences* 14, 1–11.

Verhaar, John W.: 1973, 'Phenomenology and Present-Day Linguistics', in Maurice Natanson (ed.), *Phenomenology and the Social Sciences*, Volume One, pp. 361–464. Evanston, Ill. Northwestern University Press.

Vidich, Arthur J.: 1974, 'Ideological Themes in American Anthropology', *Social Research* 41 (4), 719–745.

Voget, Fred W.: 1975, *A History of Ethnology*, New York: Holt, Rinehart & Winston.

Wald, Henri: 1975, 'Reflections on Language and Thought', *Dialectical Anthropology* 1 (1), 51–60.

e, Maria-Barbara, and Lawrence C. Watson: 1975, 'Understanding in ology: A Philosophical Reminder', *Current Anthropology* 16 (2), 247–262.

lbrecht: 1969, *Critical Theory of Society*, New York: Herder & Herder

Albrecht: 1980, 'Rationality', Unpublished Manuscript.

A. D.: 1896, *A History of the Warfare of Science with Theology*, 2 volumes. w York: Dover.

te, Haydn: 1973, *Meta-History: The Historical Imagination in Nineteenth-Century Europe*, Baltimore: Johns Hopkins.

Wilden, Anthony: 1972, *System and Structure: Essays in Communication and Exchange*, London: Tavistock.

Wilson, Bryan R. (ed.): 1970, *Rationality*, New York: Haper Torchbooks.

Wilson, H. T.: 1977, *The American Ideology: Science, Technology and Organization as Modes of Rationality in Advanced Industrial Societies*, London: Routledge & Kegan Paul.

Winch, Peter: 1958, *The Idea of a Social Science and Its Relation to Philosophy*, London: Routledge & Kegan Paul.

Wolf, Eric: 1969, 'American Anthropologists and American Society', in Stephen A. Tyler (ed.), *Concepts and Assumptions in Contemporary Anthropology*, pp. 3–11. Athens: University of Georgia Press (Southern Anthropological Society Proceedings, Number 3).

Wolf, Eric R. and Joseph G. Jorgensen: 1970, 'Anthropology on the War-Path in Thailand', *The New York Review of Books* 15 (9), 26–35.

Wolff, Kurt H.: 1972, 'This Is the Time For Radical Anthropology', in Dell H. Hymes (ed.), *Reinventing Anthropology*, pp. 99–120. New York: Pantheon.

Zinn, Howard: 1967, 'History As Private Enterprise', in Kurt H. Wolff and Barrington Moore (eds.), *The Critical Spirit*, pp. 172–186. Boston: Beacon Press.

PART III

THE HUMANITIES

ON THE RELATION OF DISCIPLINARY DEVELOPMENT AND HISTORICAL SELF-PRESENTATION – THE CASE OF CLASSICAL PHILOLOGY SINCE THE END OF THE EIGHTEENTH CENTURY

REINHART HERZOG

Universität Bielefeld, Bielefeld, B.R.D.

> "Classical education – useful education for uselessness becomes useless itself. Where tradition rationalizes itself, it has already ceased."
>
> M. Horkheimer (1950)

It is no accident that one of the very oldest disciplines in the humanities is represented in institutes that have such disparate designations as 'Institute for Classical Philology', 'for Humaniora', "de langues et de Littératures Grecques et Latines", 'für Altertumswissenschaft' (which corresponds to the departments for Ancient Literature and History) and for 'Literary Science'. It is clear to a philologist that this state merely reflects simultaneously all phases of the history of the discipline since the eighteenth century and there is no lack of investigations in philology on its own history tracing this development. What has not yet been investigated is the question of a possible interdependence between the history of the discipline – especially cultivated in philology – and the development of the discipline itself.

Philology is suited for such a case study for several reasons:

(1) An interdependence of the type mentioned can be shown in at least four paradigmatic instances. This interdependence has determined the self-image of the discipline of its paradigm shifts and the periods of its own history.

(2) The function of the 'history of classical philology" since the end of the eighteenth century reveals in exemplary fashion the "strong use of

281

Loren Graham, Wolf Lepenies, and Peter Weingart (eds.), Functions and Uses of Disciplinary Histories, Volume VII, 1983, 281–290.
Copyright © 1983 by D. Reidel Publishing Company.

historiography" in the sense of a programmatic steering of future planning of research.

(3) It is especially in the nineteenth century that these historical inventions with a steering function were closely related with contexts of institutional history and politics of research.

(4) Finally, philology is a special case in that in its most recent phase of self-reassurance it regards itself in part as finished and past and in that it connects this conclusion with a new programmatic outlook. We, therefore, encounter the phenomenon of a programmatic post-disciplinary history of science within the discipline itself.

Four paradigms will be portrayed in the following.

(I) The first history of classical philology which deserves this name was written in 1833 by F. W. Ritschl with the title 'On the Recent Development of Philology' ('Über die neuere Entwicklung der Philologie') (1). Today it is no longer well-known, but at that time it strongly influenced the field until almost 1880 — and it was written as a result of a controversy regarding the development of philology.

Since Humanism, philology was understood as the study of ancient texts. After the rediscovery of ancient Greek and Latin texts during the Renaissance, philology no longer had the task of providing an ideological foundation or methodological reflection of an unquestioned normative and not yet historically mediated identification with antiquity. Such identification was given outside of science; philology, as 'techne', limited itself up into the eighteenth century to an extremely refined instrument of text production. Even though philology thus was not required to legitimate itself, it was on the other hand in danger of losing its connection to the (extra-scientific) understanding of antiquity when this became historically reflected upon by the eighteenth century. In fact, the discipline's evaluation in public faced a severe crisis from Huet to Winckelmann; 'internal' history of science shows — for instance in the philological catalogues of Ernestis Lexicon technologiae, 1762 — that the discipline no longer allowed itself to be affected by it (2).

The awareness of the historical tension to the world of antiquity and its release in the concept of 'classical antiquity' first in the eighteenth century with Winkelmann proceeds from the ahistorical positions of opposition or identification of the 'Querelle des Anciens et Modernes'. However, at least with W. von Humboldt it led to the constitution of an early — and in a normative sense 'first' — world of antiquity as 'classic(al)' which can only be understood historically. The final goal of such a hermeneutic, though, remains up to Hegel the recourse to a normative phase of the humane, thus it also constitutes a presupposition of philosophy of history. In this form between normativity and historicism, philology — even as classical philology — could develop its method as the first field of the humanities. It thus inaugurated the methodology of the historical humanities, participating for the first time in an extra-scientific normative task of legitimation.

The two first methodological plans mirror this situation. In F. A. Wolf's 'Einleitung in die Altertumswissenschaft' (1807) philology is identified — through the new concept of 'Altertumswissenschaft' (ancient history) — with a general historical discipline in the humanities (3). A Boeckh's 'Enzyklopädie und Methodologie der philologischen Wissenschaft' (a series of lectures from 1809–1865) already defined philology, in close reference to Schleiermacher's hermeneutic, as a subdiscipline in such a general science; it thus became Classical Philology (4).

This paradigm change actually meant a great expansion of the discipline: all of ancient history, even its inscriptions and its artistic monuments became virtual objects of study in philology; its main work still lay in the interpretation of texts, but according to this program no longer concentrated only on text production and text criticism, but also on an understanding of the spirit of the author, on the discovery of the discovered (Schleiermacher).

This paradigm change occurred during an institutional shift. This was connected with the founding of the reform university of Berlin in 1810 to which Schleiermacher summoned his former student Boeckh. G. Hermann (Leipzig), a Kantian and student of Reinhold in Jena, had declined the chair in 1810. He had remained opposed to the new hermeneutic program, stressed instead the orientation of philology toward formal language phenomena and entered a vicious and prolonged controversy over the project of a 'Corpus inscriptionum Graecarum' with Boeckh.

This controversy brought about the forementioned 'Entwicklung der Philologie' written by Ritschl, a student of Hermann. Around 1830 it became obvious that philology as text criticism and as science of language reacted strongly against the 'Berlin' program. This could be seen in the work of the text critic Lachmann in Berlin as well as in the establishment of the 'Bonn School' (Ritschl, Jahn, Bücheler, Usener). In this situation, the history of science emerges as a restorative and not a programmatic venture. Paradoxically this was the first application of the historical aspect to the subject itself. Ritschl says very clearly that the reproduction of the life of classical antiquity should not only be historical but also be directed to the production of literary momuments (5). Ritschl legitimated his plan historically by linking the philology of his time directly to the traditions of the fifteenth through the eighteenth centuries.

In practice, the subject — under the guiding star of conjectural criticism — has maintained this self-image over fifty years; philologists such as Peerlkamp and Madvig have helped spread it also outside Germany.

(II) The next paradigm change is documented again by a little known programmatic paper which had its effect, a very substantial one, first as an action paper in university politics before it was integrated thirty years later into disciplinary history: 'Philologie und Schulreform' by U. von Wilamowitz-Moellendorff (1892, in 1977 included in his 'Geschichte der Klassischen Philologie') (6). In the very first sentence Wilamowitz outlines a new concept of the discipline: "Philology which still carries the adjunct 'classical' although it no longer claims the primacy that is connotated in this designation ... ". This new orientation, an immediate product of institutional conflicts, can be interpreted as a result of the crisis of positivism within the fully developed philology which realized its historical claim against the text-critical tradition. Up until the years after the founding of the 'Reich', the 'anti-Berlin' program of text philology had determined the practice of the field. It was anti-historical but at the same time retained the claim to 'classics'. G. Welcker's 'Über die Bedeutung der Philologie' (1841) signifies the victory in the controversy with Boeckh (7). The classicist facade and with it not only the legitimation of the subject since Wolf, but also its representative function for the German school and educational system since Niethammer was retained at the price of a growing awareness of the factual equality with other humanist disciplines, if not already the positivist decadence. This can be seen in the inaugural speeches of Mommsen (1858) and Kirchhoff (1870) (8). The tension was released through a radical resumption of the positions of Schleiermacher and Boeckh — radical insofar as the historical approach of German idealism was carried forward to its positivist dangers. This happened through H. Usener and Wilamowitz. Usener, Dilthey's brother-in-law and a successor of Ritschl in Bonn (a position which he gained with the latter's support) participated strongly in Dilthey's reform of Schleiermacher's hermeneutics. The expansion of the interpretation of Schleiermacher to Dilthey's triad of experience, understanding and expression ('Erlebnis, Verstehen und Ausdruck') transcended the customary rational grammatical interpretation of texts to unconscious ('lebensphilosophisch 'eigentlich'.') ways of acquisition. The concept of a classical antiquity could not be upheld in view of this hermeneutic. Usener's speech as rector, 'Geschichte und Philologie' (1882) (9) for the first time integrated pre-, post-, and unclassical antiquity, as de facto the antiquity of the mythology of history of religion and of ethnology into one discipline which now could no longer be rightly called philology. The concept 'Altertumswissenschaft' (ancient literature and history) became prevalent, successfully shaping the disciplines outside of Germany, above all in Anglo-Saxon countries until today.

This success can be attributed primarily to Wilamowitz. Not philosophically oriented, he in turn owed his new concept not to Dilthey but, after a classicist beginning, to a rediscovery of Boeckh. As Boeckh had delineated and reorganized the discipline against Wolf, so did Wilamowitz against Usener. As organizer of the 'Großbetrieb: of ancient history (Mommsen)', he reorganized the 'philologische Seminar' in Berlin into the 'Institut für Altertumswissenschaft' and put his concept into practice. This he carried out in opposition to his older colleagues Kirchhoff and Vahlen and with the hlep of his former students and new colleagues Jäger, Heinze, Reinhardt, Diels, etc. Ancient history was now, through renouncing the adjective 'classical' accepted as one historical science among others. It included all historical aspects of the world of antiquity – although not of Christian antiquity. Wilamowitz himself had introduced research on Hellenism into ancient history or rather: he institutionally integrated 'old history' into this ancient history. Archaeology and art history became equal branches of ancient history. For Wilamowitz they were even preferred research areas over the science of text interpretation. This integration also became institutionally anchored in ancient history. The union of philology, ancient history and archaeology has prevailed up until a few years ago in German, English, American and Italian universities and still exists in the German 'Mommsen-Gesellschaft' for ancient history. This science

of antiquity no longer carried any privilege in being called classical. Characteristic now was the pressure of legitimation which the subject carried as
exponent of bourgeois general education. Wilamowitz went so far as to
separate responsibility for teacher education from the tasks of ancient history.
However, it can be observed that the disciplinary field itself, i.e. antiquity,
assumed the pathos of a privilege which was pseudo-religious and nationalistic
at the same time, even without the concept of classics. This made possible a
specifically Wilhelmian justification of its own practice. The encounter of
German and Greek culture, which in the recession of idealist philosophy of
history had been considered as congenial and crucial for the development of
mankind, as well as the work ethos of positivist asceticism were the elements
that supported the completion of the historicist paradigm shift. It did not
occur through disciplinary history as a reaction (as it did with Ritschl), as
legitimation through tradition, but as a future oriented program which at
most had to integrate disciplinary history as a completed phase which could
itself be subjected to objective historical research. Only in this way has the
history of classical philology been written in this phase by Sandys, Bursian,
Kroll and Gudemann.

(III) It is again a programmatic paper which destroys this precarious balance
of normative and historical science in philology and which marks the most
fundamental paradigm shift since German idealism: Werner Jaeger's inaugural
lecture 'Philologie und Geschichte' (1914) (10).

    Jaeger, a neo-Kantian and philologist confronted the Wilhelmian historicism
of ancient history programmatically with the concepts of 'Humanism' and
'Classics' ('Humanismus und Klassik'). It was, for the first time, a restorative
program but, as it turned out soon thereafter, it could not reestablish the link
to earlier phases of disciplinary history. Instead, by way of its consequences,
it led to an abandonment of science altogether. In the turn against historicism,
relativism and positivist science as well as in the proclamation of existential
acquisition ('Aneignung') and subjective interpretation of the history of ideas,
the discovery of transhistorical constants, Jaeger participated in a general
change of the style of the humanities and their institutions. This change,
which occurred between 1905 and 1930, was specifically German and can be
linked to the specific needs of legitimation of the philosophy of history in
German idealism. In philosophy this change took place through the reception

first of Dilthey's hermeneutics in phenomenology, then of existentialism philosophy of values; in theology since K. Barth we witness the opposition of dialectical theology and soon also of existential exegesis against 'liberal' (historicist) theology; in history it was marked by the debate over historicism especially through Troeltsch.

Philology, which once again called itself 'classical', according to Jaeger's concept of a 'third' humanism (after that of the Renaissance and German idealism) reversed the constellation between normativity and historicism: the function of antiquity as an ideal shattered the humanist methodology of the nineteenth century. The core sentence of Jaeger's program thus reads: "Philology discovers in order to understand". For Jaeger, its subject matter, the world of antiquity, was no longer the unquestioned classical norm, but in the process of its humanist learning it may be 'understood' and constituted as such. The noteworthy consequence for such a philosophy is that the pre-classical and the non-classical, in the aftermath of Wilamowitz, exist side by side in antiquity and that antiquity itself knows a development toward the 'humane' which reaches its fulfillment only in philological understanding and education. (This was a theme of the Naumburg Conference in 1931). The expulsion of the school from the science of antiquity was thus reversed. The reconstruction of this development was provided by Jaeger in his 'Paideia' (1933) (11). The classical philologist as humanist and educator may therefore not fall back behind historicism in a direct identification with 'Antiquity', he must see the development of antiquity towards the humane and has to bring it to its fulfillment by discovering and teaching it. The representation of the humane, which had been the concern since German idealism, thus increased its need of justification to such an extent that not only the historicist methodology broke apart but also the coherence of the ideal of the world of antiquity was fractionated: individual, subjectively 'understood' values and traditions of antiquity were selected. The reception of an encompassing normativity was replaced by that of the 'heritage' of antiquity which from 1930 on became characteristic, particularly for the ideological appeal to antiquity outside the discipline. At first, this encouraged the establishment of a sub-discipline, 'Latinistik' (Latin studies), a specifically German development of 1907 when the requisite program of R. Heinze appeared, until the Second World War (12). The independence of 'Latinistik' was supported by the institutional decay of 'Gymnasium' education and the increasing

elimination of Greek from the schools. But it made it also possible to interpret the political thinking of antiquity as part of its heritage. The distance
between the philologist and his environment, between his ideologies and the
phenomena of antiquity became smaller, their acquisition politically short-
breathed. This process is also characterized by the distance between Jaeger's
approach and the 'fourth' humanism — of national-socialist coloring — of
Jaeger's students remaining in Germany. Institutionally this distance meant,
for the first time, the dissipation of the philological chairholders through
emigration, opportunistic regime supporting, or isolation, amounting to a
radical discontinuation of tradition. But this process also signals that the
potential for these developments was already provided for by the anti-his-
toricist paradigm shift.

(IV) Jaeger's concept was first criticized in Karl Reinhardt's 'Die Klassische
Philologie und das Klassische' (1942) (13), but neither the philological
emigration nor representatives of the discipline until the foundation of
the German reform university after 1960 have fundamentally questioned
the paradigm shift of the twenties. (The last 'Geschichte der Klassischen
Philologie' written by R. Pfeiffer ends around 1850 — before the paradigm
shift in ancient history.) (14) Again, similar to the situation in 1810 the
institutional reform made possible a new conception. This is most evidently
represented by M. Fuhrmann's programmatic papers 'Die Antike und ihre
Vermittler' (1969) and 'Wie Klassisch ist die Klassische Antike' (1970) (15).
Both comprise a disciplinary history which is further elaborated by other
publications that followed. The situation seems the reverse to that of Ritschl's
work of 1833: the history of the discipline is not supposed to defend the
status quo against a reform concept but to lead it to its completion, to take
stock. The discipline of philology itself — this is the novelty — is to be taken
out of the traditional structure of ancient history, 'Latinistik' is to be liberated
from its limitation to a national literature and disconnected from its 'classical'
twin, 'Gräzistik' (Greek studies) so that it be freed of the constraints of any
normative, historically mediated claim. It is apparent that the discipline has
thus lost completely its traditional contours and according to this concept has
been dissolved as a discipline sui generis altogether. Fuhrmann summarizes
his review of the history of the discipline: "Consequently, nothing stands in
the way of letting classical philology dissolve in the greater whole of literary

science". ("Folglich hindert nichts, die Klassische Philologie im größeren Ganzen der Literaturwissenschaft aufgehen zu lassen"). After the passage of philology through historicism, the 'whole of literary science' according to his concept could not longer be a historical discipline in the humanities, into which Boeckh or Usener saw it integrated. Fuhrmann separates ancient history and archaeology from philology with this task of integration. Characteristically this separation is promoted by a further weakening of humanist education in the schools. Philology, however, with Fuhrmann regains the rank of a transnational science of text interpretation by seeking to participate in a hermeneutic literary science. (Any integration into a structuralist literary science has so far helped to eliminate the subject of antiquity from such a science; the structuralist cannot grasp the historically distant reality of texts, the philologist depends on literary theories which encompass the phenomenon of historical mediation). After Fuhrmann, this return was understood programmatically and institutionally, at least during the seventies, as the end of the discipline of philology even though a history of the discipline conceived with this perspective in mind has not yet been written. This could be attributed to the fact that such a claim of finality is too radical and may be considered unrealized in practice. This claim may even be connected with the radicalism of the Jaegerian paradigm shift and the need of legitimation since the philosophy of history of German idealism. On the other hand, the continued practice of the discipline in German and foreign universities, owing to the changing presence of the cassical language in the schools has responded so meagerly to Fuhrmann's program – be it in the form of disciplinary history, be it in the form of a counter program – that the dialectic of both forms as it existed since the beginning of the nineteenth century has indeed come to an end.

Notes

1. Ritschl, Friedrich, 'Über die neuerste Entwicklung der Philologie (1833)', in ders., *Opuscula philologica*, Vol. V, Hildesheim: Olms (1978) 1–18 (Repr. of the ed. Leipzig: Teubner, 1879).
2. Ernesti, Johann, Christian Gottlieb, 'Lexicon technologiae (1762)', 2 Vols., Hildesheim: Olms (1962) (Repr. of the ed. Leipzig 1795 and 1797).
3. Wolf, Friedrich August, 'Einleitung in die Alterthumswissenschaft (1807)', in ders., *Vorlesungen über die Alterthumswissenschaft*, Vol. I, Leipzig: Lehnhold (1839) 1–46.

4. Boeckh, August, 'Enzyklopädie und Methodologie der philologischen Wissenschaften (1809–65)', Leipzig: Teubner (1877).
5. Cf. Ritschl, *op. cit.*, 13.
6. Wilamowitz-Moellendorff, Ulrich von, 'Philologie und Schulreform (1892)', in ders., *Reden und Vorträge*, Berlin: Weidmann (1901) 97–119.
7. Welcker, Friedrich Gottlieb, 'Über die Bedeutung der Philologie (1841)', in ders., *Kleine Schriften*, Vol. IV, Osnabrück: Zeller, (1973) 1–16 (Repr. of the ed. Bonn: Weber, 1861).
8. Mommsen, Theodor, 'Akademische Antrittsrede (1858)', in ders., *Reden und Aufsätze*, Berlin: Weidmann (1905) 35–38.
9. Usener, Hermann, 'Philologie und Geschichtswissenschaft (1882)', in ders., *Vorträge und Aufsätze*, Leipzig: Teubner (1907) 1–35.
10. Jaeger, Werner, 'Philologie und Historie (1914)', in ders., *Humanistische Reden und Vorträge*, Berlin-Leipzig: de Gruyter (1937) 1–17.
11. Jaeger, Werner, 'Paideia: die Formung des griechischen Menschen (1933)', Berlin: de Gruyter (1934–37).
12. Heinze, Richard, 'Die gegenwärtigen Aufgaben der römischen Literaturgeschichte', in *Neue Jahrbücher* 19 (1907) 161–189.
13. Reinhardt, Karl, 'Die Klassische Philologie und das Klassische (1942)', in ders., *Vermächtnis der Antike*, Göttingen: Vandenhoeck und Ruprecht (1960) 334–60.
14. Pfeiffer, Rudolf, 'Geschichte der klassischen Philologie', Reinbek bei Hamburg: Rowohlt (1970).
15. Fuhrmann, Manfred, 'Die Antike und ihre Vermittler', Konstanz: Universitätsverlag (1969); 'Wie klassisch ist die klassische Antike', Stuttgart: Artemis (1970) 12.

EPILOGUE

This volume illustrates convincingly that the history of science is used for a great variety of purposes: to strengthen a particular approach to science; to glorify the achievements of great scientists; to identify a new discipline; to justify a particular political order; to establish links with antecedent philosophical systems; to herald a conceptual overturn; to laud science as the only progressive activity; and so forth. Most of these goals can be subsumed under the general term of 'legitimation'. Historians of science, or scientists turning to the histories of their fields, have found history extremely useful in order to legitimate a particular goal of which they are partisans.

This view that history legitimates is not, of course, original, but it is much more commonly accepted for political history than it is for the history of science. The history of science has picked up a bit of the aura of science itself, commonly held to be objective. If science is the truth, then a good history of science ought to be true also, or at least some people thought. Politics and prejudices might riddle "normal" history, but the history of science should be above all that. The chapters in this book illustrate just how mistaken the people who believed this about the history of science were. It has become clear that it is just as impossible to write a history of science without serving some sort of legitimating goal as it is to write any other kind of history.

Pointing to the legitimating role of the history of science is the achievement of this book. As one of its editors, I am delighted to be associated with that achievement. While I do not agree with every point of view that the book contains, I fully subscribe to the thesis that legitimation is one of the most important functions of the history of science.

However, there has been disagreement among the editors over an implication of the book which is why we decided to divide our comments into an introduction and an epilogue, both reflecting our diverging views. That implication, one with which I disagree, is that there is no way of choosing among the various legitimating functions that the history of science serves, that one legitimation has the same qualitative status as another.

Loren Graham, Wolf Lepenies, and Peter Weingart (eds.), Functions and Uses of Disciplinary Histories, Volume VII, 1983, 291–295.

The authors of this book have been so busy slaying the dragon of progressivist, objective science (and its history) that they have not noticed that another species of dragon is lurking in the brush which will devour them if they do not take proper action. The name of that dragon is 'total relativism', the belief that since science and its history are social constructs there are as many equally valid forms of science and its history as there are societies, or even members of societies.

As the book stands, its function is almost totally destructive (although in the positive sense). Armed with the critical tools that the authors have given us, we can now pick up any book or article on the history of science and rather quickly identify what legitimating role that particular version of the history of science serves.

Is it not surprising, however, that none of the authors in this book (with one or two fleeting exceptions) explicitly asks, "Of all the legitimating functions that we see the history of science serving, are not some 'better' than others?" On second thought, this omission is not surprising at all, because if any of us admitted that some legitimations are superior to others, the old bug-a-boo of progressivism would creep back in to the history of science. This history of science would be progressive to the degree that it increasingly relied on "better" legitimations. But since one of the major goals that we have in this volume is to show the simplicity and the error of the old view that scientific knowledge is inherently progressive, we can hardly dismiss progressivism with one hand and yet bring it back with the other.

And still, in the final analysis, I think that we will have to perform that complex acrobatic act. Perhaps we can give our performance the necessary scholarly cachet by calling it a Hegelian synthesis on a higher level.

In this brief epilogue, I do not pretend to be able to solve this problem by giving a rigorous definition of what the "better" legitimations are. The most important goal at this point is to name the problem in the hope that many of us will work on it together. But I will give a few hints of the directions in which I think we should move.

In order to begin addressing the problem, we should notice that while the authors of this volume do not explicitly raise the question of which legitimations are better than others, many of them indicate that they posses implicit criteria for evaluating legitimations. It is quite clear that they dislike some legitimations intensely. Thus, Rolf Winau in his discussion of the uses of the history of medicine refers to the teachings of Galen in the following way: "These teachings were abridged and simplified, they fossilized into rigid dogma ... I need nöt stress how severely progress was hampered by this attitude." A few pages later, when describing the history of medicine as taught in nineteenth century Germany, he observes, "Thus until the beginning of this century the chair for the history of medicine was used, *wrongly*, (my *underline*, LRG) to accomodate well-deserving scholars from other medical disciplines, or to get rid of unpopular professors." And Winau does not restrict himself only to criticism of legitimations; he praises those varieties of the history of medicine which look at medicine in terms of its cultural and social foundations. So here is at least one implicit positive evaluation.

In her treatment of the heroic legend of Lavoisier, Bernadette Benseude-Vincent also clearly possesses implicit criteria for the evaluation of legitimating histories of science. After sketching out the standard literature on Lavoisier, she states: "All that remains now is to examine the influence of these *imaginary dimensions* (my *underline*, LRG) on the history of chemistry and on chemistry itself." By using the term 'imaginary' Benseude-Vincent indicates, just as Winau did by his use of terms like 'dogma' and 'wrongly', that she holds unstated positive criteria by which she could distinguish a 'good' legitimating function of the history of science from a 'bad' one. What would the opposite of 'imaginary' and 'dogma' be? One is tempted to say 'objective knowledge' but that might be premature in our current state of suspicion of such a term.

Benseude-Vincent goes on to criticize histories of science that are written as the story of great, infallible men; that are ahistorical, basing themselves on a concept of absolute truth; or that attempt to justify a given political order. She calls these the 'tricks of history'. Can we take away the tricks, or lessen their influence, by constructing positive criteria that are the opposites of Benseude-Vincent's and Winau's negative ones? The result would be something like this: good history of science examines science in its social and cultural foundations, placing much emphasis on the historical antecedents of scientific ideas and their social contexts; it is not based on a concept of absolute truth, but on relative truth, with some concepts more adequate than others; while it is inevitably intertwined with the political and social order, it should not justify one particular political system.

This description of the way to write history of science has some merit, although it surely approaches the banal. But what legitimating function does it serve? And here a final trick emerges.

Maintaining that the only "good" history of science is that which examines science in terms of its social, cultural, and historical foundations legitimates professional historians and sociologists of science, who are the only people who, as a group, possess the necessary qualifications. Indeed, it would not be going too far amiss to say that this volume, criticizing a whole raft of legitimating functions of the history of science, could, itself, be taken to be one large legitimation of professional historians and sociologists of science; this legitimation is carried out to the detriment of all others who have in the past attempted to write the history of science, especially professional scientists.

Is there an essential difference between, on the one hand, the professional historian of science who legitimates his or her approach to the development of science by criticizing the "naive" histories written by professional scientists, and, on the other hand, the professional scientist who legitimates his or her scientific ideas by comparing them with the 'naive' conceptions of his predecessors? I think there is a way out of this dilemma, but it is exceedingly difficult, and raises the most perplexing philosophical problems. It will inevitably bring us back to the issue of objective knowledge.

Before taking a few steps down that path, I think that we should recognize that by seeing that all histories of science perform legitimating functions — even those written by professional historians and sociologists of science, in other words, by us — we have already made a great deal of progress (yes, I will use the word). The most important thing is to know that histories of science inevitably perform such functions, and to identify the functions when they confront us. So armed, we should not commit the worst distortions, and we should be able to gain a great deal even from histories of science that are written with legitimating functions far different from our own. The social contexts of previous histories of science are as much a part of the concern of historians of science as the history of a discipline itself, however that disciplinary history may be defined. And the day will come when a following generation will mercilessly identify our social context and our legitimations. More power to them.

As Ulf Geuter observed, "What has to be asked is from which interest of knowledge and how — and with what distortions — history is perceived". The mere identification of these interests and these distortions is a significant step forward.

Does it not follow from this question that the broader the interest that is served (i.e., the more society as a whole is served rather than a particular group or profession) with the least distortions, the 'better' the history? If this is so, then the ultimate 'good' legitimation is the furtherance of social welfare by providing reliable knowledge that benefits society.

Since we can not eliminate legitimation, we must channel it toward goals that are worthy of our efforts: the benefit of society and the creation of reliable knowledge.

It is important to see that this 'good' legitimation contains two rather independent requirements: first, that the knowledge be of broad social benefit; and, second, that this knowledge by reliable. If one requirement is fulfilled without the other, then the legitimation is no longer 'good'. And it therefore follows that if one wishes to benefit society and provide reliable knowledge, one must answer both a normative question and a cognitive one. The normative question obviously is: "What is 'good' for society?" and the cognitive question is: "What is reliable knowledge?"

These are the ultimate questions upon which not only good history of science but every other form of scholarship depends. It would be ridiculous and arrogant for me to pretend that I have the answers to the questions. But it would be irresponsible not to recognize that the questions lie underneath all our endeavors.

I hope that the next conference on legitimation in the history of science raises these issues. The normative question asks what kind of society we want, and the cognitive one asks what kind of knowledge we want. I strongly suspect that the questions can not be adequately answered without making commitments both to a democratic society and to some form of objective knowledge, but I leave the tasks of working out these answers to another day.

LOREN GRAHAM

NAME INDEX

Abraham, M. 39
Ach, Narizss 209
Adams, Frank 101
Adler, M. 210
Adorno, T. 265
Ahlers, Rolf 258
Alexander, J. 122
Allport, Gordon 175, 202
Althusser, Louis 267
Amselle, J.-L. 249
Ampère, J.-M. 36, 70, 78
Anderson, W. C. 77
Aquinas, St. Thomas 133, 134, 199
Arduino 89
Aristotle 81, 107, 133, 134, 149, 165, 186, 199, 202, 203
Artelt, Walter 115, 117
Asad, Talal 239, 259, 266
Ash, Mitchell xiv, xxi, 143–190, 218
Auge, Marc 249
Avogadro, A. 70, 78
Avicenna 107

Babbage, Charles 99
Bacon, Sir Francis xvi, 158
Badash, L. 50
Bakan, David 186
Baldwin, James 146, 183
Banaji, Jairus 269
Barnes, Barry 243, 250, 253, 258
Barth, K. 287
Bateson, G. 241
Battig, K. 186
Baudrillard, J. 263
Bauman, Zygmunt 267
Becker, Ernest 257
Bell, Ch., 151
Benedict 234
Ben-David, Joseph. 244
Bensaude-Vincent, Bernadette xi, xxi, 53–78, 293

Bernstein, Basil 246
Bernstein, Maxine 188
Berthelot, M. 60, 64, 68, 69, 70–77, 78
Berthollet, C. L. 36
Berzelius, J. J. 75
Biot, J.-B. 36
Bismarck, Otto von 110
Blasius, Dirk 113–115, 117
Blight, James 143–144, 183
Bloch, Marc 125, 138
Bloor, D. 33, 232
Blumenthal, A. 169–171, 187, 188
Bodenheimer, Sussane 235
Boeckh, A. 283–285, 189
Böhme, Gernot 31, 184
Bohr, Niels 51
Boltzmann, Ludwig 17, 18, 28, 33
du Bois Reymond, Emil 8, 9
Boon, James 268
Bourdieu, Pierre 238–240, 242, 249, 263
Boring, Edwin 148–156, 159, 161, 166, 170, 172, 179, 184, 187, 196, 201
Born, Max 43
Bozeman, T. D. 183
Braginsky, B. B. 188
Braginsky, D. D. 188
Braroe, Niels 264
Brett, George 146, 149, 183
Brocchi, G. B. 89, 101
Brown, Phil 188
Brozek, J. 162, 187
Bruder, Klaus-Jurgen 213
Bruno, F. 186
Bucheler, 284
Buchwald, J. Z. 50, 52
Buck, Morss, 174, 188
Buckland, William 102
Buckle, H. T. 29
Buffon, G. 81, 89
Buhler, Karl 205, 208

297

Burnet 81, 89
Burnham, John 184
Burridge, K. 240, 261
Bursian 286
Burt, Cyril 177
Butterfield, H. 102, 125, 138, 195

Calkins, M. 188
Cannizzaro, S. 71
Capretta, P. 186
Cattell, J. M. 146, 147, 183
Celsus 106
Chomskii, Noam 170
Clark, Terry 245
Clausius, R. 17
Coan, R. 187
Collier, Kathleen 102
Collingwood, R. G. 125, 138
Collini, Stefan, 139
Colombo, R. 117
Comte, A. 60, 77, 175, 189, 202
de Condillac, Abbe 58, 59, 77
Conze, Wlater 115
Copans, Jean 266
Copernicus, N. 125, 133
Cox, Allan xi, 87, 96, 98, 101, 104
Cravens, H. 184

Dalton, J. 69–71, 74, 78
Danziger, Kurt 171, 178, 179 181, 187, 189, 195
Darnell, Regna 241
Darwin, Charles 15, 24, 28, 99, 260
Daumas, Maurice 53, 76
Davy, H. 69, 70
Delfendahl, B. 269
Derham 81
Descartes, Rene 36, 50, 54, 81, 203
Dessoir, Max 147, 183, 199, 200, 203, 206
Diamond, Solomon 187
Diamond, Stanley 236, 241, 247, 249, 255, 256, 260, 263, 264
Dickson, David 255
Diels 285
Diepgen, Paul 114, 115
Dilthey, W. 6, 29, 199, 200, 285, 287

Dirac, P. A. M. 43, 44, 51
Dolby, R. G. A. 188, 256
Douglas, Mary 252, 254
Droysen, J. G. 6, 7, 21, 22, 29, 30, 32, 34
Duhem, P. 66, 67, 78
Dumas, J. B. 61, 62, 62, 67, 68, 71, 72, 75–78
Dumont, Louis 263, 266
Dunn, John 134, 139
Durkheim, E. xiii, 124, 129, 133, 139
Dwyer, K. 240, 268
Dyson, Freeman 44

Easlea, Brian 268
Ebbinghaus, Hermann 149, 191, 198, 200–203, 223
Ebel, Volker 191
Eder 259
Ehrenberg, C. G. 109–111
von Ehrenfels, Christian 153
Einstein, Albert 39–42, 45, 49, 51
Elias, Norbert 254
Ernesti, J. C. G. 282, 289
Esper, Erwin 161, 187
Eulner, H. H. 117
Everitt, C. W. F. 50
Eyferth, Klaus 210

Fabian 233, 261, 263, 269
Facastoro 89
Fahim 264
Fechner, Gustav Theodor 13–15, 19, 26, 27, 29, 32, 199
Fernberger, S. 184
Ferguson, Thomas 267
Feyerabend, P. 231, 238, 240, 250, 252, 261
Feynman, R. 44
Fichte, J. G. 171
Finison, L. J. 175, 188
Finnegan, R. 249
Firth, 244
Fitton, W. H. 102
Fleishman, E. 186
Flugel, J. C. 161, 186, 191
Foppa, Klaus 209

Forman, Paul 29, 34
Fortis, 89
Foucault, Michel, 253, 263
Fought, John 232
Fourcroy, A.-F., 55, 76, 77
Fox, R. 50
Franck, 238
Frankel, H. 102
Franklin, V. P. 188
Frazer, 260
Freind, J. 117
Freud, Sigmund 186, 260
Frobenius, L. 245
Friedrichs, R. 126
Fuchs, A. 166, 187
Fuhrmann, Manfred, 288–290
Furomoto, L. 188

Galen 106–108, 293
Galileo 133
Galison, Peter, x, xxi, 35–52
Galtung, Johan 245
Garfinkel, Harold 245
Garvey, C. R. 183
Gay, Peter 268
Gay-Lussac, J. L. 70, 71
Geikie, Archibald, 101
Gellner, Ernest, 250, 251, 257, 269
George, François 267
Georgi, H. 46
Generelli 89
Geras, Norman 253
Gerhardt, C. 71, 76
Geuter, Ulfried xiv, xxi, 144, 191–
       229, 295
Gibbon, Edward ix
Giddens, Anthony 234, 268
Gillispie, Charles 102, 127
Glashow, S. 46, 51
Glazer, Nathan 139
Goethe, J. W. 3, 4, 9, 10, 22, 31
Goldman, 257
Goody, Jack 249, 268
Gould, S. J. 188
Grace, George 232
Graham, Loren, xxi, 291–296
Gran, Thorwald, 254

Graumann, C. F. 195
Grew 81
Grimaux, E. 77
Gruber, Jacob 241
Grunwald, Harald, 197, 216
Gudemann 286
Guerlac, H. 53, 76
Guthrie, R. 188

Habermas, J. 259
Hall, G. Stanley, 145, 147, 183, 184
Hallam, Anthony, 78, 96, 101, 104
Hallowell, Irving 269
Halpern, Joel 268
Hammel, Eugene 268
Harms, Friedrich 201
Harris, Ben 177, 189
Harris, Marvin 256, 259, 269
Hartmann, Eduard v. 200
Hawking, Stephen 47, 48, 51
Hawthorn, Geoffrey, 126, 139
Hazard, P. 260
Hearnshaw, L. S. 191
Hearst, E. 180, 189
Hecker, J. F. 109
Hegel 5, 8, 9, 10, 21, 24, 133, 134
Hehlmann, Wilhelm 210, 223
Heidbrenner, E. 158, 185
Heidelberger, Michail 34
Heinze, R. 285, 287, 290
Heischkel, E. 117
Heisenberg, Werner 3, 4, 31, 43, 44
Helm, Georg 19, 24, 34
Helmer 264
Helmholtz, Hermann 4, 8, 9, 10, 11, 12,
       13, 15, 16, 17, 19, 22, 23, 25–
       29, 31–33, 149, 150, 171, 188
Henderson, L. J. 150
Henle, Mary 185
Herbart, J. 191
Hermann, G. 283
Hermann, Theo 210
Herrnstein, R. 187
Herschel, John 94, 99
Kerskovits 234
Hertz, H. 38
Herzog, Reinhart, xv, xxii, 281–290

Hess 83
Hiebsch, Hans 194, 195
High, Richard 172, 188
Hillix, William 166, 167, 187
Hippocrates 106, 108
Hirsch, August, 110–111
Hobbes, T. 202
Hochberg, J. 185
Hodgson, Shadworth, 173, 188
Hoeveler, J. D. 183
Hofstätter, P. R. 208
Hollingworth, L. S. 188
Hollis, Martin 253
Holzkamp, Klaus, 195, 212–215
Holzner, B. 209
Honigman, John 256
Horkheimer, M. 264, 265, 281
Horowitz, I. L. 186
Horton, R. 248, 249, 259, 269
Hsu, F. L. K. 261
Huarte, Juan 203
Huet 282
Hull, David 102
Humboldt, W. v. 283
Hume, David 137, 139, 203
Hutton, James, 82, 89, 90, 91, 103
Hyman, S. E. 260, 263, 268
Hymes, Dell, 231, 232, 236, 252

Ibn-an-Nafis 107
Iggers, Georg 31
Itkohen, Esa 267

Jaeger, S. 20, 214, 215
Jaeger, Werner, 286–89, 290
Jäger 285
Jahn 284
James, William 146, 153, 173, 183, 188
Jarvie 232
Jaulin 261
Jay, Martin 255
Joncich, G. 183
Jones, Robert Alun xiii, xxii, 121–142
Jorgensen 235
Jung, C. G. 209

Kahane, E. 77

Kahn, Joel 270
Kamin, L. J. 188
Kanamori, H. 87
Kant, Emanuel 5, 7, 12, 31, 131, 165, 203
Kaplan, D. 232, 267
Katz, J. E. 186
Kawash, C. 166, 187
Kehoe, Alice 268
Keil, G. 117
Kirchhoff 20, 284, 285
Kitts, D. B. 104
Klemm, Otto 200, 201, 203, 204, 147, 183
Klemperer, J. 117
Kluver, Heinrich 156
Koch, R. 111, 117
Koffka, Kurt 151–153, 185
Köhler, Wolfgang 151, 152
Kowach, J. 186
Krieger, Leonard 32
Kroll 286
Kronus 138
Krueger 208
Kubrin, David 102
Kuhn, Thomas, (see also *The Structure of Scientific Revolutions*) ix, xiii, xv, 33, 79, 96, 97, 98, 100, 104, 121, 122, 124–129, 138, 143, 164, 172, 173, 216–218, 230–237, 239, 240, 243, 244–248, 253, 254, 258, 260, 266–268
Kuklick, B. 184
Külpe, Oswald 189

Lachmann 284
Laguna 253
Lakatos, Imre 268
Lamprecht, Karl 29
Larrain, J. 258
Laudan, Rachel, xi, xxii, 79–104
Laurent, A. 76
Lavar, A. B. 186
Lavoisier, A. xi, 53–78, 96, 293
Law, J. 239, 263
Lazarsfeld, Paul xvi, 139
Leach 232

Leacock, E. 234
Leahey, T. H. 186
Leary, D. 172, 173, 188
Leclerc, G. 250, 266
Lefebvre, Henri 267
Leibniz, G. W. 81, 171, 199, 206
Leiss, William, 254
Lemaire 234, 245, 255, 264
Lenoir, Timothy 11, 12, 31, 33
Lepenies, Wolf, ix–xx, xxii, 139, 140, 144, 183, 189, 195, 201, 213, 219, 230, 243, 244, 252
Lepsius, R. 223
Lersch 208
Levi-Strauss, Claude 244, 269
Lewis, C. I. 184
Lewis, Diane, 250, 254
Lichtenthaeler, Charles 117
Littman, Richard 181
Llobera, J. R. 231, 269, 270
Locke, John 170, 171
Lomonosov, M. 65
Lorentz, H. L. 33, 39, 40, 49, 51
Loschmidt, Joseph 17, 18
Lotze, Hermann, 32
Löwith, K. 260, 263
Lowry, Richard 186
Luchins, A. 167, 185, 187
Luchins, E. 185, 187
Lukacs, G. 263
Lukes, Steven 139, 253
Lyeli, Charles, xi, 79–100

McCartney, Paul J. 101, 103
McCormmach, Russell, 33, 51
Mach, Ernst, x, 15, 18–22, 25–29, 31, 33, 34, 150
MacIntyre, Alasdair, 134–136, 139
McKenzie, D. P. 103
McKie, D. 77
MacLeod, R. 164, 187, 196
Macquer, J. 60, 77
Madvig 284
Magubane 250
Maikowski, Rainer 215
Maimonides 163
Malecki 262

Malinowskii, B. 244
Manners, Robert 232, 267
Mannheim, Karl, 8, 242
Marcus, George 268
Martens 232
Marvin, Ursula 78, 96, 101, 104
Marx, Karl 129, 135, 177, 213, 220, 234, 239, 254, 260, 264
Marx, Melvin 166, 167, 187
Masterman, J. 246
Mattes, Peter 215
Matthews 85
Maxwell, James Clerk 16, 36–38, 40–41, 45, 48, 49, 50
Mayow, J. 66
Mead 234
Meili, Richard 208
Mendeleev, D. I. 65, 78
Mendelsohn, Everett 127, 243, 254, 257
Merleau-Ponty, J. 265
Merton, Robert xiii, 126–129, 131–135, 137–140
Merz, F. 209
Messer, A. 205
Metraux, Alexandre 194, 202
Metzger, Wolfgang 206, 223
Michelson, A. A. 38, 50
Miller, A. I. 51
Miller, George 186
Minkowski, H. 39, 40
Misiak, Henrik 186
Misner, C. W. 51
Mok, Albert 267
Mokhtar, A. M. 117
Mommsen, T. 284, 285, 290
Monod, J. 232
Montaigne, M. 234
Moro 89
Morveau, L. B. Guyton de 54, 55, 61, 77
Mudimbe 261, 263
Müller, Johannes 151
Müller-Freienfels, Richard 204
Murphy, F. 248
Murphy, Gardner 155–157, 159, 161, 162, 164, 184–186

Needham, Joseph 243, 244, 269
Nelson, B. 244
Neumann, C. 20
Newton, Isaac 3, 4, 9, 64, 90, 94, 133
Nickles, Th. 102
Niethammer 284
Nietzche, F. ix
Nowotny, H. 236

Oberschall, Anthony 139
O'Donnel, J. 183, 184, 196
Oldroyd, D. R. 101
Olszewski 262
Ospovat, Alexander 101
Ostwald, Wilhelm 18, 22, 23, 24, 25, 27,
    28, 33, 34, 66, 78

Pagel, Julius 111
Pallas, P. 89
Panoff, M. 266
Parmenides 203
Parsons, Talcott, 122, 127, 138, 139
Paul, Robert 269
Pauli, W. 44
Peerlkamp, 284
Pfeiffer, Rudolf 288, 290
Piaget, J. 174
Pillsbury, Walter 184
Planck, Max 17, 18, 33, 40
Plato 4, 165
Playfair, J. 91
Pliny 106
Poincare, H. 39
Pongratz, Ludwig 187, 195, 204, 205,
    211, 212, 223
Popper, Karl 232, 239, 242
Porter, Roy, 101, 102
Posner, L. 117
Poynting, J. H. 39
Price, Derek 127
Priestley, J. 61, 66, 67, 77
Pythagoras 108, 186
Puschmann, Theodor 111

Quirini 89

Rabinow, Paul 269

Rand, Benjamin 147, 183
Ranke, L. 8, 29
Rauh, H. 219
Reinhardt, K. 285, 288, 290
Reinhold 283
Richards, R. 183
Rieber, R. 189
Ritschl, F. W. 282–285, 288–290
Robinson, D. N. 186
Rose, Stephen and Hilary, 174, 188,
    264, 268
Rosemeier, H. P. 210
Rosenfeld, Leon 43, 44, 51
Ross, Barbara, 187
Ross, Dorothy, 146, 183
Roth, Erwin 209
Rott, Gerhard, 215
Rousseau, J. J. 234
Rudinger, G. 218, 219
Rudwick, M. 101, 102
Ruse, M. 103
Russell, Bertrand 42, 51
Russo, N. F. 188

Sahakian, William 186
Sahlins, Marshall 238, 216, 263
Said, E. W. 239, 243, 261, 263, 269
Salam, S. 45, 46
Samelson, Franz, 175, 176, 177, 184,
    189, 196, 202
Sander, Friedrich 209
Sandys, 286
Sanford, F. H. 186
Sapir 234
Saran, A. K. 261
Sarton, George 123, 138, 150, 163
Sartre, J.-P. 238
Saupe, E. 205
Saussure, H. 89
Savart, F. 36
Scheele, K. 61, 66
Schelling, F. 8, 10
Schelsky, H. 223
Schiller, Paul v. 204, 223
Schipperges, H. 117
Schleiermacher, 283–285
Schmid, Rudolf 215

Schmidt, A. 254, 257
Scholte, Bob, xv, xxii, 229–280
Schönlein, J. L. 109, 110
Schorske, Carl 34
Schrödinger, Erwin 43
Schultz, D. 181, 186, 187, 189
Schweninger 110
Schwinger, J. 44
Scilla 89
Seeger, Falk, 211, 217
Senghor, L. 245
Sève, Lucien 215
Sexton, V. S. 186
Shapin, S. 243, 253
Sheehan, Mary 186
Shields, S. 188
Shipley, T. 187
Siebeck, Hermann, 194, 198, 199
Sigerist, Henry 114, 115
Simoneit, Max 207, 208
Simmons, Anthony 232
Skinner, B. F. 138, 150, 185
Skinner, Quentin 134, 138, 139, 140
Skolimowski, Henryk 254
Smith, Lawrence, 173, 188
Smith, William 139
Socrates 165
Sokal, M. 183, 184, 185
Sontag, Susan 264
Staeuble, Irmingard 205, 213–215
Stahl, G. E. 57, 60, 65, 70
Stefan 16, 33
Stehr, Nico 232, 258
Steiner, George 246
Stocking, George, 122, 123, 126, 138,
    194, 207, 212, 256, 260
Sudhoff, Karl 112, 113, 117

Tambiah 259
Takeuchi, H. 87, 101
Targioni 89
Tedlock 240, 268
Terman, Lewis 104
Testa, 89
Thackray, A. 185
Thenard, L. 70
Thies, H. J. 117

Thomae, Hans 186, 216, 217
Thompson, E. P. 267
Thomson, William 17, 38, 50
Thorndike, Edward L. 146, 183
Thorne, K. S. 51
Timpanaro 256
Titchener, Edward 148, 150–152, 161,
    166, 170, 171, 181, 184
Toellner, R. 117
Tomonaga, S. 44
Toulmin, Stephen 173, 188
Treitschke, H. 6
Troeltsch 287
Turner, R. Steven 171, 188
Tweney, R. D. 188

Usener, H. 284, 285, 289, 290
Uyeda, S. 87, 101, 103

Vahler 285
Vallisneri 89
Verhaar, John 267
Vesalius, Andreas 107, 117
Vico, G. 234
Vidich, Arthur 264
Vine 85
Virchow, R. 110, 111, 117
Volhard 78
Voget, F. 256
Voltaire, F. 90, 91

Wald, Henri 246
Watson, John B. 177, 189
Watson, L. C. 245
Watson, Robert I. 160, 162–167,
    172, 186, 187, 220, 221
Watson-Franke, M.-B. 245
Weber, Ernst Heinrich 14, 19, 26, 29,
    201
Weber, Max 8, 125, 133, 220
Weber, Wilhelm 13, 15, 16, 20, 26, 27,
    28, 32, 33
Wehner, Ernst 211, 212, 218
Weinberg, S. 45, 47, 49, 51
Weiner, Walter 143, 144, 173, 183
Weinert, Franz 212
Weingart, Peter, ix–xx

Welcker, G. 284, 290
Wellek, Albert 206, 208, 209
Wellmer, 233, 259
Wenzel 71, 72, 74
Werner, A. 83, 89, 90, 91, 101
Wertheimer, M. 154, 162, 182, 186,
        187, 189, 220
West, J. 186
Westerdiep, Anne 267
Westmeyer, Hans 218
Weyl, H. 45
Wheeler, J. A. 41, 47, 51
Whiston 81, 89
Whitley, R. 184, 186
Wien, Wilhelm 39, 50
Wilamowitz-Moellendorff, U. v. 284–
        287, 290
Williams, L. P. 78
Wilson, B. R. 269
Wilson, H. T. 232
Wilson, J. Tuzo, xi, 86, 87, 91–93, 95–
        98, 100, 102–104
Winau, Rolf, xii, xxiii, 105–120, 293
Winch, Peter, 139, 252, 267, 269

Winckelmann, J. 282
Windelband, W. 6
Wise, W. Norton x, xi, xxiii, 3–34, 50
Wittgenstein, Ludwig 129, 139
Wolf, E. 269
Wolf, F. A. 283, 284, 285, 289
Wolff, Charles, 203
Wolff, Kurt 255
Woodward, W. 89, 187, 188
Woodworth, Robert S. 155, 158, 159,
        161, 172, 185, 186
Wozniak, R. N. 183
Wundt, Wilhelm, 150, 165, 168, 169,
        170, 171, 172, 173, 178, 187–
        189, 191, 192, 194, 195, 200,
        202, 203, 211
Wurtz, A. 65, 70, 71, 74, 75, 78

Yachanin, S. A. 188
Young, Robert 143, 144, 173, 183

Zermelo, Ernst, 19, 33
Zinn, Howard 258

SUBJECT INDEX

Akron, University of 160
American Philosophical Society 92
American Psychological Association
  146–148, 159–161, 168, 191
American Psychologist 168
American Sociological Association 136
anthropology, critical, 263; cultural,
  history of, xi, 229–280
archeology 285
art history 285
astronomy, Copernican 96
atomism, xi, 15, 17, 28, 33, 71, 72, 74,
  75, 78; anti-atomism, 75

behaviorism 151, 159, 161, 166, 176,
  181, 183
Berlin Society for Experimental Psy-
  chology 200
Berlin, University of 109
Bonn, University of 216, 222

Calvinism 137
Cambridge University 47
centralism 167
characterology 207
chemistry, history of, ix, 53–78, 293
Cheiron Society for the History of the
  Social and Behavioral Sciences
  160, 174, 221, 223
Chicago, University of 160
Clark University 150
cognitivism 159
Columbia University 155
Cosmogony, 81, 82, 84, 89, 90, 91, 95,
  99
cultural relativism 255

electrodynamics, 16, 28, 36, 39, 41, 44,
  47
electromagnetism 13, 33, 38, 39, 49

empiricism 58, 144, 167, 170, 173, 188,
  239, 244
energeticism xi, 19, 22, 23, 24
ether, 38, 39

Frankfurt School, 177
formalism 233
France, atomism in, xi; chemistry,
  history of, xi, 53–78; College de,
  62;
  psychology, history of, 178
French Revolution 61, 62, 78, 90
functionalism 155, 166, 171

geognosy, 81, 83, 84, 90, 91, 95
Geological Society of London 83, 91
geology, xi, xviii; history of, 79–104
German Democratic Republic 192
German Scientists and Physicians Society,
  111, 112
German Society of the History of
  Medicine and Science 112
German Society for Psychiatry, 209,
  212, 224
Germany, chemistry, history of, 65–67,
  70; geology, history of, 83;
  medicine, history of, xviii, 105–
  120; physical sciences, history of,
  3–34; psychology, history of,
  145, 156, 171, 178, 181, 188,
  189, 191–228
GUTS, 46, 47

Harvard University 148, 150
Heidelberg University 9
historicism, 6, 7, 8, 14, 17, 19, 23–28,
  32, 125, 179, 286

idealism, 170, 188, 284, 286, 287, 289

Institute for the History of Medicine
(Frankfurt), 111
International Union of Psychologists, 191

Johns Hopkins University 146
*Journal of the History of the Behavioral
Sciences,* 168, 169

Marxism, 195, 236, 240, 256, 263, 264,
177
materialism 110
mechanism (see also teleomechanism),
8, 12, 17, 25, 164, 171
medicine, history of, xii, xviii, 105–120,
293
molarism, 166, 167

National Institutes of Mental Health, 159
National Liberal Party (Germany), 30
National Socialism (Nazism, see also
Third Reich), 197, 206–207,
209–210
nativism 167, 176
New Hampshire, University of 160, 172
New York University, 155
neurobiology, 174

objectivism, 165
oceanography, 93
Oxford University 171

paleomagnetism, 85, 93
paleontology, 93
philology, classical, history of, xv,
281–290
phlogiston, theory of, 54, 56, 60, 61, 67,
70
physics, history of, 3–52
physiology, 11, 13, 106
plate tectonics, 79, 80, 84–87, 91–
93, 95–103
positivism, xi, 13–15, 19–21, 28, 32,
171–173, 175, 238, 239, 281
prescriptivism, 165–167
psychoanalysis, 157, 159, 160, 166, 181
psycholinguistics, 169, 170
Psychological Abstracts, 167, 168

Psychological Institute (Berlin), 213
Psychologische Rundschau, 208
psychology, clinical, 214; cognitive, 174;
critical, 214; Ganzheits, 207, 209;
Gestalt, 151–157, 161, 165–167,
181, 185, 206; history of, xiv, in
France, 178, in Germany, 171,
178, 191–228, in the United
Kingdom, 191, in the United
States, 143–190, 206, 208, 209,
218
Psychonomic Society, 180–181
psychophysics, 29
psychotechnics, 213

qualitativism, 167
quantum electrodynamics 44, 45
quantum mechanics 41, 42–44

Reform University of Berlin 283, 288
Renaissance, 282
Russian Chemical Society 65

Society for Psychological Study of
Social Issues, 175
sociology, 240; French, 245; history of,
xiii, 121–142
stratigraphy, 93
structuralism, 166, 181, 238, 239
Structure of Scientific Revolutions, The
(see also Thomas Kuhn), xii, 94,
104, 125, 229, 231, 232, 236,
237, 241, 246, 252, 254, 257,
266, 267
subjectivism, 165, 167

Technical Universities, 210
teleology, 12, 17, 18, 22
teleomechnism, 12, 14, 15, 27
thermodynamics, 17
Third Reich, 111, 197, 205–210, 223
Third World, 236, 262

uniformitarianism, 79, 80, 94
Union of Professional Psychologists, 191
United Kingdom, psychology, history of,
191

United States, psychology, history of, 143–190, 206, 208, 209, 218

Veterans' Administration, 159
Viet Nam War, 212, 234
vitalism, 11, 12, 164

Wehrmach, 207–208
World War Two, 156, 159
Würzburg, University of 212

York University (Toronto), 179